EDITORIAL WRITING

Principles of

EDITORIAL WRITING

by Curtis D. MacDougall

Professor of Journalism Emeritus
Northwestern University

WM. C. BROWN COMPANY PUBLISHERS Dubuque, Iowa

Copyright © 1973 by Wm. C. Brown Company Publishers

Library of Congress Catalog Card Number: 72-92053

ISBN 0—697—04318—5

Printed in the United States of America

This Book Is Dedicated
to the
Membership of the National Conference
of Editorial Writers
(the cream of the journalistic crop)

Contents

Preface

This is a book for journalism students who look forward some day to becoming editorial writers. Professionals already making a living writing editorials will obtain a few refreshing ideas and viewpoints—or at least that is the hope. And laymen, readers of editorials, should find herein clues to a better understanding of how editorial writers attempt to influence their opinions and actions.

The chapters are arranged in such logical order as the instructor of a class in editorial writing might want to present the topics. The emphasis is on the practical application of policies and principles. How these policies and principles can be translated into practice is illustrated by the use of 243 full length examples from newspapers in 37 states, the District of Columbia, Puerto Rico and Canada; in five magazines, and partial quotations from innumerable other editorials.

To avoid "dating," it is customary for authors of reporting and other basic journalism texts to use recent examples or to disguise the age of examples and quotations which are more than a few years old. This practice has been disregarded in this book for several reasons: to illustrate the fact that some of the best practices herein recommended are long established and are certainly not the invention of the author; to provide some historical perspective and continuity and to include several editorials of yesteryear which have come to be considered editorial classics.

Care has been exercised to avoid selection of editorials whose contents would not be understood by youthful readers. In almost all instances the examples would be as fresh as when they actually appeared if the dates were changed to the present. In other words, the impact would be the same if the date were 1940, 1950, 1960 or 1970. Included among the examples to illustrate the good use of the rules and practices promulgated in this book are most of the Pulitzer and other prize winning editorials of recent years. The overwhelming majority are only a few years old.

A distinctive feature of this book is the analysis of bad examples in 27 cases, indicated by means of marginal notes, paragraph by paragraph, in columns parallel to those of the faulty editorials. These notations point out deficiencies in research, poor logic or faulty composition. It is hoped that these comments by the author will stimulate class discussions regarding the contents as well as the techniques of the editorials under consideration.

There are some examples of editorials which were altogether too long, and that fact should be apparent to the student as it probably was to the subscribers for whom originally intended. During his long career of teaching editorial writing, the author applied this rule: if you feel tempted to write more than 500 words, stop and consider whether you can do it effectively, as usually about half that many words would be better. In this book it would be impossible to teach the lesson of the importance of brevity without presenting examples that violated the rule. One sobering effect the book should have on all kinds of readers is the extent to which weak editorials appear in otherwise first-class publications and, by contrast, how often some of the best are found in comparatively obscure publications.

This book is based on the premise that there is no "one right way" to write an editorial. Rather, the controlling factor in determining an editorial's success is the extent to which its author achieves his purpose. That purpose should be clearly stated, unequivocal and strongly supported by evidence and argument. Throughout most of the book the emphasis is on principles and rules and techniques. The author tries to be as objective as possible in enumerating and explaining the tricks of the trade: how to be effective in editorial writing.

In Chapter 9 the emphasis shifts in part from consideration of form to that of content, and the author provides some examples of practicing what he has been preaching. That is, he editorializes on what positions editorial writers should take in several important fields. Following the rules he has promulgated in earlier chapters, he provides facts and figures, based on careful research, and logical arguments flowing therefrom. Stated another way, the author of a book on editorial writing editorializes to show how it should be done, and some student readers should be inspired to compose editorials in rebuttal, in which case the author would like to receive copies of their work. His address is 537 Judson Avenue, Evanston, Illinois 60202. Happy to hear from you.

The author believes that it is difficult if not impossible to teach anyone how to be a hard-hitting editorial writer without setting an example. He hopes that many of his comments on editorials throughout the book, especially in Chapter 9, will provoke vigorous class debates. The extent to which any reader agrees with the author's views is of much less importance than the extent to which he is aroused to strong expression himself. Any successful teacher of a subject encourages questioning and disagreement. The American ideal of democratic education is a quest for truth and a weighing of all alternatives in solving any problem. Such an attitude of mind—querulous and skeptical—is especially important in an editorial writing class. The atmosphere of controversy must be encouraged. The purpose of the professional editorial writer is to convince and persuade. A course in editorial writing consequently should provide practice in both written and spoken argumentation. If there is any weakness in National Conference of Editorial Writers critique sessions, it is excessive politeness. This is encouraged by the practice of confining discussion to matters of technique rather than content. For several years, however, special sessions devoted to discussion and debate of issues and policies have been growing in popularity. Certainly students must be trained in *what* to write as well as in *how* to write and that means free and open and unrestricted discussion of controversial issues in the classroom with the instructor's role being largely to prevent mayhem. There is no sense in learning how to write editorials unless you have something worth writing about. Classmates and colleagues make the best guinea pigs for the testing of ideas.

This book sets high standards for editorial writing on the assumption, several times stated, that it would be folly to write a how-to-do-it book which advocated anything but the very best practices. The sincerity of all concerned is assumed. That means the editorial writer and all of his superiors and all of the readers. Pitfalls to avoid in achieving this ideal situation are enunciated and methods to avoid them are explained. The nature of readers—their culturally conditioned attitudes and opinions—are taken into account.

This book's author believes that a career as an editorial writer offers a great opportunity for public service and intellectual development. The editorial writer lives constantly with ideas. His profession requires that he know what is going on in the world. For any measure of success he must be a perpetual student of contemporary affairs. He is as free of so-called pressures to thwart his free expression as anyone else in jour-nalism or, in fact, as anyone else anywhere in our free enterprise economy. In other words, it's nice work if you can get it. Hopefully this book will help aspirants to achieve that goal.

Acknowledgments

The following answered the author's requests for assistance and made valuable contributions to the effort.

Barnum, Charles, Quincy (Ill.) *Herald-Whig*
Bates, Albert W., Orange Coast (Calif.) *Daily Pilot*
Black, Creed C., Philadelphia *Inquirer*
Breed, Donald L., Freeport (Ill.) *Journal-Standard*
Carpenter, Clifford E., Gannett Rochester, N. Y. newspapers
Clemon, James, Omaha *World Herald*
Clendenin, James, *Tampa Tribune*
Conover, Theodore E., University of Nevada
Crane, Frank, Indianapolis *Star*
Croft, Duane, Toledo *Blade*
Fleming, Louis B., Los Angeles *Times*
Gissler, Sig, Milwaukee *Journal*
Halpert, Leonard, Buffalo *Evening News*
Holden, W. Sprague, Wayne State University
Host, David, Marquette University
Jensen, Jay, University of Illinois
Linford, Ernest, University of Wyoming
Little, William, Peoria *Journal-Star*
Lunger, Philip, Buffalo *Courier-Express*
Marquardt, Frederic S., Phoenix *Arizona Republic*
McKalip, Paul, Tucson *Daily Citizen*
Perlik, Charles A., The Newspaper Guild
Reynolds, Sam, Missoula (Mont.) *Missoulian*
Sarbey, Irene, Kent State University
Soth, Lauren, Des Moines *Register and Tribune*
Strohmeyer, John, Bethlehem (Pa.) *Globe-Times*
Thomas, William, Los Angeles *Times*
Trescott, Paul, formerly Philadelphia *Bulletin*
White, Robert M. II, Mexico (Mo.) *Ledger*

I

Why Editorials?

After a few polite remarks about the value of editorials, President Harry S. Truman jolted attendants at the first annual meeting of the National Conference of Editorial Writers in July, 1947 by adding, "Still, I'd rather have a good headline writer on my side."

The late Donovan Richardson, longtime editorial writer for *The Christian Science Monitor*, recalled the incident in the Summer, 1962 issue of *The Masthead*, quarterly publication of the NCEW. Protested Richardson: "No editorial writer worth his salt will accept that heresy." According to Richardson, "Hope that someone, somewhere will read his stuff and the world will be changed" is "the essential ingredient of his (an editorial writer's) work. A man must believe he has something to say and trust someone will listen."

For more than a quarter century now, the approximately 400 editorial writers, representing perhaps 10 per cent of all editorial writers for daily newspapers in the United States and Canada who belong to the NCEW, have engaged in agonizing soul-searching to find answers to innumerable questions, none more important than these:

1. What is the role of the formal editorial in the contemporary daily newspaper?
2. How effective are editorials?

3. What are the satisfactions of editorial writing as a career?

THE ROLE OF THE EDITORIAL PAGE TODAY

Skepticism regarding the present-day value of the formal editorial is not tantamount to a challenge of the importance if not the obligation of the daily newspaper to do more than merely report the news. Rather, it is the result of the development of other methods by which the function of explaining, interpreting and commenting upon current happenings can be performed. The multiplicity of signed columns, weekend review and magazine sections, roundup and interpretative articles by knowledgeable reporters and others, supplements the formal editorial and makes it obsolete, some contend.

The defense of the formal editorial is the obligation of the paper to go beyond news gathering. Other forms of interpretation, often on the editorial or opposite-editorial page, are signed, indicating that they express the viewpoints of particular authorities. The anonymous editorial represents the newspaper as an institution. This anonymity has been attacked often. Legislators have even attempted to pass laws requiring that all editorials be signed. Although the editorial "we" is seldom used today to mean the newspaper as an institution, the formal editorial remains the voice of the paper as a whole. Realistically "we" may mean a single individual, perhaps the owner or publisher or editor or someone else, but the anonymity indicates that the paper endorses what is said. Possibly a poll of all employes in a newspaper plant would result in support for contrary viewpoints, but in a capitalistic society those who own are the ultimate decision makers. The newspaper is a business bent on making a profit and management manages just as it does in a shoe manufacturing factory or an ice-cream parlor. Employes unionize and bargain for their rights as relate to wages and working conditions. Experiments with labor-management committees or other devices whereby the rank-and-file of workers share in decision making usually develop because of the existence of either liberal-minded or frightened bosses. Since the death, early in its existence, of its founder, Heywood Broun, the Newspaper Guild has been interested in the nuts and bolts of labor-management negotiations. It is only in recent years, the trend accelerated by the beating up of newsmen at the 1968 Democratic National Convention in Chicago, that newsroom rebels have agitated above a whisper for some say-so in the selection of editorial personnel and in matters related to news and editorial judgment. Maybe the trend will continue, but it will be a long time before what is said in formal editorials is determined by anything like a majority vote of even those who write them.

Most other veteran newsmen would endorse what Sevellon Brown, editor-pubisher of the Providence *Journal-Bulletin,* told the American Press Institute which gave rise to the NCEW: "There has never been a great newspaper without a great editorial page. There will never be an outstanding newspaper without an outstanding page." Frank-

lin B. Smith, editorial page editor of the Burlington (Vt.) *Free Press,* used virtually the same words in a convocation address at Champlain College: "I have never known of a good newspaper which lacked a good editorial page. The editorial page is often described as the newspaper's conscience, and this is true."

On the other hand it is contended that "press" in the phrase "freedom of the press" no longer means just newspaper. Granted the intention of the Founding Fathers was to permit the free flow of news and comment and create the marketplace of ideas to enable enlightened citizens in a democracy to govern themselves. Sacred as this First Amendment stipulation is, so that journalistic organizations wage a relentless war against governmental encroachments on what they correctly call "the people's right to know." Nevertheless, today, in addition to newspapers, there are radio, television, news magazines and other media of communication. Nobody has to rely on a single newspaper for thoughtful evaluation of current events. In fact, one would be foolish to do so. Not pertinent to this particular book but certainly so to any discussion of modern journalism are several factors that come to mind: (1) the steady drift toward fewer daily newspapers and the consequent reduction in the variety of editorial viewpoints; (2) the trend toward joint ownership of newspapers and other media, including all of those just cited, so that whole communities are deprived of the diversity of viewpoints which the authors of the Bill of Rights envisioned; (3) the gigantic costs involved in reaching a sizable audience by any of the media today, which means that minority groups are handicapped.

About the most cynical viewpoint one encounters relating to the continued existence of the formal editorial is that its presence makes possible the perpetuation of what is called a myth: the separation of news from opinion. Some scholars suggest no malice but demonstrate the impossibility of pure objectivity in reporting. Others contend that many journalists don't even attempt to approach the ethical ideal. Twenty years ago, Adlai Stevenson II, while the Democratic candidate for the presidency, charged that the United States has a "one party press" which is Republican conservative-reactionary. It is ironic that many who agreed also appointed Spiro Agnew, two decades later, when he accused the same press, and the broadcasting industry as well, of being too left-wing, ultra-liberal, or radical. This inconsistency is frightening for what it reveals concerning the extent of public ignorance regarding the nature and importance of a free press and also concerning the gullibility of large numbers of persons. Public education deserves the blame for the existence of widespread ignorance of the nature of the media of communication which affect the daily lives of students and their parents alike much more than most of the knowledge which tradition insists must continue to be imparted to school children. To most people journalists are mysterious, possibly even romantic individuals. Because there are so few of them comparatively, they have fewer opportunities to correct misinformation and to answer abuse than is true of almost anyone else who earns his living in a different business, trade or profession.

The unpopularity of the news media also is traceable in part to the centuries-old habit of scapegoating the bearers of bad tidings. Almost any item of bad or disagreeable news inspires telephone calls and letters of complaint. Most people think that some type of news is overemphasized or underplayed. Granted that the owners of most journalistic media are conservative in their economic, social and political outlooks, it is also true that the pages of almost any newspaper are full of exposés of crime, graft and corruption in the political and business world as a result of courageous diligence on the part of enterprising newsgatherers. Regretfully it is possible to cite examples of suppression, distortion, exaggeration and other kinds of mishandling of news. Too often overlooked, however, is the fact that no matter how much it may gall them personally, owners, publishers and editors do expose the chicanery and worse of many whose views on public matters coincide with their own. Weeks or months of persistent probing by investigative journalists are required to uncover stories about a massacre at My Lai or secret machinations in the Pentagon or hypocrisy in the White House during international negotiations and a great many other activities which are obstacles to the best functioning of our economy. As the Chicago *Daily Tribune* says on its editorial page daily:

> The newspaper is an institution developed by modern civilization to present the news of the day, to foster commerce and industry, to inform and lead public opinion, and to furnish that check upon government which no constitution has ever been able to provide.

Books have been written to elaborate upon all of the issues raised so far in this chapter. As for the formal editorial, which is our subject of interest, and how it fits into the situation heretofore described, no matter what the validity of any argument, pro or con, involving it, *it is here to stay as far as the foreseeable future is concerned.* If it is an anachronism or atavism or useless appendage, it is at least a healthy one at present. In fact, its health and consequent chance for survival have been improving steadily during the past quarter century. This has been due in some part to the growth in influence of the National Conference of Editorial Writers.

The NCEW was born in July, 1947, the outgrowth of a routine seminar for editorial writers conducted by the American Press Institute at Columbia University in January, 1947. The 26 editorial writers, all from comparatively large newspapers, decided to repeat the experience of exchanging ideas and comments on their work. So, six months later, they met again and formally organized. Three-day conferences are held annually, in October or November, in a different city every year. The "backbone" session is always a full day of critique sessions. The members split up into small groups of a half dozen or so to criticize each other's work. They previously have exchanged papers by mail, either promiscuously or to illustrate their yearlong handling of editorial comment in a particular area of interest. There is no more prestigious or hard working group among professional journalists, and none has any better Basic Statement of Principles than that adopted Oct. 22, 1949 in New York as follows:

Journalism in general, editorial writing in particular, is more than another way of making money. It is a profession devoted to the public welfare and to public service. The chief duty of its practitioners is to provide the information and guidance toward sound judgements which are essential to the healthy functioning of a democracy. Therefore the editorial writer owes it to his integrity and that of his profession to observe the following injunctions:

1. The editorial writer should present facts honestly and fully. It is dishonest and unworthy of him to base an editorial on half truth. He should never consciously mislead a reader, distort a situation, or place any person in a false light.
2. The editorial writer should draw objective conclusions from the stated facts, basing them upon the weight of evidence and upon his considered concept of the greatest good.
3. The editorial writer should never be motivated by personal interest, nor use his influence to seek special favors for himself or for others. He should hold himself above any possible taint of corruption, whatever its source.
4. The editorial writer should realize that he is not infallible. Therefore, so far as it is in his power, he should give a voice to those who disagree with him—in a public letters column and by other suitable devices.
5. The editorial writer should regularly review his own conclusions in the light of all obtainable information. He should never hesitate to correct them should he find them to be based on previous misconceptions.
6. The editorial writer should have the courage of well-founded conviction and a democratic philosophy of life. He should never write or publish anything that goes against his conscience. Many editorial pages are the products of more than one mind, however, and sound collective judgment can be achieved only through sound individual judgments. Therefore, thoughful individual opinions should be respected.
7. The editorial writer should support his colleagues in their adherence to the highest standards of professional integrity. His reputation is their reputation, and theirs is his.

THE EFFECTIVENESS OF EDITORIALS

What can someone who adheres to such high principles accomplish? What is the effect or influence, for good or bad, of editorials? Is there any way to obtain a credible answer?

Presumably the second half of the 19th century was a Golden Era of Personal Journalism in the United States. Dedicated to high ideals and well-defined progressive or liberal political programs and social objectives, owners, who often were their own publishers, editors and editorial writers, supposedly thundered so loudly that lawmakers, business tycoons, public officials and other decision makers could not avoid hearing. And so Lawrence, Bowles, Godkin, Greeley, the Bennetts, Hearst, Pulitzer and others were king makers and policy determiners. Their editorial pages were avidly read and the advice therein contained was carefully weighed and often followed.

Despite the glamorous auras with which journalistic biographers and historians have surrounded these giants of the press, there is little or no evidence to substantiate the mightiness of their power. In their days newspaper readership was confined to a minority of the populace, the educated minority, and so a larger proportion of the total subscription list perused the editorials than today when the mass appeal paper, with "something for everyone," is read by a much larger audience. Probably, in relationship to the population as a whole, subscribers and nonsubscribers alike, the proportion of those who read editorials today is just as great as it was a century ago, though such readership now constitutes a small proportion of the paper's total circulation. Reader interest surveys which show large readerships of the page are suspect because of the statistical "halo" error: the desire to "look good." Most special sections of any newspaper have comparatively small readerships, but those readers may be devotees who subscribe for the designated feature only.

Generally cited as the outstanding example of newspaper influence during the late 19th century was the propagandizing of the New York Hearst and Pulitzer newspapers prior to the Spanish-American War. That the papers in question—Hearst's *Journal* and Pulitzer's *World*—sensationalized and manufactured stories of Spanish atrocities in Cuba cannot be denied. Nevertheless, no sober evaluation of the political situation would lead to the conclusion that it was the swashbuckling reporting of Richard Harding Davis or the fake photographs of Frederic Remington that caused Congress to declare war. The motivating force behind the United States war of alleged liberation for Cuba was economic imperialism. The postwar acquisition and retention of the Philippines, not exactly nextdoor neighbors to the Cubans, proves that, as do all of the other terms of concession which this country obtained from Spain and imposed on Cuba libre as the United States took a gigantic step toward becoming a world colonial power. Maybe Hearst and Pulitzer aroused the unthinking or unlearned and made the war seem to be a holy crusade. The press and the church of all conquerors have done the same thing since the beginning of recorded history. The economic and/or egoistic motivations of victorious Alexanders the Great, Julius Caesars, Napoleons and Mussolinis, however, have not originated with newspaper cartoons or line drawings. It is utterly naive to say that Hearst and/or Pulitzer caused the Spanish-American War or that any newspaper ever caused any war. The extent to which editorial endorsement of a war affects civilian morale and upholds the hands of those who direct the military operations is something else again. And it's mighty difficult to determine, too. When crowds show up at events which you have endorsed, it's only human to believe you were of some help. All you may have done, however, is to direct attention to something the majority wanted to do anyway. It's the same gamble that any advertiser of a new product takes. Every case demands separate study and consideration. Common sense dictates taking advantage of the opportunities which exist when public interest is aroused by some events, as a sports contest, space exploration, election campaign or the like. To put it simply you don't sell souvenir baseball caps and bats outside of Carnegie Hall but at the entrances to Yankee Stadium. So, the editorial ballyhooers of the "go west, young man" expansionist period may seem to have been powerful persuaders merely because they were in tune with the times, rode the wave of public sentiment, acted as defenders and promoters of the status quo or went the way the wind was blowing. Choose your own figure. Too many persuaders of all sorts are like the witch doctors who danced for weeks and when it finally rained claimed credit. Certainly superstitions just as easily debunked abound today and are perpetuated by most city desks. Editorial writers, however, are supposed to consist of sterner intellectual stuff. Certainly they should be more rational in their evaluation of their own prowess. If they require an enormous amount of satisfaction, then their self-inflicted therapy should be to confine themselves to their ivory towers and not venture forth into the real world. Such a fool's paradise is, of course, not possible today so the more sensible course is a calm and modest evaluation of one's achievements.

Anyone's success in persuading another about anything always depends upon the extent to which he offends or supports prejudices, taboos, myths, legends, stereotypes, superstitions and other factors which determine a person's attitudes, beliefs and opinions. You cannot clash head-on with a traditional popular behavior pattern or custom or law and expect anything except strong rebuff. You appeal to and try to manipulate feelings, emotions and sentiments, rather than to destroy them. You are most successful when you can make what you propose seem to be exactly what another has wanted all the time. It takes not only courage but a great deal of patience to effect changes in deep-seated opinions. It can be done. It has been done but probably not by many who have been eulogized posthumously for merely going with the tide. While you're reeducating your public, step by step, don't get discouraged at your seeming lack of progress. There are just too many different factors which enter into decision making, either by individuals or groups, including voting publics, to make predictions or analyses of surprises absolutely certain. Traumatic events, either personal or public, can cause change much more rapidly than months of brilliant oratory or miles of copy containing sparkling prose. It's the uncertainty that makes the game interesting, keeps hope alive, and inspires the best in one.

Most tangible evidence of the impossibility of cajoling people to act contrary to what they think their best interests are is provided when, as usually happens, the overwhelming majority of daily newspapers support the most conservative candidate for the presidency of the United States but he doesn't win. The same negative correlation between newspaper endorsements and voters' behavior may be noted in state and municipal elections also. In some communities the support of a particular newspaper may laughingly be called "the kiss of death," but the laugh is on the other fellow when that's the way it turns out. Many explanations are given and have validity. When a newspaper spends three and a half years exposing corruption and incompetency in a city administration, it cannot expect its readers to shed the attitudes it has helped create and vote for the incumbents just because the paper inconsistently endorses them. This happens regularly in some places, notably Chicago, and occasionally or often in other places. In March, 1971, after their managements endorsed Mayor Richard J. Daley for reelection, 88 editorial staff members of the Chicago *Daily News* and 61 Chicago *Sun-Times* staffers paid for large advertisements to recall the shortcomings in City Hall about which they had written for years and to endorse Richard R. Friedman, the rival candidate.

A valid defense of the editorial writer who has apparently failed to persuade voters to his way of thinking is that the favorable, or at least fair and adequate, treatment given a candidate whom he opposes in the paper's news columns has been more effective than editorial arguments in opposition. After Adlai Stevenson made his one-party-press charges in 1952, Prof. Nathan Blumberg, then an assistant professor of journalism at the University of Nebraska, studied the coverage given the campaign by 35 daily newspapers, all circulation leaders in their states. In his book, *One Party Press* (University of Nebraska Press, 1954), Blumberg concluded that four of the 26 pro-Eisenhower papers showed partiality in favor of their candidate in their news columns and two of the seven pro-Stevenson papers demonstrated partiality in favor of the Democratic candidate. The other 29 papers gave the two candidates an even break in their news columns regardless of their editorial attitudes. Thus, as far as column inches were concerned, the press seemingly was fair. Blumberg did not try a qualitative analysis of the news coverage. Another journalist, however, did so of the handling of the Nixon and Stevenson campaign fund stories. He was Arthur Edward Rowse, a copy editor for the Boston *Traveler*. He reported his findings, based on analyses of 32 newspapers, in *Slanted News* (Beacon Press, 1957). With the possible exception of the New York *Times*, he concluded that all papers, both Republican and Democratic, showed evidence of favoritism in their news columns. Almost every example of such favoritism coincided with the paper's editorial feelings, but precise methods of evaluating newspaper bias just do not exist.

As a result of the charge of partiality by Stevenson which President Harry S. Truman echoed, presidential campaign coverage every four years since then probably has been more fair. Thus, readers can make up their minds independently of the editorial page, and what remains in question is how much reading of any part of a newspaper plays in causing voters to reach a decision. Paul Lazarsfeld and associates showed as long ago as their study of the 1940 campaign that voters tend to read and listen only to arguments in favor of candidates whom they already tend to favor. The original Lazarsfeld study, which used Sandusky, Ohio, was published as *The People's Choice* (Columbia University Press, 1944).

The part that newspaper reading of news and/or editorials plays in causing voters to make up their minds cannot be determined with any accuracy. Angus Campbell and associates in *The American Voter* (John Wiley & Son, 1960) and other books demonstrate that how one votes is consistent with

his entire life style. All researchers cite the existence of cross-pressures—religious, ethnic, occupational, geographic and others—that complicate the situation and make predictions difficult. Since the fiasco of 1948, professional pollsters have been cautious in their predictions of the outcomes of elections. In that year they should have known better than to be so emphatic in forecasting a Thomas E. Dewey victory over Harry S. Truman. They had developed their sampling and other techniques during the unique period when one man, Franklin Delano Roosevelt, was a candidate four times. Using the same sampling techniques that they had used in previous elections made failure inevitable, just as utilization of telephone books had doomed the *Literary Digest* poll in 1928.

William Allen White once said that dust storms defeated more Kansas governors than campaign oratory, which suggests that it is the pocketbook appeal that is paramount in causing a voter to make up his mind. Any Democratic candidate could have defeated Herbert Hoover in 1932 at a time when the depression's effects were being felt from coast to coast. It has been charged that most voters were irrational. Is it irrational to vote against the status quo when one is suffering as a result of it? How much investigation and listening to both sides does one need to do to know that almost any change would be worth risking? In the face of the economic conditions which prevailed, the majority of editorial writers who advocated the reelection of President Hoover didn't have a chance.

To offset the chagrin that an editorial writer feels when voters reject his advice is the fact that almost all candidates for public office seek endorsements. It is not infrequent, in fact, for someone to investigate his chances of receiving the backing of some newspaper before making his final decision on whether to run. Furthermore, nobody likes to read an editorial adversely critical of himself. He may glibly declare that "nobody reads editorials," but he screams loudly when that which people would read if people did read editorials is injurious to him.

Kenneth R. Byerly, then an associate professor of journalism at the University of North Carolina, cited several cases to establish the appropriateness of the title of his article, "Some of the Best Editorials Are Never Written," in the Summer, 1963 *Masthead*. One example was that of an editor who refrained from lambasting Negroes for eating only in restaurants with lunch counters in the front to demonstrate their success in bringing about integration. Instead of recommending that places with counters not quite so conspicuous deserved support also, the editor quietly talked to some black leaders and the situation corrected itself without a public airing which might have been explosive.

More than one public official has mended his ways by taking hints so subtle that others didn't understand them in editorials. Sometimes an editorial writer may not care whether he has more than a single reader if he gets results from the use of innuendo or some other rhetorical form certain to be meaningful to the target reader, to let him know that the editorial writer knows where the body is buried or in which closet the skeleton is hidden. Since, in order to test direct effectiveness, purpose must be considered, such editorials are effective even though the overwhelming majority of readers ignored or disliked them. If the purpose of an editorial is to explain or interpret a news event, it is effective if it achieves its purpose with any appreciable number of persons. With how many? Who can say? If the purpose is to persuade any person or persons to behave in a particular way, the results can be determined by examining their behavior. One never knows, however, how much silent opposition he may stir up ultimately to offset the apparent immediate success. It is not uncommon that a public official acts promptly in line with what seems to be a good editorial sugges-

tion but later it turns out that both the editorial writer and the official made a mistake. What is effectiveness anyway? No simple answer is possible.

Editors judge their effectiveness sometimes by the responses they get by means of telephone calls, letters and visits. Anyone who takes the trouble to make his opinion known in such a way has more than average interest. Other modest or lazy people may share this interest but remain uncounted. It seems sensible to conclude that when the sample of responses is diversified—that is, comes from different segments of the population or areas—an idea is of widespread importance. If only members of a particular group—nationality, racial, religious or otherwise—make their reactions known, can one conclude that the editorial struck a responsive note? Or might it be that a leader or propagandist agitated to bring about the supposed spontaneous outbreak of public opinion? A lot of research is necessary to be certain about many such matters.

Two strong factors determining what influence an editorial page has are the general prestige of the medium as a whole and the competence of the writer. If a publication has a reputation for fairness, intelligence and other virtues, its editorials will carry more weight than if it lacks respect in the community. A good reputation is earned, incident by incident, over the years. It's not a basic ingredient but an end result of journalistic performance and anyone in any way connected with the operation is a factor in it. Nothing can compare with "a good name" if you set out to influence your fellowman.

Many editorials, it is often cogently said, are not read because they're not worth reading. On many smaller papers particularly they are considered more or less as space fillers and the use of syndicated or "canned" editorials is widespread. The editorial page persists because it always has been there and management does not want to risk loss of prestige by abandoning it.

Nobody within the ranks of journalists ever took a dimmer view of editorial writing than the irascible Henry L. Mencken of the Baltimore *Sun*, a prominent caustic critic of pretense and superficiality in all aspects of American life. He not only tickled the vanity of the yokels whom he ridiculed in his magazine, *American Mercury*, and his syndicated newspaper column, but at the 1947 NCEW meeting in Washington gave vent to impromptu remarks that are considered classical in the annals of editorial writers: "Why have editorials at all?" the sage of Hollins Street asked, ". . . filling three or four columns of space with the opinions of unknown and in many cases not-worth-knowing men?"

Mencken charged editorial writers with being ignorant and devoid of both ideas and courage to express them. "An editorial writer," he said, "has only one excuse for existence: that he has a positive opinion about a subject on which he is well informed, on which he knows more than the average man. And yet all he has to say is what you could hear in any barber shop— not from the customers but from the barbers. . . . I say the thing to do is to put your editorial writers to learning something first. . . . You are wasting time on the moron. . . . The editorial page has one aim. That is to appeal to the more intelligent reader in his more intelligent mood. . . . You can't escape it. A man that is worth reading at all has opinions. He has ideas."

Mencken obviously was pessimistic. By contrast, obviously holding a higher opinion of the ability of editorial writers, Eugene Patterson, then editor of the Atlanta *Constitution*, wrote an article, "Editorials Get Things Done" for the Summer, 1968 *Masthead*, saying, ". . . the longer I live the more I believe the value of the editorial is not so much to carry the day, to convince everybody, or to comfort the good and convert the evil. To achieve these goals the average editor would have to be a lot smarter than he is. The true and lasting value lies in getting people to think for themselves, to talk and to argue, and finally to decide whatever they want to decide."

Offhand that might seem to be a modest goal. It means that the editorial writer shouldn't look out of his window when the paper hits the street and expect to see the rascals scurrying out of the sinful edifices whose walls are starting to crumble.

THE REWARDS OF EDITORIAL WRITING

So the obvious question is, "Why would any talented and ambitious person want to be an editorial writer?" What rewards does it offer if it is so difficult to determine effectiveness and whatever the results, they are intangible, subjective, long-range and unconscious?

In an article written for the *Pelican Press Messenger*, publication of the Louisiana Press Association, Edwin A. Bemis, field manager of the Colorado Press Association, wrote: "An idea—a desire to express it— writing it—publishing it. There you have the entire framework of the editorial." And therein you can find hints as to why so many top-notch men and women find satisfaction in doing it: (1) it provides an outlet for self-expression; (2) it is fun to do.

In this day of the organization yes man, these are cardinal advantages. You have something to say, something that needs to be said, something that your mental health, in extreme cases, might demand that you say. As an editorial writer, except for the restraints on freedom of expression already suggested and to be elaborated upon in later chapters, you have the way to say your say. You may not be telling off the boss but he's about the only one not on the editorial writer's list of targets for his wrath. Whereas the overwhelming majority of other people go about their daily routine of earning a living by keeping their mouths shut, taking out their frustrations on close friends, relatives and pets, the editorial writer can blow his top on his typewriter.

Of course he wants his pearly words of wisdom to be widely read and he's over-joyed at any evidence that he has gotten under the skin of some phony or that action follows his suggestions. But even if nothing happens, as is the case after the majority of his pieces appear, so what? He's gotten it off his chest, he's done his duty and he's able to hope that somewhere there is some-one who was affected beneficially by his effort. Who is able to prove more effec-tiveness? The preacher? The speaker? The book author? They attract crowds and audi-ences but the success of their efforts de-pends on the same social psychological principles as in the case of the editorial writer. Maybe it's more fun to be a rabble rouser and lead rallies, demonstrations, parades and mobs, but one can hardly make a career out of such behavior without ceas-ing to be considered heroically glamorous, or without landing in jail. Whereas the demagogue arouses popular emotions, en-tertains large groups and sways opinion, his popularity is dependent on the presumed needs of the times. He can't keep going at white heat incessantly. There comes a time when he has to level off. If he is a political power he learns to rely more on censorship and control of the media of communication than on propaganda. Without the former the latter lacks effectiveness. Adolf Hitler was the past master of both censorship and propaganda in our times and his example should be a frightful reminder to everyone of the danger of succumbing to the bland-ishments of a political savior. Hitler went to war before his domestic power and popu-larity began to wane, and he became overly ambitious as had been the downfall of many conquerors before him.

Religious revivalists have their cycles of influence. They come and go to satisfy the frustrations of many. Get-rich-quick swind-lers, blatant medicine show men with snake oil to cure anything and everything, gold brick salesmen and their slick equivalents in almost any aspect of contemporary life fail ultimately. No matter how much self-hyp-nosis they engage in, they cannot have the self-respect that most editorial writers have as they plod along doing their honest best day after day and becoming miserable only when they feel that they may have com-promised too much or fallen short in crafts-manship. Much less glamorous than other ways of trying to influence the masses, no doubt about it, but indubitably offering greater opportunity for self-esteem and ego satisfaction.

Unfortunately, of course, all editorial writers are not the paragons of ethical and idealistic virtue that the foregoing might suggest, but their occupational opportuni-ties to be the kinds of hidden persuaders that they aspire to be are greater. It's not easy to stick it out in strict observation of the moral rule book no matter what you do. To repeat, however, editorial writing offers one of the best opportunities for the public-spirited and honest person who wants to make his influence felt.

An outstanding example of an editorial writer who has practiced what he preaches regarding high moral purpose and social responsibility is Robert M. White II of the Mexico (Mo.) *Ledger.* Only he and Vir-ginius Dabney of the Richmond *Times-Dis-patch* have ever won the Sigma Delta Chi award twice for distinguished editorial writ-ing. In accepting his second award in 1968, White demonstrated why he is admired so widely when he said:

> I think of a newspaper as a wheel. The rim is the newside—touching the good earth, the real world as it rolls along. The rim is the newside bolstered by the ad-side which gives it strength—an economic strength assuring independence. The spokes of the wheel are integrity, vigilance, courage, loyalty, dedi-cation to truth, respect—for man himself, for talent, for hard work, for purity in

language (the right use of the right word at the right time).

The editorials are the hub of the wheel. They set the character of the paper. Their first responsibility is to the reader—to make a public accounting of the newspaper's prejudices, opinions, hopes and hates. So editorials set the character of the paper and in doing it chart the heights to which the newside of the newspaper must rise to serve its readers well.

White wrote the author: "I live by the philosophy that being honest and sincere in editorials is more important than being right. Although it is nice to be right too. I figure readers will tolerate your being wrong, but won't tolerate insincerity or inconsistency—a lack of character. I suppose this means editorial writers don't have to be bright. I have another conviction. I write for as many people as possible. My thought is to be constructive and to sell my point of view. And if I am going to sell it, I might as well try to sell it to as many people as possible."

White has the advantage of being not only editorial writer but editor and publisher as well. Most other editorial writers must be responsible to some higher-up whose political, ethical, and other views might not exactly coincide with theirs. And therein lies the most commonly heard complaint of students and other journalists against editorial writing, to explain why many do not want to do it. They feel they would sacrifice freedom and conscience if they were merely the means by which their superiors reached their publics. Most such fears are groundless. In the first place prospective editorial writers and their employers explore each other's viewpoints in advance of hiring, to determine if they coincide sufficiently to reduce conflict to a minimum. In other words, most editorial writers agree with their superiors. When there is a difference of opinion it seldom is required of anyone to write contrary to his convictions. On papers with fair sized editorial writing staffs there usually is someone willing and able to express the opinions of whoever decides what is to be said. This is so, not just to allow the writer to preserve his integrity but, more important, for the very simple reason that few people can do an effective job of advocating a point of view contrary to that which they sincerely hold. Outstanding exception to this rule was Reuben Maury who wrote pro-New Deal editorials for *Collier's* and strongly anti-New Deal editorials for the New York *Daily News*. His defense, or at least his explanation, was this:

> When a hired editorial writer is writing editorials he is not writing out of either side of his mouth or out of the middle or any part of it. He is acting as mouthpiece(s) for the publication(s) for which he works. His job is to express the publication's policies with all the force and skill he can summon up and without regard to his private opinions. There is nothing "deadly" about all this. No editorial writer owes any apologies for it to anybody. It is merely a phase of the editorial writing job.

This viewpoint is similar to that which motivates most lawyers and press agents (public relations counsel), but it is by no means representative of how any sizable proportion of journalists regard their role.

Critique sessions at the November, 1964, National Conference of Editorial Writers in Tampa and a symposium in the Spring, 1965 *Masthead* revealed that more publishers than usual wrote their own endorsement editorials that year, provided they supported Sen. Barry Goldwater. Few writers reported any difficulty in being excused from the assignment. Wrote Sig Gissler, then on the Waukegan *News-Sun*: "What if the publisher had prevailed on me to write the editorial heartily endorsing Goldwater? I would have respectfully declined and I am confident our publisher would have accepted my decision without malice." Gissler explained the "enlightened arrangement" that prevailed in his office,

"Of course, if irreconcilable differences of opinion continually occur between editorial writers and publisher, the only honest answer is reassignment or resignation."

Most editorial writers would act in accordance with that common sense advice. Long before the breaking point is reached, however, there is no denying that there can be strain and discontent. The unconscious as well as conscious fear of offending management and thus endangering one's position is ever present. But the same is true almost anywhere in our capitalistic economy. One should ask where are the greener pastures before acting rashly.

Anyone willing to sell his talent à la Maury welcomes the cloak of anonymity. With many journalists, however, it is the anonymity which formal editorial writing involves that makes the job unattractive. They feel that if they are going to extend effort to produce first-rate treatises, they want to reap the reward of recognition outside as well as inside the office. They cherish the by-line which interpretative writers in other parts of the paper enjoy. A century ago owners and publishers wrote their own editorials and readers knew their origin. Even though a particular piece was unsigned, it was recognized as the thunderings of the strong personality whose views permeated all parts of the publication. In the business world today anonymity is generally the rule, which fact explains a great deal of the unrest and so-called alienation characteristic of the economy. In journalism opportunity is offered for public as well as private recognition. Some people prefer the protection which anonymity provides them and do not crave the limelight. Fortunately there is a place for all types in the total journalistic structure.

An even greater gripe, if that is what it can be called, of editorial writers is the sense of futility which results from the pressure of deadlines. As the world and all in it becomes complex, the task of obtaining knowledge and using it aptly grows. This is increasingly an age of specialization and most newspapers are departmentalizing to take cognizance of increased reader interest in many fields, such as the environment, population control, urbanization, mental and public health, many branches of science and so forth. No newspaper, however, can afford to have an editorial writing staff of sufficient size to cover all the possible specialties. That means that it is inevitable that editorial writers handle many different kinds of topics and the resulting frustrations can be imagined.

No matter how much education he may have, the best editorial writer—or the best of anything else—can feel woefully ignorant as regards many, perhaps most, fields other than that which he studied intensely. How much is enough background knowledge? When can one safely stop researching before drawing conclusions and starting to put thoughts on paper? Some editorials can be handled with a minimum of effort, but they are the ones which follow the news and emphasize the obvious. They are the kind that most persons tire of writing after a short time. Anyone worth his salt wants to do more than congratulate the mayor because the city won a safety award, memorialize a dead civic leader, boost the Community Chest drive or deplore the existence of antisocial behavior as revealed by a government report. There is not a single topic, including the commonplace ones just mentioned, about which extensive research could not be conducted. A good editorial writer has somewhat the attitude of a research scholar and he thrills at the discovery of an obscure fact or opinion with which to enliven his copy. Too often he learns the meaning of the old saw about ignorance being blissful, as he has an uneasy feeling he may have gone off half-cocked on some subject because he lacked the time for adequate research. Some editorial writers protect their egos by assuming arrogant stances and hypnotizing themselves into super-self-confidence. Thus they thrive on prejudice and protect themselevs psychologically by becoming bigots. These ignorant fanatics are a menace and fortunately are in a minority. Most editorial writers are quiet and modest, more aware than their critics of their own inadequacies and determined to correct them as best they can.

To offset all of the disadvantages or possible pitfalls of editorial writing, there is the prestige which comes from the position and the nature of the work. Maybe the humble editorial writer is unhappy in the realization that his ignorance is profound. How many other persons, aware or unaware of the same, have jobs which provide the opportunity—rather, involve the requirement—for a full day's work trying to correct the deficiency? The editorial writer spends his time seeking knowledge, and he is one modern craftsman who is able to feel pride in his creations. He surveys the result of his labor and he knows if it's good, even though recognition is slow in coming to him.

Editorial writing generally is pleasant work. The hours are usually better than those of other members of the newspaper's news and editorial staff, and the pay is usually better than average. Editorial writing, in other words, is considered one of the best opportunities on any paper. Usually the editorial writer has a private or semi-private office (in which case he shares it with other editorial writers) and he may have secretarial and researcher help. He is closer to management than reporters or most subeditors. Owners, publishers, and editors meet with him daily in editorial conferences so he has a chance to express opinions and to argue points of view. He's very much on the inside of what's going on in the plant. What he writes may be anonymous but he is decidedly not unknown in the office. Outsiders seek him out also, newsmakers and all who would like to have the editorial page support their pet causes. Unless office policy disapproves, editorial writers can become more involved in civic affairs than others, possibly serving on

boards and committees and giving speeches. Even if such activities are discouraged or forbidden, it is nice to be asked.

From the standpoint of the student beginner, practice in editorial writing is of considerable value as will be elaborated upon in the chapters to follow. No other form of journalistic composition calls for more precise writing. The editorial writer says as much as he can effectively in the fewest possible words. The discipline of researching a topic, outlining the subject matter, stating and defending a point of view is beneficial no matter what field of journalism one enters. There is, in other words, carry-over value, just as the English composition teachers insist there is in poetry writing exercises. It is the thesis of this book that editorials could and should be better and that the better they are the more effective they inevitably will be.

THIS BOOK'S SCOPE

As stated in the Preface, this is a "how-to-do-it" book. In frank recognition of the facts of life, including the pressures of all sort which affect policy-making, maybe the purpose should be stated as telling how editorials should be written. With due warning as to the obstacles to be met and overcome, it nevertheless is assumed that everyone is "on the level" from the owner down to the reader. It doesn't seem to make sense to presume anything else or to try to provide training for anything except the best possible performance. There is need for better editorials which means there is need for better editorial writers.

And that's what this book is all about: better editorial writers to serve the public interest which means contributing to an enlightened public so that democracy can work better than it does. To reiterate, the editorial page is here to stay, as far as the foreseeable future is concerned. It calls for more and better talent, and it provides a very pleasant and profitable opportunity for self-service and worthwhile experience.

This is a textbook and the concentration will be on the first steps that a beginning editorial writer will usually take. The book will deal primarily with how to learn to write effective editorials about domestic problems. It is a safe presumption that no newspaper worth working for would start a cub on the intracacies of international affairs or foreign policy. Just as you begin to gain experience as a reporter by covering police, the lower courts and city hall, so you develop editorial writing skill and especially knowledge by starting with topics with which you are most familiar or which are easiest for you to investigate.

Few if any young persons fresh out of college should begin a career in journalism by writing editorials. Fortunately there are few newspapers stupid enough to hire them to do so. A good background as a news-gatherer is essential to later success as a commentator on the news. It is not easy to pontificate about conditions with which one is completely unfamiliar. Granted the editorial writer gets out of the office much less often than the reporter. If he has a background of reportorial experience, however, he will know what the reporter on the assignment is talking about when he is briefed on any editorial to be written.

Hal Liston, editor of the Bloomington (Ill.) *Daily Pantagraph,* gave University of Illinois journalism students some sound advice in a speech from which the following extracts are typical:

> Ruffling the feathers of the local Establishment—of which the newspaper is both a part and an interloper—is dictated to any good newspaper. The shortcomings of even small-town life are so apparent that the temptation to accept them as inevitable is almost overpowering. None of us, or none of you, need sneer, therefore, when I say the best of our news and editorial brains should be concentrated on local issues. . . .

> Human life, as it is lived individually, is local. . . . It is the lot of catching the attention of that local living that is important to the newspaper.

Examples used to illustrate techniques and other aspects of editorial writing in the chapters to follow will be mostly related to domestic or local news, presumably the kind of editorials that a comparative newcomer to the editorial writing staff could tackle. Anything or everything learned while writing on such topics will be valuable in handling any future assignments related to national or international affairs. In another part of his lecture Liston warned against excessive narrow specialization and stressed the need for generalists. A few more typical sentences from his speech follow:

> How can the editorial writer avoid knowing less and less about more and more when the opposite tragedy has struck most of the other professions—knowing more and more about less and less?

> Salvation lies, if it is obtainable at all, in the man willing to be the general practitioner. This man will not be a lazy man, nor will he be a man obsessed with the arcane. This editorial writer will be the man who recognizes that the age of technology, the age of specialization, demands generalists who understand human hopes, ambitions, weaknesses and strength. The good editorial writer, the essayist, the best novelist, the philosopher, the best politician find their strength in the belief that wisdom may, after all, be more important than knowledge.

> One need not be a physicist to understand the fearful consequences of a nuclear war. Incineration is not a new concept for even simple persons; mass incineration as public policy is an issue all of us can understand. . . .

> If we are dealing with future shock, my guess is the specialists in all fields must listen more to the generalists. The informed generalist is my ideal of the editorial writer. An informed generalist recognizes that no event is important save for its impact on human beings.

It is impossible to improve on Liston's perceptive statement to explain the general perspective of this book. As previously implied, the highest motives are assumed on the part of owner, publisher, editor, editorial writer and all others who might be involved. They are all considered to be sincere and that includes readers whose open minds must be assumed. One of the most poignant remarks Liston made was this:

"What most towns need is fewer stupid readers, not necessarily better newspapers. The Pantagraph, in my view, is a better newspaper than many of its readers deserve."

Sounds utopian, doesn't it—a book on how ideally it should be done? Well, it wouldn't make much sense to write a book on how to do it badly, would it?

II

The Editorial Writer
at Work

Who should write editorials? What are the qualifications necessary for success at it?

PROFILE OF TODAY'S EDITORIAL WRITER

First, who *does* write them today? Under the sponsorship of the National Conference of Editorial Writers, Prof. Cleveland Wilhoit of Indiana University, assisted by Dan Drew, analyzed questionnaires returned by 372 of 389 NCEW members and 284 non-members who were asked to cooperate on the project. The results were published in the Fall, 1971 *Masthead* and were analyzed by *Editor & Publisher* in its issue of Aug. 7, 1971, from which the following is an almost verbatim extract:

The editorial writer's median age is 48.4 years, slightly younger than the median of 50 years reported in 1962. Only 4.7 percent of the respondents were under 30, and 45.3 percent were over 51 years of age.

Women number about the same among editorial writing ranks as they did a decade ago, 2.4 percent.

Baccalaureate degrees are held by 82.8 percent of the respondents, an increase of about 10 percent over the decade. M.A. degrees are held by 20.5 percent. An additional 19.6 percent have done some grad-

uate work, and half of the respondents have participated in special fellowship programs at colleges and universities. Journalism was the major subject at either the undergraduate or graduate level for 43.7 percent of the editorial writers.

A 1962 study suggested the editorial writer was "well rewarded" for his work, and the latest survey suggests he remains so in the 1970's. The median salary estimate has risen from $12,300 in 1962 to $16,751. The Consumer Price Index, however, indicates the median salary figure for 1971 is a gain of only $606 over the decade's rise in cost of living.

An overwhelming majority (83.7 percent) of the respondents say their salaries compare well with those of other newspaper staff members. One-fifth of the respondents are under American Newspaper Guild contracts, and they, too, say overwhelmingly that their salaries are higher than other departmental personnel salaries.

About one third of the editorial writers have part-time jobs such as teaching, lecturing, consulting, or freelance writing. Most say these activities are performed primarily for financial gain. Investments provide additional income for 23.5 percent, and 5.9 percent are officers, directors, or substantial stockholders in corporations.

Most editorial writers (71.4 percent) work in staffs ranging from one to four full-time editorial writers. About half of the staffs have a full-time cartoonist; 44.2 percent have one or more full-time columnists. Only six percent say their editorial staffs have a full-time research assistant.

About 80 percent of the respondents are full-time on the editorial page, but only 36 percent of them say they spend three-quarters or more of their time researching and writing editorials.

Slightly less than half of the editorial writers (48.5 percent) say they are never assigned a specific field on which to comment. About three-fourths of the respondents write signed columns, but only 21.8 percent do so regularly.

In researching and writing editorials, the most frequently consulted human sources are beat reporters and public officials. A majority say they seldom (38.3 percent) or never (46.3 percent) are compelled to write editorials that are contrary to their own ideas about an issue.

An overwhelming majority of the editorial writers say they are very satisfied (67.27 percent) or satisfied (29.7 percent) in newspaper work. A closer look at the data suggests the older respondents are more likely than the younger to report they are very satisfied with their job. Most (63.95 percent) say they expect to remain in editorial writing, but 22.5 percent, primarily the younger editorial writers, expect to move into management.

Only 31 of 129 Newspaper Guild contracts with 162 daily newspapers contain a specific reference to editorial writers. In 26 of the 31 contracts a higher minimum rate is established for editorial writers and for reporters. In 14 other contracts some or all editorial writers are exempted from contract coverage. A quick rundown of the wage comparisons of the 26 of 31 contracts provided by Charles A. Perlik, Jr., Newspaper Guild president, follows:

Baltimore Sunpapers, editorial writers receive 10% higher rate than a fully-experienced reporter; Washington Star, 92%; Battle Creek Inquirer and News, 1.5%; Boston Herald Traveler, 4% higher; Brandford Ontario Expositor, 5% higher for a combination editorial writer-reporter; Buffalo Courier Express, 13.8% higher; Buffalo News, 12% higher; Cleveland Plain Dealer, 12% higher; Cleveland Press, 12% higher; Denver Post, 5.6% higher; Detroit Free Press, 7% higher; Elizabeth N. J. Journal, 4.8% higher; Manchester Union Leader, 8.5% higher; New York Times, 10% higher; Pittsburgh Post Gazette, 1.6% higher; Pontiac Press, 4.2% higher; Providence Journal and Bulletin, 7% higher; St. Paul Dispatch and Pioneer Press, 5% higher; San Antonio Light, 3.1% higher; Seattle Times, 3.4% higher; Stockton California Record, 10% higher; Toledo Blade and Times, 7.9% higher; Toronto Globe and Mail, 16.7% higher; Toronto Star, 13.6% higher, and the Vancouver Sun and Province (those are separate newspapers but have joint production arrangement), 2.3% higher than a reporter top minimum. We find no evidence where an editorial writer was paid less than a reporter top minimum.

Understaffing is a big problem, Perlik says, citing an article, "Many Pages Wretchedly Understaffed," by Laurence J. Paul, Buffalo *Evening News,* in the Spring, 1972 *Masthead.*

Several of the virtues which are advantages for editorial writers to possess were suggested in the preceding chapter: humility, integrity, a sense of social responsibility, versatility and so forth. The same qualities doubtless would be assets for others engaged in a number of other professions. Such characteristics as courage, imagination, good judgment, curiosity, independence, conscience, courtesy, self-confidence, cooperativeness, enthusiasm and others are qualitative or subjective descriptive nouns. They are relative and must be illustrated to be of practical value to anyone in any particular situation, in this case that of editorial writer. They need to be spelled out, and they were spelled out by Irving Dilliard when he was editorial page editor of the St. Louis *Post-Dispatch* in an article, "The Editor I Wish I Were," written for the Summer, 1957 *Masthead.* For example, a typical paragraph was as follows:

My editor is cooperative. He joins with his associates to produce the best newspaper possible. He knows that this process has no place for wasteful jealousies and personalities. He makes his decisions on the merits of the issues regardless of their origin or support. He solicits and welcomes the suggestions of those who work with him. He does his part in creating on his newspaper an atmosphere of free and friendly exchange.

This is still rather general but it does indicate that the editorial writer must be a notch or two above his fellows, somewhat the cream of the journalistic crop. In an address at a Champlain College convocation, Franklin B. Smith, editorial page editor of the Burlington (Vt.) *Free Press,* created very much the same impression according to the account in *Editor & Publisher* for May 1, 1971. Smith stressed two traits above others: a sense of humor and a thick skin. Both he and Dilliard insisted upon the necessity for incessant and diversified reading; each article contains specific recommendations of newspapers, magazines, and other reading material.

Eulogies to the highmindedness of those on the top rungs of the ladder of success in any field are commonplace. Goals are one thing; paragons striving to reach them are not so numerous. Dilliard and Smith were describing what editorial writers *should* be like. As the profile put together by Wilhoit and Drew indicated, the circumstantial evidence seems to be that a majority of them do possess the technical backgrounds, educational and otherwise, to qualify them to approach the high-minded summit of aspirations.

So once again, the iconoclastic H. L. Mencken and the obviously exaggerated counter-picture he painted of editorial writing colleagues in his autobiographical *Newspaper Days:*

> He (the M. E.) was himself, in fact, the chief editorial writer, and on most papers his only help in that line came from two or three ancient hulks who were unfit for any better duty—copy-readers promoted from the city-room to get rid of them, alcoholic writers of local histories and forgotten novels, former managing editors who had come to grief on other papers, and a miscellany of decayed lawyers, college professors and clergymen with whispered pasts. Some of these botches of God were pleasant enough fellows, and a few even showed a certain grasp of elemental English, but taking one with another they were held in disdain by the reporters, and it was almost unheard of for one of them to be promoted to a better job. Everyone believed as an axiom that they lifted four-fifths of their editorials from other papers, and most authorities held that they botched them in the lifting. If anyone in the city-room had ever spoken of an editorial in his own paper as cogent and illuminating he would have been set down as a jackass for admiring it and as a kind of traitor to honest journalism for reading it at all. No editorial writer was ever applied to for a loan, or invited to an office booze-party.

THE DIURNAL ROUTINE

To some of their colleagues and to others editorial writers may seem to live "the life of Riley." Writing one or two comparatively short pieces daily appears to be an easy way to make a good living. Actually it's not so simple. Editorial writers have duties other than just composing on the typewriter. Someone has to proofread, edit and dummy the page or pages; and the mail, telephone calls, visitors and conferences consume hours. The short editorial which reads so simply may have required days of painful research, and the constant complaint of frustrated editorial writers is lack of time for more painstaking digging. Eleven writers contributed to a symposium on the subject in the Fall, 1967 *Masthead.* Their pieces include quite a number of valuable suggestions for reading, cultural and civic activities. The shortest summary of what a day's work is like was contributed by William G. Peebles of the Louisville *Courier-Journal* as follows:

My day falls into a pretty definite pattern, although it can be and is broken on occasions. It is bounded by the editorial conference and the daily deadline. Beyond these it is flexible.

Our editorial conference is held at 10:30 A.M., Monday through Friday, and it runs anywhere from thirty minutes to an hour but probably averages around forty minutes. Before the conference, I try to read thoroughly the late home edition of *The Courier-Journal*, the Indiana edition, and the first edition of the afternoon *Times*—and some out-of-town papers. From this reading I draw up a list of possible editorial topics. Occasionally I might check the library or our files for some specific information on an issue before the conference.

After the conference, and depending upon the subject matter I am dealing with, I might do some research before lunch. Or I might be tied up on a telephone call. I usually break for lunch in our cafeteria around 11:45 and take about thirty minutes. Then I come back to the office and get ready to write. Our deadline is 2:30 P.M. for the next day, which doesn't give much leeway. After that I am free to work on another editorial without the pressure of a deadline. Or to see visitors. Or to just read. I leave the office around 5:00 P.M.

However, as I said, this pattern is variable. Some days I go out to lunch; on others I might go to a meeting. On those days I try to arrange things so that I am not under the deadline gun.

When people call and want to come to see me, I always try to set a time after the 2:30 deadline. Mornings are out because of the conference. As for pests, I usually try to get off the hook by telling them to write a letter. I have sometimes contemplated screaming as an alternative, but I haven't tried it yet.

When I am not writing, I am usually reading, in the course of which I have actually read an NCEW exchange when the fancy strikes me. For a break from the reading, I now and then watch girls from my window, particularly on windy days.

If the editorial writer on the large newspaper feels overworked, he still remains the object of envy of his small city counterpart whose duties may include many that do not relate to the editorial page. In fact, many one-man editorial pages are put out by managing editors or other staff members with full-time newside responsibilities. No wonder that many nonmetropolitan papers make occasional or frequent use of syndicated (canned) editorials. A possibly somewhat hyperbolic account of the plight of the small city editor who tried to write his own editorials was composed by Thomas T. Wilson, editor of the Cynthiana (Ky.) *Log Cabin*, for the Nov. 26, 1960 *Publishers' Auxiliary*:

Writing editorials, we are told (pardon the slight interruption, but we just had to wait on a customer who wanted to pay his account up to date. Part of it was already on the books and some of it hadn't been posted yet, so we had to refer to three different books before we get the complete answer).

Now let's see, where were we: "Writing editorials, we are told." But what the heck were we going to say about it? Oh yes, writing editorials, we are told, is easy. Sometimes there is no particular subject on which the editor is feeling in a (what word would be best here?) campaigning spirit. No, that word isn't so good for right now while the political campaign is on. Guess we better go back and scratch out campaigning and substitute crusading, it seems to fit just a little better.

Our old friend Sag Kash, he of the editorial bent, used to say (pardon us again, the intercom just buzzed and we find that we have a long distance phone call from Cincinnati. Oh boy, we can hardly wait to tell the rest of the gang, the call okayed using a page ad in both papers for two weeks instead of just the one paper as originally ordered. O-o-o-o, don't we wish this was an every week experience, getting orders for full pages and for two weeks at a time! ! !) Now what was it Sag used to say? We remember that we thought a few moments ago that it was worth repeating, but . . .

yeah, got it now. "Some weeks you just have to sit and suck the ideas and the words right out of your thumb."

So, you can see that writing editorials is an easy task. All that's necessary is a good subject, plenty of words and a little peace and (hold everything again. Eddie Webster has gotten another job on the press and wants it given a final check. As usual, when Eddie has charge, there isn't too much to worry about but we always like to give 'em that last check, just in case) quiet. Or is that "quiet" so cock-eyed far from the begining of the sentence that you are completely lost? If that is the case, don't feel too badly about it. You're no more lost than the editor is! ! !

During all this an air hammer is tearing up the alley just outside the window, so we do not have much peace and quiet even without the interruptions. And Charlotte White just stuck her nose over our shoulder and having read thus far, remarked only, "Oh, you crazy thing." Admitted.

So after getting the thought well (here comes Howard "Inky" Ingles' voice saying, "Tom, don't you hear me paging you in 96 point type? This . . . well, you name it . . . is being set in 10 point type so you can see he is indicating that he is paging in an emergency voice. So back to the back room for a little consultation with the foreman to see if we can't ignore what the customer presented to us and do it a little different way, so that it is possible for us and satisfactory to the customer).

"So after getting the thought well" and here the train of thought has to send back to the round house for a wrecker outfit to see if the 'train' can be gotten back on the track. Let's see, what do we do now? "So after getting the thought well" in mind, we can get the typewriter under way again and see if we can continue with sufficient words to carry out the meaning and make a sensible paragraph out of it.

(Pardon us again, but Juanita Myers just informed us that she needed more envelopes so she can continue to mail out notices to the subscribers that the time is about to expire and she wants to know the proper procedure to follow. That one was easy, all she had to do was get the money out of the register and go to the post office after the stamped envelopes.)

And so, back to the subject again. Let's check back to Page One of copy and see if we can remember what the subject was. Sure, sure, sure! We're telling how easy it is to (slam on the brakes again. Bill Hill wants to explain to us a tricky portion of an ad. Bob Whitaker had left the instructions with him before leaving for camp, and Bill wanted to be sure the editor understood it before getting the proof to the office).

Anyone can tell by now that coming up with an intelligent, well-written, cohesive editorial (Mr. Clyde Struve of Mt. Olivet just in and he tells us that he is having trouble getting his paper on time. Jug Russell at the post office is most cooperative in digging up information and making a suggestion which he hopes will solve our difficulty) is relatively simple. You need only to keep your mind on (Chuck Garrett just walked up to the desk; but he didn't want anything) what it is you're writing about and the thoughts flow quite smoothly from the keyboard of (well, what do you know? ? ? An interruption! ! ! The job ticket calls for a tan cover on the booklet and we have run completely out of tan and a new shipment isn't due for at least a week. Customer says green is quite satisfactory with him) the typewriter.

(Oh, oh, no use starting this paragraph. At least we'll get the interruption between times about now. Here comes John Harris. He wants to tell us to write a job ticket for 500 special statements. And the customer is not in a great big hurry for them . . . we love customers like that.

And so you can readily understand, why it is that sometimes the thoughts in an editorial sometimes (daggone it we forget . . . got to go tell Freddie Preston, who wraps the mail, about the change we made on Mt. Olivet . . . almost let that slip by us) seem to change abruptly and the reader wonders, "What is he trying to say?"

You will please note that Ruth Furnish hasn't bothered us at (Roger Osborne says, "Is that woman going out the one who was in Tommy's office a minute ago? I've got to see him") all on account of this is being written on her (Ruth Jacobs can't quite make out one of our ad markings for two reasons: 1—we do not write too well and 2—fingers which are well graphited smear over the stuff anyway) day off. And mostly, Tommy Preston just doesn't bother us anyway.

Honestly, each of the interruptions outlined above occurred during the process of writing this, except one which we manufactured and which could have happened. And, this is not a particularly unusual occurrence.

And so we repeat a portion of the second paragraph above: (Tommy Preston finally got into the act, he wanted to know if the mail had been picked up). Writing editorials, we are told, is easy.

SELECTING TOPICS

The procedures whereby decisions are made as to what and how topics shall be discussed differ depending largely on the size of the editorial writing staff. If only one or two write the editorials, especially if it's part-time work, any consultation between editor and writers is very informal. When the number of full-time editorial writers reaches three, however, some sort of formal conference is likely, usually in the late morning. In attendance, in addition to the editorial writers, may be the publisher, editor, managing editor, cartoonist, possibly the political editor and others, all depending on the size of the total operation.

Whoever presides at the meeting, large or small, makes and receives suggestions for topics to be the subject matter of editorial comment. Even with a writing staff of only three there may be some standing division of labor, possibly local, national and international, so the discussion of a current news item may be led by the person into whose field of interest it naturally falls. Not necessarily, however, and how decisions are made depends on the way in which politics are determined—by managerial fiat or by democratic deliberations.

After a decision is reached, by no matter what method, the person to actually compose the editorial is designated by the chief editorial writer or another higher-up. Then comes the research and the actual composition in time to make the deadline.

Newspapers seldom engage in shop talk for the benefit of readers. Thus, the editorial on "The 'How' of Chronicle Editorials" which appeared in the San Francisco *Chronicle* for July 6, 1947, was a rare example. It follows:

This will be an editorial about editorials. Chronicle editorials, specifically, and how they come into being. In approaching the subject we knowingly risk the accusation of self-indulgence at the expense of leaving world and local events to go shift for themselves, but we have a purpose. It is to afford the reader of this page some understanding of how we reach conclusions, and perhaps some basis for judging the worth of those conclusions. Omniscience is not one of our virtues. But in the preparation of this page we start from the single premise that we've got to be responsible, and the rest of the process is a system calculated to implement that responsibility. It isn't fool-proof, sometimes we're wrong. When that happens, and we discover it, we admit—that's part of the obligation incurred when one accepts responsibility. At other times, when we come up against one of these imponderables that crop up with increasing and vexing frequency in this twentieth century, we can do no more than give you our best judgment, and when that happens we label it as such.

But most times we deal in convictions, and it is chiefly about those convictions, and how they're hammered out in our shop, that we're going to talk now.

The Chronicle editorials are not the product of one mind in any case, but of a half dozen minds turned loose upon an idea. That idea may come from the mind of the editor, or the editorial page director, or any of the five editorial writers, or any of a hundred, or thousand, different sources. In any case, the process is the same.

The idea is turned loose in a morning editorial conference, during the initial phases of which the editor is absent.

Sometimes the Idea Just Doesn't Jell

The ball is pitched, and everybody who likes takes a cut at it. It may be batted around for only five minutes before its worth is tested and its form becomes discernible. Sometimes it's kept in the air for a half hour. Sometimes it never comes down at all—it depends upon the nature of the idea itself, the amount of information available upon it and the degree to which it squares with the composite convictions of the group as modified by the fresh information available.

There are, of course, some long-standing, underlying convictions held by the editor and the entire group. These are likely to be pretty basic, more basic—for example—than a political party lable or a man's religion or nationality. The desirability of lasting peace, for example, is hardly debatable; neither is the necessity for the advancement of human dignity; neither is the ultimate inevitability of One World; neither is the proposition that the recovery of Europe depends upon resumed production; neither is the necessity for the most foolproof possible system of atomic control. As in any other thoughtful American forum where common sense is held in higher esteem than spite, hate, fear, or any of the blinding passions, these things are accepted as truths.

But the means of achieving them often provides the very meat of editorial conference discussion.

Since we opened with a disavowal of omniscience, we are not going to try to persuade you that the results of the discussions which are in evidence here day after day have any superhuman merit. A half dozen men can be as wrong as one man—but we think they are not so likely to be.

And, too, the systematic lessening of that likelihood is one of the principal jobs of the Chronicle editorial staff.

Apart from the banging together of ideas, there are two chief means by which we go about whittling down that likelihood. We read everything we can get our hands on, and we go out into the field as often and extensively as possible and see for ourselves how things are.

Sources Are Numbered in the Hundreds

The written matter is, we suppose, more or less standard in all editorial offices. The Encyclopedia Britannica is always there—a faithful, stolid pillar of information. Unfortunately, a compendium like Britannica cannot be brought out every week, or even every year, so the research must chiefly be in documents of more current vintage. The laws introduced and adopted at Sacramento and Washington are a never-ending source of knowledge; the opinions of the Supreme Court, the utterances and written works of the recognized atomic scientists; informed foreign publications like the Manchester Guardian and the London Economist; and, of course, the daily and ever-growing grist of day-to-day news as recorded by the great wire services and the Chronicle's own staff of reporters. The sifting, weighing, collating and correlation of the information that comes from these and hundreds of other sources provide the bulk of the background against which opinions are examined.

But this is not enough—exclusive resort to the ideas formulated and predigested by other people would in itself make for an editorial page that lacked at least individuality and at most a deep personal sense of conviction.

So to supplement the ideas of others, the editorial page staff goes out to prospect with its own pick and pan.

A Chronicle editorial writer periodically shows up at the Legislature, probing about for the facts in one or another field of current lawmaking. Prior to writing an extensive piece on conditions at the Preston School for Boys another Chronicle editorial writer spent several days there, getting a mass of evidence and opinion from all quarters, out of which ultimately an editorial crystallized. During the past 12 months still other members of the page staff have been in New Mexico, Wright Field at Dayton, Ohio; Washington, New York, the American occupied zones of Western Europe, and Bikini to gather material which later went into Chronicle editorials. All this in the interests of keeping our antennae up and our incidence of error down.

So (we're back in the conference now) the three or four or half dozen topics in the day's news asserting the most demand for comment are talked out through the morning and tentative decisions reached on the angle for attack and the man who's to write the piece.

The Editor Exercises Final Authority

Then the editor comes in, lights up a cigarette, tilts back in his chair and receives a summary of each projected editorial from the man who's going to write it. Sometimes the synopsis is approved as offered; sometimes the editor amends it; sometimes he tosses in a new angle that starts the discussion all over again; frequently, in his own mulling over the day's events, he has been struck with the significance of some piece of news the initial conferees have passed over. In any event, as editor of the Chronicle he holds the responsibility and exercises the authority of final judgment regarding what the editorial space of the following day is going to say. When that judgment has been rendered, the writers turn to their typewriters and go to work. In this activity as in others, the editor is the representative of the publisher, with whom he frequently hammers out basic policy decisions—usually out of normal working hours.

The supervision, of course, doesn't end there. Each editorial as it comes out of the typewriter is read by at least one other editorial writer. Then the original goes to the editor of the page, with duplications to the editor and the "make-up" man, responsible for the physical composition of the page. The original, if approved, goes to the composing room to be set up in type. Proofs are run from the type when set and read for typographical errors. The editor of the page then determines, under direction of the editor of the whole newspaper, where each piece shall appear in the page—what "play" to give each for maximum effectiveness and best appearance. And when the page has gone into the mold, proofs of the whole page are pulled and studied by the entire editorial page staff for any "bugs" that may have shown up.

Handicaps to Chronicle Type of Policy

You may by now have a rough idea of how the Chronicle editorial page—and the policy it pursues—comes out.

There are certain handicaps to such a policy, so evolved—handicaps that must afflict any organ of opinion that clings to just a few rudimentary principles and endeavors to give each day's news its due in the modification of its own thinking.

It's a lot easier to make up your mind in advance and watch for events to bolster your opinions. It would be easier, for instance, to be a rock-ribbed Republican paper and read baleful and portentous meaning into every act committed by these addle-brained characters in the Administration. It would also be easier to run a whole-souled left-wing sheet and damn every move of the National Association of Manufacturers, or any member thereof, as calculated to shove the little guy still deeper into the mire. Anyone who has ever written for a living knows the sheer exhileration of being able to get hopping mad, and stay that way day after day, bedeviling the opposition with endless volleys of short, hard, succulent, colorful invective. It's fun and it's effective—you have your ready-cut audience of like-minded citizens, and even though they know exactly what you're going to say before you say it, you always roll them in the aisles.

Newspapers like the Chronicle have to forgo that fun—but there are some deeper satisfactions in our way of doing.

For one thing, we can live with ourselves, not in any spirit of complacency but with the knowledge that we've called the shots to the best of our ability, and if we erred it was honestly and not maliciously.

But There Are Likewise a Few Compensations

For another thing, we have a feeling of rendering an honest service. Whether you agree with us on any given editorial or not, we've at least taken the time to marshal the facts, to weigh them and hammer them and hold them up to the light, and finally to write down an interpretation that represents the best thinking of the whole group of us. We thus are able to give you not one man's viewpoint, but one newspaper's viewpoint, reached on the basis of all the information that comes within the grasp of a modern newspaper.

We're not in all this expecting or asking for your agreement in all our ideas. If in these troubled times we can contribute even a little to the public awareness of the issues we're all facing, and their importance to all of us and the role free Americans can play in their resolution, we shall have done what we set out to do.

Where do ideas for editorials come from? Probably the majority are what might be called "must" editorials, depending upon the scope of the editorial page's interests. For large metropolitan papers mostly the entire world is their news and editorial responsibility, so they cannot ignore a revolution in the Middle East, a speech by the Secretary of Defense, a new tax bill introduced into the state legislature or a championship won by a local professional football team. The same universal outlook may be taken by smaller papers that are isolated and whose circulation is dominant in restricted areas, with few readers seeing papers from outside. Other small city papers may be more limited in the range of topics about which they think it is essential to comment, possibly because their readers also read other papers, presumably those published in nearby large cities. Some of the strongest editorial pages are in small circulation dailies that confine themselves almost entirely to local problems. Whatever the yardstick by which to judge, there are almost always more potential subjects "crying" to be handled than there are facilities for meeting the responsibility. So there really is no problem finding subject matter for daily comment.

It's not the topic that's difficult to come by but the angle from which to tackle it.

Even the most open-minded objective research can be, perhaps must be, motivated. The fact finder goes after the financial aspect of the topic at hand or he delves into the personalities involved; he may seek lessons from parallel situations in the past or in some other way restrict himself to what he can reasonably be expected to accomplish given the time and resources at his command. A fault of beginning editorial writers often is that they try to cover too much territory in a single piece. When you know a lot about a subject of importance, it is better to write more than one editorial than to try superficially to suggest every idea you have in a single piece.

In addition to the front page all an editorial writer's other reading is suggestive of editorials. Like the off-duty policeman, the editorial writer is on the job around the clock. He thinks in terms of editorial interpretations, so every television show or motion picture or play is potentially valuable to him. Or he becomes aware during some conversations with other people that there exist misconceptions or mysteries regarding certain matters of contemporary concern. He assumes the obligation to investigate so as to set the record straight. A first-class example of such an editorial is the following from the New York *Times* for July 30, 1971.

The Worst Drug Problem

This country's worst drug problem—in terms of number of individuals seriously affected, annual economic loss and similar indices—is neither heroin nor marijuana nor any other of the drugs newly come to fashion. Rather it is that terrible old and reliable destroyer of lives: alcohol.

The victims of what might well be called alcohol-abuse are estimated to number in excess of ten million Americans; the economic toll annually is now measured in the billions of dollars. At least half of the nation's traffic fatalities are the result of accidents involving drunken drivers, while tens of thousands of persons die each year from alcohol-related ailments.

Given the immense dimensions of the problem, it is curious that alcoholism has received so little medical or public attention until recently. In retrospect this country went from one extreme—the vain effort two generations ago to ban alcoholic beverages under prohibition—to the other extreme of almost ignoring the matter. Now at last there is evidence of rising concern and of major efforts to meet the problem. President Nixon signed into law last January the Alcohol Abuse, Prevention, Treatment and Rehabilitation Act; New York City announced last March a new program aimed at reaching more of the city's estimated 300,000 alcoholics; and now a philanthropist, R. Brinkley Smithers, has set a useful example for others by donating $10 million for an alcoholic treatment and rehabilitation center at Roosevelt Hospital.

Even more important than treatment of alcoholics, however, is prevention, though it is hard to be optimistic about such efforts in this superpermissive era. Nevertheless, the attempt desperately needs to be made, and society needs to view excessive alcohol consumption with at least as much public distaste as it does excessive cigarette smoking.

Often the origin of an idea for an editorial is inspirational. It may come as one is falling off to sleep or shaving or driving to work. All writers of any kind have the experience of what seems to be a revelation. Many keep pads and pens handy, at bedsides and in convenient pockets so as to jot down ideas and effective word combinations before they are forgotten. Among the saddest words a writer can utter are, "I had a wonderful idea in the middle of the night but I didn't get up and now I've forgotten what it was."

Just as the reporter composes leads for his news stories on the way back to the office, so does the editorial writer concoct effective phrases as he walks or rides or reposes. Says Robert White II, "Editorials are written before you sit down at the typewriter. That is to say, the thinking is more important than the writing. If the thinking is clear, the writing can be. It's only when the thinking isn't clear that the writing gets muddied." White recalls Arthur Sulzberger's phrase, "the well-stocked mind" and declares: "I try to fill my mind with as much material out of the daily news report as possible. My scheme is to have that information available to measure up editorial possibilities of news breaks as they come along."

White also provides an excellent case study of the unconventional handling of a personal experience with significance to many others. He explains:

It's local, it says something—it criticizes the parent who thinks that he is an expert in coaching; and hopefully it is amusing and interesting too.

It happened exactly the way it is written —I had no intention of going. I had no intention of writing anything, and the experience was so pertinent I, of course, wrote it.

I wrote it even though it is not a normal editorial because I don't think editorials should be personal. But in this case it was the exception and an exception that I felt was worthwhile. I should add I ran it on a Saturday when the paper somehow is a little less formidable and permits a little more levity than any other day of the week.

The editorial was as follows:

Who Is Best At Coaching?

This editor writes about being a coach with perhaps more authority than he has on most subjects.

For two years he coached; he used to be a sports editor; he has friends who are coaches; he likes sports; in fact, he is a sport nut. . . .

This summer his seven year old son, Mitch, was in the baseball program for 7-, 8- and 9-year-olds. He worked hard at it. However, he had a long way to go. We asked him one day if he "did better today." "No," he said, "I did badder."

Well, the most important moment of the entire summer for him was the final game. The Hardin Park team (that's Mitch and his friends) played the Plunkett Park team.

Mitch was almost too excited the night before to sleep.

He asked this editor to come watch the game. We explained we were too busy to leave the office.

The next morning at breakfast, Mitch said he sure would appreciate it if we would come watch. We explained we were too busy.

As we were getting in the car to come to work, Mitch came running out of the house.

"Dad," he said, "If you get even a minute please try and watch. It starts at 9."

So we left the office at 9:30 and went out to Plunkett Park to watch. We watched Mitch sitting on the bench until 10:30. While he sat the bench fairly well for a beginner, we were getting mighty nervous about getting back to work. Besides, why didn't they put him in? Maybe that coach didn't know about the importance of a little boy getting to play; maybe he didn't know how much Mitch had practiced in the backyard. Maybe . . . and suddenly we realized we were guilty of something called parent-coaching. We never had any patience with parents who get all excited about the coach and criticize him because he didn't let their youngster play, or played him too much, or whatever. Usually parents are not good judges of their youngster's ability. Usually the coach is. We knew better than to be a parent-coach. But there we were watching our son sit that bench and, of all things, found ourselves thinking critical things about the coach.

It was now the 7th inning and the score was about 14 to 21, one way or the other. We ambled down to the coach and asked, "You know, I'm desperate to get back to work, could you help. . . .?"

"Sure," the coach said, "Mitch, go in there at center field."

Mitch jumped up and said, "Yes, sir, where is it?"

Moral: coaches usually do know what they are doing.

One never knows when something he learned at any time in the past will be of value to him. Some *bon mot* of his second grade teacher may come in handy years later; or the lesson learned in a history class; or the experience of being a good winner or loser in a spelling bee or debate or athletic contest. It's not really so much what you know as how smart you are in putting it to use.

Editorial ideas are obtained from callers and correspondents. There are many people who request that editorials be written to boost a cause or to condemn some situation. Colleagues in other departments of the paper sometimes come up with ideas, although the general practice is for them to ignore editorial writers while often wondering why their views are not solicited.

So, to summarize, where do ideas for editorials come from? They come from anywhere and everywhere, all over the place. An imaginative editorial writer gets inspiration where a humdrum one doesn't. It's immaterial whether the gift is inborn or cultivated. By the time he obtains the opportunity to write editorials for a regular publication, one must have acquired the knack of seeing opportunities without much trouble. If he lacks the ability to do so his job will be torture.

STORY OF AN EDITORIAL

Among the responses to the form letter that this book's author sent out to professional editorial writers soliciting their assistance was the following from James Clemon, chief editorial writer for the Omaha *World-Herald*. It could be called a diary as it pertains to a particular editorial, as follows:

Friend author:

I'm sitting here with your letter staring at me, and it suddenly occurs: What the hell, why not send him the stuff I'm working on right now as a case study?

It's a pretty run-of-the-mill effort—an editorial plugging the youth voter registration campaign. But a great share of all our efforts are run-of-the-mill, meat-and-potatoes pieces. This probably is as representative of my day-in, day-out work as anything.

The idea originated with a young man working this summer as an intern in our advertising department. He was editor of the Nebraska U. student daily last semester, deeply interested in public affairs, attracted by opinion writing. Some would describe him as a long-hair peacenik.

He told me about the Young Voters League, what it is and what it wants to do. He said the effort would have a much better chance of success, particularly in enlisting some Establishment help, if it had some respectable publicity. We'd had a couple short news items, but after talking with this young fellow I decided it was worth an encouraging editorial. The editor agreed.

In addition to my conversation with our young man, I read the items we'd run about the league. I also read the background of young voter registration in our state, which led to the remarks in the editorial about apathy. I had a hell of a time finding out how many 18-21-year olds there are in Nebraska, but our chief political reporter finally dug it out for me. Other references came from the Census Bureau, second-hand in a voter profile book by Jerry Friedheim.

The main problem, aside from assembling factual data, was finding an approach that might help allay some of the fears of some of our older readers about the "young radical political machine." I hope I achieved that goal. On policy, no problem. We have supported the 18-year-old vote right along.

I almost always work out my first draft longhand, with pen. It slows me down, which helps keep me from wasting words. I have an unhappy facility for fast typing, which makes it too easy to rattle on and on. Second draft went through the typewriter, without too much change. When you see the words typed, it's easier to polish. So the third draft concentrates on style—changing construction from passive to active, shortening sentences, putting in names to give it "people power," punching it up here and there. (Frosting.) Copies of these drafts are enclosed, for whatever they're worth.

The third version of the editorial, which was the one that was printed, was as follows:

Young Nebraska
Gets Ready To Vote

Young Nebraskans are wasting no time getting ready to take advantage of their newly-won right to vote.

The Nebraska League of Young Voters, a fledgling organization of the fledgling franchised, is making ambitious plans to stimulate registration and interest in political activity among the state's 191,000 first-time voters.

Cochairmen are Michael K. Nelson of Omaha and Dave Holst of Hastings. Many others are in on the start of the effort.

They will work this summer to build organizations at the county and congressional district levels. They will open a storefront office in Lincoln. They are asking the help of both political parties. They are approaching adult civic and political leaders for ideas and money.

The organizers want to enlist a broad cross-section of the state's youth in reaching out to the farthest grassroots. They want the help of college and high school students, those out of school and working, young people in such institutions as trade schools, and youth organizations such as 4H and FFA.

As we see it, the two main problems facing the young workers are apathy and the danger of partisan taint.

Young people do not have the best reputation for citizenship in voting. The Census Bureau says persons under 25 have the lowest election participation rate. Secretary of State Allen Berrman said last week that so few of the newly enfranchised youths have registered that he isn't even bothering to keep statistics on them yet. He said that in many counties only one or two have registered.

However, Berrman also noted that the youths have plenty of time to register before the primary election next spring. And the ratification of the Twenty-sixth Amendment last Wednesday is expected to excite many 18-year-olds.

The young organizers seem to be acutely aware of the other problem, the danger of losing credibility through the intrusion of partisanship. They plan to achieve the best balance they can in their use of political party help, and want to try to interest their peers in politics without advocating specific postions on issues or personalities.

The point they make, wisely, is that there are plenty of other outlets for partisan interests. The movement to encourage young voters should cut across party and ideological lines.

It may prove difficult to hold down the red-hots and avoid giving opportunists a vehicle. But at the outset, the league's founders seem to be sufficiently sensitive to the danger of alienating adult Nebraskans and potential young voters by showing political favoritism. (Some adult-run organizations, such as John Gardner's Common Cause, should have been as wary.)

Many adults have shown an unreasoning, unreasonable fear of the possible consequences of lowering the voting age. Other grownups have taken a so-what attitude on the grounds that "those kids won't bother to vote anyway."

The Nebraska League of Young Voters, and other young people working to make the franchise mean something, have a chance to prove these elders wrong. We wish them success, and urge Nebraskans of all persuasions to support their efforts.

TAKING A STAND

Perhaps the strongest adverse criticism that can be made of editorial writing as a profession, in the United States today at least, is that decisions as to what stands to take on issues are made before adequate research has been done. Daily there are "must" editorials, meaning there has been news within the preceding 24 hours on which it is deemed essential that there be editorial comment immediately.

The "here is a problem" type of editorial never is strong and is justifiable only in cases in which the existence of the so-called problem has been newly discovered and all of the pertinent facts necessary to make a decision are not available. The paper

which "smells a rat" and alerts everyone to the fact that "there's something rotten in the state of Denmark" may perform a public service even though it leaves the reader in a quandary as to who the good and bad guys are.

Ordinarily, in such situations, the good and bad guys have been identified by a reporter but the timing of the editorial still is important. Fairness and common sense alike dictate waiting until enough facts are known before commenting. If the issue is not a clear-cut one of virtue versus righteousness but of alternative courses of action or differences of interpretation, it's smart to hold off until the city room has done a little more thorough job of fact-finding. Especially in one-newspaper cities, editors should restrain themselves and not feel they must rush into print before there has been time to learn all the facts and soberly evaluate the alternative attitudes toward them. Insinuations of wrongdoing may be injurious if not libelous and certainly are unfair; also they are bad for a newspaper's reputation for veracity and good judgment.

Basic policy or underlying philosophy often makes it possible to come to a quick decision on a specific issue. Few newspapers any more print platforms at the heads of their editorial columns, to advocate better garbage collection or lower taxes or the like, but the social, economic and political views of management may be consistently for or against certain proposals. A newspaper whose ownership believes strongly in developing public welfare programs, for instance, might not be so enthusiastic about a money-making drive for private charities as would a paper with a strong "government keep hands off" viewpoint. An editor who believes only an uplift of the spirit or a revival of moral and religious feeling can save the world probably would not be so enthusiastic about proposals to spend millions on additional policemen and crime detection devices to compel obedience to the law.

These illustrations suggest that sometimes the reaction an editor has to a specific proposal may not be consciously consistent but nevertheless be rooted in his deep-seated convictions which in turn come from many personality traits and psychological factors. Avid readers of any editorial page can often predict the attitude that they will find expressed there on a particular matter. This may indicate laudable consistency or it may indicate stubborn refusal to weigh issues on their merits. There is less fanaticism in daily newspaper editorializing than one would expect to find in special interest publications such as those put out by religious or minority groups of almost any kind. The so-called "regular" press makes more of a conscious effort to be objective than does a special interest or dedicated press. Maybe everyone is being self-deceptive but even pretentious attempts deserve some commendation.

Readers prefer editorials that take clear-cut stands. The editorial that "views with alarm" or "points with pride" usually is an innocuous collection of words which anyone can safely ignore. The editorial page which specializes in that sort of wishy-washy or fence straddling type of editorial could use the space to better advantage in some other way. Certainly it would be a waste of time to illustrate in a how-to-do-it book of this sort how to write such editorials. You don't need a book to learn how. You don't even need to go to school. In fact, you'd be happier if you didn't do so.

The exception to the rule of fence straddling is when it is desired to emphasize something which may have received inadequate attention in the news columns or which merits repeating and emphasis. Even so an editor may be suspected of just being lazy. It seems likely that almost any editorial of this sort would be strengthened by some original research to localize its appeal. Such certainly was true of the following example from the Quincy (Ill.) *Herald-Whig* for Jan. 10, 1972. The last

paragraph contains the kernel of an idea for elaboration into a localized piece. The handling the paper gave Missouri would be called Afghanistanism, meaning that altogether too often editors are courageous in discussing problems faraway but timid about tackling similar situations within their circulation areas.

Hunting Accidents

A study of gun hunting accidents made by the University of Missouri and the Missouri Department of Conservation can be summarized, says the department, with: "Remember the magic words—horseplay, and 'I didn't know it was loaded.'"

If one could cut out the two problems, it was added, "gun accidents virtually would disappear."

During the period of the study, 1962 through 1968, Missouri had 280 firearms accidents, an average of about 46 a year. About 27 per cent of the 280 accidents were fatal. Such carelessness as crossing a fence with a loaded gun and dropping guns—which the report classes as horseplay—accounted for 19 per cent of the accidents.

Hunters involved shot themselves 43 per cent of the time, the study determined. The remainder were shot by hunting companions who were swinging on game, which occurs largely in bird shooting accidents, or were mistaken for game. The last occurs especially in deer hunting, and in its news release on the cooperative hunting accident survey the department noted that during the recent 1971 deer season there were two fatal accidents in which hunters were mistaken for deer, despite the fact one victim was wearing bright red clothing.

Neither shooter in these two accidents had had gun safety training. Such training is considered essential to safe handling of hunting arms and in Missouri schools departmental personnel is conducting an intensive safety training program for both boys and girls. In 1970 instructors certified 17,233 students.

The cooperative study of hunting accidents showed, among other things, that the

13-25 age group is involved in 65 per cent of hunting accidents.

Half of the accidents involved shotguns, but .22 caliber rifles were responsible for 24 of 75 deaths. Feared, high-powered "deer rifles" took only six lives, and defective guns killed an equal number.

Bud Eyman, hunting safety coordinator for the Missouri Department of Conservation, says: "Hunting is a safer sport—considering the many thousands of people who do it and the relatively few accidents—than nearly any other activity. But one accident is one too many. Maybe when every Missourian has had hunter safety training we can relax a little."

Local sportsmen here in Quincy, it should be noted, have launched a program of offering hunting safety training to youths. It is a most commendable effort.

That this newspaper is not afraid to take a stand is illustrated by the following editorial from its issue of Oct. 10, 1971. It refers to a series of stories and pictures and probably was a factor in the discharge of the highway superintendent from the post he had held for 18 years.

County Highway Post

During the last ten days The Herald-Whig has published a series of stories and pictures dealing with Adams County highways. They were inspired by the fact that the Adams County Board of Supervisors now has under consideration the application of John Treuthart, county superintendent of highways, for reappointment to a six-year term of office, at a discussed salary increase of approximately 50 per cent.

Our study of the highway system which Treuthart has superintended for nearly 18 years has raised serious doubts as to whether Treuthart should be retained. The decision, of course, is up to the Board of Supervisors. It is their responsibility, but they are accountable to the voters and taxpayers of Adams County. Before entrusting the county highway system to the direction of John Treuthart for another six years we believe the supervisors should do some careful thinking.

Citizens of Adams County have been thinking and have been asking questions. The supervisors should do no less.

Our county roads have been developed—where developed—largely to only minimal standards. One result has been what seems an abnormally high maintenance cost. We have old and inadequate bridges in many locations. Our roads are poorly marked . . . if marked at all.

Many of our roads, including some busy ones that carry heavy traffic in the urban area of outlying Quincy are narrow, lack safe shoulders and present dangerous roadside ditches.

It may seem unfair to blame one official for all the shortcomings of our county roads, but a county superintendent has a lot of authority and must assume responsibility—accountability. He, after all, is the professional employed to plan, design and superintend construction and maintenance. And Adams County, under John Treuthart's guidance, has not acquired the kind of road system to which its residents are entitled—and are paying for.

Both planning and delivery by Treuthart seems at times to be haphazard, if not downright capricious. Promised and badly needed major developments have hung fire for far too long. Enumerating them is unnecessary. They are—or should be—well known to the citizens of Adams County. They should especially be known to members of the County Board.

Excellent country road systems have been developed in many places. One need only cite the county systems one finds in neighboring Missouri, and especially in the counties of our neighbor state to the north, Wisconsin. We, in contrast, have a few good county roads, many that are inadequate.

It is time, The Herald-Whig believes, for members of the Adams County Board of Supervisors to face up to reality and consider naming a county superintendent of highways for the next six years very carefully.

The task of the decision makers is not difficult regarding many if not most matters, as they clearly relate to situations or propositions for which there is precedence.

The paper's stand on such matters is known and it merely remains to update it as regards whatever the immediate news item happens to be. Nevertheless, it is hopefully presumed that at some time adequate research was conducted and alternative viewpoints given full consideration. In other words, it is to be hoped that viewpoints are not come by lightly, as a result of ignorant or superstitious unconscious prejudice or selfish interest. No doubt one can always find a stupid and biased audience for his ignorant and prejudicial effusions, but if one has any confidence in the ability of man to think and act rationally, he believes that ultimately the intellectual charlatan will fail. What follows is a thoroughly ignorant and prejudicial editorial, together with marginal notes pointing out its obvious shortcomings. This is an example of what happens when editorial writing becomes a matter of frenetic red-necked rabble-rousing rhetoric. Informed and other intelligent people are not impressed favorably. The editorial fails in the long run because of its palpable idiocies.

Whither Are We Drifting?

Comment

In the confusion of labels, political philosophies and ideologies, it is not strange that the average citizen asks: Just what is Socialism?

This is a trite rhetorical device to make the editorial seem more important than it is.

The term is vague, and often misused to cover a multitude of beliefs. As such, it may appear either as a harmless brand of idealism or else as something alien and remote from the American system, which ostensibly is based on the true liberalism of individual enterprise, initiative, incentive, and freedom. It can't happen here, too many Americans believe.

Text and reference book definitions are clear. That of the *Random House Dictionary of the English Language* is typical: "A theory or system of social organization which advocates the vesting of the ownership and control of the means of production, capital, land, etc., in the community as a whole." A synonym with a more favorable connotation is "government ownership."

Essentially Socialism is the system whereby governments, rather than individuals, control the wealth of the nation and apportion it out to each citizen as the state deems advisable. Under the system on which the United States was founded and has grown to greatness, its citizens control and support the government under the principle stated by Abraham Lincoln: "In all that the people can individually do as well for themselves the government should not interfere." This is essential for as Woodrow Wilson observed: "Freedom exists where the people take care of the government."

This picture of government apportioning out wealth as it sees fit is a humorous caricature of reality.

This is a fantastic distortion of both socialism and the American form of government. It creates a false separation between government and governed. In a representative democracy the people elect the government; they *are* the government. There is no force separate and apart from the people.

In the opposite system—Socialism, under all its manifold labels and in all its deceiving guises—the state supports the people. And those whom it supports, it naturally controls. That is the death of freedom, of incentive, of opportunity. The birth-right of liberty has been bartered for the pottage of so-called security. The test, then, of the degree of Socialism in any given government is simple: To what ex-

This seems to be a not-so-eloquent appeal for anarchy.

tent do its citizens depend upon the government for support?

It is startling, therefore, to learn from figures compiled by the United States Department of Commerce that aggregate government payments to individuals came to a record $45,200,000,000 last year.

In other words, one dollar in every six received as individual income by the American people last year came from the government—state, local, or federal. The camel of Socialism not only has its head under the flap; it is already one-sixth of the way into the tent.

It is equally significant, too, that this is the result of an accelerating trend. The proportion of government payments to total income payments has risen from 7.3% in 1929 to 16.2% in 1950—an increase of approximately 122% This is more than creeping Socialism: it is a government galloping toward the socialistic goal of control of all wealth and allocation of all income.

Nor is there any indication that the trend is likely to be reversed unless the American people awaken and reverse it themselves. For, as the United States Chamber of Commerce reported last week, President Truman has collected more taxes from the American people than all other Presidents combined and has spent more than one-third of all the money ever spent by the United States government.

War and defense expenditures are responsible for part of this, but not all. Much of it has gone to make big government bigger and more powerful. The National Small Businessmen's Association, for example, reports that in the last 10 years the peace-time spending of the Department of Commerce has increased 1,049%; the Department of Interior, 696%; the Department of Labor, 1,283%; the Department of Justice, 158%; the State Department, 1,634%; and the independent offices, 176%. And each dollar of increase represents a drain on Ameri-

This could mean farmers who receive subsidies; airplanes, shipping and multitudes of businesses that get handouts, tax exemptions, and other forms of financial aid. Are they controlled by government, or is exactly the opposite true—do they control government?

This $1 for every $6 is obtained by counting every cent spent by government: local, state, and federal, as "payments to individuals." In 1950 the total national income was $238,963 million. The federal government spent $40,167 million, about 50 percent on the Korean war and other military activities, buying goods from American businessmen. State and local governments spent $13.2 billion that year. The "camel of Socialism," therefore, is everything that is not anarchy—to include the costs of public schools or the post office, publicly owned utilities, police, the army and navy and all other governmental activities.

Percentages are statistically deceptive. Federal governmental expenditures in 1950 were about 16% of the national income. In 1929 they were nearly 4%. So the increase in percentages was 400%. In 1929 the federal government spent $3,249 million; in 1950 it spent $40,167 million. The former year was the peak year of the so-called Coolidge Prosperity era, a year of world peace. In the latter year World War II debts still were unpaid and the Korean War was raging. The increase in expenditures was not due to creeping socialism unless it is defined as foreign war in the interest of and with the support of Big Business.

Article I, Section 7, of the United States Constitution provides: "All bills of revenue shall originate in the House of Representatives. . . ." No president can collect taxes after the manner of a bad king in the Old Testament or a fairy tale.

The National Small Businessmen's Association is a front for the National Association of Manufacturers and by no means controlled by or representative of small business. In 1953 it urged President Eisenhower, in office after "20 years of treason," to sell the Tennessee Valley Authority and turn the post office over to Wells Fargo or Western Union.

Again, percentages are meaningless. When a man marries his family size increases 100%. When a

can productivity and an additional lever over the freedom of the individual.

The answer is clear, then, to the question: whither are we drifting? We are drifting, and rapidly, to the complete Socialism of the all powerful state.

If you value your freedom, it is time to check that drift.

child arrives it goes up another 50%. One can increase a donation 50%, from $10 to $15, whereas the $100 which another adds to his $1,000 gift is only a 10% increase. Thus, five times as much in actual amount is only one-fifth in percentages. Completely ignored is what the taxpayer gets for his money. Government has expanded its services mostly as a result of strong urging by different elements in the population. That "each, dollar of increase represents a drain on American productivity and an additional lever over the freedom of the individual" is just complete nonsense from any standpoint than that of a pure anarchist.

It is frightening that such careless practices should appear in a leading American newspaper, in this case the Indianapolis *News* for Nov. 26, 1951.

CANNED EDITORIALS

Even worse is the syndicated or "canned" editorial. Most notorious are those distributed by the Industrial News Review operated since 1913 by E. Hofer & Sons of Portland, Ore., a public relations firm. Financed by private power companies and other big businesses, this service sends a dozen or so well-written editorials to about 12,000 editors every week. According to the late Sen. Richard L. Neuberger, a longtime newspaperman, in an article reprinted in the *Nieman Reports* for October, 1949, "In doctrine they reflect a viewpoint on American economic life which faded at about the time Teddy Roosevelt succeeded McKinley."

One of the first exposés of the Hofer operation was by Louis M. Lyons, then curator, in the July, 1948 *Nieman Reports*. Lyons revealed that 59 newspapers with a combined circulation of 390,008 had used an INR editorial which he said distorted the viewpoint of a speech by Harvard President James B. Conant. Lyons concluded his piece by stating, "The medical profession has a procedure for malpractice. So do the lawyers. There is an American

Newspaper Publishers Association and an American Society of Newspaper Editors, and there are ethical codes for journalism sponsored by these and by state press associations. This exhibit is offered to any who accept any responsibility in these matters."

Neither of the groups Lyons mentioned nor any other has ever taken any action. In the 1920s the Federal Trade Commission confirmed the source of Hofer income as being various private utilities, a fact which Hofer never has tried to disguise. In fact, Hofer says it "is supported financially by industry, business, and professions, including public utilities, retailers, railroads, mines, manufacturers, food processors, petroleum, financial institutions, and others who believe that community prosperity and growth, sound government and reasonable taxation, must accompany individual and corporate prosperity."

Senators McNamara of Michigan and Metcalf of Montana spoke against Hofer for its campaign in opposition to Medicare in the mid-sixties. Metcalf pointed out that each week "one editorial glorified the drug industry, the oil industry, the railroad industry, and the chamber of commerce taxpayer groups," and two of the editorials "sang the praises of the public utility industry." On alternate weeks editorials were sent out praising Pan-American Airways, Railway Express Agency, American Meat

Institute, chain stores, the timber industry, etc., as Charles A. Sprague, editor and publisher of the *Oregon Statesman* of Salem, Oregon summarized it in the Spring, 1966 *Masthead*.

The extent to which the INR editorials are used was demonstrated by Dennie Lowery, a student in a University of Colorado journalism seminar conducted by Prof. A. Gayle Waldrop. After his findings were turned down by most other journalism publications, *Nieman Reports* printed them in its July, 1955 issue. Of 96 Colorado editors who returned Lowery's questionnaire, 32 said they used INR copy, at least occasionally, and several stated they use 100 to 200 items a year. Lowery estimated that the INR editorials reached about 100,000 Colorado subscribers a week. None of the papers gave credit to INR for the material.

Over the years the main target of INR editorials has been public power operations. At their Nashville meeting in 1967, NCEW members heard Frank E. Smith, a Tennessee Valley Authority director, lambast "newspapers of the country who prostitute their editorial responsibility by publishing as their own editorials the products of anonymous propaganda boiler-plate sweatshops," to use words in a subsequent article Smith wrote for the Summer 1971 *Masthead*. Smith exposed errors of fact and interpretation in anti-TVA editorials distributed by Hofer and called the editorials "paid propaganda, subtly introduced as independent opinion and aimed as much at 'educating' the editor as the general public." Of approximately 200 anti-TVA checked by the TVA library, more than 60 percent appeared in more than one paper "but with no indication that they were not the individual product and opinion of the paper which printed them," Smith wrote. "When the same critical editorial, word for word, appears without attribution in widely dispersed newspapers (which he named) . . . it is not the result of some suddenly awakening public interest in the Tennessee

Valley Authority but it merely indicates that the Hofer canning factory has distributed another product."

A report on Smith's NCEW speech appeared in the Winter 1967-68 *Masthead* and the entire speech, together with the subsequent question-and-answer period, was reproduced in the convention proceedings printed in booklet form in November, 1967, by the Nashville *Tennessean*.

Hofer's does not have a monopoly on pressure tactics through canned editorials. Rep. Frank Thompson of New Jersey inserted in the *Congressional Record* for April 6, 1966, a statement by Ray Dennison of the public relations department of the AFL-CIO which appeared originally in *The American Federationist*. It pertained to the drive to prevent repeal of section 14(b) of the Taft-Hartley Act. In part, as Robert U. Brown reprinted it in his "Shop Talk at Thirty" column in *Editor & Publisher* for April 23, 1966, it told the following story:

Readers of the weekly Forsythe, Mont. Independent and the Winona, Miss., Times, have something in common. They have been the unknowing victims of a fraud perpetrated on them in the name of objective journalism.

They and tens of thousands of other readers of small town daily and weekly newspapers have been fed a steady diet of identical "canned copy" directed against the repeal of section 14(b)—all of it written, paid for, and distributed in behalf of the right-to-work advocates under the guise of news.

What subscribers to the Independent and Times paid for and believed to be news from recognized and responsible sources, or to be the creation of their local editor's mind and typewriter, actually has been the slick writing of right-to-work lobbyists in Washington, D. C.

The barrage of editorials and news on 14 (b) which occupied the news and editorial pages of hundreds of American small town daily and weekly newspapers got there because the lobbyists paid Washington news services a fee to send them to editors. They appeared in content or headline in virtually every State of the Union. . . .

The reader could be expected to assume that the editorial was the conclusion of the local editor—respected Rotarian, community leader and doting parent—who had examined facts and figures and the economic climate around him (most of the stories appeared in the right-to-work States).

This editorial, however, was the product of National News-Research, a "boilerroom" operation in Washington, and had been distributed to hundreds of weekly and small town dailies.

The cost to the local editor was nothing. The tab had been picked up by the right-to-work sponsor, as was the cost of the steady stream of similar out-pourings by other "news services."

The sad story of how the U.S. Press Association floods the small town press with canned editorials supporting conservative American interests and some foreign governments is told by Ben Bagdikian of the Washington *Post* in his book, *The Effete Conspiracy* (Harper & Row, 1972). Bagdikian points out the "profound difference between the identical National Association of Manufacturers editorial appearing in six hundred newspapers and six hundred local editors thinking and writing about what the NAM has to say. The effect of the canned editorial is to make more rigid what is already a limited political and intellectual environment and to inhibit the individualistic responses which defenders of the rural life say they value."

LEARNING TO THINK

So that should be enough for a while on how not to do it, neither by surrendering your good sense to your emotions nor by delegating the job of thinking and decision making to a public relations-advertising firm.

If one has the slightest ambition to amount to something in this field he's going to have to cultivate the habits of mind conducive to that end. How does one learn to think, then? As long as humans are humans there will be no perfect answer. All of the social psychological factors already mentioned—religious, ethnic, economic and social backgrounds, cultural taboos and superstitions, prejudices, stereotypes, myths, legends and the like—affect everyone, including editorial writers. All anyone can do is his best. Awareness of the existence of unconscious psychological conditioning factors is an asset. Determination to do the very best possible job despite such obstacles is even more important. In no other field is there a more deliberate attempt on the part of many (not enough, of course) to circumvent human frailties. In many if not most other fields training emphasizes how to attain goals, how to utilize human shortcomings or characteristics to one's own advantage. In other words, there is nobody with purer motives than the first-class journalist acting as such.

If anyone believes that statement to be Rover Boyish, let him prepare his own list of more ethical and public-spirited economic groups. But if the foregoing is occupational chauvinism, nevertheless this book can be dedicated to the purpose of assisting any and all who want to train themselves to approach the ideal. The importance of journalism to the health of a democracy makes it essential that the effort be made to create as large as possible a corps of journalists dedicated to high principles and purposes. It is of extra importance that such persons be encouraged to become editorial writers.

To illustrate the mental gymnastics in which a truth-seeking editorial writer (or anyone else for that matter) should engage, let us postulate a hypothetical situation. Suppose that Peru and the United States were to announce that they intended to enter into a reciprocal trade agreement and that, for some reason or other, it was decided that there should be an editorial on the subject. What should someone know in order to be qualified to write such an editorial? The minimum would seem to be somewhat the following:

I. General background
  A. Definitions
    1. What is a reciprocal trade agreement?
    2. How does it differ from a low tariff? A high tariff? Free trade? Export visas?
  B. History and record
    1. When did the American program originate?
    2. What gave rise to it?
    3. With how many and what countries do we have such agreements?
    4. What is the general nature of these agreements?
  C. General purposes and arguments
    1. What are the pro and con arguments regarding the theory and purpose of such agreements?
    2. What about the economic, social and political objectives?
    3. How successful have they proved to be? Criteria by which to judge success or failure
II. Peruvian-American trade
  A. Its nature and extent
    1. What are the exports and imports of each nation to and from the other?
    2. What changes or fluctuations have occurred in this trade over the years?
    3. How does trade in the same commodities between these countries and others compare?
    4. How vital is the need each has for what the other produces?
  B. Provisions of the proposed agreement
    1. Comparison between it and similar agreements with other nations
    2. Unique features of this document

  C. Objectives and anticipated results
    1. Effect on Peruvian-American trade
    2. Effect on other nations, Ecuador and others
    3. Economic and political ramifications
    4. Who stands to gain and lose and how much?
  D. Pro and con arguments
    1. Identify groups for and against
    2. Balance sheet of possible gains and losses

This is a skeletal outline but it would be utterly unrealistic to believe such systematic investigation precedes the writing of many editorials today. The knowledge of veteran staff members makes a great deal of such detailed background probing unnecessary in most instances. The example suggests, however, that it is easy to fall short of the minimum standards which should prevail if editorial comment is to be adequate.

The Peruvian-American reciprocal trade agreement assignment is an unlikely one. Probably a large majority of editorial writers would consider themselves unqualified to handle it without the extensive background the brief outline just given suggests. It would be as absurd to expect someone to editorialize about the English game of crickets without having ever seen a game or familiarized himself with the rules. The point is raised here as to how much better prepared the editorial writer often is to tackle the topics that he does handle. The author of the "Whither Are We Drifting?" editorial was not qualified to write that editorial. That editorial indicated that you just can't write editorials off the top of your head, in an emotional heat, or to expound one's prejudices. To be qualified to write about any subject you've got to go through the one, two, three learning process suggested by the hypothetical reciprocal trade agreement piece, deliberately invented because it is quite certain that few readers of this book would consider themselves able to handle the assignment. The lesson which is intended and which cannot be stated too strongly is this: be sure you know what you're talking about every time you write. If you don't know enough about your subject, either take the time to learn more or abandon the assignment.

III

Preparing to Write

1. Seeking Facts   3. Economic Experts
2. Seeking Figures   4. Statistics
5. Indices

Learning what to write about means research. That may simply entail talking to reporters, consulting the newspaper's clipping file, making a telephone call or two and refreshing one's memory. In such fact-finding the editorial writer acts as a reporter, probing until he has explored every necessary avenue. Specifically he interviews, cross-examines and double-checks his informants and what they tell him, to the fullest extent necessary. Not all assignments require such exhaustive preparation, but no investigation should stop until it has been completed.

SEEKING FACTS

If the firsthand original research proved to have been inadequate, the editorial writer must assume blame for not having done his job thoroughly. When, however, the kind of research he must do takes him to printed sources, he may have an alibi if he errs. It should not be true but it is: many if not most of the supposedly reliable reference books are far from infallible. Familiar are the different interpretations of historical facts and figures by different biographers and historians. They are not what causes the editorial writer his worst

headaches. Rather, it is the discrepancies which exist even in the standard books of reference regarding simple facts. In the *Saturday Review* for Dec. 13, 1969, Tracy Early related some of his difficulties. For example, the *Encyclopedia Americana* gave the date of Inigo Jones' death as July 21, 1652; the *Encyclopedia Britannica* gave it as July 5, 1651 and the *Dictionary of National Biography* said it was June 21, 1652. On page 352 of the *World Almanac & Book of Facts* for 1972, under "Noted Personalities," the year of Alexander Hamilton's birth is given as 1757. On the very next (opposite) page, in a list of "Statesmen of the Past," it is given as 1755.

In 1938 it was revealed that Dr. F. Donald Coster, president of McKesson-Robbins, a leading drug company, was really an ex-convict, Philip Musica, who had even succeeded in getting an impressive biography of his make-believe self inserted into *Who's Who in America*. In 1960 the biography of a nonexistent Septimus Cadwallader Tisington-Henrint-Brown appeared in *The Authors and Writers Who's Who* published by Burke's Peerage. Most important literary hoax of this type was perpetuated on the editors of *Appleton's Encyclopedia of American Biography* whose 1886 issue included the biographies of at least 88 fictitious people, which fact went undiscovered until 1918.

Once published, anything, including the worst hoaxes, exists in perpetuity. Although debunked over and over again a spurious book or other writing can be discovered decades or centuries later by some jubilant researcher who then starts it on its way again to impress others as ignorant of its background as he. The author's book, *Hoaxes* (Dover, 1958) abounds in accounts of such occurrences. Truth seekers, including—perhaps especially—editorial writers must be constantly on the alert. It's not just a matter of choosing between the contradictory interpretations of some political or military event by differently biased historians. Rather, it's a question of whether anything ever happened at all. There seems to be adequate proof that a Civil War battle was fought at Gettysburg, but many if not all accounts of how Abraham Lincoln composed his famous address dedicating the cemetery there are without substantiation; and the same is true of the much-quoted letter to Mrs. Bixby concerning the deaths of several sons who were Union soldiers. A comparison of the supposed facsimiles of this letter indicates that not all could be genuine. According to the Lincoln scholar, Dr. William E. Barton, who investigated, if Lincoln wrote the beautiful prose accredited to him, "it was a beautiful blunder and well worth while for the sake of the letter." Most of the alleged facts of the missive, however, were proved incorrect.

And then there are the legends of George Washington's cherry tree, Pocahontas and Captain John Smith, Betsy Ross' flag, Paul Revere's ride and many, many more. *The Military Memoirs of Captain Carleton* appeared in 1723 and for a century was the standard reference for historians interested in the Queen Anne wars. Today it is believed that either Jonathan Swift or Daniel Defoe, both great jokesters, was the author. *The Memoirs of Li Hung Chang*, Chinese diplomat of the late 19th century, was written by an American journalist, William Francis Mannix, to avoid ennui while serving time in a Honolulu jail for forgery. The book was originally published in 1913 and was reissued a decade later with an introduction confessing its spurious nature. Many libraries continue to have only the allegedly authentic 1913 edition.

Perhaps the most persistent hoax of American origin, one which is kept alive by small reference books, careless authors, and plumbing equipment advertisers especially, is the story of the origin and early history of the bathtub in this country. It was invented by the satirical H. L. Mencken in the New York *Mail* for Dec. 28, 1917. "My motive," Mencken explained when he tried to stop circulation of the misinformation in a syndicated article May 23, 1926, "was simply to have some harmless fun in war days. It never occurred to me that it would be taken seriously." The story was that Adam Thompson of Cincinnati displayed the first American bathtub Dec. 10, 1842, with the result that he was denounced by physicians who said the bathtub was injurious to health. Cities and states either forbade the use of tubs or levied heavy taxes on their installation and/or use. The innovation triumphed when President Millard Fillmore had one installed in the White House, which fact President Harry S. Truman was fond of telling visitors as he escorted them on tours through the residence when it was being renovated. The Mencken hoax has been exposed so many times that it is fantastic. It persists in cropping up even in reputable publications every few weeks or months.

And, of course, there are also Bridey Murphy, the Abominable Snowman, the Loch Ness monster, and all kinds of quacks and charlatans who allegedly deal in the supernatural in one way or another. Newspapermen are suckers for astrologers, fortune tellers, prophets, spinners of tales of miraculous escapes or acts of divine favor, the efficacy of prayer, ESP, ghosts, goblins, leprechauns, fairies, angels, gremlins, elves, poltergeists, werewolves, warlocks and other unseen forces which allegedly affect the destiny of men. If these magical and psychic phenomenal influences did exist to indicate fatalistic predetermination of human events, they surely would make editorial writing superfluous. So skepticism becomes an occupational necessity if nothing else.

SEEKING FIGURES

If it's not just facts but figures that are desired, the same caution is necessary. Suppose it is needed to know the popular vote for president in 1968. So you consult the 1972 *World Almanac & Book of Facts.* On page 718 are given the statistics by states and the totals: Nixon, 31,385,480 and Humphrey, 31,275,166. On the next page, 719, in the compilation of Major Parties Popular and Electoral Votes for President 1779 Through 1968, the totals are: Nixon, 31,783-783 to Humphrey, 31,271,839. The former set of figures is that given in both lists in *Information Please Almanac.* Until its 1970 edition, that source book had contrasting sets of figures for the 1960 election. One showed Kennedy beating Nixon, 34,221,-485 to 34,108,684 and another by 34,227,096 to 34,107,646. Beginning with the 1970 edition new sets of figures were substituted in both places, showing Kennedy the winner by 34,226,731 to 34,108,157.

Maybe these inconsistencies are not important because everyone knew anyway that prior to 1972 whether Richard Nixon won or lost the margin was close. In other instances, however, the conflicting statistical data may be important, even in these days of billions and trillions. For a typical example, take the national income for 1948. In terms of millions of dollars, *Information Please Almanac* for 1950 gave it as 226,204; in 1952 the almanac changed this to 223,459 with which it stuck until 1955 when the figure became 221,641. In his State of the

Union speech Jan. 6, 1950, President Truman said his Council of Economic Advisors told him it was 190,800, but the National Association of Manufacturers stuck to 21.6 in a September, 1955 report. So did *Information Please Almanac* until 1959 when it gave 223,487 to which it has been true ever since. It still, however, can't make up its mind about the national income for 1945. In 1950 it said it was 182,691 but from 1955 it remained loyal to 181,248 until 1971 when it gave a new figure, 181,485. In 1970 it gave the national income for 1951 at 279,333; in 1972 it became 277,978.

Believe me, these samples are random. Try it yourself. In 1938 this book's author became editor of the *Chicago Daily News Almanac* and reedited the entire volume to make it into the *National Almanac & Year Book.* The labor involved checking the statistical tables on every page of both the *Chicago Daily News Almanac* and the *World Almanac.* There was hardly a page in either reference book without error. The high point was 26 mistakes on a single page of the *World Almanac,* all in figures accredited to supposedly reliable governmental sources: Bureau of Labor Statistics, Department of Commerce, Federal Reserve Board, Bureau of the Census and the like. Gremlins? It was impossible to determine, but the experience was of lifetime value to all of us who participated in it. None of us thereafter ever accepted any figure, no matter how supposedly reliable the source, without painstaking examination. Unfortunately there often are no guidelines as to which sets of contradictory figures to accept. No editorial writer can repeat the research of the Bureau of the Census to determine its reliability. In many instances if the governmental statistics are unreliable, there is no alternative. But it is often impossible to decide which allegedly irrefragable government statistics should be accepted and to guess which almanac or other reference book employs the best proofreaders.

Most trustworthy, virtually in a class by itself, and consequently the most widely used service for editorial writers and other interpretative journalists is Editorial Research Reports and Congressional Quarterly Service, 1735 K Streets, N. W., Washington, D. C., 20006. The Congressional Quarterly Service includes: (1) a weekly report digesting congressional and political activity, mailed every Saturday night; it includes full texts of presidential press conferences, major statements, messages and speeches; (2) a quarterly index of news and subjects in the contents of all preceding issues of the Weekly Report for the year; (3) timely, exclusive stories ranging from 300 to 1,000 words each three times a week; and (4) weekly news features mailed every Wednesday, listing upcoming significant events for the coming three weeks and citing background information already published in Congressional Quarterly Service or Editorial Research Reports.

Editorial Research Reports are issued four times a month. Each includes the basic facts about some basic issue in 6,000 words with a 500-word digest, suitable for use as an editorial page piece under the byline of Editorial Research Reports. The Daily Service, mailed Monday through Friday, supplies succinct background on a single spot news development in about 550 words. Each piece usually carries marginal cross-references to prior coverage in the Reports or the Daily Services.

It might seem at first glance that this is "editorial writing made easy," but it's not that simple. This service is a tremendous asset in helping to build files for reference purposes, but no editorial writer worth his salary is going to rely on it exclusively, even if such were possible which it is not, if for no other reason than that there's always a later development in the news.

ECONOMIC EXPERTS

Presumably, in the light of the foregoing evidence, the fact-seeking editorial writer would be fortunate if he needed not precise facts or figures but interpretations of them, to indicate trends and make possible predictions. Tough luck! The nation's best economic brains are no better than the reference book editors. For the past half century at least these authorities, from the extreme right to the extreme left, have been almost unanimously wrong on everything. They haven't known what is going to happen and they have not understood it when it has occurred. One can almost safely study what the orthodox economists say to be certain exactly the opposite will come to pass.

The late Roger Babson advertised that he predicted the depression of the thirties. He did no such thing. The closest he came was in September, 1929 when he forecast a crash in the stock market, which it never occurred to him would cause a decade of depression to be ended only by our entrance into a world war. Speaking on the basis of the best advice obtainable in the best financial circles, President Herbert Hoover refused to admit that there was any permanency to the failures and layoffs that threw approximately 14 million people out of work. "Prosperity," he said "is just around the corner." After the crash came, newsman Edward Angley gathered together the economic malapropisms and worse of Hoover and his associates into a nasty little book, *Oh Yeah* (Viking, 1931). In the mid-fifties the United Rubber Workers did the same thing for the "gloom and doom" statements of leading Republicans who attacked the New Deal of Franklin D. Roosevelt. According to Alf Landon, who carried Maine and Vermont against FDR in 1936, "The Democratic administration's program for Federal Bank Deposit Insurance will destroy the entire banking system," to which Rep. Robert F. Rich of Pennsylvania added, "The Roosevelt program for Social Security will wreck the nation."

These critics were professional politicians from the opposite party. George V. McLaughlin, however, was president of the

New York State Bankers Association and expressed the public viewpoint of the overwhelming majority of business and financial leaders when he warned, "There would be a wholesale liquidation of national securities if the national debt should exceed $32 billion." This was in comment on FDR's request that the legal debt limit be raised to permit work relief and other programs intended to bolster the purchasing power of the working man. This approach constituted economic reform and relief from the bottom up rather than in the traditional manner of relief and reform from the top down through loans to banks and assistance of many sorts to Big Business. Where are the pessimistic prophets today when the national debt is well over $450 billion which means about $2,000 for every man, woman, and child? Some cynic has remarked that the continuous hot and cold war economy means a perpetual WPA for the rich so the calamity howlers of New Deal days are silent. The fact remains that they couldn't be right both times. Either they were right in saying FDR was ruining the country spending money on the poor or they are wrong today for not protesting spending it on the rich. Either they don't know what they're talking about or they don't say honestly what they do know.

Just as wrong were the New Deal economists who predicted that Keynesian economics would solve the depression. The depression continued until World War II when spending and recruitment of the unemployed into the armed services and war industries changed the situation. Then came postwar reconversion of industry and the discharge of millions of GIs into the work force. Dire were the warnings of inevitable depression, or at least recession (a depression in short economic pants). When Franklin D. Roosevelt, in one of his last campaign speeches, called for a postwar goal of 60 million jobs and when Henry A. Wallace took up the slogan, even publishing a book by that title, there were loud jeers from the traditional economists. Couldn't happen, they said, and they had charts and graphs and logic to prove it. They didn't know what they were talking about and college students who read their books while attending school on GI loans were handicapped for the rest of their lives in trying to understand the economic facts of life. Succinctly, the basic fact is, as Calvin Coolidge put it, "the business of America is business," which means that the goal of the economic machinery is profits, profits, profits. It is just as simple as that and all theories are merely rationalizations, either to deliberately befuddle the suckers whose dollars are sought, or a form of self-hypnosis leading to belief in an economic dream world in which competition is the life of trade and there are laws of supply and demand, marginal productivity, diminishing returns and lots of other "realities" to guide the destinies of men.

In the interval between the wars it became generally recognized that the United States went "back to normalcy" (the slogan with which Harding was elected in 1920) too swiftly, to the detriment of the economic best interests of the entire world. We loaned large sums of money to former allies for reconstruction purposes. They were incorrectly called war loans and when the beneficiaries, with the single exception of Finland, defaulted when the depression became worldwide, we were called Uncle Shylock for continuing to insist on payments. Congress guarded against a recurrence of such bad business deals by passing the Johnson act to require "cash on the barrel head" in any future transactions. Franklin Roosevelt cleverly circumvented this restriction with his lend-lease plan to aid the British and other World War II allies both before and after Pearl Harbor.

Actually the United States went back to normalcy faster after World War II than it had a generation earlier. One of the nation's first unfriendly acts toward the Soviet Union occurred immediately after V-E Day when President Truman recalled ships on the high seas carrying lend-lease supplies to the Russians whom we at the same time were holding to their promise, made at the Yalta conference, to enter the war against Japan. Arguing that unless natural classical economic laws of supply and demand and the like were allowed to operate, there would be inflation, the National Association of Manufacturers flooded the country with propaganda to induce Congress to repeal price controls and the National Association of Real Estate Boards did the same to end rent controls and to discourage a low cost veterans' housing program. Wilson Wyatt, who had resigned as mayor of Louisville to head the program, quit after what he considered broken promises by Truman and intransigent opposition from Secretary of the Treasury John Snyder and Reconstruction Finance Corporation head, George Allen. A similar victim was Marriner Eccles, chairman of the Federal Reserve Board who stubbornly refused to go along with demands that restraints on credit be lifted. So Truman demoted Eccles from the chairmanship but Eccles didn't oblige by quitting. Instead, he continued as a member of the board for the rest of his term during which time he fought a losing battle against the greedy.

The cupidity of the economic experts who supported these postwar demands by Big Business was proved as early as January, 1948 when Truman made his annual state of the union speech to Congress and the nation. He confessed that between July, 1946, when most controls were lifted, and October, 1947, wholesale prices had gone up 60 percent and retail prices 33 percent. Between then and the time of his report, wholesale prices had climbed another 10 percent and retail prices were going up at the annual rate of 19 percent. No wonder that the period was characterized by strikes to make it possible for the workingman to survive during the inflationary period which, the economic royalists had assured

him, just couldn't possibly occur if government would just stop interfering with free enterprise. By comparison with 1939 the consumer's dollar was worth 57 cents in 1948, as reported by the Northwestern National Life Insurance Company which operates one of the best statistical departments.

So, after inflation came despite the theorists, the next wave of predictions by the alleged experts concerned imminent deflation, possibly depression. So forecast Standard & Poor; so also did the Public Affairs Institute, founded by the Brotherhood of Railroad Trainmen. In July, 1949 the institute reported the existence of 3.3 million unemployed which, it forecast, would become 6 million by the end of 1949 and 9 million by mid-1950. Everybody got into the act, conditioned to think in terms of what the supposedly leading thinkers thought. So Sylvia F. Porter, leading syndicated economist, wrote Aug. 18, 1948:

> BOOMS DON'T happen all at once. They come in waves: first one industry feels the quickened demand, the intensified activity; then the movement spills over into another area, into a third, a fourth, a fifth and suddenly, there is one unmistakable national pattern: boom.
>
> Busts don't happen at a specified hour on a specified day, either. They too come in waves: the change in subtle at the start, becomes obvious only after the slump is fact.
>
> Even as today's front pages shout inflation, today's back pages murmur of deflation.
>
> As the headlines tell of another boost in automobile prices, another rise in steel prices, the small type tells of bargains in shirts and sheets, of a sag in magazine and book sales, of price wars in liquor and luxury items.
>
> And the dominant economic truth is that the more justified the headlines on inflation, the more inevitable will be the headlines on deflation. . . .

In its issue of Jan. 30, 1956, *Newsweek* asked, "What's Wrong With the Top U.S. Economists?" and ran a chart to indicate, with a red line, "what really happened in industrial production" from 1946 to 1956 and with arrows to show what the economic predictions had been. There wasn't an arrow pointing in the right direction, not one of 15, which mostly indicated what J. A. Livingston, Philadelphia *Bulletin* financial editor and columnist, had learned by polling 53 top economists.

Both Miss Porter and Livingston have sobered up and have made readers aware of the inaccuracy of most economic predictions. Typically, Miss Porter began her March 22, 1966 column as follows:

Last Jan. 20 President Johnson and his Council of Economic Advisers submitted to Congress the administration's official forecast for the economy in 1966. Two months later, the economists well might echo the immortal words of boxing's late Joe Jacobs, "we shuda stood in bed."

For few of the key statistical predictions— on which the White House has so far based crucially important policy decisions—are holding up.

Forecast: Gross national product (the total value of all the goods and services we produce) "is expected to be within a $10 billion range centered on $722 billion, given the $675.6 billion level now estimated for 1965."

Updating: The 1965 GNP actually turned out to be substantially higher, which by itself made the $722 billion forecast too low. Meanwhile, in the first months of 1966, industrial production has been surging and economic activity generally has been much stronger than the most optimistic prediction. Some private estimates of GNP in 1966 now run as high as $735 billion.

Forecast: Inflation is a clear threat but "no major departure is expected from the 1.8-per cent increase of over-all prices in 1965."

Updating: This one was suspect from the day it was published and the accelerating pressures of January-March make it among the most dangerous of under-estimates. Even with today's historically tight money squeeze and even assuming income tax hikes this

year, a price rise of less than 2 per cent seems wistful thinking. Many economists believe we'll break the 3-per cent mark. . . .

Livingston's Jan. 12, 1967 column began as follows:

Along about Jan. 20, President Johnson's Council of Economic Advisers will set forth the administration's promises and prophecies for the new year.

This prompts Barron's Weekly to look backward. How good were the prophecies in the 1966 economic report?

Chairman Gardner Ackley and his two co-members were "false prophets," concludes Barron's because they:

- Underestimated by half the 3.6 per cent rise in prices, a 100 per cent error.
- Said that residential construction "on balance is likely to change but little," when it almost collapsed.
- Declared that the position of sterling had improved, yet in midyear, a group of central banks put up additional funds to protect the pound.
- Asserted that the United States has the determination and the means to continue the sharp improvement effected last year in bringing its balance of payments into equilibrium," but improvement, if any, has been slight.

AVERS BARRON'S: "The President's Council of Economic Advisers is not a disinterested body of scholars, competent or otherwise. Cloaked in academic robes, it has turned an organ of political and economic propaganda.

"Far from seeking to appraise business and financial trends, a difficult task at best, CEA's three wise men have been more concerned with defending the worthless guidelines and meddling with wages and prices. Like all manipulators, they have proven hopelessly inept either at grasping or coping with cause and effect or supply and demand."

Those are harsh words.

A CASE CAN BE made that the council didn't do too badly. It forecast a 6.9 per cent increase in dollar output of goods and services—gross national product—to $722 billion, give or take five billion. The final tally (when it comes) is apt to show a gain of 8.4 per cent to $738 billion. Further, the Council said the "real gain" (after inflation) would be 5 per cent, and it is likely to be 5.4 per cent.

That ought to be good for a B-plus or even an A-minus at any graduate school of business. The council was right on direction —whither went production and employment —and "in the infield" on magnitude of gain.

But Barron's argues that a good result from offsetting errors hardly constitutes creditable forecasting. Underestimations of increases in inventories, defense spending and outlays on plant and equipment were counterbalanced by the dramatic drop in housing. Can four wrongs make one right?

Moreover, wrong forecasts lead to wrong policies. Didn't a loose fiscal policy force on the Federal Reserve System an over-tight monetary policy? Didn't the President try to compensate for the underestimation of demand with wage-price guideposts? . . .

Even the Associated Press had become aware of the situation. On Aug. 15, 1967 it sent a story from New York with the following first few paragraphs:

By Associated Press

NEW YORK (AP)—This has been a rugged year for the forecasters, most of whom have been kept busy updating, correcting, painfully readjusting and—in the U.S. Treasury's case—revising downward.

The errors are so widespread—and generally on the low side when measuring anticipated revenues—that mankind has a right to wonder if the electronic computer is his friend, or is at least as reliable as a friend should be.

The computer, and its tendency to look unemotionally into the future, is the machine that has made us so dependent, so reliant not just on the present but on what is yet to come.

Among the recent statistical revisions are federal income tax revenue, the death rate, state lottery returns, retail sales, the stock market.

The list is literally endless, but it is most painful and treacherous when it includes forecasts of revenue much higher than produced in reality. . .

Also, on May 20, 1962 when the stock market suffered its sharpest loss since Oct. 28, 1929, the AP account included the following:

As stocks have sunk lower in recent weeks, however, some technicians said that all the clues and guidelines they rely on to forecast probable market movements had gone by the board. The ordinary guidelines were swamped in a sea of emotionalism—just plain fear on the part of many investors, big as well as small—that prices would go much lower before they go higher.

In the midst of the worst of Monday's selling, one security analyst said, "The big question is—'Who's doing the buying?' "

What happened on that occasion, as occurs not too infrequently, was deliberate conniving by large investors to wipe out small ones. The recovery was rapid once that end was achieved.

Elmer Roper exposed the fact that economics is decidedly not an exact science when he polled members of the American Economic Association and businessmen who serve as trustees of privately endowed colleges, universities, and foundations on the validity of the arguments in Kenneth Galbraith's book, *The Affluent Society* (Houghton Mifflin, 1958). The results were printed in *Saturday Review* for June 6, 1959 and indicated wide discrepancies. Whereas about 41 percent of the professors were mostly in agreement with Galbraith, only 16 percent of the businessmen-trustees were.

In summary, economics is not an exact science. The classical laws exist in the minds of their believers and only coincidentally in real life. The journalist wishing to become an expert in this field should train himself by observation and study of actual occurrences. He should handle the business-financial beat as skeptically as he would any other and if he has been trained to investigate thoroughly every possible angle of any story, he will in time be as learned as many newspapermen have become in science since Hiroshima, a comparatively short time ago.

Ernest Linford, professor of journalism at the University of Wyoming, sounds a warning based on 19 years as editorial writer for the Salt Lake City *Tribune:*

> Research: telephone calls; clips; interviews with reporters and so on. My colleagues were always complaining that I over-researched my editorials. I dug up everything I could about a subject and then had a compulsion to put down everything I knew, thus killing off a good editorial. If the writer leaves just a little element of mystery, the subject remains interesting. After spending a couple of days or weeks studying a subject or incident, I sometimes go flat and the material is blah.
>
> I found I courted dissatisfaction and ineffectiveness on occasion by too many phone calls, learning too much about a problem. If an editorial writer is all set to blast the mayor or the fellow down the road, he will have to have a great deal of strength of purpose to survive a telephone call asking for the mayor's side of the controversy. If he is human at all, he will find himself watering down the editorial if he deliberately seeks to get all the other side too. We all have had experiences with an editorial that turned itself around in the middle of research, and more power to us, but in too many cases the end result was just an on-the-other-hand piece.

STATISTICS

It is impossible for an editorial writer, possibly for anyone, to ignore statistics. First consideration is naturally their accuracy. Every ten years there are cities and towns that do not believe the census takers have done a thorough job of counting the population. The complainants are invariably those who had hoped for larger totals, in the spirit of "bigger and better" so important during the long frontier days. Loss of population also means a decrease in a state's

representation in Congress as the total membership of the House of Representatives remains the same and is reapportioned every decade.

Some statistics, such as the outcomes of elections, total sales of commodities, the amount of bank deposits, athletic records and similar ones should be correct because there is a total count, not an estimate based on a percentage sampling. Nevertheless, as the preceding section indicated, even such presumably easy-to-get figures are often untrustworthy, at least when they appear in standard books of reference.

Vital as it may be to have reliable information about the batting averages of major league baseball players, the voting records of congressmen, the number and value of building permits issued annually and the like, it is even more important that there be proper interpretation of the meaning of statistics. Editorial writers need to know only a modicum about the mathematics of statistics, which knowledge is contained in a short book, *Elementary Statistics for Journalists* (Macmillan, 1954) by David Manning White and Seymour Levine. The most important warning against the misuse of statistics still is *How to Lie With Statistics* (W. W. Norton, 1954) by Darrell Huff, the outgrowth of an article by the same title in *Harper's* for April, 1950.

A first lesson to be learned by anyone who seeks to protect himself against improper use of statistics is the differences between mean, median and mode and their value in interpreting factual data. Mean simply means average. You get it by asking everyone how many hats he has and then dividing the total number of hats by the number of persons. Sounds simple, yes, but it may not be meaningful. Note, the average of 1, 2, 3, 4, 6, 7, 8, 9 and 10 is 5.5, which indicates that there are as many numbers below the midpoint as there are above it. Such is so because the items counted are equally distributed. Suppose, however, the list is 1, 2, 3, 4, 5, 6, 7, 8, 9 and 30. The midpoint still is the same in terms of items counted; that is, 5.5. However, the average becomes 7.5 with 7 below and 3 above the average. So, to say that the group being studied owns an average of 7.5 hats is misleading. One affluent hat owner has thrown it off.

In 1939 Edward Lee Thorndike and associates published *Your City* (Harcourt, Brace), which evaluated more than 300 American cities of more than 30,000 population on the basis of 23 factors, typical ones being low death rate, high per capita expenditure for education, high proportion of home ownership and the like, to get a GG (general goodness) score. The criteria were indisputably good and using them as a yardstick Pasadena, Calif., was adjudged the best all-around American city. Tied for sixth place were two Illinois suburbs, Evanston and Oak Park. The book appeared at a time when local studies had spotlighted bad conditions on Evanston's west side where Negroes, who comprised about 12 percent of the city's total population, lived. Misuse of the Thorndike book to oppose proposals for local reform enraged Prof. Murray Leiffer, sociologist at the Garrett Biblical Institute. He prepared a critical reply and lectured publicly to all audiences he could obtain. Such reports as Thorndike's, based on averages, always tend to hide unsavory conditions. The United States boasts of being an affluent society and all of the statistics related to prosperity seem to substantiate the claim. Nevertheless, Franklin Delano Roosevelt saw a nation one-third of which was poorly housed, poorly fed and poorly clothed. A generation later, after the New Deal reforms and a couple of lucrative wars, Lyndon B. Johnson declared war on poverty because one in four Americans had an income below the minimum needed for a decent living. Not much of an improvement, one-third to one-fourth, and even this discouraging fact doesn't minimize the tremendous needs of the underprivileged

groups in any field that might be cited. So any editorial writer who goes off the deep end congratulating the city administration, Chamber of Commerce or anyone else for attaining all-American city status or awards for excellence in any field, must be certain that he is not doing more harm than good by directing attention away from bad conditions and discouraging efforts to correct them.

Median is more meaningful than mean in describing any important social situation. It is the midpoint above and below which are equal numbers of whatever is being considered. It is more meaningful to report that there are as many persons with incomes under a certain level as there are with incomes above it than to take an average of all the incomes. People are what count, not their relation to money.

Mode refers to points on a scale where most of the scores are recorded. For instance, the median of weekly incomes of members of a group may be $100, meaning there are as many who receive less than that as there are those who receive more. If a horizontal scale is drawn and individual scores indicated, however, it might show that a majority of those below $100 got $50 and the majority of those over $100 got $150. Perhaps there were more than two modes—high points on the scale, "where the action is." Few statistical curves are smooth with the peak in the exact middle except when school teachers make a deliberate effort to "mark on a curve," so that there seems to be an even distribution of achievement. All that may be even is the teacher's grading system; the results may not correspond to the distribution of students' achievements.

With the population what it is today few if any other projects attempt to reach 100 percent of the "universe," to use the statistician's term included in the study. Instead, there is sampling and the validity and value of the results often depend on the representativeness of the sample. Professional pollsters try to have all significant elements represented in their study samples in the same proportion as these elements exist in the population as a whole. Some of the pollsters like to say that the procedure is as foolproof as taking a sip of the contents of a bottle of milk to determine if it is sour—not necessary to drink the complete contents of the bottle to draw a sound conclusion, it is contended. True, but people are not milk and the analogy is palpably absurd. For the purpose of determining whether it was sour the homogeneity of the milk could safely be assumed. Such might not be the case if the purpose were some sort of chemical analysis and the fluid were unstirred. However, people are not so conveniently studied in the aggregate as are drops of milk in a bowl. Thus, you have to try to get all pertinent elements represented in your sample in the same proportion as they are found in the population as a whole. The first problem is to determine what the significant factors are. Straw vote pollsters use age, sex, economic status and past voting record, sometimes religion, education, geography, and other factors. The prodigious failures they have experienced, from 1948 on, indicate that theirs is not an exact science. Issues do not remain the same from one election to another. Different circumstances exist to determine what oratorical appeals will succeed and which candidates will be considered personally popular. If it were possible to guess correctly what those factors were and the certain effect on different kinds of persons, it would be unnecessary to conduct a poll. Maybe the sample should be based on psychological factors and contain a proportionate number of those who fell out of their cribs at six months and of those who didn't do so until they were a year old. Who knows what the factors should be?

Huff facetiously analyzed a report that a Yale class averaged $25,011 a year income a quarter century after graduation.

"You could," he wrote, "lump one Texas oilman with 200 hungry free-lance writers and report the average income as $25,000-odd a year." Huff discounted the survey by suggesting why some questionnaires were not returned: by unsuccessful alumni ashamed of their incomes, by those with unknown addresses, and by those who took a supercilious attitude toward the experiment. "This," he commented, "leads to a moral. You can prove about anything you want to by letting your sample bias itself . . . no statistical conclusion can rise above the quality of the sample it is based upon. In the absence of information about the procedures behind it, you are not warranted in giving any credence at all to the result."

An example of how the adequacy of a certain type of sample can be important in a debate over a major issue occurred when the National Industrial Conference Board, a research group close to if not technically a part of the National Association of Manufacturers, attacked the report of the Heller Committee for Research in Social Economics, a private agency associated with the University of California.

Year after year the Heller Committee issues reports on the adequacy of the incomes of lower income groups based on estimates of what constitutes a minimum standard of living and a subsequent necessary family income. The NICB charged that the four-person family used by the Heller Committee in making up its budget is not typical of the responsibilities of the average wage earner. Rather, it said, the average size of families is 3.39 persons. "About three-fourths of all families were smaller than the hypothetical four-person family, excluding single individuals, who are regarded as family households for census purposes, 55 percent of all families of two or more persons were smaller in size," commented the NICB.

Other ways to attack the Heller reports would be to question the proposed diet and cost items for different necessities, the definition of what constitutes a necessity, the wisdom of certain expenditures for apparent luxuries, entertainment and so forth. Welfare agencies, both public and private, are constantly being examined according to such criteria.

An editorial writer is handicapped in evaluating all aspects of any research project. He has to rely on the best evidence and advice he can obtain and be guided in the future by how accurate or valuable every source of information turned out to be in the past. Experience, in other words, becomes his guide.

In an article, "Caution: Medical Statistics at Work," in *Harper's* for January, 1953, Leonard Engel cited the false scare in California when state and United States Public Health Service workers reported several hundred low-grade cases of encephalitis. It was the intensive survey that was responsible for a distorted conclusion. Actually, Engel explained, "Central California had more an outbreak of sleeping sickness reports than of sleeping sickness."

Health situations often require common sense interpretations which a competent editorial writer can provide without being either a statistician or a medical authority. A rise in the average life span, for instance, does not mean that people are living longer and is no basis for projections into the future with the earth peopled by Methuselahs. Rather, the fact that the average age of death today is over 70 instead of 50 as it was in 1900 means only that we have reduced infant and maternal deaths considerably and, through preventive medicine and better health care, have learned how to keep more people alive longer. The fact that heart disease and cancer are the leading killers today does not necessarily mean an increase in susceptibility to either. Rather, these are diseases of the older years after expert obstetricians and pediatricians have kept alive millions who in any earlier generation would have died from diseases which are now under control or virtually nonexistent: smallpox, tuberculosis, infantile paralysis, yellow fever, scarlet fever and many others. Medical science is still a long way from eliminating death altogether, so more humans die later and geriatrics becomes the most important area for the medical researcher. The time has not yet come, however, to rewrite the biblical edict that man's normal life span is threescore years and ten.

Just as the probing reporter constantly asks "Why?" to get to the bottom of any story, so the former reporter turned editorial writer should do the same regarding even statistics about the accuracy of which there seems to be no doubt. What caused the situation they describe? Professors of logic, criminology, social problems and other subjects warn students never to accept what seems to be the obvious. A may not be the cause of B. Possibly there is a not-so-visible C that causes both A and B and maybe D, E and F also. Such thinking may lead to results disturbing to entrenched convictions. It's quite catastrophic, for example, to have it proved to you that it's not the bad boy across the alley who has been poisoning dogs but your own son. However, there is always the mother who refuses to accept the evidence or who is able to concoct an explanation to exculpate her offspring and remain prejudicial against the shanty Irish or the wops or the niggers or whoever happens to be more likely culprits than her flesh and blood. Editorial writers, if they are to serve a useful purpose, must steel themselves against bigotry. Perhaps a good rule for them to follow is to be most skeptical of whatever seems to fortify their own preconceptions. One of the most slipshod editorials ever written was the following from the Phoenix *Republic* of June 16, 1951.

Pretty Well Off

A nationally known engineer who now makes his home in Phoenix delivered a talk to a luncheon club recently on "The Mess

We're In." He then proceeded to show the remarkable material advances mankind—especially in the United States—has made since the invention of the internal combustion engine and concluded that we're not in such a mess after all.

But perhaps an even greater advance, reflected in improved living conditions, has been noted in the last 10 years. In spite of high taxes, high prices, and the horrible war in Korea, the people of this nation are physically better off than ever before. On the average, they are better fed, better housed, better clothed, enjoy more leisure and more comfort than their parents, or even they themselves possessed at any other time.

Cold statistics show this to be true. Extensive research by the U.S. News & World Report reveals that of 100 homes, 79 had electricity 10 years ago and 95 today; 59 had running water then and 84 today; 72 had passenger cars then and 82 now; only 46 had refrigerators then and 78 now. Other figures are: Baths or showers, 61 and 74; flush toilets, 65 and 77; telephones, 41 and 79; electric washers, 44 and 65; television sets, none 10 years ago and 24 out of 100 today.

Times are tough for a lot of us, to be sure, but sometimes it helps to count our blessings.

One can imagine how this waste of space came about. An editorial writer in need of copy for next day's page thumbed through the current *United States News & World Report* and came upon the article containing the statistics he used. These were not the result of "extensive research" by the magazine, as any journalist, including Arizona editorial writers, should know. They probably were from some Department of Commerce or other report and should be taken as authentic. They evoked a "mental click" in the lazy and/or harassed editorial writer. He recalled having attended his Rotary or Kiwanis or Lions or Optimist or some other kind of luncheon club some weeks or months earlier and hearing so-and-so or whatever-his-name-is praise the American economy and way of life. Had

he remembered the man's name or had he not been too indolent about consulting the paper's clips or phoning the club's president or secretary, he would not have written "a nationally known engineer." Otherwise, why the secret? If the name, which the editorial writer couldn't remember, was important, it would have added to the value of the editorial.

A possible reason for not mentioning the name was that the speech occurred so long ago that its value as a news peg would be further reduced by its mention. "Recently" is a vague term, especially as used here.

Warning already has been given about "on the average," the phrase this Pulliamite used to list the blessings Americans enjoy. Marshall McLuhan hadn't been heard from in 1951 so there's no telling what "hot" statistics as contrasted with the "cold" ones here cited would be. Anyway, instead of presenting the figures in this form, the situation could be turned around: 5 percent of Americans still have no electricity; 16 percent have no running water; 18 percent have no automobiles; 22 percent have no refrigerators, and so on. It's like whether the glass is half full or half empty of water.

No doubt that the topic of the effect of material progress is important for editorial writers' consideration. It's something about which one can have superficial or profound thoughts. The situation is comparable to making the assignment, "Write a composition about cows." If a first-grader came up with, "A cow is an animal with four legs. It eats green grass and gives white milk which we drink," the teacher would inform the parents that they had a genius in the home. If, however, a high school student couldn't think of anything more to say about cows he would be referred to the special teacher who handles what is euphemistically called "exceptional" children, meaning the dummies. Great words are merely expressions of great thoughts, and one acquires them by study and experience and the development of habits of observation, retention and recollection and maybe some other valuable traits about which they teach in psychology courses.

By contrast with the Phoenix editorial, the following is offered. It's a wee bit dull and it requires at least two readings to get its significance. It is consistent with Christion Science philosophy, logical and well presented within the framework of that ideology. Quite obviously several intellectual notches above the other example, it appeared in the *Christian Science Monitor* for Oct. 18, 1958 as follows:

Higher Standards of Living

One characteristic the year 1958 has in common with the year 1908: a large part of mankind's effort, if not in a sense nearly all of it, is devoted to improving something called the standard of living.

Sociologists speak both of a "standard of living" and a "level of living." The standard of living is the body of conditions which a society strives to achieve and maintain. The level of living is that at which a society actually exists.

At the beginning of this century, particularly in America, the level of living and, loosely speaking, the standard of living were usually measured in terms of material belongings, advantages, and conveniences. For that reason this newspaper was and still is careful to refer to the physical standard of living when dealing in those economic terms.

But a standard of living, truly envisaged, embodies much more than mechanical invention and development of natural resources, valuable as progress in those respects may be. It includes religion, education, fine arts, political organization, individual rights, and social customs, including compassion in human relations.

This is a factor for newer civilizations or developing countries to remember—though in some respects certain parts of the Orient and Western Europe can speak that reminder to the industrialized United States and the machine-minded Soviet Union. "Man does not live by bread alone," nor by nuts and bolts, television screens, or radio jamming.

The peoples of the earth who have come lately to the use of modern mechanics naturally aspire to a fuller use of technology and its products. This calls for accumulation of capital and skill; it involves intellectual development in mathematics and physical sciences; it gains from a certain religious impulse, from a code of moral justice, and from political independence. It calls for a sharing of knowledge and a lending of wealth by the industrially advanced.

But for the advanced nations a great part of their energy and wealth goes into the necessary defense of the level they have attained not only in material goods but more especially in governmental practice and personal security. At the same time they and their lesser neighbors are intensely concerned that preoccupations with military power do not end in a holocaust of nuclear war.

In this sense the search for peace and particularly the building of such a mediatory institution as the United Nations, with its many agencies, is part of the protection and production of a higher standard of living, material and cultural.

Through all these levels, from coal mine to council chamber, the improvement of standards and levels of living involves not alone physical activity but better thinking. It calls for the earnest search for facts, free exchange of information, honest drawing of conclusions, greater charitableness in areas of difference, and ideals that have a touch of altruism. For before a higher level or standard of existence can be lived it has to be thought.

An overabundance of chauvinism plus a lack of knowledge regarding the proper use of statistics made the following editorial one of the few poor ones ever to appear in the St. Louis *Post-Dispatch*. This was from the issue of Nov. 27, 1956.

Let's See What Can Be Done

A subject to which Gov.-elect Blair can turn with profit even before his inauguration is the decline of Missouri in the population standings of the 48 states. When Mr. Blair takes office three years of the 10-year span from 1950 to 1960 will remain. That will be time enough to find out why Missouri has not kept pace with the growth of the country as a whole and to see what can be done about it.

The latest report of the Census Bureau on population changes by states shows that Missouri ranks thirtieth in rate of increase with 7.6 per cent as against a national average increase of 10.9, for the same years, 1950-56. If this situation is not improved Missouri stands to lose still another seat in the national House of Representatives after the 1960 census.

Obviously the number of residents does not constitute the only measure of a state's contribution to the Union. Indeed population does not provide the most important measure. But rate of growth or decline does suggest how the state is regarded by new homemakers and operators of new industries. It is something to analyze for what it is worth in terms of the state's future.

Here is a list of the states with their percentage of growth or decline since April 1, 1950 together with their percentage of change between 1940 and 1950:

		1950-56 % Gain or Loss	1940-50 % Gain or Loss
1.	Nevada	54.6	45.2
2.	Arizona	41.0	50.1
3.	Florida	36.0	46.1
4.	California	26.9	53.3
5.	Delaware	26.4	19.4
6.	Colorado	21.7	18.0
7.	Maryland	20.0	28.6
8.	New Mexico	19.6	28.1
9.	Michigan	18.0	21.2
10.	Utah	17.9	25.2
11.	Texas	15.7	20.2
12.	Ohio	14.5	15.0
13.	Oregon	12.9	39.6
14.	Indiana	12.2	14.8
15.	Washington	12.1	37.0
16.	Louisiana	12.0	13.5
17.	New Jersey	11.7	16.2
18.	Connecticut	11.2	17.4
19.	South Carolina	11.1	11.4
	U.S. Average	10.9	14.5
20.	Kansas	10.4	5.8
21.	Wyoming	10.4	15.9
22.	Virginia	10.0	23.9
23.	Wisconsin	9.6	9.5
24.	New York	9.2	10.0
25.	North Carolina	8.9	13.7
26.	Minnesota	8.7	6.8
27.	ILLINOIS	8.3	10.3
28.	Montana	8.0	5.6
29.	Georgia	7.8	10.3
30.	MISSOURI	7.6	4.5
31.	Nebraska	6.7	.7
32.	South Dakota	6.6	1.5
33.	Idaho	6.1	12.1
34.	North Dakota	6.0	−3.5
35.	Tennessee	5.3	12.9
36.	New Hampshire	5.1	8.5
37.	Rhode Island	4.5	11.0
38.	Pennsylvania	4.4	6.0
39.	Iowa	2.7	3.3
40.	Massachusetts	2.6	8.7
41.	Kentucky	2.5	3.5
42.	Alabama	2.4	8.1
43.	Oklahoma	.1	−4.4
44.	Maine	−.4	7.9
45.	West Virginia	−1.1	5.4
46.	Vermont	−2.0	5.2
47.	Mississippi	−2.5	−.2
48.	Arkansas	−5.0	−2.0

It is apparent from only a little study of this table that the problem of Missouri is also the problem of Missouri's neighbors—Iowa, Nebraska, Oklahoma, Arkansas, Tennessee, Kentucky and Illinois. And so we hope that Gov.-elect Blair will take the lead in assembling representatives of this group of Middle Western states to plan a regional attack on this common problem of relative population decline.

The alternative is to drop lower and lower and to lose prestige and influence in the unflattering process.

The continuance of the Westward Ho migration in search of jobs and good weather and scenery is seen in the names of the states heading this growth list. The fallacy of using percentages is seen by this fact: the Nevada gain of 45.2 percent between 1940 and 1950 meant that the state's total population increased from 110,247 to 160,-083. In both years Nevada was the 48th state in size out of 48. Missouri's 4.5 percent increase meant she went from 3,784,664 to 3,954,653 which meant she went from 10th to 11th in rank according to population. Why this caused so much alarm by the *Post-Dispatch* editorial writer seems strange almost two decades later when the threat of over-population is so widely felt. The complaint here, furthermore, is comparative rank, as the rate of increase actually went up from 4.5 to 7.6 percent, which the author of this piece, however, did not consider a "comeback." The wisdom of reproducing the long list, especially since the first column is a matter of estimation, can be questioned.

Enough for bad examples. What follows is an illustration of how a statistically-minded editorial writer can straighten out readers who might otherwise be confused by a news report. Herein is combined proper use of statistics, their smart interpretation and wise comments on the total situation. The editorial appeared in the New York *Times* for June 17, 1971.

Can America Grow Up?

In 1950, there were 151 million Americans. Today, there are 208 million. By the year 2000—only 29 years from now—that number is expected to swell to roughly 300 million. In other words, if present growth patterns persist, the population of the United States will double in the last half of the twentieth century.

Citing those statistics, Senator Cranston of California and 26 other Senators have introduced a joint resolution putting Congress on record in favor of zero population growth. The fact that the co-sponsors come from both parties and across the political spectrum from Barry Goldwater to George McGovern is proof that the population issue has moved to the forefront of public concern.

There are several misunderstandings concerning this country's population problem. There is the belief that the introduction of the birth control pill and the wider availability of abortion are rapidly reducing the birth rate. It is true that the birth rate which stood at 25 live births per thousand in 1957 declined during the subsequent decade. But that decline leveled off in the last two years. Last year, it was approximately eighteen per thousand or nearly twice the death rate. As we noted yesterday, multiple births are rising because of increased use of hormones to combat infertility, and in other respects as well there is nothing less than a scientific revolution going on in the field of human reproduction.

Women in their twenties produce the most children. This country is beginning to have a rising number of women in that age bracket. These young women and their husbands are the babies born during the population boom of the late nineteen-forties and early nineteen-fifties.

* * *

A second myth is that excessive childbearing is primarily a phenomenon of the least-educated, low-income elements in society. It is true that this group has proportionately more children. But seven out of every ten children are born to middle- and upper-income families. In other words, even if the poor began to have children at the same rate as the society as a whole, this country would still have a rapidly rising population.

Yet a third mistaken belief is that if every American family began immediately to have just two children, the problem would be solved. Because of the post-World War II population boom, even the two-child family would mean continued population growth until the year 2037, when America's population would level off at 277 million, more than one-third greater than it is now.

The joint resolution introduced in the Senate proposes no drastic remedies. It urges stabilizing the population by voluntary means consistent with human rights and individual conscience. Its objective is to provide a declaration of national policy and a positive context in which the necessary attitudes, policies and research can evolve.

If zero population growth is to be achieved, many popular attitudes and expectations will have to change. For three centuries, Americans dwelling in a nearly empty, richly endowed continent developed a cult of growth. Small towns dreamed that the railroad would bring growth or that new industry would boom land values. The "booster" became an American stereotype and unending growth a national obsession. But now Americans have to develop the self-discipline to prevent an overcrowded and impoverished society. The question is no longer whether America will grow but whether Americans can grow up.

INDICES

Editorial writers must understand the nature of index numbers, their use and misuse. Sometimes a labor-management dispute can hinge in large part or entirely on the base year to be used for making comparisons to show the extent of need for wage raises or the opposite. Why selection of the base year is important can be demonstrated easily. Consider the following, using round numbers for ease in illustration.

Year	Income	Outgo
1	1,000	900
2	1,000	2,000
3	1,500	2,000

Comparing 3 with 1 shows income up 50 percent and outgo up 400 percent. Comparing 3 with 2 shows income up 50 percent and outgo up none. It's easily seen how parties to a dispute could disagree as to whether Year 1 or Year 2 should be used for comparison with Year 3.

An index number, the *Random House Dictionary of the English Language* says, "is a quantity whose variation over a period of time measures the change in some phenomenon." There is plenty of inconsistency by environmental and other agencies in their choice of base periods. The trend, especially in labor contracts, is toward using three-year averages. Formerly the monthly average for the years 1923-25 was widely used; for instance, by the United States Bureau of Labor Statistics for its

Index of Prices of Building Materials and Costs and by the Federal Reserve Board for its Index of Industrial Production, now based on 1957. The United States Bureau of Mines used 1918 for its Relative Rates of Growth of Coal and Water Power in the United States. The International Labour Office used 1929 for its Index for Worldwide Employment and Unemployment, and the United States uses 1958 for its indexes to show industrial production in West Europe and the USSR.

Few journalists are adept at analyzing and interpreting index numbers. A rare exception was the late Robert P. Vanderpoel, longtime financial editor for Hearst and Field newspapers in Chicago. The following is the first part of his column in the Chicago *Sun-Times* for Nov. 16, 1952.

Last February the United States Bureau of Labor Statistics launched a new wholesale price index, declared to be more modern, more accurate and more comprehensive than the old index. It was based on average prices during the years 1947, 1948 and 1949 while the old index was based on average prices of 1926.

The index was criticized in this column at the time on several grounds. First, it had been expensive to prepare; second, it was to cost 20 per cent more; third, and most important, it was based on a very high plateau—the very peak of the postwar years prior to Korea—and a period during which price relationships quite obviously were topsy-turvey due to the aftermath of the war.

Statisticians, we were told, could iron out these discrepancies. To this I replied that after all there were few statisticians and for the average man on the street the new index would always be "telling lies."

Let us look at this new index today. First of all, wholesale commodity prices as measured by this index are now at the lowest level since it was presented to the public on Feb. 26. The average of all commodities is down about 2½ per cent. Compared with early last year, however, the index is down around 6 per cent.

Other more sensitive indexes such as that of Dun & Bradstreet show declines of around 15 per cent or more.

Despite these sizable reactions in wholesale prices the bureau's consumers' price index (commonly known as the cost-of-living index) has moved upward. Inasmuch as most of the wage contracts with escalator clauses are based on this index there have been continued wage increases, with their inflationary influence, even in the face of the declines in wholesale prices. Incidentally, the consumers' price index also is about to be distorted by being placed on a new postwar plateau as a base level.

10 Pct. Above Postwar Highs

The new all-commodity index on Nov. 4 stood at 110.1. One might surmise from this that prices are only 10.1 per cent above "normal." That, of course, would be a great mistake. Prices average 10.1 per cent above the extremely high levels that prevailed in the years 1947 to 1949—the highest in the history of this country until the Korean war was started and sent them even higher.

The farm product index on Nov. 4 was 104.3. The casual observer could hardly conclude otherwise than that relatively speaking farm prices today are low, the index being more than 5 per cent under that for all commodities. That is not correct, however, because during the period the Bureau of Labor Statistics adopted for its base farm products which were way out of line on the up side.

The two best known and hence most controversial indexes are (1) the United States Department of Agriculture index for per capita farm and nonfarm income, and (2) the Dow Jones daily stock and bond market indexes.

It is on the basis of the farm income indices that the parity income ratios used to determine governmental subsidies are erected. Still in use is the 1910-1914 period during which presumably the economic balance between rural and urban dwellers was correct. The parity ratio has been called a statistical "monstrosity" but all efforts to replace it with another system have gotten nowhere in Congress. Within a generation the political Farm Bloc has become more urban than rural, consisting of representatives of banks, insurance companies, and conglomerates that now own the farms and pull more political weight than the farmers who were split into special interest groups—cattle, corn, wheat, cotton and the like—and had to rely on charismatic leaders such as "Cotton Ed" Smith and the Bankheads to obtain their clout, usually exercised through judicious logrolling. The city slickers who now own the farms are quite content to continue the federal largesse that they used to criticize—before they became the beneficiaries. There seems no chance that the basic principles underlying federal governmental farm policy will change. It's still essentially what the much maligned Henry A. Wallace concocted as a relief measure in early New Deal days.

The process by which to determine parity is something like this: suppose farm income per capita to be 461 as compared with 100 in 1910-14 and suppose nonfarm per capita income to be 272 on the same basis. The index of farm income (461) divided by the index of nonfarm income (272) yields the parity income ratio (168). In other words, it's a sort of ratio of ratios. Henry C. Withers did a competent job of explaining it to nonfarm owning city slickers in the Dallas *Evening News* for Jan. 20, 1954, as follows:

If you want a real tough nut to crack try to explain in simple language, within reasonable length, just what is meant by parity prices for farm products.

Fred Pass, agriculture editor of The News, when asked define the term in thirty or forty words, came up with the following:

"Parity prices are prices which would give farm products the same purchasing power per unit, in terms of things farmers buy, as prevailed in a base period considered average years for farmers' income. That base period is usually 1910-14.

"If that is too complicated for you, how about this: If a farmer could take a bale of cotton to town in 1910-14 and sell it for enough to buy a suit of clothes, then he should be able to sell a bale today for enough to buy a suit of the same quality."

Perfectly simple, isn't it? Now you understand thoroughly and are surprised that members of Congress, all of whom want to help the farmer, especially in an election year, have to talk so long about the kind of farm law that shall be passed.

The difficulty is not in agreeing upon the continuance of approximate parity but upon the formula to be applied in arriving at true parity.

Not only is the higher cost of living involved but the higher cost of production also. A farm hand used to get $15 a month; now he gets almost that much a day in some seasons. Everything the farmer buys costs more.

So a cost of living index has been established, covering 176 items and services. It works like this: In the base period cotton averaged 15¢ a pound. The cost of living index in 1953 stood at 300, three times what it was in the base period. Full parity price for cotton in 1953 would be 45¢ a pound.

But there were other factors which reduced the price support for cotton in 1953 to 30.8¢ a pound for upland cotton and 73.9¢ a pound for extra-long staple.

If the farmer can't sell his cotton for that price on the market the government stores it and lends the farmer the support price without interest. If, later, the market price exceeds the support price the farmer can sell. If the market price continues to be lower the government is stuck with the cotton.

What is true of cotton is true of all other basic commodities. On Dec. 14, 1953, the government owned $2,618,575,000 (billions) of farm commodities acquired under the support plan. It had, in addition, $2,000,841,000 (billions) outstanding loans on farm commodities to be acquired in 1954.

The total of federal funds invested in taking crops off the market now exceeds $5,-000,000,000 (billions) and is expected to go to $6,000,000,000 (billions) by July 1, 1954.

You don't raise cotton or any other farm product. What is your interest in the problem? The government now is losing money on this operation at the rate of $1,000,000,-000 (billion) a year. You pay your share of that in federal taxes.

Unless some revision is made in the law the agricultural act of 1949 will go into full effect in 1955. It provides that the government must continue to support prices on a basis of 90 per cent parity.

No one in authority has proposed to discontinue price supports for farm products. The disagreement is between those who wish to retain the mandatory supports, based on the most recent 10-year period, and those who propose to vary the price support level as the total supply varies and to determine the level before crops are planted.

The latter solution is that recommended by President Eisenhower to Congress Monday.

The avowed purpose of the Dow Jones averages is to give a general rather than precise idea of the fluctuations in the securities markets and to reflect the historical continuity of security price movements. The daily publication of an average consisting entirely of stock began May 26, 1896. Today this average is based on the sales of 30 industrial stocks on the New York Stock Exchange. The other Dow Jones reports today are based on 20 transportation stocks, 15 utility stocks, and 40 bonds. What relationship there is between investments and economic well-being is unprovable. No doubt the ups and downs of the market indicate what Wall Street investors believe. To them the status of the stock and bond markets is a harbinger of what to expect. In 1929, however, the Dow Jones average had peaked at 381.17 just before the great crash of October after which it slumped to 41.22 in 1932. Stock market operations are at best speculation; at worst they are just plain gambling.

IV

Structure and Style

There is no one correct way to write a good editorial. As is true of any form of creative activity, however, there are some rules that the beginner is wise to master, even though his future success may depend on the originality with which he modifies or violates them.

GENERAL CHARACTERISTICS

Since there are no rigid stylistic rules to adhere to—that is, no 5 w's or inverted pyramid structure—an editorial, good or bad, must be defined in terms of its purpose. It is that part of a publication which management dedicates to the purpose of influencing the thoughts, opinions and actions of its readers. Such a definition includes the biblical quotations which, on Christmas or Easter, may occupy the position otherwise used for formal editorials. It also includes dramatic skits, poetry, cartoons, illustrations and other devices which are sometimes used with the frank intention of bringing readers to a predetermined point of view or attitude. They are all editorials in purpose despite their stylistic dissimilarities.

A good editorial is one which succeeds in achieving the intention of its author to communicate a particular message. It does not merely view with alarm or point with pride or direct attention to the existence of a problem. Rather, it makes a point clearly and it provides facts and arguments in support of it. The best editorials are written by persons who feel strongly about what they have to say, know what that is, and are willing and able to say why they feel as they do. A good case could be made for the contention that any other kind of so-called editorials are a waste of space which could be better utilized for other printed material. Anyway, to repeat a point already made, there's no sense studying how to write bad editorials even though it must be sadly admitted that there are quite a few people making a living by writing them.

One of the first lessons a beginner learns is that writing a good editorial is not so easy as it may seem. The short one or two paragraph piece, which appears to be a filler, may have taken hours, days or even weeks to research and possibly as long to rewrite and edit to size. Many a writer has testified to the fact that it is much more difficult to condense than to expand an idea. Because space is so limited, the editorial writer is faced with the task of saying more in less space than almost any

57

other kind of author. Every word has to count and the reason some of the editorial classics of all time seem so superior is because of the effort expended to cut them down to size. By substituting short for long synonyms, one comes up with the most pertinent to be found in *Roget's Thesaurus of English Words and Phrases*, an essential for any writer's library. Its user should, however, look up the meaning of any synonym in a standard dictionary if he has any question as to its precise meaning.

Editorial writing is the tightest kind of commercial writing that there is. This is true of long as well as of short pieces. They are longer, not because of verbosity but because they contain more information which couldn't be crowded into less space. Long-windedness is completely out of place in effective editorial writing. Because of the drill it provides in eliminating superfluous verbiage from one's copy, editorial writing is tremendous practice for almost any other kind of composition. It provides especially good experience for journalism students who will become reporters upon graduation and, with few exceptions, won't qualify for good editorial writing positions for a few years. Enrollment in an editorial writing class will be time well spent for the writing discipline it provides, if for no other reason. In addition there is the necessity of mastering the technique of effective research and of logical argumentative thinking. No course in communicology can come close to offering the same advantages despite its heavy emphasis on mental processes, Marshall McLuhan fakery and the like.

THE SUMMARY SENTENCE

An editorial fails if it does not get across the point its author wants to make. The test should be this: is it possible to condense the point of the editorial into a single summary sentence? If not, there must be something the matter with it. Maybe it straddles, pussyfoots, tries to avoid being definite, showing courage only in admitting that a problem exists. Or maybe it's fuzzy because the writer doesn't know what he's talking about. Such editorials are superfluous; any newspaper could find better use for the space they occupy. Maybe the editorial's point is obscure because the writer commits an error quite common among beginners; that of trying to cover too much in a single piece. Students especially feel the temptation to say everything they know or think about a given subject in a single piece. Possibly they can be excused because they have professors whom they wish to impress by revelation of the amount of research they have done and because they won't have the opportunity to follow up a first editorial with others on the same subject. To meet the course requirements they have to tackle something different for the next assignment. Professional editorial writers are not under the same handicap. They can return to the same subject as often as they deem prudent. Consequently they can adhere to the sound rule: one editorial, one point.

Recall the hypothetical example of the signing of a reciprocal trade agreement between Peru and the United States in Chapter II. Summary sentences of editorials from a variety of viewpoints on that news event might be as follows:

The agreement should not be signed because it would anger Ecuador.

The agreement would be good because it would cause the exports of each country to the other to nearly double.

The agreement is essential if we are to keep the friendship of Peru in the United Nations.

All of the reciprocal trade agreements to date have failed so the success of this one would be doubtful.

Play the game yourself: think up more possible summary sentences which, old timers will recognize, are similar to the topic sentences that high school teachers required whenever someone wrote a theme.

Unfortunately, or perhaps fortunately, there is no literary composition in post-high school days that in any way resembles the themes which high school students are laboriously taught to compose throughout their elementary and secondary school years. Nevertheless, the topic or summary sentence idea is good as a testing device for the editorial writer who wants to check his own effectiveness. Students can use it in critically analyzing editorials. If they don't get the point of an editorial, or, worse still, if there is no point to get, they can resolve to do better the next time when their turn comes.

What follows is one of the editorials which won for Duane Croft of the Toledo *Blade* the Sigma Delta Chi distinguished service for editorial writing award in 1966. It was published Feb. 5, 1966.

Welcome 'Encroachment'

The Federal Government has come to the aid of Lucas County's most forlorn school district, Spencer-Sharples.

The $157,000 community school program obtained through the local anti-poverty headquarters will not fill all the gaps cited in a report just two weeks ago by an inspection team of the State Department of Education. But the money from Washington will shore up some of the weakest spots through guidance counseling for high school students, remedial reading and arithmetic classes for elementary pupils, in-service training for teachers, a vocational education course for adults, and other supplements to the undernourished S-S educational fare.

This is a great deal more help than the people of the district could expect from any other source. And in that lies a moral that should be of particular interest to those who fret and fume about federal encroachment on local control of the schools.

It was the hallowed principle of local control which created the Spencer-Sharples situation in the first place. Applying the tenet at the ballot box, the better-heeled neighbors of the S-S area were able to pull away from it, relieving themselves of any share of responsibility for it and leaving it isolated without a place to educate its children or enough tax revenue to provide one.

It is the revered principle of local control which stands in the way of a permanent solution to the district's terrible poverty problem. The state furnishes more than 77 per cent of the district's operating budget, which still is inadequate compensation for the lack of a broader tax base. Absorption into a larger district would provide such a base, but the state—under the principle of local control—is for all practical purposes powerless to demand this for Spencer-Sharples.

Closer to home, the county board of education has authority in state law to propose some sort of merger. But—under the principle of local control—this authority becomes a worthless theory because the county board's proposal would be subject to referendum. Why would the areas which voluntarily divorced themselves from Spencer-Sharples vote voluntarily to help support it again?

Besides, S-S is now a local district itself, under its own control. And if, despite the willingness of its residents to vote themselves the highest tax rate for school purposes in Lucas County, the district still hasn't enough money to maintain an adequate educational program—well, under the principle of local control, that is the S-S district's tough luck.

Enough said about local control of the schools. In spite of it, thanks to the Federal Government, the people of Spencer-Sharples see some prospect at last of improving their educational opportunity.

The $157,000 from the anti-poverty program is probably only a starter. Plans are under way for more help through the aid to education act passed by Congress last year. There should be assistance possibilities beyond that.

It may be "encroachment," but it is just what Spencer-Sharples and thousands of other locally controlled school districts need more of.

The summary sentence for this editorial obviously is something like this: "Local control fails when a district, such as Spencer-Sharples, cannot properly finance its schools."

On the other hand it is impossible to compose a summary sentence for the following from the Baltimore *Evening Post* of Aug. 10, 1953.

Jersey Turnpike

Perhaps it's because engineers prefer to err on the conservative side or perhaps it is because there are too many variables to make accurate forecasts. Anyway it is becoming increasingly evident that if a modern toll facility is built to serve a real need it will attract users beyond the most optimistic estimates.

True the initial cost of these projects is exceedingly high. But look at what they take in. As of June, two months short of a year of its opening, the Bay Bridge had already taken in upward of $2,800,00 or $400,000 more than the take predicted for the entire first year. Now glance at the travel trend on the Jersey turnpike for the first six months of 1953. Traffic has already exceeded the estimates for 1971 and revenues have reached the level predicted for 1968. Average daily traffic on this high-speed facility now amounts to 53,700 cars, more than twice the engineer's estimate for this year. And recently with many drivers vacation-bound it has soared to 76,700 cars a day.

One of the difficulties that has plagued these high-speed facilities such as the New Jersey and Pennsylvania turnpikes is the high accident rate, particularly in the rear-end-collision category. Here, too, the latest report on the New Jersey turnpike authority shows marked improvement. Fatalities were 4.1 for each 100,000,000 miles, a rate ranking with the lowest for five state highway systems. Additional safety measures and increase in State police patrol are credited by the report for bringing the accident rate as a whole down from 90.0 to 60.1 per 100,000,000 miles as compared with the same half-year period last year.

Of course one hesitates to predict whether the rate of usage will continue at these high levels. However, past experience indicates that use of gasoline is one thing which does not fall off by any wide margin in a depression, if, indeed, such is in store. But

the most encouraging thing to be drawn from the New Jersey report is that it is possible to have good fast highways and hold accidents within bounds with alert but conventional police work.

The closest it is possible to come in summarizing this piece is: "Random thoughts on the Jersey turnpike." The editorial makes several points and suggests others: the rapidity with which new highways become obsolete; the huge costs involved; accidents; the role of the police; the gloomy outlook. It develops none of these or other ideas, however, and takes no stand on anything. It is weak because it violates the one editorial-one-point rule.

THE THREE UNITS

A good editorial makes three things clear:
1. The subject or news peg—the news event or current situation or occasion evoking editorial comment.
2. The reaction—clear-cut for or against, pro or con; what the editorial writer wants the reader to think or do.
3. The reasons—facts or logical arguments to back the stand.

In his *Editorial Writing* (Houghton Mifflin, 1924), M. Lyle Spencer, then director of the School of Journalism at the University of Washington, described the three-unit editorial:

> In it, one division, usually put first, gives the news, facts or truths on which the editorial is based. Another unit, usually in second place, gives the reaction of the writer toward the news, facts, or truths presented in the first part. The last unit gives the reasons for the writer's reaction. For the sake of clarity these three divisions may be called respectively the informative, the reactional and the deliberative units.

The 1-2-3 organizational order is not only usually the most logical but it is the easiest for the beginner to learn. Good editorial writers have adhered to it for years as the dates of several of the examples to follow indicate. Here is a good example of how it is done from the Miami *Herald* of July 30, 1946.

On the Level

Sidney Hillman left an estate consisting of insurance policies made out to his family of a face value of $60,000 and $9,900 in Amalgamated Bank shares and certificates.

A probate showing that he lived well inside his official salary is the finest possible tribute to a labor leader or a public official. Not all the glowing obituary notices received by the late Samuel Gompers were worth the revelation that Sam left an estate of about $1,000.

Hillman's insurance and stock represent less than the average accumulations of a businessman or corporation executive with an income of $15,000 per year—the amount of Hillman's salary.

Not all records of "friends of labor" and leaders of labor have been such testaments of sincerity as those of Hillman and Gompers.

Note that paragraph one differs from the 5 w's news story lead in that it ignores specificity as regards the *when* and *where*. A regular news story lead would relate that the will was filed today in the probate court of a certain city. The editorial lead, however, clearly has a timely news peg and there is no indication of what the reaction of the editorial writer is to the occurrence.

This reaction is strongly stated in paragraph 2 and permeates the rest of the piece which is the deliberative unit consisting of facts and reasoning.

Another way of emphasizing the reaction is illustrated by the following introduction to a good-sized piece, "Impeach Judge Atlee," in the Philadelphia *Record* for July 16, 1936:

Two members of the Pennsylvania House of Representatives have asked an investigation of Judge Benjamin Atlee, of Lancaster.

They believe he should be impeached if he was correctly quoted in his recent speech from the bench, in which he deplored the fact that a Negro prisoner before him had not been lynched.

The Record agrees with the two legislators.

For emphasis also the reactional and informative units may be combined. The St. Louis *Post-Dispatch* did it by means of a single adjective in its July 15, 1936 piece, "Politician, Spare That Tree," as follows:

A justified protest has been made by the Greater St. Louis Association of Gardeners against the practice of nailing political posters to trees.

Eliminate the "justified" and the style could become that of the preceding Philadelphia *Record* piece somewhat as follows:

A protest has been made by the Greater St. Louis Association of Gardeners against the practice of nailing political posters to trees.

The Post-Dispatch agrees with the gardeners.

A common editorial beginning, combining information and reaction, is illustrated by the following from the Chicago *Daily News* of April 19, 1955:

New Bill; Old Racket

A thoroughly bad bill (S.B. 263) passed the Senate at Springfield on April 14 and is now waiting the action of the House. It needs such fundamental revision that it would be better to kill it and start all over again.

A different rhetorical method of doing the same thing is shown by the lead the Kansas City *Star* used for its editorial, "A Mill for the Library," May 4, 1956:

Within a very few days Kansas City should know whether the library is to have its own tax—an absolutely necessary measure to help save both the school system and the library.

There is no mistaking the editorial's stand in such editorials. The Boston *Globe* didn't pussyfoot in its editorial, "Unbalanced Vote on Schools," Sept. 23, 1971, which began as follows:

> In an outstanding display of faint-hearted defeatism, a majority of the Boston School Committee has turned its back on a timid first step toward compliance with the state's six-year-old law to end racial imbalance in the schools. Only Chairman Paul Tierney and committeeman James Hennigan had the sense to realize what now lies ahead for the city and its impoverished school program.

It is, of course, impossible to have a reactional unit divorced from an informative unit. The news peg, however, may not be a specific incident headlined on yesterday's front page. Rather, it can be a series of events or a continuing situation. In the following example from the Louisville *Courier-Journal* of July 21, 1971, the reactional comes first and the informative is blended throughout the bulk of the piece which is almost entirely deliberative.

Deepening Economic Trouble

NEITHER BULLISH RHETORIC nor impressive but misleading statistics can conceal the truth: Economically, the country is in deepening trouble.

The clock in the Commerce Department's lobby in Washington keeps ticking off increases in our gross national product, but it counts inflation as real output, which it isn't. The June figures showed a drop in unemployment, but the labor-force sample taken in June, on which the figures were based, came before schools closed for the summer and therefore did not reflect the usual June influx of students into the labor market; those who fail to get employment will have to be counted this month, and that will change the picture.

After seasonal adjustments, what the June figures actually revealed was that the number of people with jobs declined by 500,000 between May and June, and 310,000 of this total involved jobs in the non-agricultural area. Moreover, the cutbacks in employment were not selective, were not the result of special situations, but occurred over a broad spectrum of the economy; this economic downturn differs from others in recent years in that it is hitting white-collar workers, executives, scientists, technicians, as well as assembly-line workers and others in the production end of manufacturing.

Yet despite the unemployment and the sluggish rate of economic growth, inflation perversely continues rolling along. The figures released in June showed that the wholesale price index edged up four-tenths of one percent, and this index is based on the prices of 2,300 commodities.

One doesn't need to see this kind of figures to know that the cost of living is still rising. The realities are all too apparent. People who are out of work know the realities, too, and it is cold comfort to them to know that, statistically, they have a lot of company.

The unemployment figures, by the way, don't include those persons who are unfeelingly described in current lingo as the "hard-core" unemployed, those who have simply given up hope of finding jobs and have stopped looking. They don't include the ill, disabled and handicapped who also want jobs but are unable to get them.

The relative inertia of the Nixon administration in the face of all this is hard to understand, economically or politically.

Summary: Bad economic conditions are growing and affecting more elements in the population.

Sometimes such a technique results in what is virtually an editorial essay, the timeliness of which, however, is clear because of contemporary references. Such an editorial was the following from the Philadelphia *Bulletin* of June 17, 1964.

'The Fifth' in Fifty States

There is no area in which the rights of the individual walk a more precarious tightrope between the rights of society than in application of the Fifth Amendment to the

U.S. Constitution—the clause which protects against self-incrimination.

Heroes and rogues both have taken shelter behind this Bill of Rights bunker. Often this has been to the righteous indignation of decent citizens, who hate to see a knave get away with something. Yet most Americans have realized that the concept is indispensable to our way of life—on a level with the doctrine that a man is innocent until proven guilty.

The Fifth, by ruling of the U.S. Supreme Court, now is the law of the several states as well as of the federal government. While rascals have this protection, the important thing is that so do all citizens; for the basic purpose of this doctrine is to prevent tyranny on the part of governmental agencies. Because of it, all Americans have been the freer.

The Supreme Court's extension of the Fifth came, as almost every other pronouncement of importance seems to come these days, by way of the Fourteenth Amendment, with its sweeping demand for equal protection of the law. Therefore, the Court said in effect, one jurisdiction cannot demand information which could be used against an individual in another jurisdiction.

It is an insistence on uniformity which dissenters find objectionable; and since the voting split 5-4, the dissenting view cannot be waved off.

Yet the sense of this historic decision is in keeping with a long trend of the high court. In a series of decisions going back some 40 years, "Age of Enlightenment" guarantees of individual rights which the Founding Fathers wrote into the Bill of Rights have gradually been imposed upon the state governments. Extension of the Fifth is simply one more example, though a notable one.

Summary: The United States Supreme Court has extended the vital protection against tyranny provided by the Fifth Amendment to all Americans.

The following lead, which the New York *Times* used on its March 24, 1971 editorial, "Progress Against Hepatitis," comes as close as possible to combining all three units into a lead.

The rising incidence of illness and death from serum hepatitis in recent years has been a cause of growing concern, especially as the disease is usually transmitted through blood transfusions or infected needles. The report yesterday of Dr. Saul Krugman of New York University that he and his colleagues have apparently demonstrated two means of immunizing patients against the disease is highly encouraging. Dr. Krugman was properly cautious in his announcement, but the possibility of an effective vaccine against serum hepatitis now appears brighter than ever before.

At the other organizational extreme is the following from the Chicago *Sun* of June 9, 1942 which deals entirely with a situation and has no suggestion of a specific news peg.

Sacrificing?

It would be bromidic, of course, to reiterate that war requires sacrifices by every civilian—man, woman and child. There is another side to this sacrifice business, however, of which Americans rapidly are becoming aware.

Succinctly, it can be put this way: under the necessity of war we are learning to do a great many things which we should have been doing all along.

Walking, for instance. In anticipation of rationing in these parts, some motorists are getting in a last fling, but many others have found that footing it to streetcar, bus or elevated surprisingly doesn't kill them.

If the shortages increase, furthermore, we shall begin to eat better—more of the right things, that is—thus further braking the much-advertised "softening" of the American public.

For what we eat and buy generally again, we'll pay prices for which there are ceilings, and we won't be able to yield to the temptation to commit ourselves to too many installments, thus mortgaging our future.

For what we buy we'll use more carefully. For generations teachers have told their classes that the average Japanese family can live for a week on what the average American family wastes in a day.

Summary: War has some good effects on civilians.

If an editorial is almost entirely informative, the observant critic may wonder why the city desk fell down on the job. If, however, the information did appear in the news columns and the editorial is not much more than a rehash, the critic may ask if the editorial writers are either lazy or devoid of ideas. The following editorial, from the Houston *Chronicle* of March 27, 1971, is mostly informative, probably repetitious of some news story; but the author cleverly added his own reactions throughout. In effect he made the news story more readable.

Tourism: Billion-dollar Industry

Americans have more free time these days, and more money to spend on travel and recreation. With improved freeways and fast air travel, tourism has become a major American industry. In Texas last year, 21,116,000 out-of-state visitors spent $1,469,115,000, according to the Texas Highway Department.

These figures show just how important tourism has become. A few years back, it was hardly recognized as a business worth worrying about.

Average spending by auto visitors was $11.34 per person per day. The auto tourist party averaged 2.8 persons, and they spent 5.7 days in Texas.

Those who come here to visit apparently like it, for the highway department figures show that 70 percent of the out-of-states had vacationed in Texas before.

Ninety percent were favorably impressed by what they found here. They were most complimentary of Texas highways. What they liked next best was the friendliness of the Texans they encountered.

Houston was the state's favorite tourist city, followed by Dallas, El Paso and San Antonio. But most of the tourists were just touring.

This is a big state. There is much variety here to see.

What we should remember, however, is that tourists go where they are well received and welcome and where they can find pleasant accommodations and interesting things to do. That means we cannot take tourists for granted. Hotels, restaurants, resort areas, service stations, the entertainment industry, sports, and all others who profit from tourism must continually seek to improve their facilities and their hospitality.

As for Texans generally, the best thing we can do is to keep on being friendly to those who come to visit our state.

Some cities of America have grown big and cold. The people in them have become too busy and too rushed to take time to be nice to visitors. Let's hope that time never arrives in Houston. As we grow into a major metropolis, we don't want to lose the neighborliness and friendliness characteristic of the small towns from which so many Houstonians come.

It makes life a little more pleasant. And for the tourist business, it adds to our economic well-being.

Summary: Let us be friendly to tourists who bring us so much revenue.

By contrast with the Houston editorial, which was mostly informative, the following approaches the opposite extreme of being almost entirely reactional. Hardly a fact is mentioned without the writer's passing pertinent comment. The writer utters a strong cry of alarm but he offers several specific suggestions. The piece appeared in the Tucson *Arizona Daily Star* for March 27, 1971.

More Water Needed

The Lower Colorado Region Interagency Group estimates that the Lower Colorado basin will have a population of 8 million and will need an additional 2.25 million acre feet of water 50 years from now. The estimates were prepared by 40 state and federal agencies and probably are on the conservative side.

Not included in the water estimate is the 1.2 million acre feet that Congress already has authorized for Central and Southern Arizona. That is essential in getting Arizona through the remainder of the century.

The estimate of population and need—one being based on the other—is timely, especially in emphasizing that precious time is being wasted in the construction of the Central Arizona Project. Construction funds are expected from Congress once Arizona is able to present evidence that the users will be able to pay off most of the cost.

This is a matter of prime importance because it affects the immediate future of Arizona, which is one of the fastest growing states in the Union. The legislature, now in session, is moving to establish a water resources commission before it adjourns. Such a commission is a must in getting the CAP under way.

The longer range future is another thing. The biggest question is where Arizona, and small parts of Nevada, Utah and New Mexico, can get another 2.25 million acre feet to support a population of 8 million. The study did not go into this since the legislation authorizing the CAP precludes official studies of importing waters from other river basins until 1978.

Unofficial studies can be started—in fact probably are under way—at any time but the organization making such studies would lack the authority to enter into any type of agreement.

There is one study that should be pushed, and pushed hard. That is the study of desalinization of sea water and its eventual transportation to the arid Southwest. This, in turn, presents the problem of reaching accord with Mexico if such water is to be exported across Sonora to Arizona.

Arizona and her sister states cannot take a defeatist attitude regarding future supplies of water. Other civilizations have withered and died because they lacked the knowledge of how to get supplemental water once the underground supplies had been exhausted. Such knowledge is available today.

Cost will become a minor factor because none of the Southwestern states can let that stand in the way of survival.

The problem will be solved because even more sophisticated solutions will be devised in the near future.

Summary: Greater effort by several agencies is necessary to solve Arizona's water supply problem.

The following editorial, which won the Illinois Press Association best editorial of the year in 1935 for the Evanston *Daily News-Index*, illustrated a device whereby a number of reactional points can be presented. This style is handy when it is necessary to withhold editorial comment for weeks or months, in this case until a long trial ended.

It Might Not Have Been . . .

The Lindbergh baby might still be alive;

Its illustrious parents might have been spared the harrowing experience which will haunt them all their lives;

A sum estimated at about $629,000 might have been saved individuals and the state;

A young man, skilled in a trade, with a wife and baby, might not have been sentenced to die;

A number of other kidnapings, some involving loss of life, might not have been perpetrated in imitation of one which seemed to have been highly successful;

An entire nation might not have been demoralized and brutalized for almost three years, and who knows how much longer—

If—

Mankind were more intelligent;

If, instead of clinging ignorantly to outworn theories and methods of safeguarding itself against lawlessness, it had utilized scientific knowledge and technique.

Bruno Richard Hauptmann is an ex-convict. Were he to return to Germany he would be arrested as a fugitive from justice. Twice he attempted to enter this country illegally and on his third attempt succeeded. Able to tell the truth only with difficulty he made a practice of deceiving his wife, his friends and police authorities with whom he came into contact. His sullenness, stolidity, taciturnity and stubborness suggest a warped mentality—not, by any means, insanity in the legal sense of the term—the instability which, from the standpoint of society, is potentially more dangerous than outright craziness.

Hauptmann's career of crime should and could have been prevented after his first conviction years ago in Germany. Under the laws of that country, which are similar in this respect, to those of our own, Hauptmann could be imprisoned only for a definite period prescribed as suitable punishment for the offense he committed. At the termination of that sentence it was mandatory upon his jailers to release him.

"How," it may be asked, "were the court and prison officials who handled his case at that time to know what the future would be?"

The answer is that, of course the average judge, juror, police or prison official is incompetent to pass judgment on the potentiality of a human personality.

But—there are men of knowledge who can pass such judgment. They are the psychiatrists, the mental experts, whose concern is not the circumstance of a crime or its gravity but the individual committing it. Although today employed quite extensively in police and juvenile courts to work with first and minor offenders, these specialists are powerless to enforce their prescriptions. Potentially dangerous as the petty thief may be discovered to be, there is no legal procedure by which he can be removed from society. Instead, he must be released after serving a sentence and allowed to roam until he commits a crime sufficiently grave to warrant his legal murder or life time imprisonment.

Make mistakes? Of course the psychiatrists make mistakes. But so do judges and juries, pardoning governors, parole and probation boards. Their mistakes are those of scientific diagnosis whereas those of laymen dealing with a scientific problem are ones of ignorance.

It cannot, of course, be maintained with certainty that a mental test would have caused Hauptmann to be adjudged a dangerous character deserving of removal from society years ago. What is certain, however, is that were the findings of mental experts enforceable there is many and many a Hauptmann who would be taken out of circulation before he had a chance to commit murder or some other major crime.

The existence of capital punishment as a deterrent from crime is proof of society's failure to cope with its criminal element rationally. The death penalty is a gesture of impotence.

Summary: The Lindbergh child murder might have been prevented had scientific knowledge been utilized in time.

THE EDITORIAL "WE"

Examples so far have been typical of the vast majority of editorials in that they have been written strictly in the third person. In a couple of instances the name of the paper was used that way. No formal editorials, of course, ever are written in the first person singular. If a writer says "I" he signs his article or column or is so well known that his authorship is understood. Use of the first person plural, the editorial "we," persists but seldom to create the impression that the entire staff of a paper, or anyone other than the writer, in fact, is meant. In the following example the "we" does not create the impression of either a skull session by experts or any hypocritical attempt to make it seem extra-prestigious through the supposition that it is the result of some sort of group thinking. It's really a legitimate and effective rhetorical approach, as used by the Los Angeles *Times* Jan. 28, 1971.

Fostering Intellectual Stagnation

If we had a penchant for censoring what books others should read and what films they should view (although we haven't), our target would be the Los Angeles County Library Department.

County librarians must be jittery enough by now, we suspect, to knuckle under to the most elementary sort of criticism.

This suspicion is based on the peculiar result of a strange meeting held in the office of Supervisor Frank Bonelli between two Hacienda Heights women and County Librarian William Geller.

Bonelli, who denies he wants to impose censorship, called the meeting to talk over films shown at youth discussion groups held at a branch library in the Hacienda area.

The women contended the short movies, selected from the system's 1,100-film collection, were "anti-American, blasphemous, revolutionary and anti-business." And they were even more unhappy over the "dangerous" discussion periods held later.

We aren't sure how the confrontation went. But we are both dismayed and annoyed at what followed.

Geller ordered all 1,100 films, many award winners and most of them shown many times before on television, withdrawn. Then he rescinded the order on all except 19 to which the women objected. They will be reevaluated by the library's citizen advisory groups.

"I guess I lost my cool," Geller conceded later, "and I suppose lots of people are going to look at this as censorship."

We agree, Mr. Geller, on both counts, especially after checking into some of the withdrawn films. They include a film based on an epic poem by a Chicago activist, a religious allegory produced by the Protestant Council of New York, a Canadian film on white-collar crime and a Yugoslav film about a pig that did not want to become a pork roast.

We don't object to a review of library subject matter. The library has an obligation to offer a balanced collection of materials, even those that are controversial and thought-provoking.

We do object, however, to our librarians' bowing to small, vocal groups or, for that matter, powerful establishment ones, who would purge the stacks of materials they consider objectionable.

We happen to believe strongly that residents of this county, including our youth

and young adults, are capable enough to view controversial films and discuss them afterwards.

Summary: County Librarian Geller should resist pressure to censor films.

In the following editorial from the Chicago Lerner community newspapers of Sept. 27, 1970, the "we" is a forceful substitute for "our reporters," and the point of the piece is to demonstrate the nature and extent of the cover-up which the paper tries to expose.

Those Police Photographs

Recent events on the North Side, in which legal aide lawyers and the director of the Uptown Hull House were followed and photographed by police undercover agents, raise a number of questions which have not been satisfactorily explained by police.

We asked the police, for example, what is done with information gathered by the Subversives unit of the Intelligence division, and were told that it is given to other agencies of federal and state governments only at the discretion of the department.

We asked if police officials didn't consider that the photography could lead to charges of harassment, and were told that no photographs are taken to harass people.

At one point we were told not all the pictures are taken by intelligence ("red squad") police but that most are taken by police from the graphic arts section. Asked if it wasn't true that many of these graphic arts pictures wind up in "red squad" files, police authorities admitted that they do.

We asked the police their definition of "subversive," and what criteria they use to determine if a citizen should be photographed. We were told that the police must protect the secrecy of their operations and could not divulge their criteria.

We concede that perhaps some information police might gather should be secret. But must the methods used for gathering information be kept from the voting and taxpaying public?

We wonder if the veil of secrecy exists because the police are gathering intelligence by questionable methods, and about law-abiding people and organizations.

The public is paying for a service which it is unable to evaluate in terms of either cost or political consequences. It is paying thousands, perhaps hundreds of thousands, of dollars to have dossiers built on large numbers of people.

Additionally, one of the many ways voters may judge a candidate is by the appointments he makes. An appointee, in turn, is judged by the job he does. If the voters are not permitted more information on police department operations they will not be fully informed in judging the performance of the mayor and the city council in directing the police force.

In what seems to be a zeal to photograph every participant in current events, we have seen undercover police photograph clergymen, nuns, political candidates, reporters, scientists, lawyers, members of community organizations, teachers, administrators and even other undercover policemen.

We can't help but wonder if the Intelligence unit's definition of subversive is not too broad, and takes in people who are in no way a potential danger to Chicago. Police surveillance of such people can have a chilling effect on their willingness to speak freely and participate in our democracy.

In determining the worth of such methods, we would like to know if information gathered in such a way has ever led to a conviction, or how many convictions?

The framers of the U.S. Constitution wrote an elaborate series of checks and balances so that no arm of the government could operate without disclosure. And with good reason. For even good men who are allowed to operate without public scrutiny are often tempted to go bad.

Perhaps such public scrutiny and control over police activities would make the task more difficult. But only in a police state is the job of a policeman supposed to be easy.

Summary: The photographing activities of the police red squad are deplorable.

Sometimes the "we" in an editorial means the readers as well as the editorial writer, maybe the public or the entire human race. The following from the Corvallis (Ore.) *Gazette-Times* of Feb. 25, 1964 is an excellent example of how it can be done.

Privacy in the United States

Studies! Studies! Studies! Some group in this country is always conducting a study of human behaviors, animal behaviors, fauna and flora behaviors, moon patterns or something. We are studied to death.

The most recent one to come to our attention is a "major" study of the effect which recent scientific and technological advances are having on privacy in the United States.

This sounds like another one we can do without.

But reading into the news release, we find there are some things they might discover which would be of interest, if not of value. For instance, the purpose of the study "is to assess the extent to which recent scientific developments threaten the essential balance between the needs of society and government for information and the competing needs of individuals and institutions for privacy."

At last someone is thinking about the individual instead of the masses. Just think, someone out there cares!

Actually, science certainly has robbed us of our own individuality and privacy. They now have Laser beams which can eavesdrop on conversations; many stores have closed-circuit concealed TV surveillance; micro-miniaturized radio transmitters which can be hidden in tiny objects of common use; lie detector tests which can even be administered without the subject's knowledge.

We have subliminal and subaudial projection of messages to audiences on television, radio and motion pictures; drugs which might be administered to unlock secrets of persons without their awareness, there are prospects of learning an individual's emotions and attitudes from brain waves. Personality tests now delve into the recesses of attitudes, beliefs and behavior and there is the increasing pace of computer processing of information about millions of private persons.

This study has been conceived by the Bar of the City of New York, the money comes from the Carnegie Corporation of New York and all sorts of important scientists, sociologists, psychiatrists and other people will do the work.

The results of the study will be published later this year. You will have to wait that long to find out how much your privacy is being abused. Trouble is, even when you know, there will be nothing you can do about it.

Summary: Maybe the study of encroachments on privacy will be good.

An entirely different type of "we" editorial is the one in which the writer counts himself double and substitutes the first person plural much as kings and queens often do. Ordinarily this sort of writing is signed; many columnists engage in it. Occasionally, especially in feature topic editorials, it is effective as in the following from the Washington *Evening Star* for Dec. 9, 1963.

For Freeways

As we took our customary route homeward over the Southwest freeway the other day, the blurred outlines of an idea that had been forming suddenly became sharp and clear.

Perhaps it was the view of St. Dominic's Church from the vantage point of the westbound lanes. Perhaps it was the graceful curve of a granite faced ramp contrasted with a stretch of green grass. Or perhaps it was a view, difficult to see unless one is up on something, of the great tower of the National Cathedral rearing up from Mount St. Alban.

Whatever it was, the idea came into focus in the form of a question:

Why is there so much talk about the "ugliness" of freeways? Why is somebody forever glooming about cutting up our cities with "great swathes of concrete" put there

to gratify lazy Americans who wrongheadedly like to drive cars instead of traveling around some other way?

We happen to like freeways. We see not only practical value in them but also a very real esthetic value. They are like rivers, from which one enjoys ever-changing vistas that would hardly be seen from any place else.

And freeways are not just good to look from. When properly designed, they are, like bridges, also good to look at. Bridges have been accepted for centuries as among man's greatest works. Freeways, too, can possess a beauty and grace of their own.

Let's worry about whether our freeways are well or poorly designed, and quit just damning them on general principles. This much is sure: They are not going to go away.

Summary: Freeways are not all bad.

DIRECT ADDRESS

This type of editorial comes as close as it's possible to come in dragging the reader into the editorial himself. The following hard-hitting piece from the Denver *Post* of Dec. 1, 1961 does it by use of the first person plural.

Here in America, Let Freedom Shout!

If any of us were to walk into a Denver bus station and see five of our fellow citizens being slugged and kicked, we would—depending on our degree of courage—either take it upon ourselves to save those being beaten and punish those doing the beating, or we would shout to high heaven until somebody else did the job.

We would, in short, not tolerate in our city such violence and such brutal disregard of humanity.

But when such an incident takes place elsewhere, we show a great depth of understanding and tolerance—especially if our fellow citizens happen to be Negroes and the incident takes place in the Deep South.

On Wednesday five Negroes were beaten and pummeled after they were refused service in a McComb, Miss., bus station.

Two reminders: 1.) The Negroes were completely within their legal rights—to say nothing of their moral rights as citizens of the democratic United States—in requesting service, for federal law now prohibits segregation in bus and rail terminals. 2.) Although there may be understandable confusion on this point, Mississippi is, indeed, still one of the 50 United States and therefore under the jurisdiction of federal law.

On the basis of these two points, federal authorities are investigating the incident, and at this point most of us—however revulsed or disgusted or infuriated at the beatings—are content to let the matter rest. Let the feds do it!

We justify our own inaction and long-term indifference with the old dodge "What can I do about it?" and with a bouquet of pretty rationalizations that smell of magnolias.

● We say: "You can't expect the South to be integrated overnight; segregation is part of Southern culture, and culture can change only slowly."

Ignorance and bigotry always die slowly, if at all; remove them from incessant attack and in the atmosphere of indifference they feed upon themselves and grow and thrive and prosper.

● We say: "Those who use violence to prevent their fellow citizens from obtaining their rights are only a small, fanatical segment of the Southern populace; the great majority of Southerners are 'right-minded, correct-thinking people.'"

But they passively allow such violence. Beatings and sluggings could not take place, even if perpetrated by fanatics, unless a permissive atmosphere existed, unless the rights of their fellow citizens—Negroes—didn't essentially mean so little to the white Southerners that they are willing to sit back and see such outrages occur.

● We say: "You can't hope the offenders will be punished, because no Southern jury would ever convict a white man of attacking a Negro."

So we sit back and allow our indignation to dissipate itself in a chorus of weak "tut-tut's." Because the incident involves Negroes in the South, we allow our whole system of laws—than which nothing is more basic to our democracy—to be reduced to a shambles.

● We say: "Isn't it a shame this racial incident happened. Think what the Communists will make of it."

Instead of indulging in searching but essentially profitless international concern, think rather of our separate, distinct fellow citizens who have not only been beaten but, more importantly, have been denied their rights as Americans and as human beings. Think of the hundreds of thousands of little pictures and the Big Picture will take care of itself.

So what can we do? We can get angry. We can get angry enough—and sufficiently vocal about it—to get something done. This is what democracy is all about: the people, free within freely accepted laws, utilizing their freedom to make life better for themselves and their fellows.

We can raise our voices in support of prompt and effective federal action against those who brazenly ignore federal law.

If our mistreated fellow citizens have no recourse to local courts in the South, we can loudly and persistently demand that the federal courts try the offenders.

We can't just say: "Let the feds do it." Through our active and vocal interest, we must let the federal government know that it has our wholehearted support in taking whatever vigorous action is necessary to wipe out this national shame.

We can get angry—and say so! Patience is a noble virtue—when it's not used as an excuse for being lazy!

Summary: The South does not deserve sympathy for using violence to prevent racial integration on buses.

Most direct address editorials are written in the second person and the "you" meant to be unmistakably the reader. The technique is well illustrated by the following editorial from the Calumet City (Ill.) *Sun-Journal* of Jan. 7, 1971.

A Sobering Thought

If you are reading this at home in your favorite easy chair, and not a hospital bed, consider yourself one of the lucky ones. You have survived one of the most dangerous weekends of your life.

No fewer than 454 persons lost their lives on the highways New Years Eve weekend. Thousands of others now find themselves confined to emergency wards in hospitals across the nation. In Illinois 21 persons are no longer with us, holiday accidents snuffed out their lives. How many of these drivers were drinking or hit by drinking drivers is not known. But we do know that by the time 1971 ends, more than 86,000 persons will be killed or injured by drunk drivers. That's right, 86,000.

It's not a wild, inflated figure. We know it is accurate because it is near last year's figure, and the year before that. Something must be done. And we know what that something is.

Illinois is one of only 4 states that does not have a mandatory breath test for motorists suspected of drinking. In the Lansing-Calumet City area alone, four innocent persons were killed by drivers apparently under the influence of alcohol. In each case the offender refused the drunk test and was booked on a lesser charge. We are not crying for their blood, we are crying for an end to senseless slaughter by inebriated drivers.

How do we end it? First, Illinois needs a law that requires anyone arrested for drunk driving to take a breath test. If the motorist refuses, the penalty would be loss of license for one year. Similar laws are on the books in 46 states. We know the law is a good one. It's working in other states and is recommended in standards set by the National Safety Bureau. Illinois needs this law, and you can help get it for us.

Politicians are just like all of us. It takes a little push now and then to get started in the right direction. You can provide that push by writing your Illinois state Senators and Congressmen and telling them you want a law making a drunk test mandatory. It may seem a harsh step, but 86,000 persons a year don't think so.

Write today and get the drunks off the road before they get you.

Summary: Illinois needs a compulsory breath test for drunken drivers in accidents.

Even more direct and personal, because it discusses the topic in relation to the specific effect on any reader, is the following from the Las Vegas (Nev.) *Review-Journal* of Aug. 20, 1966.

Uncle Sam Is Watching You

Have you done anything you would just as soon keep to yourself?

Then let's hope you can. But don't be too sure.

For the fact is that as of right now you are of sufficient interest to your government that 20 U.S. agencies and departments may have taken the time and trouble to collect some sort of information about you.

And that isn't all.

The Bureau of the Budget is now proposing that a National Data Center be established to assemble all this miscellaneous information, feed it into a computer and end up with a complete, it's-all-in-here dossier on you and your life for handy use by anyone who may have the "right" and the opportunity to see it.

Any way you look at it, this seems to add up to a startling invasion of privacy. And it is all the more alarming because some of the information on file about you may not have been obtained directly from you, or from undeniable facts about you, but from what other people have told government investigators about you.

Now, all such second-hand information may be absolutely true and unbiased. On the other hand, it may not. Whichever it is, there it is in the big, family-sized dossier.

And since you don't know what's in the file, or who may be seeing it, you, of course, have no chance to deny or explain it.

Perhaps you are so fortunate as to have no qualms about what anyone may know about you or your affairs, regardless of who he is, what his motives are or how private the subject matter may be.

But many of us are not so lucky. We have our little secrets that we'd just as soon keep secret.

The National Data Center, by greatly increasing the availability of such personal information, could go a long way toward putting private citizens and their private lives in a grand, governmental goldfish bowl.

This proposal ought to be sidetracked.

Summary: The proposed National Data Center would continue the dangerous trend toward invading privacy.

THE GRAMMAR OF EDITORIALS

Editorial writers obey the rules of grammar and rhetoric which they learned in school. They make their subjects and predicates agree and they put modifiers in the proper places in sentences. If they deviate from the orthodox rules, they do so deliberately for special effect.

Perhaps the most important rules of rhetoric that the editorial writer must obey are those for unity within and between paragraphs. An editorial must "flow," meaning its ideas must follow each other in logical sequence. The New York *World Telegram* began its editorial, "Good Things Badly Done," July 14, 1936 as follows: "There is both good and bad news in the announcement that the government this week is paying railroad men's pensions out of the Treasury." There was only one possible way to continue that piece: "It is good news that after all these years the veterans of industry at last are receiving benefits to care for their old age. It is bad news that Congress and the courts have permitted a sound principle to be turned into a dangerous precedent." And so on. Many teachers of grammar insist that all that is involved is the exercise of good sense and that straight thinking leads inevitably to straight writing.

Just as there are feature leads to news stories there are feature leads to editorials. In fact, the editorial writer has greater license than the objective news reporter inasmuch as he does not have to adhere slavishly to the 5 w's and put latest developments first. His is a follow-up job. It is trite to warn him against triteness of form

or expression. Originality counts and cleverness such as that demonstrated by the following from the Richmond *Times-Dispatch* of Aug. 3, 1949.

Put Those Prepositions Where They Belong At

Columnist Robert Ruark made some strong statements Monday concerning the rule against using a preposition to end a sentence with. He said there was no logical reason why you shouldn't put one of those "lousy, skimpy little words" at the tail end of a sentence if you wanted to.

There's really nothing for Columnist Ruark to get excited about. Prepositions always are supposed to govern other words, called their "relatives" and only the laziest writer should find it difficult to arrange the sequence of his words so that the relative is last and the preposition is before.

Sometimes, with all the belittling of the old tried and standard rules, we wonder what modern literature is coming to. Instead of polishing their sentences, as did the old masters of the language, many of today's writers sit down and simply dash something off. Prepositions are left dangling naked at the end of sentences, and you can't tell where they're going to or where they came from. These unclad words, tied onto nothing, appear about to take off.

In the speaking art, too, conformity with standard rules of grammar should be striven after. Here, errors are easier to fall into. A person who wishes to leave a good impression with his listeners should use the very best grammar he is capable of. With anything less, he should refuse to put up.

It is a sad commentary on the literary world today that fundamental rules of grammar are laughed at. This is the age of skepticism when there's little left to cling to. Fortunately, however, there are a few purists in the writing and speaking arts who refuse to cut corners and whose work can be depended on.

Yes, Ruark, end your sentences with prepositions if you want to. But don't try to influence other writers, who to such a flagrant violation of rules of grammar will never give into!

The *summary* sentence to describe this piece obviously is: the rule against ending a sentence with a preposition is absurd. Granted, a few of the constructions are more than a bit strained. Nevertheless, the overall point is certainly made: a healthy cynicism toward grammatical purists. The editorial recalls Winston Churchill's famous reply to a criticism about his ending a sentence with a preposition: "This is the kind of nonsense up with which I will no longer put."

The Chicago *Daily Tribune* had a similar purpose, that of teaching a lesson in the proper use of the language, in the following editorial which it ran Nov. 7, 1953. The summary is in the last sentence of the editorial itself.

Some New Cliches

The convention of the Associated Press Managing Editors association reported the results of a poll on the 10 "most detested" sports cliches. High in disfavor are "mentor," for coach; "inked pact," for signed contract; "pay dirt," for a score, and "circuit clout," for home run.

We are glad to join in sneering at these, but, from long association with the "sports fraternity" (no mean cliche itself) we feel that the eminent editors have overlooked a few terms that yield to none in setting the teeth to grinding. High on anybody's list, for instance, would be that standby of the football broadcasters, a "teedee," meaning T.D. for touchdown.

Among baseball terms, the use of "bobble," for error has a high rasping content, while "senior circuit" for American—or is it National?—league has a suggestion of pomposity, like an overstuffed clubman in an overstuffed chair.

The search for the quaint in sports reportage (a word the dictionary says is "rare" but is not rare enough) seems to have early afflicted baseball writers especially. Thus, around 1912, it was thought picturesque to describe a ground ball as a "daisy cutter," while it never sufficed to say that So-and-So was a left handed pitcher. He had to be a "southpaw" or, better yet, a "portsider."

"Bangtails" and "hayburners" have long been at the racetracks, and it used to be fashionable in autumn to "don the moleskins," tho we hear little of them these days. The "gridiron" has survived long after it ceased to be a gridiron, and, of course, a hot basketball team "hits the hoop" rather than shoots baskets.

The prize ring, or "squared circle," as it used to be known among the more sophisticated gentlemen in press row, has been particularly productive of tired metaphors. An old boxing writer we knew was a master of this sort of patter, and we well recall the lead of a pre-fight story he turned out which began with the rhetorical question: "Can Billy Petrolle, the Fargo Express, hit the rocky road of fistiana's comeback trail?" In this instance we believe that the answer proved to be "yes."

This practitioner of syntactical genocide was never content to say that a punch drew blood; instead, the punchee "spouted claret." The aggressor never delivered a right to the jaw, but uncorked a lick on the chops. At the right moment he would invariably "swing a haymaker" that sent his adversary into "dreamland."

Perhaps the editors had better poll the membership again, for the catalog of horrors is far from complete. As an old editor of our dim past, who was noted rather more for energy than for literacy, was given to remark, "What we need is some new cliches."

THE QUESTION LEAD

Few news or feature writers are able to figure out ways of using a question lead effectively. It is easier for an editorial writer to do so for a serious as well as feature topic. Witness this example from the St. Louis *Post-Dispatch* in November, 1948.

A Notable First

What city has the most electrically-heated homes among all the cities of the world? New York? London? Tokyo? Los Angeles? None of them or others of the very largest cities. It is Nashville, Tenn., with a population of 170,000.

Twenty-two years ago Nashville had only 29 electrically-heated homes. Today it has 75,000. The reason: low-cost electricity supplied wholesale by the Tennessee Valley Authority and promoted vigorously by the city's distribution system. No smoke. No soot. No residues.

In most of the world's cities electricity is too costly for heating, except for a favored few. In Nashville it is economical. And heating provides a winter use for peak capacities demanded in summer for air-conditioning.

Nashville is an example of what other cities in other regions could do to make living more pleasant and more economical—given the low-cost electricity to do it.

Summary: The Tennessee Valley Authority enables Nashville, Tennesseans to enjoy low cost electric heat.

The following is a delightful use of the question lead and feature treatment of a subject which often stumps the ingenuity of the editorial writer. It appeared in the Philadelphia *Record* for July 16, 1936 and contains its own moral.

'I Wanna Giraffe'

What makes man different from the rest of animated creation?

The theologians say it is his soul; the poets say it is language; the materialists say it is his useful thumb; the philosophers—or some of them—say it is his inability to be content.

Give him meat, he wants salt. Give him comfort, he wants music.

Just so, Henry Breyer, 3d, wanted a giraffe.

This young man, aged 5, occupies a peculiar and exalted position in the world of boyhood. He is the son of an ice cream manufacturer, and as such in the hierarchy of juvenile dreams ranks even above the sons of Presidents, locomotive engineers and big league ball players, and just below the sons of G-men—if G-men have sons.

But true to the glorious curse of our species, Henry, 3d was not content, not even when his father took him to the Philadelphia Zoo.

A cloud came over his face as he sought for something that wasn't there. "I wanna giraffe," said Henry Breyer, 3d. So giraffes, two of them were brought from Africa to Philadelphia so Henry Breyer, 3d, can look upon them in addition to being the boy whose father makes tons and tons and tons of ice cream.

And other children can look upon them, too, and reflect that they have this instructive pleasure because the human soul can soar even above the limits of unlimited ice cream, and thus they may learn at the zoo the secret of progress and the secret of why all utopias are contrary to human nature.

And the moral, of course, is "Excelsior!" For even Alexander sought new worlds to conquer; and if he had lived long enough he might have had ice cream—and two giraffes.

Another form of question lead is the Q and A, familiar to interviewers. The *Wall Street Journal* used it editorially Feb. 27, 1957 as follows:

Out of the Mouths of Children

Q. Daddy, what is a sport?
A. A sport is a game, played indoors or outdoors, sometimes in teams, sometimes man to man.
Q. Like prize-fighting, Daddy?
A. Well, no.
Q. Like professional football, Daddy?
A. Well no.
Q. Well, what is a sport, Daddy?
A. Professional baseball.
Q. Is that the only one, Daddy?
A. Yes.
Q. That's funny, Daddy. Baseball is a sport, but football and prize-fighting aren't. How is that?
A. The Supreme Court says so.

Yep, the Supreme Court said so just the other day, Son. Professional baseball is a sport, and not a business, so professional baseball does not come under the Sherman anti-trust law. But professional football and boxing are not sports because they are businesses and so they do come under the Sherman law.

The reason for this strange discrimination, Mr. Justice Clark tried to explain in the majority decision which ruled pro football a business, comes about because 30-odd years ago baseball was ruled a sport by the Supreme Court. It was ruled not a business, because it was judged not to be engaged in interstate commerce to a great enough extent to come under the Sherman law. As late as 1953, in Toolson v. New York Yankees, the High Court upheld this ruling.

The ruling, of course, may have been meritorious all along.

But in 1955, in U.S. vs. International Boxing Club, the High Court ruled that what applied to baseball did not apply to boxing.

And now, in Radovich vs. the National Football League, the Supreme Court ruled that what applied to pro baseball did not apply to pro football.

"We continued to hold the umbrella over baseball because it was concluded that more harm would be done in overruling than in upholding" the original decision, Justice Clark explained—if that is quite the word. The reason was that "enormous capital had been invested in reliance on its permanence." Such reasons, of course, have not prevented the Supreme Court from overturning other previous decisions.

Thus what the Court has said is that baseball, with its vast farm systems and playing schedules reaching from, for example, Milwaukee to New York, is not in interstate commerce as much as boxing and pro football are, and thus that all other pro sports are businesses while baseball alone is still a sport.

Q. I don't understand the differences, Daddy.

A. Don't worry, Son. Three of the justices are still shaking their heads about the decision. They can't see any legal differences between baseball and football and boxing, either.

Q. Well, Daddy, aren't you glad the other six are just judges and not umpires.

Summary: The United States Supreme Court decisions on the professionalism of baseball and football are inconsistent.

NARRATION

The editorial equivalent of the suspended interest feature article is the narrative piece of which the following, from *Chicago's American* of March 2, 1968, is a first-class example.

The Doctor Isn't In

Thomas Schuster, 23, got his arm caught in the rollers of a printing press Wednesday at the Sleepeck Printing company in Bellwood. He hung there for five hours, in extreme pain and shock, until rescue squads got the press dismantled and freed him; Schuster was taken to a hospital where the mangled arm was amputated.

While the squads were struggling to get him free, a police radio operator was trying desperately to reach a doctor who would come and relieve Schuster's agony. It took two hours to find one.

The operator called five doctors at their homes; none answered the phone. A physician at Westlake hospital could not come because the law requires hospitals to have a doctor on duty at all times. A seventh doctor, reached at his home in Oak Brook, said it was too far to come. An all-points emergency call for a doctor, any doctor, got no answer.

The company meanwhile called the Joslyn clinic in Maywood, which handles accident cases for the firm. A nurse reported that no doctor was available. When police called back, tho, she agreed to call Dr. Everett A. Joslyn, who responded at once. He arrived to give Schuster pain-killers—two hours after the horrifying ordeal began.

Said Bellwood police chief Dwight Wulf: "The doctors won't answer their phones after midnight. Sometimes if they happen to be at the hospital you can get them there, but they won't come. We always have a terrible time getting doctors out to the scene of an accident. We've been operating under this handicap for the last 10 or 15 years."

Generally, said Wulf, a young physician just starting his practice in the area will take emergency cases, but soon becomes so overburdened that he too starts ducking them. Wulf said Bellwood officials and the

Sleepeck company are trying to work out plans for emergency medical service and are hoping to meet soon with doctors to agree on a system.

That is a need that can no longer be neglected, in Bellwood or Chicago or any other community where medical service has deteriorated to this appalling point. The Schuster case is rare only in its degree of horror. Similar cases of medical need being refused or ignored are increasingly common, and the situation cannot be tolerated. A community would not put up with a fire department that refused to answer calls at inconvenient times, and we can no longer put up with medical service that is available only when and if a doctor can be found who is willing to give it.

A convincing answer to this problem has already been offered. Six members of the Chicago committee on trauma of the American College of Surgeons have drafted plans for an area-wide medical emergency service. It calls for a main "trauma center" operating a communications network, plus a series of treatment units—teaching hospitals to be designated as centers for treating emergency cases in their districts.

The communications center would be able to rush ambulances and medical personnel to the scene of an emergency and alert the nearest receiving unit. The treatment hospitals would have the facilities and personel for handling trauma cases available at all times.

It is long past time to get this plan moving. It is already late, by several years and many, many lives.

Summary: Doctors must be made to answer emergency calls at all hours.

The 1965 Pulitzer prize for editorial writing went to John H. Harrison of the Gainesville (Fla.) *Sun* for his campaign in favor of a minimum housing code. Harrison's editorials were mostly unorthodox and heavily illustrated with camera shots. They were addressed to the city's mayor. The following, which appeared Nov. 20, 1964, was typical:

Memo to McKinney

The road was dusty, and the small Negro boy strained under the weight of the bucket he was carrying. He had brought it more than two blocks from the fountain that was provided 'as a courtesy,' the sign told us. Three to five times a week the child makes the trip.

The child lives in a house eighteen feet by twenty-four feet along with three other people.

On several of the open windows there are no screens.

There is no front door at all.

Sunlight comes through the roof in two places.

The child and his family share with another family the outhouse in the backyard.

Not only is there no lavatory in the house, there is no tub, shower or hot water supply.

The siding on the house had deteriorated, the chimney needed replacing, the foundation was out of level.

The water lapped over the side of the bucket as the child stepped up a concrete block into the house.

Now, Mayor McKinney, that's a third to a fifth of the family's weekly supply of water.

To drink.

And that family lives in the Northeast section, within the city limits, of Gainesville, Florida, and they pay $5 a week rent. That's Florida's "University City," Center of Science, Education and Medicine.

Now, tell us again, Mayor McKinney, as you have since last August, that a minimum housing code for Gainesville is unnecessary. Tell us again that you want more discussion of the minimum housing code as you did last week. After all, the League of Women Voters and the Citizens' Housing Association of Gainesville, Inc., have, since 1955, documented by studies housing in Gainesville that has no indoor plumbing or piped-in drinking water.

That's ten years, Mr. Mayor.

But tell the child that carries the drinking water down that dusty road that the minimum housing code is unnecessary.

In our mind's eye we'll try to console him with Emerson—"The dice of God are always loaded. For everything you have missed, you have gained something else. The world, turn it how you will, balances itself . . . Every secret is told, every virtue rewarded, every wrong redressed, in silence and certainty."

Summary: Deplorable living conditions make a minimum building code essential.

Harrison commented modestly on his work:

There is far more compassion than excellence in the series I did.

But the important thing is that a 13-year battle was won in one month by a newspaper doing its job.

I think there are two avenues of popularity open to newspapers—the one is to flatter, to yield, to cajole. The other is to stand for right things unflinchingly. We are, with tenacity, committed to the latter.

ARGUMENTATION

It would be extremely pleasant to be able to report that all crusaders are as successful as was Harrison. Unfortunately such was not the case with Ira B. Harkey, Jr., of the Pascagoula (Miss.) *Chronicle* who won the Pulitzer prize in 1963 "for his courageous editorials devoted to the processes of law and reason during the integration crisis in Mississippi in 1962." In his book, *The Smell of Burning Crosses* (Harris-Wolfe & Co., Jacksonville, Ill., 1967), Harkey told of the animosity and persecution which finally caused him to pack up and move north.

What follows is one of the editorials that helped Harkey win the award. It is an excellent example of an argumentative editorial.

Perfectly Capable of Closing Ole Miss

Anywhere else in the United States, the suggestion that a state university be closed down for any reason at all would not rise to the level of public discussion. Such a suggestion could not originate outside a lunatic academy.

But in our state,—where the leaders for eight years led us to believe we would not be required to obey the same laws that others must obey, whose leaders called out the mobs to let blood in senseless opposition to the will of the nation, where American GIs and marshals are referred to in terms of hate formerly used only for Huns who ravished Belgium in the World War and Japs who tortured prisoners in World War II—in this state we had better discuss the possibility. Now.

For the people who could do and say the things that have been done and said in our state during the past six weeks have proved themselves perfectly capable of closing down a university.

The suggestion has been made that Ole Miss be closed. It has been offered by the same group of false prophets who deluded the people for eight years into believing that we could maintain school segregation in Mississippi while all about us other Southern states were failing in their attempts to prevent integration. Somehow, in the face of all that is sane, they managed to convince most white people that they had a secret unknown to other Southern leaders.

If we now let them convince us that it is proper to close Ole Miss and destroy a century of cultural advancement, then maybe we do not deserve any better than to be led by owners of grammar-school intellects and of attitudes that most humans left behind somewhere in history.

It is heartening to note a resurgence of manhood on the part of the Ole Miss staff and faculty and the rallying of alumni support to keep the institution going. All alumni, all parents of present students, all Mississippians who care a hang about their state —we will exclude moral and religious considerations here and mention only the economic—all should also rally behind the university and let our leaders know that we do not regard suicide as a solution.

Summary: Leaders who have been wrong in saying Mississippi did not have to obey the laws are equally wrong in proposing to close Ole Miss.

EXPOSITION

As a rhetorical form exposition explains a process, thing or idea. In other words, it is that form of composition which tries to tell what something is all about. Often the editorial writer can make his point best by straightening readers out as regards the intricacies of some situation. He may let the facts "speak for themselves." Usually, however, in a good editorial, there must be interpretation and advocacy based on factual explanation.

The expository part of any editorial is a part of the deliberative unit. It brings the reader up to date regarding what has been going on, perhaps while his attention was lagging. An excellent example of how to give historical as well as contemporary background to a situation is provided by the following editorial from the San Francisco *Sunday Examiner & Chronicle* for July 25, 1971.

Fighting for All

A heartwarming example of good citizenship is going largely unnoticed in this country. It deserves a salute.

Almost singlehandedly, Japanese-Americans have fought for years to make sure that what happened to them never happens to their fellow citizens.

Half-forgotten now is the story of how, in panic after Pearl Harbor, 110,000 Japanese-Americans were rounded up and shipped off to detention camps, many to spend the rest of the war there.

Almost everyone who has studied that affair now agrees it was unnecessary, unjust and illegal.

But in 1950, during the anti-Communist hysteria of the McCarthy era, Congress passed a law legalizing, for future use, the kind of treatment that had been inflicted upon Japanese-Americans.

       °   °   °

This is the Emergency Detention Act, commonly called Title II.

In time of war or insurrection, it empowers the Attorney General to arrest and hold indefinitely any individual or group he believes might engage in espionage or sabotage.

This is police state law with a vengeance, and not just an academic law either. Six stand-by detention camps were set up at isolated places across the country, including one at Tule Lake.

At the time the camps were envisioned as holding places for all those Communist conspirators Joe McCarthy used to talk about.

In more recent years there have been charges—and denials—that the camps would be used to detain black militants in case of a race uprising.

There is little likelihood the law would ever be used against Japanese-Americans. Such a repeat performance of injustice would be too much for the public to swallow.

No, Japanese-Americans have less reason to fear this law than any other minority. But they know better than anyone else the injustice of it. And so for 20 years they have fought to have Title II repealed.

Occasionally black leaders have spoken against it, and this year, for the first time, Chinese-Americans went on record that the law might be used against them.

But the Japanese-Americans have led the fight, and most of the time they have been the only soldiers at the front.

Their long campaign gets little attention in the general press, but in their own newspapers every move concerning Title II is front page news.

As individuals and through the Japanese-American Citizens League, they have devoted thousands of man hours and spent thousands of dollars sending delegations to Washington to testify about the inequities inherent in this law.

Last fall the Senate passed a repeal measure by Daniel K. Inouye, the Japanese-American senator from Hawaii.

In the House, a companion bill was introduced by Rep. Spark Matsunaga, also of Hawaii, and quite a list of Congressmen signed as honorary co-authors.

       °   °   °

The Justice Department has come out in favor of repealing Title II, pointing out, as evidence of its sincerity, that the detention camps have been abandoned or converted to other uses.

With so much support, you would expect repeal to be just a formality. Not so. Matsunaga's bill was bottled up in the House Internal Security Committee by Chairman Richard Ichord, a Missouri Democrat.

So the battle had to be fought all over again, Matsunaga this time working through the friendlier Judiciary Committee.

Now his bill and a rival one by Ichord are before the full House for a showdown vote, expected in mid-September.

Win or lose, the Japanese word for thanks is arigato.

Summary: Japanese-Americans, in the best position to know, have led the fight to repeal the concentration camp law.

Good reading for all aspiring editorial writers, and for all professionals too, is the article, "How to Write Understandable Articles About Economics," by Lauren K. Soth, Pulitzer prize winning editor of the editorial page of the Des Moines *Register and Tribune,* in the Winter 1953-54 *Masthead,* reprinted in the magazine's Summer, 1967 Anthology issue. After asserting that editorials about economics "are the dullest, the least informative, the most pedantic, and the most prejudiced of any we run," Soth explained why and gave some advice for improvement. Here are direct quotations from his article:

Economics is complicated stuff . . . economic questions quickly involve social ideology . . . we pontificate on every little economic event in terms of these grand ideologies instead of trying to explain what is happening here and now, and its significance here and now to the economic well being of the people . . . most editorials about economics would be improved if the writer set out to explain and interpret an economic event to his readers instead of to give them the "word" . . . to do a good job of interpreting economic events requires wide reading in the field of economics . . .

leg work by editorial writers pays extra dividends . . . the biggest stumbling block to comprehension is faulty organization . . . much of the background material for economic editorials comes from professional economic journals or business publications . . . the main job of the writer for general readers often is to fill the gaps which the experts leave out . . . unfortunately for popular writers, economists have taken many everyday English words and given them restricted technical meanings . . . in most contexts concrete terms can be used to replace technical, abstract words . . . economics cannot be made simple and entertaining . . . the psychology of desiring to appear profound often makes editorial writers shy away from any attempt to be interesting.

Soth practices what he preaches. As evidence here is a sample of what he wrote for the Nov. 13, 1971 edition of his paper:

Price and Wage 'Restraint'

It is misleading to speak of "loop-holes" in the new wage and price "ceilings" which the Pay Board and the Price Commission are preparing to put into effect next week. The scheme of the control system is not rigid but is intended to be loose restraint. The aim is to permit the free market to operate as fully as possible.

In both wage and price guidelines, the Administration is concentrating on the major industries. In the major industries, where there is little competition in prices and little competition in wages, the government supervision will be strict. Thus firms with sales of $100 million or more must notify the price commission about proposed price increases. In the case of wages, collective bargaining agreements affecting 5,000 people or more will come under the same kind of requirement for pre-notification.

Smaller firms and smaller labor bargaining units will be required to make reports periodically about their price and wage actions to the Price Commission and to the Pay Board. The smallest firms will not have to report but will be expected to comply with the general guidelines. Agriculture, small retailing and other small business will be essentially free from control.

*   *   *

This system of price and wage guidelines is based on the theory that the elements of the economy which "administer" prices and wages can be effectively regulated by the government. In earlier attempts during wartime, the controls over "free market" business, such as farming, proved to be ineffective. Black markets in meat sprang up within a short time after controls were imposed in World War II. The administrative task of regulating prices and wages in thousands of small businesses would be even more staggering in peacetime and probably would not work.

Economists who have advocated "guidelines" believe that by concentrating administrative effort on the key price-setting and wage-setting industries, the government can get better results. They feel that the free enterprise parts of the economy will be influenced strongly by the controls in the major industries. Moreover, fiscal and monetary policy can be relied upon to hold prices down in the more competitive businesses.

By permitting numerous exceptions in the wage guideline of 5½ per cent increase for the next year, the Administration hopes to make general restraint more tolerable and elicit co-operation. The same kind of exceptions in prices will provide a loose cloak over the trend of prices rather than a rigid barrier which invites black markets.

The experience so far of wage regulation under the Construction Industry Stabilization Committee offers some hope that the Pay Board and Price Commission can accomplish their goals for the economy as a whole.

The construction industry wage rate increases have definitely turned downward this year. The wage increases still seem extremely steep compared with those in other industries. As of Oct. 22, the average annual wage increase approved by the stabilization committee stood at 10.8 per cent, calculating the average over the life of the approved contracts. However, that is a considerable reduction from the average of 15.2 per cent in the same period of 1970.

Out of 1,024 cases the committee has reviewed, an adjustment of some nature has been ordered in 320 cases. Many of these involved reducing contractors' bid prices to avoid "windfall profits" that might have resulted from the wage restraint actions.

This technique of holding profit margins down, when wages are restrained, may be applicable to other industries. The excess profits tax which was used in World War II and the Korean War, had many faults, mainly the encouragement of wasteful cost expenditures.

The Nixon Administration deserves support from labor and business for the intelligent way it is going about price and wage control this time. The Administration has learned from mistakes in previous control operations.

Summary: Nixon's price and wage control system is profiting from past experiences of others.

DESCRIPTION

The editorial writer who follows the advice of Soth and others to get out of the office while fact-finding will have occasion to compose editorials similar to the following which appeared in the Boston *Globe* for Sept. 24, 1971.

Boston's Not Washed Up

Mayor White took a busload of news people on a ride through the city last Monday, the purpose of the exercise vaguely educational and candidly political.

The itinerary covered a lot of territory, winding from downtown through South Boston into Dorchester, Mattapan, Roxbury, the Back Bay, the South End and back over Beacon Hill to City Hall. It turned out to be intensely educational and no more political than any event involving a mayoral candidate for reelection.

If you were looking for trouble, there was plenty of it.

The stench of the Fort Point Channel, the bottle and can-litterd gutters around the D Street Project, the dreary skyline of Columbia Point, the occasional, familiar wail of sirens, the broken windows of decaying buildings and the broken faces of decaying, idle men—there was no shortage of the familiar evidence of urban decline; and there is no intention here to minimize it.

Nevertheless, this mayor-guided tour was the opposite of discouraging, and the picture of a problem-ridden city, death-wish enamored of its own obsequies, lost its credibility during the morning.

Too often, outsiders learn of the city in terms of its problems. Most often, insiders, city residents, gain attention and assistance by emphasizing these very real problems as they apply to them as individuals.

Seldom does the opportunity arise to pass through a dozen or so neighborhoods, from the elite facades of Beacon street to the crumbling warrens of Bowdoin street, in the same morning, to gain an over-all picture of just what is going on.

That picture ought not to be compared with ancient Rome or modern Amsterdam, Cleveland or San Diego but with the Boston of a decade ago and the potential Boston of a decade hence.

For all the sentimental bilge accumulated over the disappearance of Scollay square, it is hard to stand in the new magnificence of Government Center without taking some hope for future progress. Around the horizon, the skyscrapers of a new, vital and growing Boston, grow daily more impressive.

Progress, too, along the waterfront and in the South Station area is increasingly manifest. Across the channel in South Boston, plans for additional industrial development are about to go forward.

There are new businesses along Dorchester avenue and new tennis courts and playgrounds in Columbus Park. Just off Morrissey boulevard, a new school site is being excavated. The Marshall and Lee Schools are educational palaces, as fine as anything in the suburbs, in Massachusetts or elsewhere.

Playgrounds and new libraries are striking contrasts to the blight in their neighborhoods, but they are there. The Fields Corner shopping center is thriving, there are new street lights, and new coats of paint on some of the houses.

Particularly in those areas in which the code enforcement program has been in effect, there are signs of residential upgrading.

It is difficult to derive much optimism from Blue Hill avenue, but it also ought to be noted that no city, in fact, no nation, has as yet satisfactorily solved the racial ghetto problem. That Boston continues to search for answers is in itself encouraging.

There is a lot of good, new housing in Washington Park, with its exceptionally fine YMCA, Unity Bank branch and new cars parked at the new row houses. Even along Columbus avenue in the South End, beyond the new tennis courts in the Carter Playground, there is new housing. Beyond, on the return to downtown, the Hancock building nears its topping-off and the plans for Park Plaza go forward.

What do we expect of a city? Have we a right to Utopia? On the record, the answer has to be that we do not. But a tour of the old town, from its poshest to its poorest neighborhood, fails to document the case that it is all washed up.

In fact, it remains an enormously exciting, intellectually stimulating, emotionally evocative, vital place, better off than it was only a few years ago and needing, perhaps, only a more general realization of the extent of progress to arrive closer to fulfillment of its promise.

Summary: It's not a bad city if you look all around.

READABILITY

Narration, argumentation, exposition, description, of which examples in editorial writing have just been given, are the leading types of composition, any school boy can tell you. Early textbooks on editorial writing devoted sections or chapters to them. Teachers of the subject assigned editorials by rhetorical types until it was realized that such straightjacketing of students was destructive of talent, not a developer of it. The student could complain, "I don't feel argumentative about labor. Can't I write my argumentative editorial about public health and do an expository piece about labor?" Any writer must have the freedom to choose the form in which he expounds whatever he has to say. Whereas one author will do a short story, another will produce a play or a poem or a magazine article or a newspaper editorial. What determines the inspiration? Go to the psychoanalyst's couch to find out but be prepared to come away disappointed with the answer. You can't tell and what difference does it make? Through trial and error and the influence of all of life's experiences, one creative artist (a term which includes the best editorial writers) does it this way instead of that. He gets his ideas from a multitude of sources and, given exactly the same assignment, a group of the very, very best writers will come up with different answers.

No editorial writer should feel any inferiority complex in relation to creative artists of any other kind. Nobody, of course, can prove anything one way or another. About the only tangible evidence to bolster the egos of editorial writers in relation to co-workers on the newspapers are the results of the studies of the comparative readability of news stories and editorials. The first was conducted by Prof. Lester Getzloe of Ohio State University in 1946, assessing the readability of foreign news stories in nine daily newspapers and of editorials on foreign affairs in 16 dailies. Eight of the newspapers were included in both studies and editorials were found to be more readable than news stories in six of them.

A more extensive study was conducted about 20 years later by James Moznette, graduate student at the University of Oregon, under the direction of Prof. Galen Rarick. They used the Flesch Reading Ease Formula and found that 64.1 percent of the editorials scored above the median reading ease score, whereas only 39.8 percent of the news items did so. Their samples were from ten metropolitan dailies on the Pacific coast. Thus, the average editorial could be readily comprehended by a person with a high school diploma. Articles in the *Journalism Quarterly* for Summer, 1968 and *The Masthead* for Winter, 1969-70 provide details. They're good for the morale of the professional editorial writer and should be inspirational for the student who thinks he wants to learn how to do it.

V
Unconventional Approaches

1. Humor
2. Sarcasm
3. Satire
4. Parables

5. Parody
6. Essays
7. Good Taste
8. Paragraphs

Most editorials are written about serious topics and are necessarily sober in tone. Probably the most frequently voiced criticism of them is that they are too often dull. To the extent that this is so may be the fault of the editorial writer. He may lack the knowledge to discourse interestingly about a subject; he may lack the time for adequate research; he may lack the ability to appeal to any but pedants, or he may not have the proper enthusiasm for the job. On the other hand, it may be the reader who is to blame. Perhaps he never was taught by parents or teachers or others to have an interest in current affairs which would condition him to become a reader of editorials. In such case our democracy is in danger, as widespread ignorance and indifference can prove fatal.

Because of the sobriety necessary in handling most topics, it is impossible to put reader entertainment first on any list of goals for editorial writing. Nevertheless, it is possible to be ingenious in the use of literary devices customarily restricted for what could be called feature topics, in order to popularize other topics. The warning that must be heeded is this: when you deviate from the orthodox sober style, be good. Nothing is worse than bad attempts at feature treatment, so if you are not cap-

able of it, keep producing for your waste basket until you have learned.

HUMOR

Most people don't know how to be funny. They don't know how to tell a joke without muffing the punch line. Their departee is better than their repartee, which means that any wit they display socially comes from a repertoire of wisecracks, most of them plagiarisms, so if their audience is not a new one, it cannot help but be bored. It often is shocking to discover that even professional entertainers lack the ability to tell jokes effectively when they are off-stage and not reciting lines written by expert gag men. In other words, they are comedians and not humorists.

Editorial writers are not exempt from the ranks of those who generally should leave comedy to others. It's refreshing then when anyone breaks this rule successfully, as a Chicago *Sun-Times* writer did Dec. 14, 1970 as follows:

Rinse, Please

A lecturer in dental medicine at Australia's University of Melbourne got 289 children to draw pictures of a visit to the dentist. The pictures were horrible—chairs were racks, instruments were monsters, blood flowed everywhere and children were depicted screaming in agony.

The idea, said John L. Godfrey, the lecturer, was to discover why children are afraid of the dentist. Well, Mr. Godfrey, we'll tell you why they're afraid. They get hurt, just as we do. This man in forbidding white (he must have just changed it so the blood wouldn't show) comes along, sticks a lot of stuff into the victim's mouth, starts up a machine which makes a noise as soothing as that of an incoming nuclear missile, and leaves the patient to contemplate the next second, when the pain is sure to come, and the first of the month, when the bill is sure to come. And with it, the victim gets canned schmaltzy music and live ambiguous political questions.

We sympathize with dentists, to a degree. They can't turn to public-relations and advertising the way politicians and detergent manufacturers do. Cartoon characters like Buzzy the Drill or Alex the Friendly Explorer Pick just aren't the dentist's bag.

Dentists do important work, and we like them; we really do. Some of our best friends are dentists. They're a great bunch of people to live with, but they're hell to visit. So we sympathize with them, but we'd draw our own pictures just the way those kids did.

Summary: Kids are right to fear dentists.

Reminiscent of the paragraph shorts which were quite common a generation ago is the following from the same newspaper of Feb. 18, 1972. The pun has been called the lowest form of humor but its clever use has made lots of people laugh from Shakespeare's day to the present.

Warranted

The U.S. District Court in Manhattan ordered the arrest of Mrs. Clifford Irving, wife of the Howard Hughes case author, at the request of the Swiss government, which believes it should have its case and Edith, too.

The following is an example of burlesqued sarcasm, absurd and meant to be a dirty dig at the Russians during the height of their unpopularity in this country. It appeared in the Chicago *Daily News* for Dec. 8, 1953.

A poll of newspaper readers, disclosed by the International Press Institute at its meeting in Zurich, Switzerland, reveals that not everybody is an avid student of foreign affairs. For instance, 40 percent of American newspaper readers who were questioned could not identify Georgi Malenkov, premier of Russia.

Well, we don't believe Georgi could identify 40 percent of American newspaper readers, so maybe that makes it even.

Burlesque is the undisguised purpose of the following from the March 8, 1957 Virginia City (Nev.) *Enterprise* where a former New York *Times* man, Lucius Beebe, entertained eastern tourists seeking a taste of the Old West with spoofs such as this. Together with his editor, Bob Richards, they "captured the flavor of the old Mark Twain days," according to Theodore E. Conover, chairman of the Department of Journalism at the University of Nevada, who added, "They approached everything from the Old West attitude—hard drinking and hard writing." Publication discontinued shortly after Beebe's death in 1967 but the plant is now a Mark Twain museum catering to tourists.

A Pestilence of Bishops

Let us briefly, so as not to be charged with wilful neglect of this peculiar pus-pocket of snivelling godliness, turn our attention to the activities of the group of mendacious bigots that calls itself the Methodist Board of Temperance whose home is appropriately in Washington D.C., the booziest town in the entire U.S.A.

The current campaign of this rancid pressure group through the agency of its sanctified shill Senator Strom Thurmond of the church-ridden poor farm of South Carolina is against the innocuous practice of serving free cocktails on air liners to while away the time on what is at once the most expeditious and most boring agency of travel yet devised by people in a mad scurry to get somewhere they have no business to be, to do something they had better leave undone.

No more classic example of the meddlesome impertinence that is the basis for Methodist existence can be imagined. The service of drinks by the airlines is an offense to nobody but the Methodists to whom the pleasant and gracious aspects of the world are as the devisings of Sodom. It endangers completely nobody, which gives the lie to the Methodist suggestion that serving Martinis to the passengers is somehow related to drunken automobile driving. It is an example of sheer, unadulterated, emetic religious bigotry comparable to the anti-Catholicism and anti-Semitism that have for decades been the other fastest moving merchandise of Methodist hatred.

That the Methodists can terrify even such a miserable lackey as the psalm-singing senator from South Carolina as a front for their gruesome activities is a comment alike on South Carolina and the personnel of the United States Senate which once, in the days it enjoyed respect and honor, delighted to number a long succession of giants from Daniel Webster to J. Ham Lewis who were handy men with a bottle. The Methodist Board has never enjoyed the respect of anyone; it is a pity its paretic bishops can corrupt even a single dim witted stooge like Snivelling Strom.

For almost 20 years this book's author handed out the following editorial to editorial writing classes and had the students vote as to whether the primary purpose of the author was antilabor or just good humor. Invariably there was an almost 50-50 split, indicating that whatever the motive, the writer failed to achieve it with more than half of his readers. No editorial can be effective if it is not understood, so the admonition should be repeated: if you want to be funny, be sure you know how. The editorial appeared in early October, 1953 in the Boston *Herald*.

Is a Birthday Happy?

A fundamental American right has been destroyed by the truckers' new contract in Boston. The contract provides that each driver will take his birthday off with pay.

We object. What right has any union or any company to tell any red-blooded American he has to celebrate his birthday? A birthday may be inevitable, but that doesn't make it time for rejoicing.

The whole business of birthday celebrations is a product of juvenile gangsterism, devised by youngsters too impatient to wait till Christmas and parents too lenient to resist.

At best, birthdays are something to be put aside with knee pants and baby dolls. No adult in his right mind enjoys the advent of another birthday.

When some unthinking member of the family does recall a birthday, the only way to react is to scorn all childish frivolity, stomp off to work and prove that you can do three times as much work as the young squirts just out of school. But what if the company and the union have entered into some devilish agreement which says you have to stay home—with pay?

What are you supposed to do, sit home and weep?

You can have your Happy Birthdays. For our part, we'll go to work and forget 'em.

SARCASM

Being sarcastic—that is, using harsh or bitter derision or irony—often results in creating sympathy for the intended butt of the barbs. Hence, it defeats its own purpose and must be used sparingly and competently or not at all.

When he was writing editorials in the thirties for J. David Stern's Philadelphia *Record*, the great I. F. Stone was already an experienced user of most literary devices, including sarcasm. The following, from the July 16, 1936 issue of his paper, was typical.

Progress

As a result of 150 years of the most amazing progress in technology, organization, production and distribution, Great Britain has reached the point where its Government can—and in a few months will—supply each and every man, woman and child in the country with a "perfect" gas mask.

In a few months, the British, or some one else, will invent a new poison gas so perfect that the perfect gas masks will be useless.

Ain't progress wonderful?

Summary: Attempts to protect against poison gas are futile.

A half decade earlier one of the greatest editorial pages in the history of American journalism ceased to exist with the death of the New York *World.* Typical of the biting satire with which the page abounded during the editorship of Frank Cobb was the following:

Old Gold Comes in Second

Do you remember the gloom that descended on the country, the lumps that were swallowed by countless throats, the bitter, scalding tears that were shed by countless eyes, when John L. Sullivan, the incomparable, the insuperable, the invincible, was knocked out by Corbett at New Orleans? The same mood possesses us as we read that Old Gold has come in second, instead of first. For until now Old Gold too has been incomparable, invincible and insuperable; it has won blindfold tests, concealed-name tests, and perhaps other tests also, in a manner that indicated that in very truth it was champion of them all. Yet there it is in black and white. At Harvard University, scene of so many classic defeats, Old Gold bit the dust. It bit the dust as must all who wear the crown; bowed its proud head and acknowledged as victor another cigaret; another cigaret of fourteen years' standing, but—another cigaret. Thus once more, in ironic fashion, we see the truth of the old adage that what goes up in smoke must come down in ashes.

One consideration, however, consoles us. The salient point about the tragedy is not that Old Gold came in second, but that Old Gold admitted it. That proves something.

That proves that Old Gold is game. That proves that Old Gold has the old fighting spirit. Old Gold will come back. Old Gold will enter more tests, thirsting only for combat. And Old Gold—mark our words—will win.

Summary: The Old Gold defeat at Harvard was a publicity stunt.

Wry and somewhat bitter is the following from the Chicago *Daily News* for Jan. 22, 1948, before Richard Daley began his reign in the Windy City.

The Mayor of Boston

Chicagoans who sometimes tire of keeping a finger on the pulse of civic virtue should now be willing to admit that things could be worse. Take, for instance, the case of Jim Curley, who on Jan. 7 became mayor of Boston for a fourth time and on Jan. 18 was convicted by a federal court of using the mails to defraud.

Curley is a political phenomenon that would have staggered even Lincoln Steffens, chronicler of the "Shame of the Cities." When he ran for mayor of Boston last fall, one of a field of seven, he was already under federal indictment. He made the race also, while holding a seat in Congress which he did not intend giving up. Still he won handily.

It is said that people get only the kind of government they deserve. But we doubt that the good people of Boston, granting their peculiar tastes in literature and drama, deserve Jim Curley.

Summary: Bostonians are to be pitied for Mayor Curley.

The contemporary style usually used only by columnists was demonstrated in this piece from the Macon (Ga.) *News* for Aug. 25, 1971.

With Deliberate Speed

The U.S. Senate, which delayed action on a number of bills during its most recent session, was not acting without precedent.

As a matter of fact, it is still deliberating over how to spend a $25,000 gift George Washington gave the country 172 years ago.

President Washington specified that the bequest, 50 shares in a Virginia surveying company, be used to endow a national university in the nation's capital. In a 1790 message to Congress, he noted that establishing such a university would be "well-worthy of a place in the deliberations of the legislature." Little did he realize how deliberative Congress could be.

The senators did come up with one idea about 70 years ago. Someone suggested giving the donation back to the Washington estate. But according to Oscar Steiner of Cleveland, chairman of the George Washington Memorial Foundation, there is "no way" the money, if it is still in the U.S. Treasury, could be returned.

Eight presidents have sent messages reminding the Senate of the gift; and in 1968, the Virginia legislature asked Congress to "investigate the provisions of President Washington's will."

Now Sen. George McGovern of South Dakota, the only announced candidate for the Democratic presidential nomination, has introduced a bill to create the George Washington Institute of Social Sciences.

It doesn't sound like such a bad idea, but it's not the sort of proposal the senators would rush into blindly. No, we've a hunch the sizzling debate will rage on a while longer yet.

Summary: Congress probably will continue to delay using George Washington's $25,000 gift.

SATIRE

According to the *Random House Dictionary of the English Language*, a satire is "a literary composition in verse or prose, in which human folly and vice are held up to scorn, derision or ridicule." The following classic from early World War II days, the authorship of which has been lost (to this author at least), is a pungent example of mild satire. It translated into football terms understandable to American readers the irritation of the English during the period of the so-called phony war, the winter of 1939-40, when British military operations were negligible.

"We Want a Touchdown!"

The Monday morning quarterbacks and the great unorganized but amply articulate army of second guessers are diagramming scoring plays on the backs of envelopes and on tablecloths. In every club and pub the wolf pack is in full cry.

"When, in heaven's name, are we ever to have a team with a scoring punch? Why can't our quarterbacks ever call anything but a punt or a prayer? Why are we always kicking from behind our own goal line? Why can't we run with the ball once in a while? Can't we ever get past the 50-yard line into the other guy's territory? If there isn't anyone on the coaching staff who knows anything about offense, why don't we fire the whole bally lot of 'em, and get somebody who knows something about the 'T' formation and the man in motion?"

Any football fan knows that when the old grads and the subway alumni begin talking that way, it's a safe bet that the head coach is likely to be fired or kicked upstairs to the post of athletic director. It doesn't always work out that way; sometimes the situation can be saved by getting a new backfield coach.

The current concern of loyal fans of old Brittania State over the failure of their teams to score any touchdowns since the kickoff of the 1939 season has all the earmarks of the usual prelude to a coaching-staff shakeup. It isn't only that the team hasn't scored against a major opponent that irks the subway alumni, but it has never taken the offensive, and shows no desire to. The fans are clamoring for a little razzle-dazzle. Frankly the subway alumni are tired of spending so much time in the tubes. From this distance, it doesn't appear that the tenure of Head Coach Winnie Churchill is seriously threatened; but no team ever got into the Rose Bowl without having a few plays designed to convoy a ball carrier over the enemy's goal line. That's what the customers pay to see; and the Voice of the Grandstand is the Vox Celeste.

Summary: The English want some action by their military.

PARABLES

Fables, allegories, parables are powerful literary tools for anyone gifted in their use. To be meaningful they must be understood. What follows is an example of an editorial which appeared originally in the Sacramento *Union* in early 1962. It was reprinted in the Chicago *Sun-Times* for Feb. 17, 1962 and was interpreted by most readers as intended to expose the ignorance and hypocrisy, or both, of persons who complained about governmental spending. Three years later, Feb. 28, 1965, however, it was used in *The Clarion*, publication of Our Lady's Catholic Parish of Glenview, Ill., rallying place for the John Birch Society, with the following editorial comment: "One of our dear, good parishioners recently called my attention to our non-taxed Credit Union which could be unfair competition to Building & Loan companies, etc. It is certainly food for thought." In other words, the piece was taken seriously at face value, no innuendo, hyperbole or irony recognized.

Do You Know This Man?

A reader has sent us the following word picture of a 20th Century American.

A young man lived with his parents in a public housing development. He attended public school, rode the free school bus, and participated in the free lunch program. He entered the army, then upon discharge retained his national service insurance. He then enrolled in the state university, working part time in the state capital to supplement his GI education check.

Upon graduation he married a public health nurse and bought a farm with an FHA loan; and then obtained an RFC loan to go into business. A baby was born in the county hospital. He bought a ranch with the aid of the veterans' land program and obtained emergency feed from the government.

Later he put part of his land in the soil bank, and the payments soon paid off his farm and ranch. His father and mother lived very comfortably on the ranch on their social security and old-age assistance checks. REA lines supplied electricity; the government helped clear his land.

The county agent showed him how to terrace it; then the government built him a fish pond and stocked it with fish. The government guaranteed him a sale of his farm products at highest prices.

Books from the public library were delivered to his door. He banked money which a government agency insured. His children grew up, entered public schools, ate free lunches, rode free school buses, played in public parks, swam in public pools, and joined the FFA. He owned an auto so he favored the federal highway program.

He signed a petition seeking federal assistance in developing an industrial project to help the economy of his area. He was a leader in obtaining the new post office and federal building, and went to Washington with a group to ask the government to build a great dam costing millions so that the area could get "cheap electricity."

He petitioned the government to give the local air base to the county. He was also a leader in the movement to get his specific type of farming special tax-write-offs and exemptions. Of course, he belonged to several farmers' organizations, but denied that they were pressure groups.

Then one day he wrote to his congressman: "I wish to protest these excessive governmental expenditures and attendant high taxes. I believe in rugged individualism. I think people should stand on their own two feet without expecting handouts.

"I am opposed to all socialistic trends, and I demand a return to the principles of our Constitution and the policies of States Rights."

Do you happen to know this man?

Summary: Almost everyone benefits from governmental spending.

PARODY

Success when one imitates, impersonates, mocks, burlesques, mimics, apes or simulates depends upon his audience's acquaintance with the object of the attack. As a literary form the parody is a humorous or satirical imitation of a serious composition. In the case of the following from the Chicago *Sun-Times* for Nov. 1, 1971, familiarity with the book mentioned was necessary for adequate appreciation of the cleverness involved, as it is written in the language which the principal character, Holden Caulfield, teenager, uses as he relates his tale of juvenile revolt.

Caulfield Commentary

There was this real big deal out in Hinsdale last week over "The Catcher in the Rye," which I told J. D. Salinger about. He wrote it up and all. You wouldn't believe what happened. I swear.

What happened was, this lady didn't want anybody in the high school to read the book. She said it was "vulgar." That word kills me. It really does. Just about any time somebody doesn't like something, it automatically becomes "vulgar" and all. The thing is, the lady's daughter didn't even have to read it. She was segregated from the rest of the class—which *did* read it—and she did something else. Anyhow, the biggies out there finally said the book'll stay on the reading list.

"The Catcher in the Rye" isn't the greatest book in the world, I admit. But it's sold around a trillion copies and all. And so far as I know it hasn't turned anybody into a Charles *Manson* or anything. In case you don't know about it, the book is all about this madman stuff that happened to me when I was going to Pency Prep, this very phony school out in Pennsylvania. I sort of got the ax and went to New York, where I was surrounded by flits and phonies and finally had to sort of take it easy and all. A lot of kids liked the book, and some of the people who run the place I finally went to said that's because they *identify* with me.

What's the matter with that? But I guess I'm wasting my time telling you this. You can't tell anybody anything. No matter how hard you try, nobody keeps listening.

Summary: Holden finds the attempt to censor his book to be phony.

It is fervently to be hoped that readers of the following editorial from the Toledo *Blade* for Dec. 15, 1963 were acquainted with the original document of which this anniversary piece was a biting parody. The editorial certainly was different from the usual flag-waving chauvinistic effusions that the occasion traditionally inspires.

A New Bill of Rights

Despite the homage paid to that part of the U.S. Constitution known as the Bill of Rights—the first 10 amendments protecting individual liberties—we all know that times have changed.

Today is the 172nd birthday of the Bill of Rights. Isn't it about time for freedom-loving Americans to modernize old concepts, bring this U.S. credo up to date, make it conform to mid-Twentieth Century conditions of peril within and without that threaten the priceless American heritage of individual freedom?

It seems fitting, at this time, to propose a new version of the Constitution's first 10 amendments:

Article 1. Freedom of speech and press shall not be abridged so long as the views expressed are popular. The right of the people to peaceably assemble and petition for the redress of grievances shall not be denied except south of Latitude 39 degrees.

Article 2. An unregulated militia being necessary to the security of the United States, the right of juvenile delinquents, adult hoodlums, and cranks to bear mail-order pistols and switch-blade knives shall not be infringed.

Article 3. No U.S. soldiers shall be quartered in or near any American community unless the right of local merchants to serve the customers of the color of their choice is maintained.

Article 4. The right of people to be secure in their homes and persons against unreasonable searches and seizures shall be violated only by police agents and vigilantes.

Article 5. No person shall be deprived of due process of law except those suspected by congressional investigators and duly chartered patriotic groups.

Article 6. All citizens shall have the right to know the nature of charges against them and to confront their accusers so long as this meets with the approval of public officials, elected or unelected politicians, and noncharitable private societies.

Article 7. The right to trial by jury shall be preserved wherever verdicts conform to local public opinion.

Article 8. There shall be no cruel or unusual punishments, and even those suspected of unpatriotic views shall only be ostracized, stripped of reputation, and barred from employment.

Article 9. The enumeration of these particular rights in no way deprives the people of other rights, especially the inalienable right of the majority at any time to deny the rights of unattractive, peculiar, or nonconforming individuals.

Article 10. All powers not given to the United States Government belong to the states; provided, however, that the U.S. Supreme Court under Chief Justice Earl Warren shall be prohibited from making any decisions that deny states the right to withhold the full privileges of citizenship from inhabitants who dwell in cities or whose complexion is un-American.

Oh, yes, there might be some objection that the similarity in form between the old-fashioned Bill of Rights as enunciated by our forefathers and the proposed, modern revision of the first 10 amendments would result in confusion. This, however, is a mere matter of semantics, and a difficulty easily resolved.

The revised, popular version need not be known as the Bill of Rights at all. It could be hailed proudly as the American Bill of Wrongs.

Summary: Better restudy the Bill of Rights.

One way to explain the nature of some historical event is to write it up as a modern newspaper reporter would do. Sam Reynolds was trying for a greater effect in the following editorial which appeared in the Missoula (Mont.) *Missoulian* for June 13, 1969. The author explains: "It illustrated an attempt to write an imaginative piece commenting on a current problem. Christ is the kids, of course—the Kent Staters and all the others with guts to put principle over conformity." Members of an NCEW critique group called it "blasphemous" but nobody explained why such would be so.

Dateline Jerusalem

JERUSALEM—A revolutionary conspiracy aimed at subverting and overthrowing Roman and Jewish civil and religious authority has been smashed here, officials said Thursday.

One Jesus of Nazareth, self-styled "King of the Jews," was arrested, questioned, tried and executed, police said. His supporters have been driven underground and one has committed suicide, according to the police.

They said at least one other suspect in the conspiracy has denied acquaintance with the executed Jesus and is under surveillance. When Jesus was arrested, police said that one of his henchmen resisted and cut off one of an arresting officer's ears with a sword.

"He (Jesus) conspired to undermine the authority of the Roman government by denying the divine status of the Emperor Nero Caesar and by otherwise stirring up civil disorder," a spokesman for Roman Gov. Pontius Pilate told newsmen.

Gov. Pilate could not be reached for comment, but sources close to the governor said that he ordered the execution of Jesus after hearing damaging evidence furnished by elders, scribes and priests who testified against the Nazarene.

A Temple spokesman, who asked not to be identified, said Jesus for many years had been actively undermining the Temple's religious authority and urging people to transfer their allegiance to his so-called Christian sect, which responsible authorities have described as a small, tightly-knit conspiratorial and revolutionary group organized by Jesus and completely subordinate to his domination.

The full circumstances surrounding the conspirator's arrest, interrogation, trial and execution were not immediately made clear, but conferences were under way late Thursday between Roman and Jewish authorities and a spokesman said a full report would be made public in due course.

One informed source said that Herod, tetrarch of Galilee and Peraea, was in the city when the conspiracy was broken, and that Gov. Pilate sent Jesus to Herod for questioning.

It is known that Jesus once publically insulted the widely-respected tetrarch, calling Herod "that fox." The informed source said that Herod personally quizzed Jesus, who refused to reply, and that in disgust Herod dispatched the self-styled "Christ" back to Gov. Pilate for trial.

Unconfirmed reports Thursday said that Pilate at first was reluctant to condemn Jesus, and that the governor's wife even tried to intervene in the case of the Nazarene's behalf, calling Jesus a "just man."

However, Gov. Pilate eventually was persuaded to condemn Jesus to death on the strength of testimony presented by scribes, elders, priests and other responsible citizens, according to an officer of the Scribes Association who attended the trial.

Jesus, he said, flatly declined to testify in his own defense, and those present felt that his default in effect was an admission of guilt.

"It's fortunate for Jerusalem and all Palestine that this conspiracy has been broken in time," the Scribes Association officer said. "We hope it is an object lesson to all those who would question long-established values, would attempt to undermine law and order or would foolishly try to subvert properly consituted authority."

Summary: The story of Jesus' travail provides a lesson regarding the dangers of timidity and bigotry today.

ESSAYS

In what are nostalgically called the good old days, the meaningful essay was commonplace on most editorial pages. Collections of the best of some all-time greats, as Walt Whitman, Henry Watterson, and Frank Cobb, are top-heavy with this type of editorial. The same is true as regards William Allen White who won a couple of Pulitzer prizes for editorial writing. Here is one of the prize winners which appeared in the Emporia (Kans.) *Gazette* for July 22, 1922.

To an Anxious Friend

You tell me that law is above freedom of utterance. And I reply that you can have no wise laws nor free enforcement of wise laws unless there is free expression of the wisdom of the people—and, alas, their folly with it. But if there is freedom, folly will die of its own poison, and the wisdom will survive. That is the history of the race. It is the proof of man's kinship with God. You say that freedom of utterance is not for time of stress, and I reply with the sad truth that only in time of stress is freedom of utterance in danger. No one questions it in calm days, because it is not needed. And the reverse is true also; only when free utterance is suppressed is it needed, and when it is needed, it is most vital to justice. Peace is good. But if you are interested in peace through force and without free discussion, that is to say, free utterance decently and in order—your interest in justice is slight. And peace without justice is tyranny, no matter how you may sugar-coat it with expediency. This state today is in more danger from suppression than from violence, because in the end, suppression leads to violence. Violence, indeed, is the child of suppression. Whoever pleads for justice helps to keep the peace; and whoever tramples upon the plea for justice, temperately made in the name of peace, only outrages peace and kills something fine in the heart of man which God put there when we got our manhood. When that is killed, brute meets brute on each side of the line.

So, dear friend, put fear out of your heart. This nation will survive, this state will prosper, the orderly business of life will go forward if only men can speak in whatever way given them to utter what their hearts hold—by voice, by posted card, by letter or by press. Reason never has failed men. Only force and repression have made the wrecks in the world.

Summary: There is nothing to fear from free speech.

Reminiscent of John Winthrop and other New England Puritans was the following philosophical treatise from the Clovis (N. M.) *News-Journal* of Aug. 17, 1958.

The Moral Climate

Surely it is true that most of us wish to live in a civilization which is based upon moral law. To consider that human beings actually desire an immoral climate, is to presume that persons would rather be dead than alive—a preposterous assumption.

The problem does not arise out of our yearning for a moral climate. It arises from our failure to comprehend one simple fact. Morality depends totally upon freedom.

How can this be, we are asked.

Freedom, functionally, relates to choice. So long as a person is free to choose, so long as it is possible for that person to choose within a moral framework. But eliminate the person's ability to make a choice, and you will have provided, not for morality, but for amorality.

Let us grant that persons who are free to choose, may not always choose courses of action which are moral in themselves. This is an obvious fact relating to man's shortcomings. Man is fallible. And as a creature who falls short of perfection it is well within his capabilities to make foolish and immoral choices.

But let us consider the alternative. Let us suppose that we pass laws and hire policemen to watch all of us at each moment of every night and day so that at no time are any of us permitted to make a foolish or an immoral choice. Would this create a moral climate? It would not. It would create a climate of regimentation, slavery and coercion which would be totally immoral.

What would be wrong? The error in such a procedure resides in the fact that no moral

virtue accrues to any individual who does what he ought to do because he is forced to do it. For example: Let us suppose that you are ushered into a room in which a great pile of money lies unattended on a table. However, you are handcuffed to a policeman: a man with a drawn gun stands guard: it is impossible for you to even think of taking that money. Are you virtuous because you do not attempt to steal? Of course not.

But let us suppose that you are ushered into the same room and the money has been placed on a table. Now let us suppose that no one else is present; the door is wide open; you are convinced that you could steal the money and make a complete getaway with it. At this point a choice is yours. You can resist temptation and recognize that the money is not yours and then it is immoral to steal. Or you can succumb to temptation and take the money.

If you choose to resist temptation, you have made a moral decision. If you choose to succumb, you have made an immoral decision. But, before you make up your mind either to be moral or immoral, a moral climate pertains. You are free. It is only when freedom exists that a person's actions can be adjudged to be either moral or immoral. And the person who confronts temptation and governs himself according to moral rules, is the only person who acquires virtue.

Modern civilization frequently attempts to compel people to be moral. In these times we urge all prone to attempt to force others to that which we think, in our own fallible judgment, is moral. Witness the prohibition amendment, various blue laws passed at various times, censorship laws, remember—the—Sabbath laws, and so on ad infinitum. Each of these laws is aimed at making people better and more moral by means of force. Each such law is an immoral means employed to obtain a moral result.

But the result is never moral. The result is simply to shift individual responsibility into the realm of governmental meddling so that an amoral climate results. A person who does not drink because of the fear of arrest, resists the temptation to become drunk because of fear, not because he feels that drinking will do him no good and could lead to an immoral act.

The decline of civilization begins with compulsion. The rise of civilization occurs when people are able to choose and constantly make moral choices. But to prohibit choice is to use compulsion and to abandon the moral law in favor of the gun and the club. And this in itself is immoral and reduces civilization to barbarism.

While all of us can be distressed over a situation in which any individual makes an immoral choice, all of us should be even more distressed when freedom is abandoned in favor of violence and coercion.

Summary: You deserve credit only when your good behavior is not the result of coercion.

The essay style has utility other than to propound deep thoughts on vital public matters. It can be used by feature writers as well, as was true of the following example, (authorship unknown). Note the effective use of alliteration and the deliberate use of what otherwise might be considered trite and hackneyed expressions. This is the type of editorial, incidentally, that evokes reader response. Anything related to food does so. Housewives, presumably not avid editorial readers, want recipes and argue about them as long as the editor of the letters' column will allow. Since such material is generally confined to a special section of the paper, the editorial page avoids the controversy generally. But it's "in for it" also if it waxes too eloquently about anything concerning pet animals, babies, old people or hobbies. A good way to test the page's popularity is to print a few such pieces.

Punkin Pie

To a man still young enough to remember sufficiently far back into his boyhood years to the time when he never had had enough dessert in his life, there is no word in the English language so suggestive of toothsome, lickerish joy as pie, plain pie—particularly "punkin."

You can't spell punkin pie with an *m* and an extra *p*. Pumpkin pie is the kind one gets in restaurants, flavored with cloves and all-spice. "Punkin" pie has cinnamon and ginger in it, and sometimes a hint of an unmentionable beady fluid about which one would not dare ask mother. And of all the smacking, ambrosial delicacies catalogued under the genus *pie* the best is "punkin."

There are other kinds, of course—apple, peach, cherry, squash, blueberry, .custard, lemon, mince—and every one probably has its value in the world. Some people even may prefer them. One never can account for different persons' tastes. But for boys, young men, and elderly men whose stomachs have not yet grown old, there is none that will approach "punkin," the khaki-colored queen of pastries.

One grows hungry at the thought of "punkin" pie—the crisp, crinkly crust; the thick, rich, pungent filling, with the dust of cinnamon tarnishing its tawny top; the creamy, dreamy, velvety, faraway taste as one's mouth closes on its prize. Some appetizing joys there are, but none that exceeds capturing a piece of punkin pie, getting it into one's hands, contrary to all social usage, biting into it until one almost mires up to one's nose, until one can scarce see over the top of the upstanding crust, and beginning the unequaled delight of devouring the first mouthful. To taste it is to love it, love but it, and love forever.

GOOD TASTE

When President Franklin Delano Roosevelt had trouble with a voting machine, he exclaimed, "The damned thing won't work." A howl of protest resulted when his exact words were reported and both the chief executive and the journalistic media that reported the president's language were the objects of the wrath of the puritanical. Shortly thereafter President Harry S. Truman popularized "s.o.b." but "son of a bitch" still is avoided in print, if possible. The commercial press has been slow to show the effects of the tremendous wave of freedom in speech that has affected many other fields. College editors still are removed from office for allowing "fuck," "shit" and similar words to appear in campus newspapers. When William Kunstler yelled "bull shit" at Judge Julius Hoffman during the Chicago conspiracy trial, it came out "a barnyard epithet" in the press. Quite shocking was Pulitzer prize winning Chicago *Daily News* columnist Mike Royko's commendation of Sen. George McGovern for calling a woman professor "a horse's ass" on an airplane flight between Springfield and Chicago during the 1972 primary campaign.

Very little obscenity, vulgarity or profanity gets into formal editorials if for no other reason than that it's still true such language is escapist, used by persons at a loss to express themselves effectively in any other way. Adroitly used, unconventional language can have high shock value. That happened Sept. 3, 1914 when Henry Watterson captioned a short 77-word editorial, "To Hell With the Hohenzollerns and the Hapsburgs" and thereafter put the sulphurous slogan in the masthead of the Louisville *Courier-Journal*. The shock naturally was due in part to his taking sides in the war waging in Europe so soon after it began and at a time when Americans were trying to follow President Woodrow Wilson's advice to remain neutral in thought as well as in action. The use of the four-letter word, however, was part of the shocker.

The gingerly fashion in which most of the press still handles other four letter words was demonstrated by the following editorial in the St. Louis *Post-Dispatch* for June 14, 1971.

The Word

If there are humorists on the Supreme Court they must have had a chuckle the other day over the dilemma they handed the daily press, not to speak of the nation's radio and television stations. The court met firmly, as it should, an issue involving the use of a coarse four-letter Anglo Saxon word held in disrepute by middle America and widely used in the military and youth culture.

The question facing editors was whether, in reporting the Supreme Court decision in the case of Paul Robert Cohen, the Court's language, including the word, should be quoted verbatim. In his opinion Justice John Marshall Harlan, as proper an Ivy Leaguer as may readily be found, said the issue might "seem at first blush too inconsequential" for the court to entertain, but in reality was "of no small constitutional significance." He is right.

The case before the tribunal involved the 1968 conviction and 30-day sentence of the defendant Cohen for peace disturbance. His offense was that he wore in a Los Angeles courthouse a jacket with an inscription denouncing the draft of which the word was a part. There was no disturbance; Mr. Cohen did nothing more than display the word in public. The court ruled this was no crime.

The word is one of an earthy and expressive group that has been floating around in the verbal English language for centuries. In the Puritanical age that now seems to be ending in America, it was relegated to alleys, back fences and college dormitories. It is now in fairly common usage among persons from about 10 to 25 years of age and among novelists who purport to mirror the modern scene. But we suspect that for most middle-class middle-aged Americans it remains offensive.

That is the source of the editors' dilemma, which is quite different from the judicial question. The word is used by the young to display contempt for their elders' mores, and also substantively, as in the case of Mr. Cohen, to express the depth of legitimate disgust with the draft and the Vietnam war. But printed in general-circulation publications it has a disproportionate impact. It becomes obtrusive, and therefore bad taste and bad style.

We have a feeling this will change; English is a living language and customs ebb and flow. When the shock-power of this particular four-letter word declines, it will become acceptable for wider usage. And at that point a new generation of young people will have to think of a better way to rile the old folks.

Summary: It's not yet possible to print "fuck" in a daily newspaper.

Regarding a less controversial word, by today's standards, the Chicago *Daily Tribune* editorialized April 8, 1961.

A Dirty Word?

Mayor Egan of Aurora was commenting on his defeat for reelection. He said he had no apologies to make for anything he had done in office and added, as reported in this newspaper: "I'd sure as —— do the same things all over again."

What we wish to know is whether our readers would have been offended if the word "hell" had been spelled out instead of being left to the imagination. We don't want to give needless offense to anyone and it's no more trouble to print "——" than to print "hell"; but these days, would anyone really care if we had spelled out what Mr. Egan said?

We doubt it. Sometimes the word is spelled out in our columns and sometimes it isn't, depending on the whims of reporters, editors, and printers, but we can't recall ever having received a protest against either version.

Incidentally, we wonder why anybody ever thought it was indelicate or blasphemous to say "sure as hell." The phrase could reasonably annoy a man who doesn't believe in hell but he would be troubled not by the impropriety of the word but by the concept that hell is certain. To those who believe in hell, the phrase should sound as an affirmation of faith.

Perhaps the explanation lies in the fact that hell is sometimes discussed in church and is therefore thought to be a sacred subject. But then why don't we feel the same objection to "for heaven's sake"? Why does no one object to calling a kind of white cake "angel food" and a kind of chocolate cake "devil's food"?

We asked these questions the other day of Carey Orr who recalled that when the late Ring Lardner ran our "Wake of the News" column, he aimed to satisfy everybody by spelling it "he-ll." This doesn't seem to be a wholly satisfactory solution.

Summary: Let's say "hell" in print.

PARAGRAPHS

A generation ago editorial paragraphs were a fixture on the editorial page. They were short, usually one sentence comments on current events. Terse and witty, they were in the form of puns, epigrams, proverbs, adages, maxims, aphorisms, and slogans, and they made use of similes, metaphors, innuendoes, personifications, insinuations, slang, plagiarisms and about any other rhetorical device that there is.

To produce successful pithy short shorts requires genius akin to that possessed by gag writers for professional comedians or by muckraking or iconoclastic columnists. Such talent is expensive and anyone who possesses it today can find a better market than the newspaper editorial page. Hence, the editorial paragraph has declined. About the only comparatively recent plug for it was an article, "Every Man a Paragrapher," by Rufus Terral, St. Louis *Post-Dispatch* editorial writer, in the Fall, 1949 *Masthead*. The piece was mostly autobiographical about the travails of a paragrapher. He quoted one of his first:

A Montana chap tried to get rid of dandelions by digging up the roots, and even had the yard gone over with a blow torch, but all to no avail. About all we can suggest to him is that maybe he should learn to like dandelions.

Terral's comment was: "Not enough of a point. Not a universal-enough experience. Too wordy. Strained. A pretty sad paragraph."

The article contains some better examples with some attempt at classification by intention. For example:

Intended only to amuse:

School is about to reopen and once again we shall see the annual parade of carefree, happy parents.

Paragraph of manners which says, "Aren't we silly creatures and what of it?"

A woman's shop advertises lingerie of "heartbreaking beauty," and also serves notice, "All sales final." Just in case, we suppose, the heart doesn't stay broken.

Philosophical:

An inquiring reader, interested in the Rocket Society's proposal for colonizing the moon, wants to know whether it has been proved that life is possible on any of the other planets. Madam, it hasn't even been proved on this planet yet.

Political:

The National Association of Manufacturers is publicizing its views with a slogan, "For a Better Tomorrow for Everybody." The better today it has in mind, however, is pretty plainly for the National Association of Manufacturers.

Terral said the most widely reprinted paragraph he ever wrote, which he felt helped editors who clipped and pasted it, to laugh off something that had irritated them was as follows:

The New York City War Council has issued an order saying, "Illumination is required to be extinguished before these premises are closed to business." Well, it means that before lockage is effected to the doors, the electricity is demanded to suspend. Or turn out the lights before you go out.

Historically the journalistic champions at this sort of writing were Finley Peter Dunne, from the Spanish-American War to World War I, and Will Rogers during the twenties and early thirties. They came as close to being court jesters as this nation ever has had. They made everyone chuckle as they irreverently unstuffed shirts and exposed pomposity and hypocrisy in high places. Presidents, from Roosevelt to Roose-

velt, gritted their teeth and made believe they liked it.

Dunne, who worked in many capacities on several Chicago and New York newspapers, created the fictional Martin Dooley, a saloon keeper, who discoursed on the day's news in Irish dialect English to his bartender, Hennessey. He exposed the shams and weaknesses of American life within the framework of traditionally American values. He was not a short paragrapher but many of his aphorisms still are quoted, as "The Supreme Court follows th' iliction returns." Of Theodore Roosevelt's immodest book, *The Rough Riders,* Mr. Dooley remarked, "If I was him I'd call the book, 'Alone in Cubia.' "

In an article, "Mr. Dooley: A Man of Great Renown," in *The New Republic* for March 22, 1948, Lloyd Morris wrote:

The basis of Dooley's universal appeal lay deeper than humor. He spoke as a moralist, and he became everybody's philosopher largely because he translated into ethical terms the major issues of the day. He addressed the American conscience, always sensitive to extreme discrepancies between what is and what ought to be. He invited it to consider the disparity of American democratic principles and common American practice.

Michael Putney explained the durability of Will Rogers' humor in an article, "Will Rogers, Satirist for Today," in *The National Observer* for Oct. 5, 1970.

. . . low-keyed, gentle barbs, which he used with such unerring accuracy to deflate the pompous and expose the dishonest.

Some typical Rogers' observations which were syndicated daily by the New York *Times* for many years were as follows:

Calvin Coolidge: He kept his mouth shut. That was such a novelty among politicians that it just swept the country. He's just the man we needed. He didn't do nothing, but nothing's what we wanted done.

U.S. Diplomacy: History shows that the United States never lost a war or won a conference.

Congress: My little jokes don't hurt nobody, but when Congress makes a joke, it's a law. When they make a law it's a joke.

Doctors: The only problem with doctors is you gotta be near dead to appreciate them.

Government: We are a nation that runs in spite of and not on account of our government.

Voters: The short memory of American voters is what keeps our politicians in office.

Journalistically, probably nothing could happen more in the public interest than the discovery of a new Finley Peter Dunne or Will Rogers. In the meantime, some competent work is being done. Among the best is the Starbeam column which Bill Vaughan writes for the Kansas City *Star* of which he is an associate editor and which is syndicated as "Senator Soaper Says." The following example appeared in the St. Louis *Post-Dispatch* for May 7, 1972:

Bill Vaughan Says

It is estimated that it takes two hours and 34 minutes of every eight-hour day for a worker to earn enough to pay his taxes. Surely, the boss won't mind you being that late, since it's the period when you would have been working for the government, not him.

Six thousand National Guardsmen will be available for duty at the Republican national convention. There is progress of a sort; what used to be dismissed as quaint circuses have finally achieved status of full-scale riots.

There seems to be a sudden upsurge in gang-style slayings. Part of the nostalgia fad, we assume.

Loud voice on the bus: "I'll tell you, it's a terrible temptation to vote straight Democratic, the party that needs the money."

The newest trend in urban renewal is toward little shops that look like those of 100 years ago. For the old home town, all that would be required would be a little modernization.

The wage earner today is likely to find that he's not even making enough to pay his deductions.

The Boston *Sunday Globe* of Sept. 26, 1971 ran these "Editorial Points."

One cure for the troubles of Ulster would be to have everybody emigrate, and stock the country with new people.

The American Legion wants to make it a crime to fly the flag of any nation hostile to the United States. How'll we know for sure who's friendly?

The crumbs-from-the-table economic theory runs up against the fact that those in the chairs are likely to be very neat and thorough eaters.

Letting a person buy a house with a 5 percent down payment will enable him to take on a real back buster of a mortgage.

Candidates for office in Saigon need health guarantees no doctor can give.

Another kind of news is all that leaks out.

Russian influence in Sudan seems to be as effective as ours in Vietnam.

The Philadelphia *Inquirer* has a "Cheers & Jeers" editorial page feature of which the following from the issue of June 6, 1971 is typical:

Cheers: To Eileen Story, the 13-year-old Columbus, O., girl who kept her cool while a hijacker held a knife at her throat during an unscheduled jet flight to Cuba.

Jeers: To the weatherman for souring the merry month of May with four rainy weekends—and then following up with five Mondays of sunshine.

Cheers: To the Boy Scouts here and elsewhere for getting a mammoth cleanup drive under way. It's the kind of good turn many of their elders can benefit from, learn from and (gasp!) even try themselves.

Jeers: To the Pennsylvania House of Representatives for again bowing to the private-club lobby and refusing to pass a bill to permit Sunday sales of liquor.

Cheers: To Sen. Adlai Stevenson III of Illinois for his vast concern over the sanctity of elections to be held in Vietnam in October; we trust he will be equally alert to any hanky-panky in Mayor Daley's Chicago when the votes are counted there next year.

And "Today's Chuckle" assists readers to get through the day. The following was on page 1 of the Chicago *Daily News* for May 8, 1972.

The way things are now, almost any girl with a good job can get married.

Otter Tail Hi-Lites

The Graffitti distributed by the McNaught Syndicate are substitutes for the formal editorial paragraph. Typical examples:

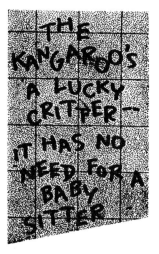

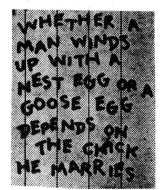

VI

Faults to Avoid

1. Dullness
2. Straddling
3. Vagueness
4. Afghanistanism

5. Ignorance
6. Chauvinism
7. Dogma
8. Bigotry

The preceding chapter illustrated numerous ways in which to be more than usually effective in editorial writing. This chapter, by contrast, will concentrate on how not to do it. Pedagogically it is supposed to be bad to direct students' attention to poor examples for fear they will unconsciously imitate them. However, since there is quite a bit more of this book to come, that risk is minimal and seems to be worth taking, especially inasmuch as the faults against which warnings now are being sounded can be observed anyway by not much more than a cursory sampling of the mine run of editorial pages. So it's impossible to protect the young learner from the bad while inspiring him with examples of the good. This chapter should help him to become a more astute critic of his own work as well as that of others and possibly to avoid some pitfalls which may come to seem more obvious to him. Most of the examples are from newspapers which ordinarily do much better, indicating that

even the best will slip if he doesn't watch out.

DULLNESS

According to a commentator on WBAL-TV, Baltimore, that city's *Sun* is one of the five or six newspapers which the President reads daily. In an otherwise generally favorable analysis of the paper, the critic advised: "I would recommend he avoid the editorials, which lack the pungency of their counterparts in the New York *Times* and the Washington *Post*. So often the *Sun* editorials are so gray, quality modified, equivocal that the President needn't bother with them."

What follows is a fairly typical example of what is meant. Perhaps this is better than average because it includes facts and figures. These, however, are already known to the minority of readers with a special interest in the topic, and they are not sufficient to impress the uninformed. The conclusion is equivocal. It appeared in the Baltimore *Sun* for Sept. 30, 1971.

Hard Fight Ahead	Comment
A new formula for state aid to local school systems has passed its initial legislative test with	Does little more than indicate the topic; it's a label so anyone already interested in state aid will read

a 4-to-1 affirmative vote by a Legislative Council committee. The ultimate fate of the measure remains very much in doubt as the proposed increase in state contributions would require both state tax increases and acceptance of the principle of equalized educational opportunity throughout Maryland.

on. Otherwise, it is vague. "New formula" is undefined and so are "proposed increase" and "principle of equalized educational opportunity." The reader who continues with the editorial must already be savvy.

The program which has won committee acceptance is the one put forward earlier this year by a special commission headed by Harry R. Hughes. In general terms the state would pay about 55 percent of statewide school operating costs, whereas currently the state pays only about a third of the statewide total of school operating costs. The additional state money, estimated at $164 million, would assure that each county and Baltimore city gets an increase in state aid to meet rising school costs, which is an immediate objective of county and city officials.

For the $164 million to be meaningful there should be total expenditure figures. How much more would the county and city get, to bring their totals to what? What is the cause of the rising school costs and how much is the increase?

But the state aid would not be pegged at 55 percent of school costs in each jurisdiction. The new formula would be based on an equalization of taxable wealth in counties and city so that the amount of state aid would range from 30 percent in the wealthiest counties up to 70 percent in the poorest ones. In practical terms, the jurisdictions which need the most help in maintaining quality schooling would get the highest percentages of state aid in meeting their budgets, and those with the most favorable local tax resources would get the smallest percentages of aid.

This implies but is not explicit that the 55 percent is the present law. Most readers don't understand what "equalization of taxable wealth" means and cannot understand the meaning of the 30 and 70 percent range. What is "quality" schooling? This is not clearly stated and doesn't clearly say that the state is to give any locality enough to bring its education up to what? An average? The best? What standard and who establishes it?

In terms of fair treatment and equality of opportunity for all Maryland children, regardless of where they may live, the Hughes commission program is a substantial improvement over the present state-aid formula, which now actually serves to bolster the disparity in school expenditures between wealthy and poor counties. The Hughes program also would move Maryland in line with the landmark California decision in which the court ruled that the quality of a child's education should not be a function of the wealth of his parents and neighbors. To get such a program through the Maryland General Assembly, nevertheless, will require tremendous public pressure to offset the resistance to equalization among wealthy suburban counties.

Good point but not substantiated. Inadequate summary of the California decision.

Weasel ending. Who should apply what kind of pressure on whom? The fact of wealthy suburban opposition seems tacked on; it might be the most important issue in the whole debate.

STRADDLING

The patience of readers becomes exhausted if, paragraph after paragraph, it is impossible to determine which side of the issue under consideration the editorial writer supports. Few will reread and ponder; instead, they'll turn to the comics. Here is an example of an editorial which seems to play hide-and-seek with the reader who may be excused for concluding that the author wasn't sure of himself. It is from the Lincoln (Nebr.) *Evening Journal* and *Nebraska State Journal* of Sept. 21, 1971.

Whither the Technical College?

Comment

The Lincoln Technical Community College Board (actually the public schools' Board of Education, wearing different hats), has adopted a passive position regarding implementation of LB759, the act creating a statewide system of community colleges.

The expression "passive position" seems to be mild censure.

* * *

Under the law, all Nebraska counties must be part of one of eight college districts by 1973. The Lincoln college, whose boundaries now coincide with those of the public school district, is designed one of the eight.

* * *

What the Lincoln board is saying, in effect, is that it won't oppose expansion of its college district—would, in fact, be receptive to counties wanting to join—but doesn't intend to go out and beat the drums for growth.

Tactically, the board's position may be sound. The question of how to set up the statewide system is causing considerable ferment in Southeast Nebraska. Some counties are looking toward the two-year vocational school at Milford, now state-operated but envisioned as part of the new arrangement. Some persons are promoting the idea of using the former Pershing College facilities at Beatrice. Others seem to feel something could be worked out involving Peru State College.

The first sentence seems to indicate disapproval but the rest of the paragraph presents extenuating circumstances.

For the Lincoln college board or staff to adopt an aggressive stance risks alienating counties or groups which otherwise, in the end, might decide joining Lincoln is the best route.

This exonerates the board.

* * *

In addition, the Lincoln board appears to favor leaving the assignment of uncommitted areas up to the 1973 legislature, rather than doing it by the petition and election method in the counties themselves. One might question how qualified the lawmakers are to decide, yet this approach possibly could avoid spirited election battles that might leave scars in some of the areas.

This says the board is wrong.

This suggests the board is wise.

* * *

From a practical standpoint, the Lincoln college can afford to remain aloof from any quarrels over implementing LB759. By the standards in that law, and by its own assessment, the college has the tax base and clientele now to continue as a viable institution. If no additional territory joins its district, there apparently will be no serious harm.

This hastens to correct any favorable impression so far created.

Yet by most yardsticks there is a great deal of logic in expanding the Lincoln college district, at the very least to include the rest of Lancaster County. The college itself stands to gain from an enlarged tax base and more potential students. And surely there would be some advantage to surrounding areas to affiliate with a strong, existing institution like the one in Lincoln, located in a community that offers a variety of other educational assets. Though the college has rejected a salesman role, there is nothing to stop others in Lincoln and Southeast Nebraska—organizations, governmental leaders, individuals—from stepping into the picture.

This passes the buck, but not very specifically.

* * *

A hard-sell campaign is not needed—should, in fact, be avoided. An effort ought to be made simply to insure that all possibilities and ramifications of LB759 are fully understood, and that whatever structure is created by 1973 will provide the greatest possible educational benefits for all of Southeast Nebraska.

Anyone inspired by the preceding paragraph to want to do something is promptly discouraged. In the final sentence the writer figuratively washes his hands of the whole controversial mess.

VAGUENESS

Even the editorial which has a strong ending can be ineffective if it loses readers because of its longwindedness and its excessive use of vague expressions, including platitudes and clichés, as in the following from the Columbia (S.C.) *Record* of Feb. 16, 1965.

S. C. Education: The University

The projected growth of South Carolina's total educational structure demands now, as it has in the immediate past, a reasoned system of priorities. A limited per capita income and a surplusage of young people compel the most judicious disbursement of funds as the state seeks to overcome the past errors of human investment that are primarily responsible for our present impoverishment.	**Comment** Too vague for ordinary reader. What is a reasoned system of priorities? A limited per capita income? A surplusage of young people? Highfalutin language, "past errors of human investments." What does it mean?
There can be no self-glorification in post-World War II accomplishments, no self-delusion that we've not a long way to go, no self-pity about state poverty. There **must** be dedication and commitment.	Trite expressions: self-glorification, self-delusion, self-pity, dedication and commitment.
There must be priorities. But these priorities *cannot* be dictated by any false standards imposed on education from pre-school training through post-doctoral research. If a need is compelling, then it must be assigned First Priority and funds must be found. If the existing revenue structure is inadequate, it must be altered.	What false standards? Who imposes them? Who determines the needs?
No educational requirement deserving First Priority can be assigned a lesser place simply because of inadequate funding.	Vague generality.
The current General Assembly is challenged with a First Priority item that has been neglected: proper direct financing of the University of South Carolina.	Finally gets to subject of editorial.
Engulfed by a gigantic wave of sons and daughters of Carolinians in 1964-65, the University is bracing itself for a second surge this coming September. The school's administrators, faculty and students know that the pupil population will have expanded by *one-third* in two years.	Trite: engulfed by a gigantic wave, bracing self, second surge.

With its physical facilities taxed almost beyond endurance, with its underpaid teaching faculty strained by overloads, the University wants, rightly, to improve the quality of education offered the state's young people. It does not want to sacrifice quality in this period of its greatest growth.

Yet, the University recommended direct increase from the state amounts to only two per cent of its last appropriations—only a meager $113,581. (The Budget and Control Board also suggested an increase in out-of-state student fees, overestimating income therefrom and stretching the disparity between in-state and out-of-state fees to an exorbitant percentage.)

Why is it exorbitant?

The recommended direct appropriation for the University amounts to only $619 per student, compared with a current appropriation of $693 per student and a 1963-64 funding of $704 per student.

If this is the crisis, it should have been stressed at the beginning of the editorial and not delayed by a long introduction.

In short, the University is being asked to submit to a reduction of $95 per student *in the very years of its greatest growth.* (Direct appropriations plus the increase in out-of-state fees would amount to $660 per student; still a decrease of $44 per student over the last normal year of operation.)

The current per capita appropriation for other state institutions include $815 for Winthrop, $953 for Clemson, $1,011 for The Citadel.

For too many years the University, which should be and is the hub of our higher educational system, has been under-funded. The future of South Carolina depends, in a very real sense, on immediate action by the General Assembly to alleviate this inequity

We recommend to the legislature, with all the strength that words on paper can command, a per capita funding of $704 for the University, plus vital salary increases; a total increase of $1,142,425.

Trite: with all the strength that words on paper can command. If the issue is that important, it should have been emphasized earlier before most readers probably lost interest.

No item in the budget of the state of South Carolina deserves a priority higher than that which should be assigned to the University.

Repetitious.

Failure to provide these essential funds would not penalize the University as such, but it would damage the young men and women of Carolina, who are its future.

Possibly there's another side. There have been cases of expensive wate and administrative costs on campuses.

Were we given the power to cast votes in the Assembly on this First Priority item, we would deliver 124 votes in the House and 46 in the Senate *for* a 27.3 per cent increase in University appropriations for 1965-66.

Finally, here's the specific point.

When the editorial writer has nothing to add to the news peg on which his editorial depends, either because he did no research or, possibly, because there really wasn't anything to add, the result is banality. In the following from the Boston *Evening Globe* of Sept. 21, 1971, the final paragraph oozes sweetness and light but all that went before it was merely a rehash of what should, at least, have been in the news story the day before. Anyone who read the news account didn't need the editorial as it added nothing whatever to his knowledge. Anyone who missed the news story would do better to unwrap the garbage and find it to read, instead of the editorial rehash.

A New Look at Town and Gown

We have all read much about the friction between town and gown, particularly as it relates to housing but in other matters as well. That is one reason why it was so refreshing yesterday to hear the remarks of Chancellor Francis L. Broderick of the University of Massachusetts in Boston before the Dorchester Board of Trade.

For two years from now, U. Mass. in Boston will move to a brand new campus at Columbia Point, Dorchester, and what Dr. Broderick talked about with considerable foresight was, quite plainly and simply, being a good neighbor.

It was good to hear that the U. Mass in Boston already has a working relationship with the Columbia Civic Assn. and with the Columbia Point Action Coalition, and hopes soon to have such a tie with the South Boston Citizens' Assn. But Dr. Broderick called for more than this—for anticipating problems instead of merely responding to them after they arise.

The state university, he warned, cannot build housing, or establish day care clinics or health centers solely as community services nor undertake projects in economic development. Yet these are eminently desirable, and he pointed out a way to realize them.

One, he said, could be a non-profit, tax-exempt community development corporation, separate from the Dorchester, South Boston and Columbia Point communities and from the university as well, and yet including them all, drawing on private investment, foundations and Federal money to develop new community facilities.

Such an agency or agencies could create new housing to prevent "blockbusting" and encourage new business activities with the university making available its staff resources for much of the organizational administrative work. And one result could be the kind of community services to be needed by the neighborhoods involved.

But merely an exchange of good intentions will not deal with the coming problems and opportunities. Dr. Broderick is right in urging that a working partnership be started now to set up the capacity to plan together, and he has offered to make available to a joint planning group within 90 days the technical staff needed to translate plans into action.

This was the forward-looking speech of a good neighbor, and his invitation for cooperation ought to be accepted enthusiastically by all concerned.

AFGHANISTANISM

Even worse than the preceding example, which had the virtue of comparative brevity but which failed because it contributed nothing new to the reader's knowledge or understanding, is the long harangue which summarizes à speech, report, or article with a few banal remarks, at the same time passing up the opportunity for any critical analysis. This is afghanistanism on the domestic front and is illustrated by the following from the Birmingham *News* for Oct. 6, 1958.

Changes Seen in Alabama Agriculture

The old gray mare ain't what she used to be, nor is the farm on which she lived what it used to be. Agriculture in Alabama is changing just as industry and other pursuits are changing. What's more we may expect more changes in the future in the farm life of Alabama.

Something of what those changes may involve was discussed last summer by Ben T. Lan-

Comment

Hackneyed expressions and trite thoughts.

News peg is old.

ham, Jr., head Department of Agricultural Economics at the Alabama Agricultural Experiment Station, in talks before the Alabama Farm Credit Clinics. Mr. Lanham's remarks recently were published in Alabama Business, published by the Bureau of Business Research at the University of Alabama.

Mr. Lanham notes that farming is and always has been a way of life as well as a business, but he thinks that in the future it may become almost entirely a business. It is a business of declining numbers now, and even now half the young men reaching working age on farms are not needed to keep up the present numbers.

Too leisurely getting into subject, and most important aspects of subject are delayed.

Farming, Mr. Lanham goes on to say, was formerly a business of arts and crafts, but now it is becoming a science.

Glittering generalities. What made farming an art or craft, a science? This is oratory on paper.

Farm products are what economists term an inelastic demand; that is to say, a small change in production usually results in a relatively large change in price. Further, there being some 5,000,000 farms functioning as small businesses, no individual producer is big enough to influence price.

In 1958 there were about 4.5 million farms compared with 6.8 million in 1935 and close to 2.5 million today. Agriculture has been steadily becoming a part of the total economic procedure; the farm size has increased from about 140 acres to over 400 acres in a half century, indicating the trend to monopoly. Farm population has declined to about 10 million or 5 percent of the total population.

Mr. Lanham says that the "most important single question facing the state's agricultural economy is in respect to the future of cotton —which is still the state's No. 1 cash crop." He thinks that cotton will become increasingly less important in relation to other enterprises in the future, both from the standpoint of acreage and income. As cotton declines, the relative importance of livestock, he believes, should grow.

A modicum of research could have confirmed this trend. No need to rely entirely on Lanham, making this not much more than a resumé of his report.

Farming, this agricultural economist observes, will continue to be risky and costly. Mechanization and irrigation, he goes on, will continue to expand in Alabama and major adjustments will have to be made in farm management methods. He sees Alabama farms as continuing to increase in unit size, with farming becoming more like other businesses. Many products will be produced to specification and sold under contract.

"By the year 1975," he says, "we may find ourselves with an agriculture in Alabama that is so commercialized, so specialized, so capitalized, and so managed, that the only alternatives open to the small farmer as a com-

The conclusion does not follow necessarily from the premises. What does it mean for the small farmer to integrate? That term, especially in the South, implies race relations.

mercial producer are to either integrate or disintegrate."

Many such prospective changes may seem regrettable to many people, farmers and city dwellers alike. But change appears inevitable and presents a challenge to summon up the courage, the determination and the wisdom to meet new conditions so as to make the most of new opportunities.

What changes are regrettable and why? Change is inevitable is a bromidic statement, meaningless. What new conditions require what kind of courage, determination and wisdom? And what are the new opportunities? This is a semanticist's nightmare, meaningless verbiage.

In journalistic circles afghanistanism means timidity in tackling local problems while taking vigorous stands on faraway matters. It was first used by Jenkin Lloyd Jones, editor of the Tulsa *Tribune*, in a speech to the American Society of Newspaper Editors in 1948, in which he said:

> The tragic fact is that many an editorial writer can't hit a short-range target. He's hell on distance. And there's a lot that is comfortable about this distance. It takes guts to dig up the dirt on the sheriff, or to expose a utility racket, or to tangle with the governor. They all bite back, and you had better know your stuff.
>
> But you can pontificate about the situation in Afghanistan in perfect safety. You have no fanatic Afghans among your readers. Nobody knows any more about the subject than you do, and nobody gives a damn.

Thus, afghanistanism is virtually synonymous with cowardice and/or laziness on the home front. In its defense Francis P. Locke, then on the Dayton *Daily News* wrote in *The Masthead* for Fall, 1953 essentially that modesty is a virtue, and Raymond K. Price, Jr., formerly chief editorial writer for the defunct New York *Herald Tribune*, explained in the Summer, 1970 issue of the same magazine:

> On a lot of papers it is of course a basic rule that editorials should be "punchy"—meaning, among other things, that they should pretend to a great certainty whether the writer feels it (or has reason to feel it) or not. These are lauded as "strong." The opposite—that familiar on-the-one-hand-and-on-the-other—devil—is derided as wishy washy. But what is better—the wishy-washy

editorial that raises the right questions, or the punchy one that gives a flip answer? Is it more important to know "where the paper stands" or to have it take "stands" only when it knows what it's standing for?

Price's point is well taken as a warning against dogmatic and premature passing of judgments. Assuming, however, that there has been adequate time and opportunity for research and thought, the fence straddling, wishy-washy editorial is to be deplored, and it is deplored by readers who shun it.

Some wag invented "The Utility Editorial" as follows:

_____ is an issue which is a challenge to us all. Every right-thinking person in _____
(state, nation, world, universe)
will (view with alarm) (point with pride) (be puzzled by) (be gratified by) (be alarmed by) this latest development, which comes at a time when _____
(state, nation, world,
_____ faces the darkest day in its history.
universe)
All men of good will should band themselves together to (see that it doesn't happen again) (perpetuate it) (encourage it) (discourage it) (deplore it) (praise it). Only in this way can we assure continued (progress and prosperity) (justice and freedom) (peace and joy) in a _____
(state,
_____ fraught with crisis
nation, world, universe)
as never before.

We must all (get behind) (oppose) this latest development in the ever changing rhythm of time, in order that the _____ may continue to _____ . On the other hand, _____ . As _____ has so well said, _____ . The future of _____ hangs in (state, nation, world, universe) the balance. We must not fail.

The test to apply to an editorial to determine whether it commits the sin of afghanistanism is: who is supposed to think or do what? If the editorial does not provide the answer, there is something the matter with it.

IGNORANCE

In an article, "Why Editorials Don't Get Read," which appeared originally in the Gannett newspapers publication, *Editorially Speaking* and was reprinted in *The Masthead* for Summer, 1969, Desmond Stone, editor of the editorial page of the Rochester (N.Y.) *Democrat and Chronicle,* recalled the first editorial he ever wrote, for an Australian newspaper. It was about the marriage of Princess Elizabeth and Prince Philip and the young author began it as follows:

At 11 A.M. yesterday, to the glorious sounds of trumpets, the marriage of Princess Elizabeth and Prince Philip was consummated before the altar of Westminster Abbey.

Stone's usually taciturn editor guffawed as he explained to his cub that consummation is not synonymous with celebration. "I can only plead the ignorance of a half-educated youth," Stone reminisces, admitting he should have consulted a dictionary. When his boss was away he admonished Stone to refrain from writing on either local or national affairs. "Obviously he figured that if I were to write again about a consummation before an altar, at least the locale would be some backward little country with customs perhaps strange enough to embrace that kind of behavior," Stone wrote. And then he gave this advice:

But if we're writing about something local or regional, then we had better be well informed. We had better be sure we know more than the people we're writing for. And we ought, of course, to write well within the limits of this knowledge. Like a good singer, a good editorial writer shouldn't be straining when he hits high notes. He ought always to have a reserve of knowledge.

And that about says it, except to add that it's hard work to avoid being an ignoramus when writing about an unfamiliar subject. Following are a few examples of editorials by authors who just didn't know what they were talking about. They were illiterates in respect to the subjects which they were injudicious enough to tackle. For example, an editorial which appeared in the Chicago *Daily Tribune* for Nov. 20, 1957.

Who Is Mentally Retarded?

A new superintendent of the Iowa school for the mentally retarded has discovered among his charges Mayo Buckner, 67, whose intelligence quotient is 120. He is said to be "a competent printer and musician."

This man of above average intellect has been an institutional inmate for almost 60 years. His mother had him committed in 1898, because he would not fight back when other children picked on him, and because he "rolled his eyes." The family doctor concurred. Five years ago, when Buckner's capacity was established, apparently for the first time, it was felt he was too old to start life on the outside. The new superintendent, tho, is willing he should have a chance. Buckner would like to see if he "could make it."

That a man of more than normal ability should spend his life in an institution for the mentally retarded is appalling. Even more so, tho, is the thought of all the mentally retarded people who are not only outside, but in positions of power.

One of the things the world could use is a periodic checkup on both the inmates of institutions and the top echelons of governments, to make sure that fate has not played tricks with others besides Mayo Buckner.

Buckner should not have too much difficulty on the outside. After all, he has expert evidence of his intelligence. A good many of us on the outside have been at large without it. As the discharged mental hospital patient well said, "I have a sanity certificate. Do you?"

This editor makes a puerile political crack in the next-to-last paragraph and demonstrates his ignorance of mental health in the first paragraph. His wisecrack would be funny if it weren't rooted in complete misunderstanding of psychological facts. The writer's ignorance includes not knowing the difference between mental retardation and mental illness. Mental retardation is feeblemindedness and can result from prenatal or birth injuries or (15 percent) heredity. There are three classifications of the mentally subnormal: morons (intelligence quotient of 50 to 69; imbeciles (I.Q. of 25 to 49); and idiots (I.Q. of 0 to 24). They are called amentias, feebleminded since birth, as contrasted with dementias, who lose mental capacity in later life from injury, illness or senility.

Mental illness, by contrast, strikes persons of medium or high intellect. It sometimes is difficult to distinguish between genius and insanity. The trend is away from the attempt to classify mental illnesses by distinct types, as pure types just do not exist. In other words, a mental illness is not like measles or mumps or tuberculosis, identifiable as a distinct disorder caused by some sort of invisible bug. There are, rather, only symptoms. Dr. Karl Menninger brought research and thought up to date in his *The Vital Balance* (Viking, 1963). Despite the contemporary recognition that pure types of mental illness are impossible to distinguish or classify, the broad difference between schizophrenics and manic-depressives still presumably has value for descriptive and diagnostic purposes. The former means split personality and the patient loses touch with reality to build his own dream world. The manic-depressive is alternately boisterous and morose. Yale University studies revealed that persons in the lower or bottom economic class were 11 times more likely to be schizophrenic than those in the higher economic classes, among whom manic-depression was three times as prevalent as among the lower classes.

Back to the editorial: a sanity certificate would not pertain to this case, one of mental retardation. When Buckner died Sept. 28, 1965 at 75, the Associated Press commented, "And with him died an era that mental health specialists would just as soon forget." Explained Alfred S. Glenwood, superintendent, the blame for awful errors such as occurred in this case resulted from "poor diagnostic procedures and an outdated philosophy that institutions are depositories for human problems."

The Chicago *Daily Tribune's* morning rival, the Chicago *Sun-Times*, also displayed ignorance in the following editorial which it ran May 5, 1952:

How's Your Mental Health?

Just for a switch, we thought it would be interesting to discuss mentally healthy people in discussing Mental Health Week. Here is what the National Association for Mental Health says are some of the characteristics of people with good mental health.

Comment

Good idea but the "switch" doesn't occur. It is difficult to believe the paper obtained this description from the source it cites. If these qualifications are valid, Diogenes would have a more difficult time finding a mentally well person than he did seeking an honest man.

They feel comfortable about themselves. They are not bowled over by their own emotions, by their fears, anger, love, jealousy, guilt or worries. They can take life's disappointments in stride. They can laugh at themselves. They can feel they are part of a group. They accept responsibilities. They think for themselves, make their own decisions.

There are many other characteristics, but this gives an idea that mentally healthy persons are good friends, good workers, good mates, good parents and good citizens.

Just as a person who is healthy physically can become ill, so a person mentally healthy can become ill. The purpose of Mental Health Week is to remind everyone that there are many services available for maladjusted people and to remind them also that more such services are needed.

For example, businessmen are urged to take advantage of increased knowledge in the mental health field. A maladjusted personality may be the trouble behind a perennial trouble-maker, a gold-bricker, one who can't give or take orders, an absentee, an undependable or suspicious worker.

According to Dr. William C. Menninger, 60 to 80 per cent of all dismissals in industry are due to social incompetence and only about 20 to 40 per cent are caused by technical incompetence. Mental health not only means happiness for the individual, it means money in the till for industry. It's as important for employers to watch their employees' mental health as to watch their physical health.

Information on the subject of mental health can be obtained by writing to the Illinois Society for Mental Health, 123 W. Madison.

Journalistic ignorance apparently was epidemic in Chicago in the early fifties. The Chicago *American* seemed the most reluctant to get abreast of modern scientific thought in this editorial from its issue of Nov. 11, 1955.

Scientists snorted at this editorial at the time. Today, two decades later, so would almost everyone else. Today newspapers and magazines frequently feature articles about the possibility of test tube babies

This suggests that mental hygiene should result in docile employees, "yes" men without questions regarding their jobs or the status quo. Many years ago Louis Bisch wrote a book *Be Glad You're Neurotic* (McGraw-Hill, 1936), in which he pointed out that much or most of what we value today in all fields originated with heretics who broke with the status quos of their time, many to become martyrs. If this is so, the mental health movement to produce conformists should be opposed, not supported as herein.

and virgin births, and the term "cloning" is fast becoming widely known and understood: the production of genetically identical copies of individual organisms, possible already for plants and some animals and perhaps soon to be the same for humans. Already sensational headlines and illustrated articles ask whether we are to go in for Adolph Hitlers or Ludwig von Beethovens.

Superman Again

We had supposed the superman idea died with Hitler and his Nazi madmen, but it has just popped up again in Chicago. It was revived by Dr. H. J. Muller, Indiana University geneticist and a Nobel prize winner, in a forum discussion of artificial insemination held at Sinai Temple.

Dr. Muller said that by using only great men as donors and "many worthy spinsters and widows" as mothers, we can breed a race of supermen "as far beyond us as we are beyond the microbes."

We will not go into the moral and ethical aspects of Dr. Muller's proposal just now. We want to discuss it simply as hogwash, of which it is a captivating example.

Briefly, the doctor's idea is that the human race has gone to the devil because modern civilization has permitted too many people he considers inferior to survive and produce children. Can't kill these people off, he says; it wouldn't be kind.

So the thing to do is to supplant the kind of average human being now being born with creatures produced by inseminating carefully selected women with "male germ cells" from "rigorously chosen donors."

Only men with "outstandingly superior characteristics" would be considered as donors, Dr. Muller explained.

We aren't quite certain what makes a man "outstandingly superior," but we feel pretty sure that under any definition of the term, Abraham Lincoln's father would never have been chosen as one of Dr. Muller's donors. Nor would George Washington Carver's father, or Ulysses S. Grant's or Joan of Arc's, or

Comment

Dr. Muller's viewpoint is completely distorted. He began predicting genetic disaster in the thirties. Since modern medicine keeps alive the weak who previously succumbed, much human breeding is by parents whose counterparts would be forbidden to reproduce by any cattleman or vegetable grower. Dr. Muller's "great man" is to offset this decline; he is not the holder of high social honors but one genetically super.

Unknown to the Hearst editorial writer, even in 1955 there was a great deal of artificial insemination going on. Today the practice is widespread.

The penultimate paragraph is a complete distortion. It confuses fame and fortune with biological background. Why would Tom Lincoln not have been chosen? From all reports he was a strong healthy individual who survived well in his environment. The extent to which a father is journalistically unknown has nothing whatever to do with the situation.

Benjamin Franklin's or Henry Ford's. They were all undistinguished men.

Dr. Muller made his reputation as a geneticist working with fruit flies. In his preoccupation with these fascinating creatures, he seems to have overlooked a few of the differences between them and human beings.

Here is demonstrated again extreme ignorance of scientific laboratory research. Most of what is known about genetic mutations and much that is known about viruses resulted from the work of Dr. Muller and others using fruit flies in their experimental laboratories.

One final example of ignorance from Chicagoland, this time the suburban Lansing *Journal* for June 27, 1963. This piece is typical of endless scapegoating of youth, slashing out at a stereotype which doesn't fit any appreciable number. It falls short of explaining why young people in all ages have been more liberal than their parents, and it certainly ignores any current situations which lead modern youth to attitudes of disillusionment and frustration. It proposes only force and punishment as correctives. The author of this should read any book or article by a contemporary criminologist. None is better than *The Crime of Punishment* (Viking, 1966) by Karl Menninger.

Let's Quit Coddling Kids

For too long we have been handling juveniles with kid gloves. We have tried being pals and big brothers with sobsisters and do-gooders carrying torches for young hoods who ought to be publicly spanked.

Still the ranks of juvenile delinquents continues to grow. We give them paroles and they commit crimes again—and bigger ones. We have tried plush reformatories with swimming pools and sports and TV every night.

Our kids aren't underprivileged . . . The boy that steals tires for his hot rod isn't under-privileged, nor is the girl who with her gang beats up other girls for the fun of pulling hair and seeing running blood.

Too long we have listened to those who blame "bad boys and girls" on society while the kids stand around and sneer at us and plan another looting or rape.

Judge William Obermiller of Whiting had the right idea when he ordered local young hoods to be spanked, their ducktail haircuts shaved

Comment

Parole is release under supervision after one has served part of a prison sentence. Obviously what is meant here is probation which suspends sentence while the young person is at liberty under supervision of a probation officer. Figures on the success of either system do not validate this claim. Many investigators, including newspapermen, have reported that most reformatories are still places of horror and breeding places for future misbehavior because of the harsh and antiquated disciplinary methods. There are no swimming pools and sports and TVs; if there were more the record would be better than it is. As of now the recidivism rate is disgraceful.

It is true today that delinquency exists in the wealthy suburbs as well as in the ghettoes, indicating that the search for an answer must go deeper than superficial journalistic squawking of this sort.

Making kids repair damage seems sound but insulting their dignity by forcing haircuts and strict

off and sentenced them to spend four week-ends cleaning up the public beaches under police supervision.

We should junk the rule of secrecy and the press should be allowed to name names when kids commit crimes. True the parents of wild kids suffer humiliation when their kids are exposed . . . but there is nothing that the kids fear more than the ridicule of the press and of public shame for their behavior.

Kids who commit crimes should be exposed . . . they should be sent to work farms and made to work. Shirkers should be put on bread and water with no privileges, workers should get good food and privileges. A few days of hard work would work wonders.

It won't cure our troubles, but at least we adults would be approaching this problem in a sensible, if old fashioned manner, instead of the juvenile way we are handling our juveniles today.

What we are doing and what we have been doing hasn't proved effective.

dress regulations is not. The battle of school administrators and others to compel obedience to styles of yesterday has pretty much ended and the elders now emulate the young's fashions.

There is evidence that hard punks revel in publicity. Juvenile officers know that most hardboiled kids are nonreaders of anything.

This fellow should read some of Dickens' novels which helped direct attention to the ghastliness of his proposals.

What this means is that adults can calm their own guilty consciences by beating their children. One would hate to be this editorial writer's pet canary.

CHAUVINISM

Friday the 13th in November, 1964 the National Conference of Editorial Writers spent the day at Cape Kennedy, inspecting the launching pad from which the first astronaut was sent into space, sites from which weather observing satellites were launched and the awesome complex then under construction from which the first manned moon flight ultimately was begun. The day's topic was "Why Go to the Moon —and How?" and it was a fascinating experience to attend the illustrated lectures by former deans and science department chairmen from leading campuses and others. The "how" of the coming flights was answered by illustrated descriptions of several alternative methods by which to get the men back home. There seemed, however, to be only one "why." That was to restore the prestige that the United States presumably lost when the Russians put up sputnik in 1957. All day long not one scientist spoke one word to elucidate any potential scientific value of the Apollo program. Today scientists and even some editorial writers can enumerate a few, but at least on that occasion those in charge of the program believed they should soft-pedal them and impress editorial writers, the supposed molders of American opinion, with the political significance of the venture.

There were some who heard and thought the message was great. They were the ones whose pages often make one believe they think every day is the Fourth of July or their readership confined to Bob Hope and John Wayne fan clubs. Patriotism is one thing, when it is properly defined; chauvinism is something else again. Flag waving and sabre rattling usually discourage rather than encourage rational consideration of a problem. They lead to vitriolic stereotyping and name calling to befuddle the issues involved.

Perfectly illustrative of the discussion so far was the following editorial which appeared in the Columbia, (S.C.) *State* for Aug. 18, 1971.

Fickle America Summon Astronauts Back to Earth

It is a curious thing. "The American public was prepared to wait ten years to see men standing on the Moon," *The Economist* observed last week, somewhat flabbergasted, "but two more to see what they can do when they get there have proved too many." The Apollo program, the British magazine notes, has been cut to ribbons.

The space program remains, in vestigal form. But the space program and the Apollo program are not at all the same things, and the Apollo program—in step with a decline in the public's interest—has petered out. Several of Apollo's rockets have been diverted to the orbiting laboratory project—nothing more than an American imitation of the Soviet sky-lab. And the space budget, pinched to $2½ billion,

Comment

Clever to use a foreign journal for the news peg. "Cut to ribbons" is an exaggeration.

Considering the nation's social needs, $2½ billion hardly seems a "pinch."

No indication of what our men on the moon should do. Total ignoring of any scientific value there might be.

probably is too small now to sustain a manned space program.

"When the last two scheduled Moon landings have been made," *The Economist* points out, "the Americans will not be able to go back there this decade." Will we go there in the 1980s? Ever again?

What is most incredible is abandonment of the lunar program at the moment of success in order, as our British critics note, to tag along after the Russians. The Soviets have made orbiting laboratories their specialty while pooh-poohing the U.S. man-in-space program they have been unable to duplicate. In terms of national prestige alone, it is a disastrous turn.

But there is more than prestige involved. It is not being visionary—not anymore—to assert that the exploration of space is linked with the future progress of man and man's civilization. When Neil Armstrong took his giant leap for mankind, he lifted history out of one groove and set it in another.

That is the urgency of the Apollo program. Try as one will, there is no way to get history back into the old rut. The only question is whether this country or some other is going to control the future development of space.

The outlook is not especially bright for the United States. America is preoccupied with other things, with down-to-earth things, with creature comforts. NASA had expected the thrill of Apollo 11 to last, but it didn't. America is calling home her astronauts, and we regret it.

What follows is a forceful exposition of the "my country, right or wrong" doctrine. Its success may mean the stifling of dissent. This editorial, with its theme that everything is the fault of a minority, outside agitators and troublemakers, appeared in the Phoenix *Arizona Republic* and the Indianapolis *Star* for May 23, 1971. Both papers are owned by Eugene C. Pulliam.

Stop It, Anti-Americans!

Stop it, you anti-Ameicans! Stop criticizing everything and everybody and every motive and every action except your own. Stop con-

What is "the moment of success"? Our men have landed and returned with rock specimens after setting up instruments for scientific experiments. What would "success" be? A permanent settlement on the moon?

Anything Russian must be inferior. The Russians are studying and data gathering also by other methods. It would seem that the international competition is what is nonsensical. Why not cooperate rather than compete so far away from home battlefields?

This is too vague.

What was history's "old rut" anyway? First indication that space is to be developed, and just what does that mean?

Why is the outlook black? Is it wrong to be preoccupied with other things? How will men on the moon bring peace and security to men on earth?

Comment

Who's he talking about? Who's doing all this? Are dissent and criticism anti-American? He says so. This is name calling without naming names.

stantly sniping at your government. What in the world is the matter with you? You have the most wonderful nation on earth, a nation that has gone to extraordinary lengths to uplift the poor, feed the hungry, comfort the afflicted, and extend justice to everyone. Yet here you are, applauding the very people who degrade and mock America, who tell you how selfish and corrupt Americans are.

Your own eyes and your own common sense should tell you that in no other land, under no other system, is the individual more respected or better treated. Nowhere is a person as free to do what he wants with his life. Nowhere in the world, despite our occasional overemphasis on getting and spending, are charity and service to mankind more practiced or revered than right here in America.

So what? That's what we all want.

For the past couple of years you have allowed a small handful of hypocritical critics to flagellate us and our government.

Who?

Be realistic, America. Where is your sense of proportion? We aren't a debased or rotten nation. We have our share of criminal misfits, but most of us are pretty decent people— hard-working, law-abiding, God-fearing. All of us want a better life for ourselves and our children, and most of us want a better life for our neighbors too.

O.K., take a bromide and cool off.

But this anti-Americanism is corrupting our national soul. It's having a harmful effect on our children, who are beginning to believe it. This false picture is making it easier for the haters, the doomsayers and the malcontents, those with the biggest mouths and the smallest consciences, to mislead and confuse us. It is twisting our values, making it difficult for our children to know right from wrong.

All what anti-Americanism? Who's hurting what children and how? What false picture?

Thousands of American boys have been killed in Vietnam by being trapped in Viet Cong villages where men, women and children were paraded as villagers, when actually they were armed with Viet Cong cocktails, bombs and what have you. Our boys were trying to be decent to the villagers and suddenly they found themselves completely surrounded by the whole village, armed to the teeth. But the poor bleeding hearts in America, these anti-American so-called patriots, instead of having

And hundreds of thousands of Vietnamese have been murdered by Americans who are far away from home.

any sympathy for our boys, who of course had to fight back, felt sorry for the old men and children who got hurt in the mix-up. Of course they would get hurt in that kind of a mess. We had a lot of boys killed in that action. The anti-Americans had no sympathy for our boys, but they had all kinds of sympathy for the poor villagers who were simply used, innocently or otherwise, by the Viet Cong. This is war, make no mistake about it, but these anti-American loudmouths seem to believe we have no right to wage it in our own defense.

The leading cry of anti-war groups has been, "Bring the boys home."

One United States senator actually made a statement that the American prisoners of war in Hanoi might as well just stay there, because they certainly wouldn't have been prisoners of war if they had had enough sense not to enlist for a useless and barbaric war. Well, the facts are they didn't enlist—they were drafted. And many of the very same men who voted to support President Kennedy when he went into Vietnam and who supported the Tonkin Resolution, later, when the war became unpopular, turned about face and blamed the whole thing on President Johnson. And now they are blaming the war on President Nixon, who didn't have a single thing to do with starting this war. But the very men who are loudest in their criticism of President Nixon and the present situation in Vietnam, which is gradually being solved, are the very ones who really helped start the whole mess. This is the worst display of national hypocrisy we have ever witnessed in this country.

Who said this? Why protect him if it's so?

Nobody had an imagination big enough to envision what it would lead to. Johnson's Bay of Tonkin resolution has been proved a hoax. Nixon is the most recent agent of the forces that profit from the imperialistic venture.

The majority of Americans thought they were voting for peace in 1964 and 1968 and applauded Nixon's statement that he had a plan to end the war.

It is unbelievable that so small a minority of Americans could create such a terrible atmosphere in this country. If it were not for the loudmouths the world would not know anything about what is going on here, because it is so much more peaceful here, and safer, than anyplace else in the world. But to hear these bleeding hearts yell, you would think Russia is a Utopia compared to America.

This is paranoic thinking, dragging Russia in. How about Benedict Arnold, John Wilkes Booth and Al Capone?

Stop this anti-American rot. Because if you don't, America's youth will be consumed by the stench of this hypocritical rhetoric.

What rot? What hypocritical rhetoric.

Stop it, America, before it is too late!—*E.C.P.*

It would be difficult to find a worse example of distorted logic, angry and ignorant name calling, nonsensical ranting and raving in support of nothing. The issue seems to be Americanism, so how about the following from the Des Moines *Register* of Dec. 15, 1951 as an exhortation to uphold that principle? This is a different kind of defense of patriotism.

When Fury Displaces Thought and Reason

One reason why a democratic people should fear the political virus known as "McCarthyism" is simply that it is so dangerously contagious. The poisonous techniques of name-calling, impugning guilt by association, character assassination, smearing, and casting "the big doubt" are easily spread—from the national level on down to states and local communities.

A lawsuit currently being held in Fairmont, W. Va., affords a good illustration. Last March, Dr. Luella R. Mundel, then head of the art department at Fairmont State College, attended an "anti-subversive seminar" sponsored by the local American Legion.

During the question period, she objected to the idea that college faculties are "overrun by Communists," and deplored the fact that genuine "liberals" and Communists are often indiscriminately lumped together.

The vice president of the West Virginia State Board of Education, Mrs. Thelma B. Loudin, was present at the seminar, and at the next Board meeting, in May, she is reported to have said: "That woman (Dr. Mundel) is not fit to be on a college faculty. She is a poor security risk." Later on, Mrs. Loudin told Dr. George Hand, president of Fairmont State College, that "by poor security risk, I meant she is a poor teacher"!

President Hand called in the FBI to check the "security risk" charge. It conducted an exhaustive investigation of Dr. Mundel's competence as a teacher, which included a thorough questioning of her colleagues on the faculty and all students majoring in art.

As a result of these inquiries, Hand recommended to the board that Dr. Mundel should not only be kept on the staff, but given a higher salary.

The Board ignored this recommendation. In July, after considering also "the allegation that Dr. Mundel had on occasion declared herself to be an atheist," the Board voted to discharge the art teacher—"for the good of the college."

Dr. Mundel subsequently filed a $100,000 slander suit against Mrs. Loudin, and the trial opened last week. Thus far, Mrs. Loudin's defense counsel, Senator Matthew M. Neely (D-W. Va.), has made Dr. Mundel's paintings and religious views the center of the whole controversy!

The Constitution of West Virginia says: "No religious or political test oath shall be required as a prerequisite or qualification to vote, serve as a juror, sue, plead, appeal, or pursue any profession or employment."

But the rabble-rousing of demagogs can pervert Constitutions, as easily as it can damage the professional reputation of an art teacher who speaks her mind at an "anti-subversive" forum.

Summary: Dr. Mundel's civil liberties are being violated.

Lest the examples so far seem discouraging, here's one in which there's an expression of progress and hope. It's brief, to the point and specific. No vague name-calling but definite details. It appeared in the Easton (Pa.) *Express* for Oct. 15, 1954.

We're Moving Ahead

The reasons why Communist intrigue has been an utter failure in this Lehigh Valley area and the nation generally are quite evident. Communism thrives most vigorously on social discontent, and here, such discontent is relatively negligible.

Every day that passes signals progress in the effort to make the United States truly the land of equal rights and equal opportunity envisioned by the men—and radical men for their era they were, indeed—who founded our nation.

In Arkansas, the Democratic party has placed three Negroes on its state committee. More Negro appointments are being considered in keeping with a pledge for proper representation.

In New York, one of the greatest singers of our age, Marion Anderson, has signed a contract to perform with the Metropolitan Opera. Miss Anderson will be the first Negro to sing in Metropolitan productions.

In Delaware, Bryant Bowles, Negro-hater and race-hatred agitator, has been arrested for conspiring to break the state's public education laws. This opportunizing demagogue was propelled into prominence by his rabble-rousing assault against the Supreme Court's anti-segregation ruling.

The 1954 baseball World Series money has been distributed. Among the players who shared were a number of Negroes, including a spectacular fellow and great American named Willie Mays.

Certainly, we have a long way to go. But slowly, solidly, we're moving ahead.

Summary: The more we practice democracy the less chance there is of communism.

And now back to earth again with the following from the Toledo *Blade* of Aug. 12, 1956 which seems to be pro-American although Eugene Pulliam might not agree.

Mr. Zankl's Signature

Gary Judd has had a disillusioning experience. He has written about it in the Sylvania Sentinel-Herald. But it is still "hard to believe."

Mr. Judd is a senior in social studies at the University of Toledo. He went out the other day with a petition, entitled "A Reaffirmation of Democracy," on which he sought signatures. This is what the petition said:

When in the course of human events it becomes necessary to dissolve the political bands which have connected them with one another, and to assume among

the powers of the earth the separate and equal station to which the Laws of Nature and of Nature's God entitle them, a decent respect to the opinions of mankind requires that they should declare the causes which impel them to the separation.

We hold these truths to be self-evident, that all men are created equal, that they are endowed by their Creator with certain Unalienable Rights, that among these are Life, Liberty, and the pursuit of Happiness. . . .

There was more to the text of Mr. Judd's petition, including a statement that "when a long train of abuses and usurpations . . . evinces a design to reduce them under absolute despotism, it is their right, it is their duty, to throw off such Government." For the petition consisted of three paragraphs of the Declaration of Independence.

But although he spent most of a day circulating his petition, Mr. Judd got just one signature. Responses varied from the indifferent ("I don't have time to sign this," or "I don't care about things like this") to the hostile ("I've read enough of this—g'wan get out of here"). Not one of those who refused to sign gave any indication of recognizing that the text was part of the document usually regarded as the foundation of American freedom and democratic principles.

There was one exception—one man who did sign Mr. Judd's document. He was George Zankl, 3331 Maher, who said "I would be proud to sign this for this is the principle upon which our great country was founded."

"I then asked him," Mr. Judd writes, "exactly why he felt so deeply about this. He told me that he was a naturalized citizen who came to this country in 1935. He chose this country to live in because he believed in freedom and our way of life."

Gary Judd is not, in fact, the first to be disillusioned at finding how few Americans today will put their signatures to the words in which this nation's aspirations first were formally expressed. His experience differs principally from those of others previously thus rebuffed in that he found one man who was proud to put down his name to endorse the principle on which the United States was founded.

George Zankl's signature may be a lonely one. But how brightly it shines there in support of those truths which some Americans no longer seem to hold self-evident.

Summary: Most Americans apparently are ignorant of and take lightly their democratic liberties.

DOGMA

It is to be expected that the publication of a special interest group should express editorial opinions consistent with the principles and objectives of the sponsorship. A Roman Catholic paper naturally favors federal aid for parochial schools; a temperance magazine opposes any extension of the right to sell intoxicating beverages, a labor union publication supports legislation for a higher minimum wage. And so on.

Such editorial stands are conscious and honest. They are what subscribers want and expect. They provide readers with argumentative ammunition for use during polemics with relatives, friends and others. They emphasize the importance and relevancy of matters which otherwise might escape the attention of the constituency. The sage editorial writer explains the significance of events in terms of the interest group's predilections. In other words, he gives his readers what they want and with which they are predisposed to agree.

The nature of the editorial writer's responsibility changes when the publication seeks to appeal to outsiders, members of the general public, in addition to the true believers already in the fold. The danger of weakening the editorial appeal and effort exists when the writer becomes so addicted to his point of view that he sacrifices credibility by his unconscious bias and/or fanatical onesidedness. Even the already converted may dislike excessive

zeal and prefer a more tactful policy. Granted, anyone "just sees things that way" as a result of his upbringing, education and experience; but the successful editorial writer must try to divest himself of mental habits that might interfere with a rational evaluation of the problem at hand. If he can force himself to assume the role of neutral researcher, he will discover reasons to justify his own convictions much more certainly than if his efforts consist only of a search to substantiate the preconceptions.

Religious affiliation may not be so important as formerly in determining how a person votes, but strong religious feeling can color an editorial writer's perspective and judgment on a specific matter. As a result his effectiveness is lowered, with all but the fundamentalist minority who don't need his fulminations to tell them how to think about anything anyway.

During its comparatively short lifetime the United States has given birth to a surprising number of new religious groups. The most important, in size and influence, are the Church of Jesus Christ of Latter Day Saints, commonly called the Mormons; the Church of Christ, Scientist, commonly called Christian Scientist; and the Jehovah's Witnesses. All three are absolutistic, evangelical, proselyting and fanatical above the average as is usual with a new movement trying to grow. The first two publish daily newspapers for the general public and examination of their editorial pages is a good way to test the hypothesis regarding bias, both conscious and unconscious.

The following is typical of what appears regularly on the editorial page of the Salt Lake City *Deseret News*, the Mormon-owned daily newspaper which declares on its editorial page, "We Stand for the Constitution of the United States as Having Been Divinely Inspired." This editorial appeared Jan. 21, 1969.

The Spiritual Crisis

Will America Pay the
Price of Greatness?

Comment

"We have found ourselves rich in goods, but ragged in spirit; reaching with magnificent precision for the moon, but falling into raucous discord here on earth.

"We are caught in war, wanting peace. We are torn by division, wanting unity. We see around us empty lives, wanting fulfilment. We see tasks that need doing, waiting for hands to do them.

"To a crisis of the spirit, we need an answer of the spirit."

This is what the Institute for Propaganda Analysis would call attempting to create the bandwagon effect. Where is this impressive list of thinkers outside the imagination of the editorial writer who creates it in his own image?

With these telling words, uttered during his inauguration as 37th President of the United States, Richard Milhous Nixon joined an impressive list of thinkers who have come to essentially the same conclusion:

That America is good not because it is great, but became great because of the fundamental goodness of its leaders, its people and its system of government;

That what a nation is for is much more important than what it is against, since no country can reach higher than its aims;

Like most aphorisms this impresses most if not analyzed. What do "good" and "great" mean? Do these leaders include presidents like Harding, industrialists like Insull, labor leaders like Hoffa, sportsmen like the Black Sox? What does "system of government" mean? At the lowest level we have strong mayor, mayor-council, and city manager plans in comparable cities. Lack of conformity also exists at the state level. There is no one system.

That if America is to emerge from the "long night" of discord, distrust, and decay in which we find ourselves, there must be a spiritual reawakening throughout the land.

This is viewing with unspecific alarm. When did the "long night" begin? Nearly two centuries ago the American Revolution was waged successfully by a minority of patriots who won only because of French help. Since then we've had a civil war, several bad depressions and wars. The "discord, distrust, and decay" need spelling out, and, especially "spiritual awakening" needs definition. Several Old Testament prophets and some latter day revivalists have sounded woeful warnings. It doesn't seem to be provable, however, that it's always the sinful who get punished by a flood or fire or earthquake or war, whether acts of God or caused by men. What so you do when you awaken spiritually?

It is the same conclusion that a leading American economist came to a few years ago when he observed: "The ultimate test of democracy is not material possessions, the condition of the economy, or the state of technology, important as these are. The ultimate test of democracy is the quality of its individuals."

If this economist is so leading, give his name. And what does "quality of individuals" mean? People like the editorial's author?

It is the same conclusion that a hard-headed French historian name Alexis de Tocqueville came to more than 150 years ago when he warned: "Not until I went to the churches of America and heard her pulpits aflame with righteousness did I understand the secret of her genius and power. . . . If America ever ceases to be good, America will cease to be great."

It is the same conclusion that can be found in the message of a prophet more than 2,500 years ago that America was a choice land, that it would remain free and inviolate so long as its people served the Lord in righteousness.

In putting his finger, then, on the spiritual crisis confronting America, President Nixon was dealing not with an empty platitude but with the most pressing and fundamental issue of our times.

Just how pressing it is may be seen from the excesses of materialism manifested in a crime rate that is growing faster than the nation's population, with more and more young people committing uglier and more violent crimes.

It can be seen in the growth of *violence* and sensuality in just about all entertainment media, a development that is bound to coarsen and brutalize the human spirit just as surely as uplifting books and plays send that spirit soaring.

Once again, definitions are needed for "righteousness," etc.

Prophets have validity only if there is predestination and it is impossible to believe in both the importance of man's free will and in fatalism.

This is an empty platitude.

The causes of antisocial acts are found in economic and social conditions among poor people; the big thieves and murderers, however, are, as always, in the upper economic brackets. There are inadequate statistics on them. Unfortunately Prof. Edwin Sutherland of Indiana University died before he wrote a sequel to *White Collar Crime* in which he admittedly pulled his punches.

Who commits the violence? The Walker Report concluded that the disturbance at the 1968 Democratic National Convention in Chicago was a police riot. The Illinois division of the American Civil Liberties Union said the same and issued an illustrated report, *Law and Disorder*. Mayor Richard Daley had an hour long television documentary prepared to counteract the Walker and ACLU Report. However, there was not one scene of any violence by anyone except a policeman. The author spent several days at a seminar conducted by the National Advisory Committee on Civil Disorders whose chairman and vice chairman were Governor Otto Kerner of Illinois and New York Mayor John Lindsay. We saw newsreels from so-called riots in the Watts section of Los Angeles, New York's Harlem, Newark, Milwaukee, and other places; there was no scene of violence by anyone except policemen. No National Guardsman was murdered at Kent State or Jackson State. No state's attorney's police were injured when Fred Hampton and Mark Clark were murdered in their sleep in Chicago. The hostages who died in Attica penitentiary did not have their throats slashed by prisoners but were shot by policemen.

It can be seen in the loss of personal freedom that results as big government grows bigger and more bloated; in the growth of federal paternalism that feeds the stomach but starves the soul, with dependency becoming a way of life instead of a temporary expedient; in intolerance and mistrust between races, generations, and social classes; in the increasing resort to violence as a substitute for lawful, orderly dissent and discourse that respects the rights and free agency of others.

As the population increases and Americans become jammed closer together, self-discipline is the only real way to avoid civil war and anarchy.

As President Nixon observed, the answer to America's spiritual crisis is to be found by looking within ourselves. But how? Mustn't a national spiritual reawakening stem from a spiritual reawakening of each of us, individually?

Government gets bigger to deal with the needs of a mushrooming population. In a democracy people are the government. Blind attacks on the system indicate disbelief in the possibility of a workable democracy and by implication favor substitution of fascism.

This would make gasp a crusader for better housing and city planning, more employment, better parks and recreational facilities and other ways to improve urban living. This recalls the I.W.W. parody on a hymn: "Work and pray, live on hay; you'll get pie in the sky when you die."

A spiritually awake president does not hesitate to accelerate a war he said he would stop, with the killing of hundreds of thousands of helpless people.

Typical of new religions, the Mormons stress belief in historical interpretations which nonbelievers call their myths, and they stress correct conduct, both in discharging their churchly obligations and in personal habits. Their food taboos include tea and coffee as well as alcohol and they forbid smoking and unorthodox dress and appearance. Although there is photographic evidence that Brigham Young and almost all the other patriarchs of the church were bearded and long haired, in 1969 President Ernest L. Wilkinson admonished students of Brigham Young University at Provo to obey the rules set forth in a pamphlet by the General Authorities of the Church entitled "For the Strength of Youth." He summarized:

At BYU we construe this to mean that we apply the strictest and highest standards of modesty and propriety, for our students are expected to set the proper examples for the entire Church. Consequently, for women mini-skirts even in moderate form, and for men long hair and beards, and for both sexes grubby clothing and unkempt appearance are not acceptable. Although in the matter of dress the world is becoming more lax, we intend at BYU to maintain vigorous standards.

Editorials in the *Christian Science Monitor* are generally more philosophical and abstract than those in the *Deseret News*. Those in the latter, as the foregoing example indicated, are vague and dogmatic but generally have a news peg. One excellent example of a *Christian Science Monitor* philosophical editorial already has been given (see page 51). The following example, which appeared in the issue of Nov. 4, 1967, is mostly informational but it concludes with a deceptively easy solution which amounts to hardly more than an evasion of the whole issue.

Unstressing Stress

As Britons survey the postwar years since the National Health Service was installed, they find an uneven record in the conquest of illness. A big problem remaining undefeated is simply the stress and strain of modern living.

The medical correspondent of the Times of London comments that death rates and maternal mortality rates are way down, and that certain historic diseases have almost disappeared. Life expectancy, which is a product of many causes including better outlook, better food, and more cleanliness, has increased to or beyond the Scriptural three-score years and ten.

Simultaneously, despite the welfare state, "doctors' surgeries are packed out, the pharmaceutical industry is making a fortune out of so-called tranquilizers and antidepressants, sickness rates are soaring, and it is estimated that one-fifth or more of the ills that doctors have to treat are, at least in part, occasioned by stress."

Responsibility is laid at the door of modern life with its stressful and anxietyridden pace, even in sedate (or swinging?) Britain.

What is the answer? The Times refers to a statement that the church can ease stress by offering, very simply, "the peace of God, which passeth all understanding."

And how to find this peace? Perhaps the prophet Micah gave a hint when he said: "What doth the Lord require of thee, but to do justly, and to love mercy, and to walk humbly with thy God?"

How do you do justly? love mercy? walk humbly with God? These are poetic terms which sound good in church but don't clear up very much for the general reader of an editorial. They do not suggest how to tackle social and economic causes of the stresses and strains which the British authority say lead to mental illness. What are those stresses and strains? What program is needed to reduce or eliminate them? In modern terms it is a "cop out" to substitute Biblical exhortation for realistic fact facing. It is this sort of failure to come to grips with mundane matters and the substitution of vague hopes that the Marxists mean when they accuse religion of being "the opium of the people." The American concept of separation of church and states implies the right to think and act as one pleases in his place of worship but to forget such behavior when he mingles with others to solve mutual problems in the here and now.

Any subject which touches on religion is ticklish. Throughout the years editorial writers have avoided them. Today, however, many matters that were hush hush just a few years ago because no one wanted to offend anyone else's religious beliefs or to start a bitter controversy have become matters of public discussion. The Milwaukee *Journal* did an excellent job of bringing one of these matters into the open and discussing it rationally in its editorial of Sept. 22, 1957 at a time when it still took courage to do so. The editorial follows:

'Not Man for the Sabbath'

In persons whose religious faith decrees Sunday to be a holy day, the wish and determination to observe it as such are admirable and laudable. Not so is the effort to strait jacket others into one's own concept of the forms that Sunday observance should and should not take.

It seems to us that this is where the Milwaukee Archdiocesan Council of Catholic Women erred in its convention resolution recently recommending boycott, the week through, of stores that also stay open for Sunday business. This goes far beyond their own perfectly proper choice not to do any shopping on Sundays themselves.

The position has several logical difficulties. Many members of the community, merchants and customers, are Jewish, for instance. The devout among them yield to none in rigid observance of the Sabbath. But the Sabbath is not Sunday; it is Saturday, the seventh day. There are good practicing Christians, too, who prefer, for themselves the Old Testament rule of seventh day observance.

The Catholic women wade into another morass of contradictions when it comes to saying just what kinds of commercial activity are "wrong" on Sunday. Do they mean to forego their Monday morning newspaper, watching TV, listening to radio, seeing a ball game, movie or play, dining out, refilling the gas tank on the Sunday drive if necessary? All these things represent a lot of people earning their living by Sunday work. Is there really a moral distinction between a restaurant and a grocery both choosing to be open Sunday?

The good ladies, if they would achieve an unassailable position, face quite a discrepany right within the organization of their own church, furthermore. The Catholic high schools schedule all their football games on Sunday. While this may not be stictly commercial activity, it certainly is profane, and not at all an act of "adoration" or "reflection," which the convention resolved to be the right uses of the Lord's day.

All who wish Sunday to be a day of worship and peace and rest can make it so, for themselves. And the more who can be led, spiritually, into that way, the better. But we are pretty well past the era (of Puritan origin, ironically) of trying to legislate it for all. Trying to pressure it economically upon all is equally misguided.

Jesus Himself had a word in point. When the Pharisees frowned on His own busy Sabbath activities, He replied: "The Sabbath was made for man, and not man for the Sabbath."

Summary: It's in the last paragraph.

Even more courage was needed for the Toledo *Blade* to attack a church's authoritarianism when it did so, before Vatican II had laid the groundwork for questioning and discussion both within and without the hierarchy. This editorial appeared Sept. 10, 1956.

Is Study Dangerous?

The action of Bishop Mark K. Carroll forbidding Catholic students of his diocese—the Wichita, Kans., area—to enroll in most undergraduate psychology and philosophy courses at non-Catholic colleges and universities is but another chapter in a chronicle extending far back into history.

Bishop Carroll is concerned lest the faith of Catholic young people be shaken and their patriotism undermined. His proscription against exposure to certain lines of academic inquiry is generally typical of a long-existent belief that learning may somehow be injurious to basic human values.

The notion that the pursuit of knowledge may lead men into areas they are not prepared to chart or track is not new. In an earlier day, Bishop Carroll might have forbidden study of the physical sciences as likely to unhinge the faith of the students. Indeed, so great was the concern of ecclesiastic powers with the contradictions which seemed to them inherent in the findings of a Galileo or a Girodano Bruno that they sought to stamp out the alleged heretical teaching at its source. One's recantation and the other's death resulted.

More recently, secular authorities as well as ecclesiastical ones have tried to prevent dissemination or study of such scientific concepts as Darwin's evolution of species. Some of the United States proclaimed it a crime to teach, or even discuss, these studies. The prosecution of one teacher under such a law in Tennessee became celebrated in its time. John Thomas Scopes, the teacher, was found guilty of the violation charged. But his trial did more to establish the validity of the Darwinian thesis in the public mind than any other one factor.

This clash between the findings and the explorations of the physical sciences and religions men live by has tended to resolve itself in the last several decades. Scientific knowledge has served to deepen and strengthen basic religious beliefs. If it has provided rational explanations for some of the mysteries which puzzled men in the past, and which they had tended to explain in terms of miraculous powers of the supernatural, it has given 20th Century man the more reason to wonder at the complexity of the universe and has tended to shore up his faith in a supreme power.

Whether the psychological and philosophical concepts which now disturb Bishop Carroll so much will have the same ultimate effect, no one can say. All that's sure is there is no way to suppress them. They will survive because they are true, or be discarded as false.

Meantime, the testing and examining of them by scholars of all faiths will continue. And we should think that those who regard these concepts as dangerous and untrue would be most anxious of all to have a part in the testing and examining process.

Summary: History proves that progress comes only when the search for knowledge is not hampered.

More than a decade ago the "Put Christ back into Christmas" movement was begun by a group of churchwomen who felt that the sacred holiday had become too commercialized. Obviously all they achieved was to encourage advertisers to use religious symbols and scenes as well as the traditional Santa Claus, reindeers, sleigh bells, holly, trees, sleds, candles, snowmen and similar figures. No matter how much they would prefer to avoid the subject, many editorial writers all over the country are forced to take cognizance of efforts, including legal action, to prevent the erection of crèches (the nativity scene) and other religious emblems on public property, including the post office and its grounds, city hall and, especially, the public schools. Jewish and free-thinking parents object to Christmas programs that expound Christian mythology and some even dislike Christmas hymns. The fact remains that the public schools all over do close for a ten day or two weeks' holiday which includes both Dec. 25 and Jan. 1, and that the winter vacation is also observed by business. It is a time for reunions of families, Christian and non-Christian alike, Atheists, humanists and free-thinkers generally can rationalize their enjoyable participation in the knowledge that Dec. 25 was an important day in the pagan Roman world and that there were many similar festivals which the early Christians plagiarized. Vern L. Bullough condensed the historical story in an article, "A Season to be Jolly," which appeared in the *Humanist* for November-December, 1965, and is good reading for any heretic who suffers a guilty feeling when he enjoys digging into his stocking on Christmas morning.

The editorial writer's problem remains, however, if the same intellectual rebel insists that the American principle of separation of church from state forbids use of public facilities to advertise Christian or any other religious beliefs. The problem is one of comparatively recent origin. A generation ago the public schools generally recognized Santa Claus, the exchange of presents by lottery, trees and other non-religious symbols which the children manufactured for window and/or wall display, using plenty of crayon, paper and paint. After school hours they hastened to their churches where they rehearsed for the Christmas party at which Santa Claus gave everyone a stocking full of goodies but most of the program was religious in nature. It just didn't seem to occur to public school teachers to assign drawings of the Bethlehem manger and star any more than it did to the Sunday School teachers to emphasize the singing of "Jingle Bells."

One puzzled editorial writer recommended a kind of released time solution which the United States Supreme Court outlawed in its 1949 decision in the case of Vashti Cromwell McCollum, the University of Illinois professor's wife who brought suit to prevent her son's being isolated in the Champaign schools during religion classes. She told about it in a book, *One Woman's Fight* (Doubleday, 1951) which is a sad commentary on the extent to which many Christians practice the teachings of their Master.

The author of the following editorial shows no venom but his "back to majority rule" would be unconstitutional in the light of not only the McCollum decision but also in more recent cases forbidding daily Bible reading in public school classrooms and the recitation of a standardized prayer. Anyway, this writer's proposal would not be a "return" but rather a continuation of the present day attempts to break down the wall between state and church. The writer failed to do his homework before he wrote the following which appeared in the North Hennepin (Minn.) *Post* for Dec. 10, 1970. Reread the preceding few pages on how the schools of yesterday solved the problem apparently to the satisfaction of everyone.

Eliminate School Religious Events?

If you have difficulty believing we are in a changing society, consider the situation which has developed in school district 281.

Recently, a committee in that district offered guidelines for Christmas programs in schools, in an effort to bring holiday practices in line with a 1963 ruling by the Supreme Court which eliminates sectarian activities in public schools.

The results? There will be no school sponsored Christmas programs in elementary buildings, but PTA groups will be allowed to sponsor Christmas programs after school hours.

Guidelines point out that the spirit of Christmas must be academic rather than devotional, and that the study of Christmas (including religious literature, art and music) will be permitted in the same manner the study of other religious beliefs and practices of other cultures is allowed.

Adoption of the guidelines by district 281 people was certain to bring some comment. One of the first to reply was Rev. Msgr. Stanley J. Srnec, pastor of the St. Raphael Catholic church in Crystal, who said: "Let those students be excused who do not care to participate, but make it available to those who want it."

With the ecumenical theme in full swing now, the name of the game is to respect the other fellow's religious beliefs, and we don't argue that.

But eliminate the religious aspect of Christmas from elementary rooms and go along only with Santa Claus, reindeer, gaily decorated trees, etc.?

Maybe it's time to go back to the "majority rules" system.

We agree with the St. Raphael pastor. Allow the practice and excuse those who have other beliefs. And we to assume then that the people who don't believe in Christ will hire private tutors to instruct their children during the annual Christmas vacation break?

Summary: The religious aspects of Christmas should be retained in the public schools.

An editor who signed his editorials and so injected an occasional first person into them, took a free swing at released time in the Sierra Madre (Calif.) *News* for Aug. 8, 1957.

What About Released Time?

Sierra Madreans are about to witness a paradox. Or so it seems from here.

Russia has Sputnik and Mutnik circling the globe. Soviet universities are bulging with young scientists, while here in the United States we are wringing our hands over the drastic shortage of trained engineers and researchers, the inadequate educational facilities and, alas, in some instances the poor quality of educational programs themselves.

Yet we, in Sierra Madre, are now proposing to take away valuable public school time from our children so they can attend religious classes during the all too short school day.

And we also will be spending the public's, the taxpayer's money to do it.

This is not to argue that moral values, as taught through organized religions, are not important. Perhaps they are more important now, in an atomic age where one madman could trigger a war of annihilation, than ever before.

But there are 24 hours a day, 168 hours a week. Our youngsters go to school, at the most, only 30 hours a week.

There are dozens of hours left over each week for religious training, hours which would not detract from the school program.

Why don't the churches use some of this time?

Friendly persuasion, apparently, doesn't work. Or at least that's what the churches are saying when they insist that the state use its power to urge students to attend classes in religion.

The clergy is also admitting that Boy Scout programs, baseball, hop-scotch and other activities are more appealing to children after school hours than is religious instruction.

Therefore, the clergy, or at least that section of it which is pressing for released time, wants the state, through the public schools, to assume what is traditionally and constitutionally the responsibility of the church and the home.

The church, it seems to me, is admitting also that its program isn't attractive enough to induce youngsters—or their parents—to attend released timed classes on a voluntary basis.

Under released time, children will be lined up and shepherded out of the school by teachers. Then presumably they will be met by instructors from the churches and taken to their classes.

Upon their return, public school teachers again will have to supervise the children. And while the youngsters are away, those who remain in class will have to be supervised by teachers.

They probably will be occupied with busy work, since it would be unfair to children not in school if those who remained were taught, for example, reading, writing and arithmetic.

Thus we have the teachers spending up to two hours a week of the time in nonproductive pursuits—all at the expense of the taxpayers.

Perhaps people who favor released time wouldn't mind this. But public schools exist for everybody. What about those parents who disapprove? Is it fair to them to be compelled to pay taxes to support a program with which they disagree?

There are many more arguments, both pro and con, on the subject. There are those who maintain that released time programs are divisive because they spotlight those children who remain in class. They are pointed out as different from the majority.

Others believe the spiritual values obtained through released time outweigh any arguments in opposition.

It can only be hoped that parents of children now in Sierra Madre School(they are the ones who will actually settle this question) will think a little before they make their decision.— H. W. E.*

Summary: A released time program takes valuable time away from students and has other weaknesses.

The Baltimore *Evening Sun* came about as close as possible to proposing a sane compromise in its issue of Dec. 9, 1960.

Church and State

The request of the Baltimore Jewish Council that the observance of Hanukkah be eliminated from the public schools is a matter of judgment which concerns primarily those of the Jewish faith. Certainly it is the duty and privilege of the Jewish community to determine the appropriate places for essentially religious observances. The decision has implications for the community as a whole, however, for it raises once again the basic question of what is meant by separation of church and state.

The Jewish Council notes that "we are opposed to government, or any instrument of government, such as the schools, taking a hand in religious education, however well intended." To this there should be no significant dissent by adherents of any faith. However, the application of this perfectly valid principle is not always easy. There are occasions, originally religious in nature, which have become a part of the community's life.

The most obvious example, of course, is Christmas. To a greater degree than most observances, this has both secular and religious aspects. It would be unfortunate if, in avoiding any semblance of religious instruction, the schools took no note of the tremendous impact of the holiday upon all activities of the community. For children in particular any such recognition necessarily involves using in the public schools some of the symbols identified with Christmas. They

---

*The initials stand for Harry W. Elwood, now an assistant professor of journalism at West Virginia University.

need not and should not be the most solemn and religious symbols. But to eliminate them entirely from the school would be to insulate it from the life around it.

We do not suggest that this will necessarily follow or that it should logically follow from the decision respecting Hanukkah. But we do think it would be unfortunate if a proper regard for the principle of separation of church and state should ever lead to a complete sterilization of school activities.

Summary: Play down the religious aspects but don't ignore Christmas in the schoolroom.

Another editorial, written in the public interest, handled the religious angle firmly but delicately. It appeared in the Dayton *Journal-Herald* for Aug. 26, 1965.

Birth Control Information

It is unfortunate that the Catholic bishops of the United States, through their national welfare conference, have seen fit to condemn a proposed federal information program on birth control.

This is a sensitive question with Catholics. We have on that account recognized the degree of restraint exercised by priests and Catholic lay leaders who, in the past, have recommended against imposing Catholic convictions on the majority. Theirs was perhaps a difficult decision. We wish the bishops had followed suit.

Most of the rest of us believe it is essential that, in grossly over-populated areas of the world, a continuing effort must be made to control births. We believe, in effect, that it is a "sin" for children to be born into an environment in which there is little hope for a decent life. For so many the future is starvation.

This conviction, implemented as a policy abroad, most certainly should become a domestic policy as well. As a nation, we cannot distinguish between poor Africans, poor Latins and poor Americans. No doubt the Reds would wish we would. They would gladly seize on such a "Yankee" distinction based on what they'd no doubt describe as national and racial origins.

The point is that a majority concern and national interest must prevail in the matter. We could not, for example, press ahead with surplus food distribution if Orthodox Jews were successful in objecting to any federal use of pork products. The convictions expressed by the Catholic bishops, though understood and respected, nevertheless should not influence a decision on establishing a birth control information program among America's needful citizens.

Summary: A minority of Catholic bishops must not be allowed to stop our national birth control program.

BIGOTRY

Religious fanatics are not the only bigots. Lamentably, prejudice exists throughout our society causing bias, discrimination, intolerance, injustice, hatred, meanness, fear and violence. Minority groups—racial, ethnic, nationality, economic—are the usual victims, but the ignoramus can have anyone or anything as his target.

Some denizens of the states that formed the Confederacy, for instance, have yet to accept the surrender at Appomattox. They continue more than a century later to fight the Civil War and to agitate and legislate for states' rights as the vehicle by which to counterbalance the improvement in the lot of the former slaves that otherwise might result. It has been a long and bitter postwar struggle. Two steps forward, one step backward, has been about the way it's been. Slowly but steadily the people of the South are accepting the verdict. The trend is accelerated by the great mobility that characterizes contemporary life. Few businessmen any more spend their entire careers in their hometowns. Instead, they're transferred by their conglomerate employers every few years. This sort of thing once was the supposedly sad lot of the poor preacher whose superiors reassigned him from parish to parish. Today, the military, educators and almost everyone else, are on the move, and it's beginning to be a badge of failure to stay put anywhere for any length of time. As a result born Southerners now live in the North and damnyankees have become voters below the Mason-Dixon line. In time it's bound to make a difference, together with all the other changes brought about by modern communication and transportation facilities. As of now, however, there are some old diehards still writing editorials while sniffing magnolia blossoms and sipping mint juleps for refreshment. Here, for example, is a strong states' right plea from the Charleston (S.C.) *Evening Post* of March 16, 1965.

What the Constitution Says

The right of the citizens of the United States to vote shall not be denied or abridged by the United States or by any State on account of race, color, or previous condition of servitude.—15th Amendment to the Constitution of the United States.

However much the President may seek to torture the langue of the 15th Amendment, the meaning of that language resists change. There it is for anyone to read who knows how.

It is simple. It is precise. It says not one word about literacy tests, pro or con. It makes no mention of federal registrars. It is silent as to whether the failure of half of the qualified residents of a state to vote shall constitute proof of the abridgement spoken of.

These matters, about which the Constitution says nothing, are the heart of the President's proposed voting rights bill. "It will establish," the President told his Saturday press conference, "a simple, uniform standard which cannot be used, however ingenious the effort, to flout our Constitution. And if state officials refuse to cooperate, then citizens will be registered by federal officials."

Under the bill the President proposes any citizen who meets the qualifications of residence and age and who is able to fill out a simple form, stating his name, age and place of residence, is entitled to vote. He is presumed, by virtue of having written his name, age and address, to be a literate member of the community. In point of fact, however, he may be no such thing. And, constitutionally speaking, it is of no particular consequence anyway.

The Constitution, to which the President pays so much respect in his public utterances, sets

Comment

The assumption is that any basis for discrimination not mentioned specifically in the Amendment is consequently permitted.

The writer ignores the fact that the specific bills are intended to implement the 15th Amendment and were consistent with its spirit: that all human beings be treated alike.

There is also the 14th Amendment which includes: "No state shall make or enforce any law which shall abridge the privileges or immunities of citizens of the United States; nor shall any State deprive any person of life, liberty, or property without due process of law, nor deny to any person within its jurisdiction the equal protection of the laws."

no standard for voting requirements over and above the brief admonition contained in the 15th Amendment: No state may deny the franchise to any citizen because of his race, color or previous condition of servitude. It says no more. As a matter of abstract legality, a state could, if it wished, deny the ballot to all but college graduates and remain within the limits imposed by the supreme law.

What President Johnson proposes is a whole new set of restrictions on the states' constitutional power to regulate voting. These restrictions have no basis in the Constitution. Rather, their justification is drawn from the administration's gauzy concept of civil rights, and the Constitution suddenly becomes (to paraphrase Mr. Justice Holmes) what Martin Luther King says it means.

This is feeble name calling.

This is not to say that none of what Dr. King says is true. A good deal of what he says is very true. Negroes are being discriminated against here and there in the South and in the North. In Mississippi only a fraction more than 6 per cent of Negroes of voting age are on the books; the presumption is strong that Mississippi registrars have kept the figure purposely, and unconstitutionally low. The remedy for such injustice is plain: Let the aggrieved persons bring an action at law, subpoena the books, demonstrate for the court how their rights are denied.

Thousands of students and northern lawyers participated in the Mississippi Summer Project to encourage voter registration among Negroes. The lawyers were overworked defending the students, many of whom were arrested and jailed. There was only one native Mississippi lawyer brave enough to take any of the cases. Several murders occurred throughout the Old South to prevent the success of the lawful methods herein advocated as adequate.

But this lawful procedure is not what our President has in mind at all. He would step upon the Constitution instead, and he would have us love him for it. "Let there be no strife between me and thee," was his Saturday remonstrance, "for we be brethren." Let there be no contempt for the Constitution, we would say to the President, and we'll think it over.

Whoever wrote the following editorial which appeared in the Mobile *Register* for Jan. 19, 1961 was about as prejudiced as it is possible to become. The editorial is rhetorically deficient, replete with clichés, hackneyed expressions and overworked emotion arousing devices. The words and phrases which add up to name calling rather than logic are in italics.

A Deluge That Threatens Under Foul, False Label

Here comes the deluge, with Sen. Joseph S. Clark, an *anti-South political extremist* from Pennsylvania, throwing wide the floodgates.

Mr. Clark is the *grandstanding political newcomer* in Congress who recently *fell flat* in demanding a committee purge of the *veteran Virginia statesman,* Sen. Harry F. Byrd.

He now rushes to the rooftop to parade as the chief legislative agent of the incoming Kennedy administration in the proposed implementing of the Democratic platform plank on "civil rights."

". . . President-elect Kennedy requested Rep. Emanuel Celler of New York and me to put into legislative or bill form the civil rights plank of the Democratic platform," he has told his colleagues.

"We have proceeded with that task, which is nearly completed."

The "civil rights" plank being put into bill form by Senator Clark is a *horrifying political perpetration* against the American people by a *conglomeration of radicals masquerading as Jeffersonian Democrats.*

That plank would *strike down* racial segregation by federal force in "all areas of community life" all over the United States.

It would do that (1) in brutal offense to constitutionally guaranteed states' rights, (2) *in ruthless contempt* for common sense and the individual, and (3) in *wanton destruction* of good will between the races.

It would open up an injunction-contempt of court process for *bludgeoning citizens into submission* to forced racial integration under penalty of being deprived of trial by jury and summarily cast into jail.

It would reach into the federal treasury for funds to use as *filthy lucre* to lure *easily-tempted* school districts into hurrying up integration.

It would create a *highhanded FEPC to ride herd* on trade unions and employers with a *federal blackjack* to saturate the nation with a racially integrated labor force.

It would make illiteracy a qualification for voting by requiring the unlimited registration of persons unable to read or write.

These are examples of the deluge that threatens the American people under the *foul, false label* of "civil rights."

Sometimes the bigot slips and falls on his face, and who feels sorry for him? The following editorial was written for the Columbia (S.C.) *State* either in ignorance or defiance of the bombshell which an honest medical examiner threw into the case the day before this piece appeared, Sept. 17, 1971. Russell G. Oswald, New York State corrections commissioner, had solemnly misled the press into believing that nine hostages among the 41 dead at Attica prison had been murdered by inmates who slashed their throats. Then came Dr. John F. Edland, Monroe County medical examiner, who reported that autopsies revealed the nine had been shot and none had knife wounds. Nobody could deny that the prisoners did not have guns but the 1,700 state troopers, National Guardsmen, and sheriff's deputies who stormed the prison were so armed. Newsmen were enraged at having been lied to by Oswald, who even described the kinds of weapons the prisoners used, and by a state police sergeant and corrections commissioner both claiming they witnessed the throat slashings through binoculars. The Greater Buffalo International chapter of Sigma Delta Chi strongly protested the handling of the press by public officials and demanded investigation. Gov. Nelson Rockefeller came in for considerable adverse criticism for his inactivity during the Attica crisis.

The South Carolina editorial writer's attitude, as expressed in paragraph 4, is that there is some sort of international conspiracy afoot and that prisoners are a leading part of it. Others were expressing this idea at the time, pointing out that the campuses had quieted down months after the nationwide protests over the United States' invasion of Cambodia and the murders of students at Kent State and Jackson State. The believers in conspiracy as the explanation for any expression of dissent sometimes charged that the basis of operation for the revolutionists had shifted from campus to jail. It is virtually impossible to refute the logic of such a fanatic. In his opinion this would be the best of all possible worlds if it weren't for evil people complaining about it and annoying their betters. All sickness is imported or imposed, none is internal, they believe. Hunt the scapegoat! Catch the witch!

The Lesson of Attica: No Compromise With Thugs

AMERICA'S worst prison riot in recent memory has left scores dead, scores more wounded and, one desperately hopes, a lesson learned. The danger is that, in the mawkish backwash one could have expected, the lesson, purchased so dearly, will be lost.

Postmortems already are suggesting that prison officials erred when, after wasting precious time on Bobby Seale and other stunt men, they finally summoned the nerve or (more likely) the permission to do what had to be done. Anytime force is employed in some grim job like the Attica uprising, those who act will be criticized.

It is particularly true in this case, for the cunning ringleaders of the Attica prisoners took care to doll themselves up as political operatives—Black Panthers rampaging against the man's injustice, blood brothers of Quebec separatists, men out of the same mold as Arab hijackers.

There was more than a little truth in the camouflage, however dishonestly it was worn. These prisoners, under the skin were in fact not *much different from the separatists who murdered Pierre Laporte* last fall as a warning to Canadian officials, then stuffed his mutilated body in a trunk. And they deserved an equal amount of consideration.

This is in no sense a moral judgment. It is a matter of praticality. Unless one is prepared to bring the whole structure of civilized order to the point of collapse, one cannot negotiate with terrorists; and the sooner this lesson is learned, the sooner this kind of terrorism will cease. Airline hijackings at last have become less common precisely because the authorities, finally and after much costly dawdling, decided to take firm countermeasures.

Just so at Attica. As long as attorney William Kunstler ran back and forth, dickering in behalf of the inmates, he kept the hostages alive. But he did so at the great cost of keeping alive as well the hopes of their captors—a thing that ruled out any chance of having the hostages released.

The convicts demanded amnesty, and the official willingness to discuss terms suggested that they might get it—that and perhaps the memory of the sorry deal Canada made with Mr. Laporte's murderers, whereby they went free and a surviving hostage was released unmurdered.

Enough of such deals, for they do no more than get us over one hump at the cost of other, higher humps further on. That is the lesson of the Attica horror; and if we can learn the lesson, it may be worth the many lives it has cost.

The conspiracy and scapegoat philosophy also permeated the thinking of the author of the following editorial from the Shreveport (La.) *Journal* for May 6, 1966.

Anarchy on the Campus	Comment
College students for several decades have been busily engaged in convincing themselves they know more about administering a college than the administrators do and more about academic freedom than their professors, but the current state of student revolt is—in a word—revolting. The latest vogue is to organize the campus hippies and revolutionaries in a raid, not on coed dormitories, but on the administration building and therein—through a series of maneuvers including sit-ins, lie-ins, sprawl-ins and	A ridiculous exaggeration. By contrast with students almost anywhere else in the world, until the past few years American students have been indifferent and disinterested in politics. Some students became active in the civil rights movement after Dr. Martin Luther King dramatized the issue with the successful Montgomery bus strike and the march from Selma to Montgomery. The majority needed the protracted American military activities in Southeast Asia and its adverse effects on their own lives to awaken them to activity.

smell-ins—effectively put out of commission the brain of the college structure.

Admittedly, capturing the offices of a college administration and forcing a campus the size of Columbia University to suspend all operations because of the student siege is about as daring a student "prank" as one can imagine. But it lacks class.

Columbia, and other schools which have been assaulted by their student bodies, have only themselves to blame for the spectacle they have presented. The age of permissiveness, particularly on the more "progressive" campuses, has exceeded all bounds. Negro demonstrators occupied the business office building of Northwestern University in Illinois for 38 hours until school officials accepted their terms.

Perhaps the age has gone beyond recall when a punk brazen enough to disrupt an entire campus would be accorded a series of stout whacks across the posterior with a paddle, but there are other ways of stopping anarchy from defiling what pass for seats of higher learning.

The most effective is expulsion. Even the most dedicated fool has difficulty plying his trade when denied a platform. Most colleges and universities today turn away applicants for lack of room. Ejecting those who prefer not to accept the responsibilities of civilization to make room for those who honestly seem to improve themselves makes good sense.

Unfortunately, good sense is a virtue not found in every college administration building. Which is why some colleges slid into the muck.

This suggests that the majority of students are sheeplike, to be manipulated by nefarious leaders. Where did those leaders come from? And what caused them to become disillusioned so as to want to influence others?

Rather than an age of permissiveness, to most young people about to enter the enonomic world on their own, it seems like an age of conformity without the opportunities or choices available to their parents or grandparents. If possible they would like to restore the real free enterprise days.

Not a paper was misplaced nor the slightest damage done and the negotiations between students and administration were at a very high friendly level. An unprecedented meeting of the entire faculty was called and the overwhelming sentiment was that most of the students' demands were justified.

This is a poor attempt at cleverness.

In other words, say "yah" or get out; Papa knows best. This is a memorial to Marie Antoinette and George III.

McCarthyism is defined by the *Random House Dictionary of the English Language* as a noun meaning (1) public accusation of disloyalty to one's country, esp. through pro-Communist activity, in many instances unsupported by proof or based on slight, doubtful, or irrelevant evidence; (2) unfairness in investigative technique; (3) persistent search for and exposure of disloyalty, esp. in government office.

Although he was responsible for this new noun, Sen. Joseph R. McCarthy of Wisconsin (1907-57) did not invent the postwar red baiting and/or witch hunting and was, in fact, much less effective at it than many others. Nobody went to jail as the result of any of Joe McCarthy's alleged exposés, which is testimonial to their speciousness. Thousands, however, suffered irreparable economic loss and consequent destruction of professional reputations as the result of the publication in 1947 of *Red Channels*, with a list of 151 persons in the radio-television industry who, the editors asserted, were affiliated in some way with Communist causes. The report was issued by *Counterattack, the Newsletter of Facts on Communism,* and the original 151 were only a minority of those in the entertainment world against whom charges were leveled. In addition there was AWARE, Inc., an organization dedicated to purging the theatrical world of subversives and fellow-travelers. Many others engaged in the scare tactics. There was the attorney general's list of several hundred organizations of alleged questionable loyalty, the relentless House Committee on un-American Activities, the FBI, American Legion, Daughters of the American Revolution, a grocer in Syracuse and others.

Any student who intends to engage in electronic journalism should read the two-volume *Report on Blacklisting,* written in 1956 for the Fund for the Republic by John Cogley, editor of *Commonweal;* also *The Judges and the Judged* (Doubleday, 1952), written by Merle Miller for the American Civil Liberties Union and *Fear on Trial* (Simon and Schuster, 1964) by John Henry Foulk who successfully defied the blacklisters to the tune of a court judgment of more than $3 million against them. The late Edward R. Murrow, radio and television's best so far, and the actress, Myrna Loy, stood by him in his travail.

The following editorial is based on *Red Channel's* information and it represents a state of mind quite prevalent throughout the United States during the fifties. Further comment on it seems superfluous. Its dreadfulness is as self-evident now as it should have been when it appeared in the *Park Cities-North Dallas News* for Oct. 1, 1959.

What Kind of Art?

The Park Cities North-Dallas News is unable to consider art as being unrelated to anything else in life. Reference here is to the opening presentation for the 1959 season of the Margo Jones Theater.

Certainly there are actors and actresses available whose political and economic viewpoints are at least middle-of-the-road if not conservative. There can be absolutely no excuse for any civic institution in Dallas county giving recognition to or making use of artists or actors whose political and economic viewpoints are liberal or left wing.

The first play for the season was financed by a grant from the Ford Foundation and will probably justify its inclusion among other questionable projects financed by this enigmatic philanthropy, such as the Fund for the Republic (But which one?).

The male star is Albert Dekker whose long acting career has been spotted with innumerable affiliations with various unusual committees such as a committee to defend the "People's Daily World," "California Political Action Committee," and "Committee for Radio Freedom." In view of this actor's ultra-liberal record as a California State Assemblyman, it is not surprising that he once served as treasurer of Connolly's "Motion Picture Artists' Committee" and supported a citizens' committee for motion picture strikers and the one for the "First Amendment."

The female star is Edith Atwater whose unusual sideline activities have been equal to those of Albert Dekker in undesirability, even if not in length and in scope. A supporter of Henry Wallace and the Progressive Party in 1948, Edith Atwater has been a sponsor of or affiliated with many groups, fronts, and committees like: "Artists Front to Win the War," "Progressive Citizens of America," "Stop Censorship Committee," "Cultural Conference for World Peace," "Entertainment Committee for Russian War Relief," and the "Hollywood Ten."

If local patrons are unable to differentiate between performers with desirable backgrounds and undesirable backgrounds, then there is little doubt but that a steady stream of performances by controversial characters is in the offing.

This is one event in the local theater which will definitely not be covered or recommended by the Park Cities North-Dallas News.

Wendell Willkie, who became the Republican Party candidate for president in 1940 by a brilliantly staged publicity campaign resulting in a convention blitz, brushed off some of the wild charges he had made as "just campaign oratory." Perhaps, therefore, the barefoot boy from Wall street as he was dubbed, deserved the kind of nasty, exaggerated comment contained in this editorial from the Detroit *Times* of Oct. 8, 1942. By that time Willkie had lost a great deal of his conservative following by supporting the war efforts of President Roosevelt, his erstwhile opponent. He had circumnavigated the world and returned to write a great book, *One World,* in which he pleaded for an end to power politics and against the kind of foreign policy which has characterized the so-called Cold War. In other words, Willkie became an internationalist and moaned to friends. "How could anyone have been so wrong?" He died early in 1944 after dropping out of contention for the Republican nomination that year following defeat in several state primaries.

Willkie Needs a Damper

MR. WENDELL WILLKIE is not as secretive as the President when he takes to the open road.

The President says nothing about it—and neither does the hog-tied press—when he goes to and fro up and down the land.

But the loquacious Mr. Windy Willkie does his daily dozen of publicity stunts in the newspapers every morning before breakfast.

First he tells the world a mouthful before he leaves for his globe-girdling junkets.

Second, he promotes his perpetual candidacy more or less absurdly, but nevertheless persistently, while he's on the way.

And, finally, when he returns, the public can count on seeing Mr. Willkie dodging eggs and cavorting in the political spotlight from one end of the American continent to the other.

✿　✿　✿

All of which would be tolerable though not agreeable if Mr. Wordy Willkie would only say something intelligent and do something commendable.

But Mr. Willkie, to please Russia, is now declaring for a second front on the part of the Allies if our military leaders approve.

Comment

"Open road" has a disparaging connotation, suggesting a tramp.

The *Times* apparently is not hog-tied. It is to conjecture who does the hog tying and why?

Clever sarcasm but not much argument.

It would not be a junket if the paper approved of the tourist.

Hardly perpetual to seek a second nomination. Many others have done it, most recently Nixon, Humphrey and Stevenson.

Dodging eggs refers to the single incident when a heckler hit him with an egg in 1940 in Chicago; a photographer got a memorable shot of the disgraceful incident and the country was horrified. Today it should be more horrified by the fact it does not become horrified at the everyday sight of such violence.

You resort to nastiness when you have little to say.

Every nation fighting Germany wanted a second front for its own sake, not that of Russia. We established one, under the generalship of Dwight D. Eisenhower, in Normandy, France in May, 1944.

The Daily Worker, the official organ of the Communist Party, took Mr. Willkie to its heart on the strength of that statement, putting his proviso, to be sure, as to the approval of the Allied military leaders in rather fine print.

But Mr. Willkie blazed forth in large type in the Russia Firsters' minds when he said of the military leaders of the United Nations:

"AND PERHAPS SOME OF THEM NEED PRODDING."

Prodding from Mr. Willkie and the Communist Party? Strange bedfellows!

*   *   *

GEORGE ROTHWELL BROWN, Washington correspondent of the Hearst papers, said in a recent dispatch:

"The Communist Party, up to its old tricks of following the Moscow party line, is the only pressure group that is trying to put the heat on the military leaders and force them into premature action."

We sincerely hope that Mr. Willkie has not been bamboozled into following the Moscow party line.

Let us indeed hope that anything untoward and un-American that Mr. Willkie may say is purely what he himself once merrily called "mere campaign oratory."

Two years hence there will be a presidential election.

No doubt Mr. Willkie will be the candidate of some party or other—only a seer in the fourth dimension can tell which one.

We hope his present tieup with the Daily Worker is merely political convenience.

But, really, some friend ought to try to put a limit on Mr. Willkie's "campaign oratory."

His open-air talks from the towers of the Kremlin to the caves of Chungking are doing a grave disservice to not only his country but to any political party to which at any time he happen to belong.

It is true that the Russians wanted it to be done earlier. So did many Americans.

Favorable mention in the *Daily Worker* was the kiss of death for many. Let any Russian endorse anything, in fact, and any American hesitated to do likewise. If a prominent Russian said he liked peanut butter, it was almost smart not to be seen buying any.

Mr. Willkie didn't write the headline. The editors did.

This was not so. The main obstacle was Winston Churchill who wanted the second front on "the soft underbelly" of Europe, the Balkans, and his inveterate anti-Russianism was the main reason. He wanted to weaken Moscow in the postwar period. The French invasion, however, was much more feasible militarily.

An irrational analogy.

At the time of his death Willkie was in indirect informal consultation with FDR over the possibility of a liberal third party. It is doubtful that the *Times* writer knew this.

Willkie had no control over any publicity they gave him. In fact, his remarks got much more extensive coverage in regular American newspapers.

This introduces a new note and is merely stated, not developed.

A seasoned Chicago ward committeeman gave the author this advice upon his becoming a candidate for public office: "In politics there are sons-of-bitches and sons-of-bitches, but as long as they're our sons-of-bitches, they're all right." That means that you excuse faults in your friends that you would condemn in your enemies. The following is a perfect example of the operation of this principle. The editorial appeared in the Grayslake (Ill.) *Times* for July 23, 1966 as follows:

Undignified News

On our Neighbors pages in this newspaper an effort is made to report such local social events as engagements, marriages and the pleasant happenings of family life.

No effort is made to carry reports of marriages out of our area.

There were two weddings recently that happened elsewhere that if they had been area events we probably would have handled them along with the police news rather than in the more dignified columns of our Neighbors page.

One was the fourth marriage of U.S. Supreme Court Justice William O. Douglas, age 67, who married a babe of 23. The other three wives of this gent from the Medicare set divorced him on grounds of cruelty. Three days after his third wife divorced him she married a man of 27. Justice Douglas is the final word on our laws and moral code.

The other marriage was the third wedding of Frank Sinatra, 50, to Mia Farrow, 21. Their vows were sealed in a four minute ceremony.

In the case of Mr. Sinatra we can turn to another TV or radio station if we aren't interested in him. Justice Douglas, however, can't be tuned out. Nor can he be dismissed by the electorate. He holds his job via Presidential appointment and it is for his lifetime unless he resigns.

Not long afterward, Dec. 8, 1968 to be exact, Sen. Strom Thurmond of South Carolina, 66, married 22-year-old Nancy Janice Moore who had represented her state in the Miss America contest in 1965. Thurmond, of course, is a leading conservative. In 1948 he was the Dixiecrat third party candidate for president. Thereafter he quit the Democratic Party on whose ticket he had been elected both governor and senator in South Carolina and became a Republican.

Mike Royko, Pulitzer prize winning columnist of the Chicago *Daily News* had this to say about the situation Jan. 6, 1969.

A couple of years ago, Supreme Court Justice William O. Douglas got married, and the nation's busybodies were so mad they couldn't gum their food.

They were upset because Douglas was 67 and his new wife was only 23 and pretty.

The way they howled, one might have thought Douglas had slipped her a spiked drink and dragged her across a state line.

The marriage touched off a genuine furore. (A genuine furore consists of angry letters to papers and the disapproval of morning disk jockeys.)

Some congressmen even suggested that Justice Douglas be investigated. U.S. Rep. Paul Findley pleased some of his Downstate constituents by suggesting that the rules should be changed so Douglas could be kicked off the Supreme Court.

Some of us defended the marriage, mainly on the principle that if something offends the busybodies, it must be pretty good.

One reader wrote that I'm probably a dirty old man myself, which was funny because I am a dirty young man who hopes to mellow into a dirty old man.

Eventually the furore died down, and everybody went back to peeking in their neighbors' windows and having unspeakable dreams.

But last month I thought it was going to happen all over again. Sen. Strom Thurmond (R.-S.C.) got married, and it looked like there would be another furore.

The senator, at 66, married a 22-year-old girl. Their age difference—44 years—was exactly that of the Douglases.

The howl figured to be even louder because the new Mrs. Thurmond is a former beauty queen—Miss South Carolina—and is rather spectacular looking.

But the furore didn't develop. There wasn't even one peep of protest from the old hens. The disk jockeys were silent on the subject. And Rep. Paul Findley and his associates didn't once suggest that our national security was threatened by the match.

It was a surprise and a puzzle.

Sen. Thurmond is no less prominent than Justice Douglas. He's been a major political figure for many years, first as a Democrat, then as a Dixiecrat, and now as a Republicat.

He is no less influential or powerful. The senator assured Richard Nixon's nomination by holding the Southern delegates in line in Miami. He was responsible for the slating of Spiro Hoo.

And it can't be that he looks younger. In fact he is bald, while Douglas had a pretty good thatch of his own hair.

What, then, is the difference between the two men?

The only answer that makes sense is that their politics are opposite: Sen. Thurmond is a conservative, and Douglas is a liberal.

And if that is the major factor, the matter should be studied by psychologists, political scientists, and people who manufacture dirty books.

It would mean that the nation's busybodies—long thought to be bipartisan—are, as a group, political conservatives.

This is a disillusioning idea because busybodies have the dirtiest minds of anybody, and conservatives have always represented themselves as America's moral backbone (pardon the expression).

They have always decided what is good and pure, and what is dirty. And we relied on their judgment. As soon as they said something was dirty, we went and looked at it.

And their judgment was accepted because they had always been consistent, if nothing else.

But now we find that they have a double standard: It is wrong if a liberal does it, but it is OK for a conservative.

I could accept half of that standard, because it is true that if a liberal does something, it is probably wrong, or will turn out that way in time. But a conservative should not be allowed to get away with the same thing, although he can be given credit for having the imagination to try.

The nation's liberals should demand that we return to the old moral standards, and conservatives should stop trying to tamper with tradition.

And what about the Grayslake *Times?* Dec. 10, 1968 the author wrote a "Dear Bill" letter to its editor:

> Please send me a copy of whatever editorial you write about the forthcoming marriage between Sen. Strom Thurmond of South Carolina, 66, and Nancy Moore, 22.
>
> I hope you write one because you did an hilarious job on Frank Sinatra and Justice Douglas in your issue of July 27, 1966. I have kept a mimeographed supply of that piece for occasional use by my editorial writing classes. I'd like to have another from you in the same field.

The "Dear Curt" reply was: "He'll probably go the way of Senator Tom Walsh of Montana—which would be constructive."

Sen. Thomas Walsh, successful prosecutor of the Teapot Dome scandal cases, was appointed by President-elect Franklin D. Roosevelt to be United States attorney general. Returning from his honeymoon in Florida, however, he died from exertion in a Pullman berth with his bride. He was 74 years old.

VII

Servicing Readers

The daily newspaper is one of any city's most important institutions without which its existence would be considerably different. The newspaper which has the respect and trust of the community is in a strategic position to exercise considerable power. It is a stabilizing influence, a matter of civic pride, and a force for progress. A newspaper which lacks the confidence of its constituents is not only at personal disadvantage as a commercial enterprise but is a social misfortune. All citizens have a profound personal interest in the development and maintenance of a strong competent local journalistic medium. They need it as much as they need good honest government, first-class schools, recreational and cultural activities and other factors which make for good community living today.

LETTERS TO THE EDITOR

A virile letters-to-the-editor column or readers' forum is a surefire circulation builder. Surveys show it is the best read feature on the editorial page and/or opposite editorial page as a whole. Its importance is obvious. On the one hand it provides a public service in the spirit of the First Amendment by being a clearinghouse for diverse viewpoints of readers. From the strictly mercenary point of view, by encouraging reader response, the newspaper keeps in better touch with public attitudes and questions and has some yardstick by which to judge the effectiveness of its own operations.

Most people who write letters to the editor are against something and protesting. Franklin B. Smith, editorial page editor of the Burlington (Vt.) *Free Press*, discussed this phenomenon during a convocation address at Champlain College in March, 1971, in part as follows:

> Perhaps it's human nature, I don't know, but much of the response to editorials appears to be of a negative nature. This is due, in part at least, to the entirely logical reason that the people who agree with your viewpoint have no cause to object while those who disagree feel compelled to present "the other side of the story."

In an article, "Handling the Daily Mail," in the Fall, 1970 *Masthead*, Barney Waters, editor of the Yonkers (N.Y.) *Herald Statesman,* gave these typical statistics on the extent of the flow of letters: the Burlington (Vt.) *Free Press* (circulation: 41,000) gets an average of 35 a day; the New Britain (Conn.) *Herald* (circulation 35,000) gets an average of 121 a month and published 1,445 in 1969; the Eugene (Ore.) *Register-Guard* (circulation: 56,000) ran 1,658 letters from 1,262 different people; the Omaha *World-Herald* (circulation: 125, 376) received 30 to 40 letters daily, used 13 to 15.

Discussing "Letter-Writers Are a Sensitive Lot," in the Summer 1971 *Masthead*, Smith expanded on the statistics regarding his paper: 2,300 letters were published and an additional 5,000 were not used. In his convocation speech Smith explained:

Why were the other letters rejected for publication? Well, we receive many letters with phony names or with signatures such as "Concerned Citizen" or "Disgusted" or "King Richard the Third." Other phony names, when you read them backward, spell obscenities. Many letters carry non-existent addresses, or a vacant lot is given as an address. A goodly number of letters are plainly libelous or in bad taste. We have several readers who write at least one letter every other day, and all of their letters cannot be published. A great many letters are from out-of-state and are of no particular interest to our readership.

And we receive a massive amount of lengthy letters, especially from college professors for some reason. All of these lengthy letters, regardless of subject, are returned to the writers for shortening. And, finally there are some issues which generate a tremendous amount of mail. In these cases, we will run representative letters covering opposite viewpoints.

There is one rule, and one rule only, which governs the publication of letters, and that is to be as fair as humanly possible to all of our letter-writers. This is an impossible and thankless task, but we keep on trying.

John R. Finnegan, then assistant executive editor of the St. Paul (Minn.) *Dispatch and Pioneer Press*, summarized the attitude of the other participants when he led off a symposium on "The Care and Feeding of Readers Who Write" in the Fall, 1968 *Masthead* with these words:

In any discussion of the letters to the editor column, one thing stands out: You can't have a lively stimulating column unless you have a lively, stimulating editorial page. Your page has to generate discussion, encourage debate, provoke thought and controversy.

As reported in the Fall, 1955 *Masthead*, Clifford Carpenter, editor of the Rochester (N. Y.) *Democrat and Chronicle*, summed it up this way for an American Press Institute seminar:

What creates letters? They are sired in four basic ways:
1. By a clear editorial policy, with fairly strong orientation to local and regional issues.
2. By other letters.
3. By what has come to be known as enterprise stuff in the newsroom, such as a prize-winning series of articles.
4. By the run of news itself.

ANSWERING READERS

Most letters are run without an editor's note. Answers, if any, come from other readers in subsequent issues. Not too infrequently, however, it is deemed expedient to make editorial comment on a reader's letter, either simultaneously with its publication or shortly thereafter. There can be several reasons or types of reply.

Sometimes it is desired to answer a reader who has taken issue with an editorial viewpoint previously expressed by the paper. So, the follow-up editorial is argumentative. Here are examples of letter and reply in the Chicago *Sun-Times* for Dec. 6, 1971, which the paper ran, as is its custom, with an overline, "Dialog."

Selection of Judges

Your Nov. 26 editorial "For nonpolitical judges," urged Gov. Ogilvie to veto legislation which set forth the procedure for the partisan election of judges. This editorial advice is obviously well motivated and aimed at taking judges out of politics. It is further suggested that this can be accomplished by anticipated legislation, not yet passed by the General Assembly, which would call for nonpartisan election of judges, probably at special elections.

Knowing that the fight for merit selection of judges has been carried on for more than 40 years, it seems to me that the substitution of nonpartisan election of judges for merit selection is short-sighted and effectively removes any possibility of merit selection.

My record as a delegate to the Illinois Constitutional Convention will indicate my complete support for the merit selection of judges. Furthermore, I was given the responsibility by the Cook County Republican Party of handling the merit selection of judges issue, known as the 2B campaign, at the constitutional referendum of 1970.

Simply stated, my position is that approval by the governor of the partisan election of judges, would not be inconsistent with the long-range goal of merit selection, because the substitution of nonpartisan election of judges will delude the public into believing that nonpartisan election of judges is similar to merit selection, when in reality, it is not. In the Chicago aldermanic and the recent Con-Con elections, both of which are nonpartisan types of elections, the major political parties exercised strong control.

Countywide nonpartisan election of judges in Cook County would be so costly without party support that only a few persons could afford to be candidates. Persons who are already well known would continue to be elected. This means that politicians, leaders of ethnic and fraternal organizations and prominent civic leaders with good public relations facilities will continue to be elected with the help of newspaper endorsements, because the newspapers already know and are familiar with such people. The sole practitioner and the attorneys from the small law firms who do not circulate in the groups above mentioned would be all but eliminated from the judiciary in spite of their fine qualifications.

The cost of special judicial elections would be prohibitive and not welcomed by the public which is interested in consolidating and reducing the number of elections in Illinois.

Proponents of nonpartisan judicial elections, who are the same people who have been actively campaigning for merit selection for the last two generations, should take a second look at the proposal for nonpartisan election of judges, because such a short-sighted goal might lead to the demise of their long-range goal for merit selection. Besides costing millions of dollars more in election expenses, would it be a step forward in improving the quality of judicial candidates? I doubt it.

Joseph A. Tecson

See editorial "Selection of judges."—Editor.

DIALOG

Selection of Judges

Disagreement with a Sun-Times editorial urging Gov. Ogilvie to veto a bill providing for nomination and election of judges under party labels is expressed on the opposite page. Ogilvie did, in fact, veto the bill last Thursday but the arguments of Joseph A. Tecson deserve attention. Until the Legislature agrees on some method of judicial selection, the Supreme Court will fill vacancies.

We agree with Tecson that the best method for putting judges on the bench is the one turned down by the voters last December; it provided for the merit appointment of judges by the governor, acting on nominations from a nonpartisan commission. The voters preferred the election of judges.

We differ with Tecson on how that election should be conducted. We favor a nonpartisan election, like that in which Con-Con delegates were chosen. So does the Chicago Bar Assn., the Chicago Council of Lawyers, and the Independent Voters of Illinois. Tecson believes such an election would not be an improvement over party label elections and could hinder efforts to get selection by appointment eventually.

We hope, with Tecson, that ultimately merit appointment will be adopted, but believe the day is now many years away. Meanwhile, we believe, the Legislature should take the opportunity the new Constitution provides to move at least a step away from selection of judges on party labels. Parties undoubtedly would exert influence in a nonpartisan judicial election, as they do in the aldermanic elections. But many able, independent lawyers who now shy from currying political favor to get on the bench might be encouraged to run.

The partisan election bill vetoed by the governor was rammed through the General Assembly with little debate. Now, at least there will be an opportunity for full arguments on how judges are to be selected.

Sometimes the reader begins the argument. The Chicago *Daily News* has a "Give and Take" feature in which it responds to letters on topical issues. The following is from its issue of Dec. 20, 1971. It was illustrated by John Fischetti's Pulitzer prize winning cartoon showing a Negro hanging from chains around his wrists, and the cutline: "Why don't they lift themselves up by their own bootstraps like we did?"

Give and Take:
Why don't blacks do something about ghetto crime?

"Give and take" is a continuing feature of the editorial page, in which The Daily News responds to letters on topical issues.
To the editor:

As a middle-class, white American who has been sympathetic to the plight of the blacks, let me say I'm now beginning to lose patience with them.

Their alleged leaders are constantly harping about the wrongs done their people by the whites. But never do they admonish blacks for violence and crime.

A minority of our population (blacks) is committing a majority of the major crimes—rapes, murders, holdups, riots, hijackings, cop slayings—you name it.

Why do our officials—and the press—condone this behavior? Instead of protecting them, why not call it as it is? I've read articles in your paper where you describe a burglar or a murderer who has escaped, and you give his physical description (size, weight, dress, etc.) but the most important characteristic—that he is black—is left out. (Not always, but you and the rest of the media are frequently guilty of this.)

Can't we do something to correct the blacks committing crimes and intimidating others? Why couldn't your paper carry the ball in a concerted campaign to let the blacks know in no uncertain terms that we will not condone these barbaric acts? Let them be deserving of the equality they seek.

Chicago   Ray Hollander

Patience—which reader Hollander says he is beginning to lose—is the key on both sides. Much of what he says is undeniable. Blacks commit crimes out of proportion to their numbers. Black leadership has been slow to rise, and much of it has been weak. And yes, we do try not to emphasize a culprit's color. To do so only reinforces the mutual sense of separateness.

But speaking of patience: The black people, kidnaped from their homeland and sold as livestock, have waited well over a century for recognition as fellow humans. That's patience.

Since the 1954 Supreme Court decision on school desegregation, the black people have waited 17 years for the logical result to ensue: desegregated student bodies and faculties, a comprehensive broadening of opportunities in jobs, in housing, in education, in society. That's patience.

Certainly there is no reason to condone black crime any more than white crime. But until white society provides social justice for the blacks, it had best exercise a bit of patience on its part.

Black crime and the scarcity of competent black leaders, black ignorance and black poverty are continuing tragedies. But it isn't the whites who bear the brunt. Whites pay out their tax and charitable money. Blacks pay with their blood, their hearts, their lives, for overwhelmingly, black criminals prey upon black innocents, so that the complete tragedies are played out in the ghettos.

Certainly, this newspaper does not condone "barbaric actions" by blacks or any others. Just as certainly, neither our failure to condone nor the law's vengeance goes to the heart of the problem.

Our central concern is not for blacks or whites, but for the society in which all hold irrevocable membership. No man who is denied an education, a decent job, a decent place to live, and a fair shot at dignity is going to pull his weight in that society. The story is pretty well told in a cartoon our John Fischetti once drew, and we reproduce it here as the Q.E.D. of our position.

Not infrequently a reader, especially a young one, ostensibly objects to even the subject matter of an editorial no matter what the viewpoint. The following is another of the Chicago *Sun-Times* Dialog editorials, from the issue of Nov. 15, 1971.

A Newspaper's Business

I am a member of a freshman English class and we have been studying the newspaper and learning what it does. I think The Sun-Times falsely leads public opinion, about President Nguyen Van Thieu and what is going on in Vietnam, in the Oct. 5 editorial "Thieu's meaningless margin."

The Sun-Times view about Thieu is that he used his people or forced his votes by his power over the people. The Sun-Times says the United States is getting too involved in the South Vietnam war and that we should leave the South Vietnamese and go home. You say the U.S. is killing off chances for the South Vietnamese to have democracy by repeated bombing in Cambodia and Laos. The Sun-Times is leading public opinion by saying South Vietnam does better without our help. This is not a newspaper's job to try and persuade the public in this direction.

Doug Lyons
Deerfield
See editorial "A newspaper's business."—Editor.

A Newspaper's Business

A member of a high school English class in Deerfield writes in today's Letters column that The Sun-Times in its editorials is "leading public opinion by saying South Vietnam does better without (U.S.) help." He also says it is "not a newspaper's job to try to persuade the public in this direction."

With all due respect, we believe that persuading the public—on the editorial pages—is precisely a newspaper's role. This is perhaps an obvious statement, but it is sometimes a good idea to restate fundamentals and to think a bit about why they are fundamentals.

What is an editorial, exactly? Is it the personal opinion of the publisher? Is it the view of the individual editorial writer? Or is it the distilling of a great many ideas—"inputs," in computer terminology—into a single argument?

The answer is that it is at times all of these things. An editorial is the view of the publisher as an individual inasmuch as it represents a position with which he does not totally disagree; after all, it's his newspaper.

The editorial writer's opinion and expertise also enter into "leading public opinion;" it's what he's hired to do. So do the opinions and expertise of the editors, as well as those of reporters.

What it all adds up to—or at least we hope it does—is the expression of opinion by the newspaper as an institution. And the opinion is not lightly held. On most subjects, we discuss and argue (Lord, do we argue!), so that the distillation is a reasoned argument, backed up by facts and experience. While we do not presume to tell the reader what to think, we try to tell him what we think he might be thinking about.

Reader objection is not always so mild. Throughout history mobs have been known to burn down newspaper plants and attack editors. There have been petitions and demonstrations and boycotts of unpopular publications. When the protests become extra strong on any particular issue, the editor may feel it necessary to acknowledge and respond. This is what Creed C. Black, editor of the Philadelphia *Inquirer,* did

Jan. 17, 1971 in a signed column, "Reflections: Shocked? The Feeling Was Mutual."

"NOBODY," Nathaniel Hawthorne wrote, "ought to read poetry, or look at pictures or statues, who cannot find a great deal more in them than the poet or artist has actually expressed."

It's obvious he was never a newspaper editor, for having people read more into something than was intended is one of the eternal pitfalls of this business.

Recently, for example, we've been publishing a number of letters protesting an editorial cartoon which appeared on this page Jan. 6. It depicted a group of Israeli soldiers whose heads were covered by American silver dollars instead of battle helmets.

Several readers have said they were shocked by what they considered a piece of anti-Semitic propaganda. Others have accused the cartoonist (and the editor) not only of bigotry but of ignorance of the facts regarding American aid to Israel. Some have simply professed not to understand the cartoon. And I have in hand a letter which takes note of the other correspondence and asks:

"Since this was in such bad taste, why don't you answer these letters? What excuse do you have for allowing this insult to be printed? How did it come about? Who is responsible? I am looking forward to an explanation. . . ."

Fair enough.

* * *

The decision to publish the cartoon was mine. I regarded it—and still regard it—as a timely and acceptable cartoon commentary on congressional approval of a $500 million appropriation President Nixon had requested "to provide Israel with the credits that will assist her in the financing of purchases of equipment that have been necessary to maintain her defense capability, and to ease the economic strain caused by her expanded military requirements."

The idea for the cartoon came from the artist himself, Ranan Lurie, whose work we purchase from a features syndicate.

And though I learned years ago that a sure way to drive a political cartoonist up the wall is to ask him what he meant to say, *I thought Mr. Lurie should be given the opportunity to speak for himself on this one.*

"I was trying," he patiently said, "to explain that the $500 million in United States aid is a very real physical shield for the state of Israel."

He didn't seem too surprised when I told him that some readers said they could find neither that nor any other meaning in the cartoon, since that is an occupational hazard.

* * *

But when I told him that others had accused him of not knowing what he was talking about or of spreading anti-Semitic propaganda, or both, it was his turn to be shocked.

Ranan Lurie, his critics should know, is a native of Palestine whose family has lived there for six generations since migrating from Russia in 1815.

He is an Israeli citizen who came to this country two and a half years ago, after working for 15 years as the cartoonist for Yedioth-Aharonoth, the afternoon newspaper in Tel Aviv.

And he is a former major in the Israeli army who left his family and a one-man show of his work in Montreal in 1967 to fly back for the Six-Day War to lead 300 paratroopers into Jordan.

"We had to end the war quickly," he says wryly, "because I had a 20-day excursion ticket."

His work first appeared in this country in Life magazine. Then the New York Times began to use it, and more recently it has been offered to other papers.

Thanks to this increasing exposure and to readers who follow Nathaniel Hawthorne's advice, Mr. Lurie will probably be asked to explain more cartoons as time goes on. I would hope, however, that he will not have to answer again to charges that he is an Arab propagandist.

RIDICULE

Usual practice is to ignore the crackpot letters and handle those which were written in dignity in the same manner, with respectful calmness. The temptation to deviate from this rule of restraint is often profound and on occasion editors have succumbed to it. Here are some examples.

The first, which appeared in the Chicago *Sunday Tribune* for May 23, 1954, naturally caused quite a stir on the Northwestern campus. A committee of student leaders visited the newspaper office to be given a secret peek at the letter so as to be able to assure their fellow schoolmates that it was genuine. Opinion was divided between those who thought it was bad taste if not downright cruel to ridicule a student, even anonymously, whereas others were aghast at the revelation that anyone could possibly pass freshman English at any university and be so illiterate, so the situation was a matter of public interest to be exposed. Incidentally, "sofomore" was an example of the *Tribune's* own "simplified spelling" to which Col. Robert R. McCormick was addicted.

Easily Misconsrewed

Uncinated is a word, all right, but it was new to us when we read about the lad from Center Square, Pa., who won the national spelling bee by reproducing this curiosity correctly and then going on to conquer transept. Happily, you don't have to know what uncinated means to lead a useful life, and there is a little additional solace to be had from the hunch that, whatever it may mean, uncinate means the same thing and is the more elegant form. Merely to have suspected the existence of uncinate is to prove you are literate.

And this brings us to a letter we received the other day from a young man, a member, as he tells us, of the sofomore class at Northwestern university. We grow in kindness every hour and, accordingly, shall withhold his name and make no effort to discover where he prepared for college or how he ever got out of the freshman class.

This young man thinks that a news item we published about a referendum at his university on segregation as practiced by college fraternities was misleading. The young man wishes us to know that the students at Northwestern "are against discrimination but reserve the right to try and

remedy the situation thru education and tolerance and not by force from without."

We quote these phrases from a 700 word letter because they come from one of the very few sentences containing no more than one error in spelling. Moreover in this sentence you can understand what he is trying to say without reading his words more than once.

It seems that the intire question was brought up by a few students who unfortunately didn't consider several points. Our correspondent finds this disquiting. He believes that certain proposals were impracable, for they have been tried without success. He speaks of unnoticeable progress. He finds that ethnic discrimination cannot be stopped by a law. In a stronger sence, he tells us people arn't going to be told what to think.

Certain princaples were involved, having to do with coersion, and these should not be skipped over. Some things are not pertanent.

"I cannot stress to strongly enough . . ." our young friend tells us at the start of one sentence. He mentions "a third and most potant point," which, he says, "can very easily be misconsrewed," and "you can see how ridiculas the reasoning is."

Indeed, we can.

Similarly, the Chicago *Daily Tribune* published the following editorial Jan. 25, 1956 with perplexed indignation with which it is difficult to disagree.

Go You Northwestern

The illiteracy of many freshmen at the University of Illinois has been receiving attention. Now it is necessary to report that we have received a letter from a Northwestern university student which says:

"Who are the two senators and congressman for the state of Illinois, and were (sic) in Washington do we write then (sic)."

There are people who believe that the privilege of voting should be extended to 18 year olds.

More significant was the Chicago *Sunday Tribune's* documentary editorial of June 26, 1949 which rather amazingly cast discredit upon a prominent Republican office-holder and held up to scorn a cross section of its readership. Some have called the editorial too long; others have answered that fewer examples would have led to the adverse criticism of lack of representativeness in the sample.

The Triumph of Reason

The failure of the house at Springfield to pass house bill 650, which would have released unclaimed dogs from downstate public pounds for purposes of medical research, has been accompanied by rejoicing in certain quarters. During what passed for debate on this measure; Rep. W. Russell Arrington, the Evanston statesman, deposed as follows:

"There have been charges that 'fanatics' are opposing this measure. I have received some 3,000 letters from responsible persons in my district . . . I say that not one of these good citizens is a 'fanatic' nor were any of the letters I received unauthentic."

The *Tribune*, too, has received a number of letters opposing the bill. Of these, a very few employed temperate or reasoned argument. The intellectual caliber of the opposition can best be conveyed by the excerpts from the correspondence. Here's "Anonymous":

May Jesus Christ curse the newspaper, the legislator, the man, Woman, or child who works for the passage of the torture bill. May the U.S. where it is written be cursed and go under. Look about the *Tribune* —lift your head long enough from filthy reasoning and see utter destruction coming down upon you. . . . Who cares when the stinking mongrel brats and the filthy men and women die?

From "Fair Play":

The doctor found that teeth which were transplanted in kittens would grow. If I needed teeth I would certainly have a difficult time finding someone to give me his teeth so that I wouldn't need to bother with false teeth, but would have new ones growing in my jaw.

From L.S.:

Reverse the spelling of dog you have God and dog is the nearest thing to perfection,

love. Something we do not find in the barbaric country . . . why doesn't the *Tribune* expose the racket on $10,000 per quart on white nice milk in the Columbia University?

In defense of Rep. Charles H. Weber, Democrat, who opposed the bill:

If he was not so modest he would have told his accusers of the children's Drum and Bugle corps he was instrumental in organizing his district. . . .

From "Eddie," a student of antique lore:

. . . the Egyptians considered them sacred unto an almost worship. . . .

From S. B.:

Anyone who walks a dog knows how many dog lovers are in this town . . . what this country needs is more boys with love for a dog and the simple virtues. These long-haired sadists from Central Europe never had a dog.

From V. E. R.:

There are other ways rather than torturing and being cruel to man's best friend, the dog, and cats too are a faithful animal.

From Mrs. E. T.:

I cannot for the life of me see why you are siding with warped minds who think they can outmaneuver God? When it is God's will to cure an ill, He, and He alone, will send somebody down upon this Earth with that knowledge.

From G. H.:

Won't you tell us Margaret Rose who paid you thirty pieces of silver to betray man's best friend? I dare you to publish this letter.

From D.A.D.; a student of science:

A dog is a natural meat eater. If evolution is true and man is a descendent of an ape, man is therefore not a natural meat eater, but is like an ape . . . frugivorious. Only taste, hunger and cannibalistic appetite, and ignorance make man a meat eater . . . the Osteopaths have definitely claimed a victory over cancer. They are curing it in Dallas, Texas, and have been curing it for the past twenty years. Has anyone heard about it? NO. The all-powerful hand of the American Medical Association has succeeded in keeping it quiet.

From L.B.:

A dog isn't just another animal. You don't see blind people being led by pigs and cows.

Mrs. E.S.S. forwarded a list of prominent anti-vivisectionists compiled by the American Anti-Vivisection society. Among those listed were A. Atwater Kent, George Arliss, Theodore Roosevelt, Clarence Darrow, Cardinal Newman, Cardinal Manning, Maurice Maeterlinck, G. K. Chesterton, and Mark Twain, all deceased.

"An American" noted:

Some animals are given a small anesthetic, otherwise with the agony they are subject to on the table they might bite these tender-hearted scientists.

G. B. K. stated:

Nobody would object, either to umbrella manufacturers holding their new models over dogs and cats to see whether they actually kept out rain.

L. G. H. threatened:

If House Bill No. 650 goes thru, every pet owner is apt to vote for Socialized medicine.

"An Anti-Vivisectionist" demanded:

How much did the A.M.A. pay you for the editorial in Thurs. *Tribune*?

C. B. K. (also represented above) came back:

How about the head of a large Illinois Medical school; his father, if one is to believe the obituary writer, was a good overall workingman. Should this doctor be cut up alive to help preserve the life of "someone of aristocratic lineage who may some day fall ill?"

A. A. F. reported:

I have wired my representatives and senators to vote against the vicious and much misrepresented House Bill #650 to vote a vigorous protest against it, so I suppose I am a "sentimentalist" which I certainly prefer to be in contrast to the sadists that are sponsoring this bill.

D. K. accused:

The writer of the article Animal Experimentation probably thinks it alright to kill horses for meat too.

J. J. S. was even more blunt:

Who ever wrote the editorial on "Animal Experimentation" . . . is almost beside himself with rage.

Anonymous subtly inquired:

Where do liars go when they die?

We could continue, but we waive the rights of our correspondents to quote a contribution to the debate rendered by Rep. Harry L. Toppin, Republican of Kankakee:

I'm fighting to save the dog that comes from the wrong side of the tracks.

With such persuasive argument from the assembly floor, and with the guidance of such appeals to reason as are indicated by our correspondence, it is little wonder that the house saw its duty and gone went and done it. As for Rep. Arrington, in receipt of 3,000 of these communications, his head may be ringing like a Chinese gong, but bells are tinkling in his heart. We commend him to the intellectual community centering about Northwestern University, which he represents. We commend his 59 colleagues who joined him against the bill to the tender consideration of their constituents.

SCOLDING

Editorials "telling off" public officials and others are everyday occurrences. It is not usual, however, for an editorial writer to excoriate any large part of the community. Directing attention to a community's shortcomings or laxity in rectifying undesirable situations is one thing; lambasting the citizenry, or any appreciable or influential part of it, is another. It's not done very often today that impersonal corporate ownership has replaced the crusading owner-publisher-editorial-editorial   writer all in one person.

One of the last of the old breed of personal journalists was Oxie Reichler who retired a few years ago from the editorship of the Yonkers (N.Y.) *Herald Statesman*. What follows is a typical Reichler editorial blast of Feb. 8, 1961.

Editorial Comment . . .

Milk, Eggs, Cream and Orange Juice Vanish From Van Onto Family Tables; How Is It Explained to the Children?

WE ARE TROUBLED about some $4,460 worth of merchandise that disappeared from a snowbound truck near the entrance of the New York State Thruway at McLean and Central Park Avenues.

Somewhere—presumably in Yonkers homes in or near that section—are to be found the 6,000 quarts of milk, the 200 dozen eggs, the 600 quarts of orange juice, the 600 half-pint containers of cream, the 300 pounds of butter, the 200 containers of cottage cheese, the quantities of buttermilk and the special milk for babies. The value of these is estimated by the company at $2,000.

There are also the 6,000 glass bottles valued at 11 cents apiece, the wooden crates worth about $3.60 apiece, representing a container value, according to the dairy firm, of an additional $2,400.

WE HOLD NO brief for the company, whose merchandise vanished from its snowy location. Perhaps the property should have been better guarded, perhaps a second sentinel should have been posted after the driver was instructed to end a vigil which had lasted 13 hours.

Perhaps the truck should have had firmer locks, or otherwise have secured more adequately its precious cargo.

Nor do we especially take to task the frail men and women who—suddenly confronted with this vast cornucopia of fresh foods available for the taking—shed their normal cloaks of integrity and morality and gave themselves over to the elementary greed that so readily seizes upon minds and bodies on some occasions.

WE MUST NEVER forget that this is one of the facets of our society—when crime is on the upsurge, when courts are so lenient as to make a mockery of law-enforcement and when it has become almost fashionable to appropriate anything that isn't locked up or nailed down.

Let him who is without sin cast the stones. We do not excuse anybody, we merely explain and understand the frailty of the human frame, the allurement of temptation, the ageold fact that it is easy to descend into Hades.

What does bother us a lot however—and bothers us most seriously, most gravely, and to the extent that it interferes with normal calm—is the effect of this bonanza inside the homes of the beneficiaries—the effect upon Yonkers boys and girls!

HOW DOES Father or Mother explain to them what has happened? With what words is the justification made that such merchandise is for the benefit of the body? Are pious words of grace said over such food—an adventure in blasphemy perhaps without parallel?

And if it is all right for the parents to appropriate or misappropriate property in this way, would it have been all right to go on—to appropriate the truck as well?

And if it isn't all right, how is the explanation made to son and daughter and to their playmates, who may have been involved in the dairy adventure? What words are used? What tone of voice? With smiles or with mischievous scowls?

AND WHAT HAPPENS when Junior or Missy bring home other items which belong to another—perhaps from a classmate or from the teacher's desk?

It must be a hundred years since James Russell Lowell cautioned us that we had better not get too snooty about the tried and true virtues, particularly the one about misappropriation. "In vain," he said, "we call old notions fudge, and bend our conscience to our dealing; the Ten Commandments will not budge, and stealing will continue stealing."

We believe that we have enough experience of years to suggest that the food thus misappropriated may not go down so easily or cheerfully, that there will be consciences that will be troubled for days and weeks, perhaps for months and years.

We are simple enough to discern a glimmer of light and hope in the fact that a few persons from among those who helped themselves actually called the dairy company and asked to have their merchandise put on their bill or said they were sending checks.

It is our prayer that there will be more who will find their souls troubled enough to repair their own spiritual and moral fabric, and who will do something to make amends.

WE HAVE TWO reasons for our hopeful exhortations to make amends—and neither has anything to do with the company's losses or gains.

The first reason we have is that we know the importance of ethics and honesty, no matter what cynics may say.

We accept wholeheartedly Ernest Hemingway's memorable way of putting it, that what is moral is what you feel good after, and what is immoral is what you feel bad after.

We wish everybody in Yonkers lives and acts so that he or she will feel good all over.

The second and far more important reason is for that boy or girl in the house who has been sharing the dairy experience.

For God's sake, let not a single child in our city be led into the mind-twisting and soul-destroying path by what he sees or hears or eats inside any Yonkers home!

Summary: I hope you choke.

The Evanston (Ill.) *Review* amazed its conservative readership by its editorial of July 16, 1964 as follows:

Vandalism Is a Community Problem

Two weeks ago, in the annual North Evanston 4th of July parade, some spectators booed when they saw a float which paid tribute to the late President Kennedy.

Last week, at a Scranton for President rally in Fountain Square, a youngster who had come just to watch was struck without provocation by a man carrying a Goldwater sign.

Friday night vandals raged through Calvary Cemetery, tipping over tombstones and toppling statues, in the latest in a surge of vandalism that also has hit the Community Golf Course, Lee street beach and other lakefront areas, and that has included tire-slashing and other acts of violence.

We believe there is a relationship in all of this.

Most vandalism is committed by youths. It was a youth who tore a watch from the wrist of a woman at the Scranton rally last week and threw it to the street. It was teen-agers who grabbed Scranton signs and stomped on and set fire to them.

Police Chief Bert Giddens places the responsibility for vandalism and juvenile crime on parents. And it is a community problem, not merely a police problem, he says.

The first answer usually heard is to increase the penalties. Fear of punishment will deter some, but experience has shown this is not a final answer.

Establishing a juvenile court locally for more control and supervision, as proposed by Chief Judge Harold Sullivan, would help.

A more positive approach than arrest and punishment is providing worthwhile activities for youngsters to channel their energies. An example—both of such an activity and the result—is in the letters column on this page.

But none of this gets at a major factor in the problem. If adults in their attitudes and expressions show little respect for institutions, for property or for the rights of others, neither will their children.

And if their children go a step further and translate these attitudes into action—vandalism and violence—it is the adults who are to blame.

Summary: Members of the community, especially those that are parents, must assume the blame for recent bad actions by youths.

Another journalistic giant of the Oxie Reichler genre was the late William T. Evjue, of the Madison (Wis.) *Capital-Times,* to whom not much was sacred. What follows was a typical blast at smugness in and out of the state capitol. It appeared March 13, 1965.

Youth Sets Fine Example, Assembly Dipped in Shame

AN ARTICLE in Thursday's GREEN in The Capital-Times by a leader of the Madison Youth Council warns that "an open season on juveniles seems to have been declared by several legislators in the 1965 legislative session."

The alarm of the young man is justified. Never in history have so many bills been introduced that would brand, condemn, and punish the youth of this state.

Milwaukee legislators in particular have been leading the pack in howling for the elimination of the safeguards in the juvenile code and depriving young boys and girls in Wisconsin of their legal and natural rights.

* * *

There is bitter irony in this. The state of Wisconsin does need protection, but it is not from our young men and women, but from some of the fearful and bigoted men who sit in the Legislature in Madison.

The contrast between the deeds of Wisconsin's youth and those of the Legislature has been dramatically expressed in the past few days.

Through their courage, dignity, and endurance, young people from Beloit College, the University of Wisconsin and Edgewood College have touched the conscience of the state by their stand for social justice and simple, decent humanity.

The march from Beloit and the rally at the Capitol against the brutality in Selma, Ala., showed the caliber of the young people of this state at its finest.

Any parents who had a boy or girl in that demonstration should be bursting with pride—in themselves as parents and in their child. This was Americanism at its greatest—idealistic, courageous, compassionate, the very essence of our Christian-Judeo tradition.

* * *

AND WHAT was the Legislature of the great state of Wisconsin doing? What kind of stirring example was it setting for our young people?

Well, over in the Senate, the senators were busy voting themselves an increase in pay.

And in the Assembly, for two days running, some Democratic and Republican members were raising objections to a simple resolution asking them to express their opposition to the "shameful occurrences in Selma, Ala."

NOBODY WAS asking the Assemblymen to do anything but express sentiments that have been voiced by the overwhelming majority of Americans—that had in fact already been expressed by Republican Gov. Knowles and Democratic Lt. Gov. Lucey in their talks to the students at the rally at the Capitol.

Still, from both sides of the aisle came objections to the resolution. Not only did the Assemblymen fail to pass it. They refused even to consider it.

The Wisconsin Assembly today stands apart not only from the young people of this state but from the leaders of their own parties and most Americans.

The legacy of George Wallace still lingers in Wisconsin and one of its strongholds is the state Assembly. This is Wisconsin's shame.

Summary: Wisconsin's youth are much more socially conscious than members of the Assembly who attack them.

It required courage for the Charleston (W. Va.) *Gazette* to run the following editorial reprimand in January, 1962 at the height of the so-called McCarthy period of red baiting and witch-hunting.

West Virginia Representatives Stand Bravely with 406 Other Timid Souls

With the courage it takes to swat a fly, West Virginia's six members of the House of Representatives joined the applauding, shouting majority to keep the House Un-American Activities Committee in business for another year.

Only six among the 418 voting congressmen dared stand against the committee which has made a mockery of patriotism and polluted the fresh air of freedom which Americans proudly say distinguishes their land from those where Communists hold sway.

* * *

In the Soviet Union today, a suspected capitalist would be hauled before a governmental tribunal and undoubtedly given a stiff prison sentence. In the United States today, a suspected Communist or radical is hauled before the HU-AAC, asked questions about his political beliefs and often cited for contempt of Congress if he fails to cooperate. Chances are he then will lose his job and possibly end up in jail, meeting essentially the same fate as his capitalist counterpart in the Soviet Union. The crime is heresy in both instances.

"Are we as ready and willing to defend our individual freedoms in the House of Representatives as we are on the battlefield," asked Rep. Thomas L. Ashley (D-Ohio), *one of the six who stood against the HU-AAC, shortly before noses were counted.*

"Fear of taking a position which may be misunderstood will never be a legitimate reason for acquiescing to an exercise of government power which violates the basic freedoms set forth in the Bill of Rights . . ." he explained.

". . . to fail in this responsibility is to invite the same shameful excesses of the Mc-Carthy period which still lie heavily upon the conscience of Congress and our country."

Obviously, Rep. Ashley is wrong. Concern over the withering away of traditional American freedoms—justified on the grounds that the American people aren't smart enough to think for themselves—doesn't even tickle the conscience of a majority of congressmen.

They (included the six from West Virginia) would prefer running with the herd to running the risk of arousing a handful of fanatical constituents, who might threaten their jobs at election time as the HU-AAC threatens the Bill of Rights the year around.

Summary: West Virginia congressmen should oppose HUAAC which is undemocratic and authoritarian.

APOLOGIZING

"It's hard to eat crow," writes Frederic S. Marquardt, editor of the editorial page of the Phoenix *Arizona Republic*, "but sometimes it's necessary. In my opinion, if you decide to apologize, you should do it handsomely."

Marquardt describes the background for a situation which ended in a correction:

The case dealt with criticism of action taken by a Phoenix justice of the peace. The Arizona Republic had never supported Justice of the Peace Renz D. Jennings, who served a term in the legislature before going on the court. Nor had it ever supported for election his father, Renz L. Jennings, who was elected to the superior and the supreme courts. However, there was no political motivation in our editorial criticizing the manner in which Justice of the Peace Jennings acted in a preliminary hearing in the case of George L. Brannin. On the basis of a news story in The Phoenix Gazette, we ran an editorial headed "An unbelievable ruling." When we learned that the facts in the news story were wrong, we ran an apology headed "Neither fair nor factual."

The editorial based on wrong information appeared June 27, 1971 as follows:

An Unbelievable Ruling

"A rank injustice" is how members of the Citizens Crime Commission described the recent dismissal of charges against a man who shot a Phoenix detective. That is much too kind a description for such an unbelievable ruling.

Here we had detective Ismael Urias shot *three times* while attempting to arrest on a morals charge a man who had been arrested four times previously, including arrests for indecent exposure and for lewd and lascivious acts. Yet Justice of the Peace Renz D. Jennings decided there were not sufficient grounds to send the case to a Superior Court jury, reportedly because the state had not proved "intent to commit murder."

What kind of justice is it that refuses to let a jury decide something so serious as a point blank shooting? How can someone shoot a law officer, three times or once, and walk out of a JP court a free man?

Jennings supposedly told the county attorney's office it could file a charge of assault with a deadly weapon against the assailant, George Leroy Brannin. But that kind of buck-passing does not justify dismissal of the shooting. What kind of extenuating circumstances could justify dismissing without jury trial an assault wherein the victim was shot three times?

And then we wonder why the crime rate is soaring and why the morale of law enforcement officials is at an all time low!

The follow-up "eat crow" editorial appeared July 2, 1971 as follows:

Neither Factual nor Fair

That special responsibility of editors, confirmed by the Supreme Court and discussed in the lead editorial above, gives newspapers great latitude. But it also imposes on editors a special obligation to be factual and fair.

With that in mind, we regret that in an editorial published earlier this week we were neither factual about nor fair toward Justice of the Peace Renz D. Jennings.

The information on which we based that editorial, contending that an assailant who shot a Phoenix detective three times had been freed because the state had not proved intent to commit murder, was simply wrong. Detective Ismael Urias was shot once and his assailant, George Leroy Brannin, was shot three times.

But the controversy centered around whether Justice of the Peace Jennings was right to dismiss the original charge and direct the county attorney to file a charge of assault with a deadly weapon against Brannin. After a further review of the facts, we believe Jennings acted properly. And we make this public apology, not because we are required to, but because we were unfair to Justice of the Peace Jennings and therefore we believe we have a moral responsibility to try to undo whatever embarrassment we caused him.

A further editorial from the same newspaper dealt with a case involving another newspaper in another city. The following appeared in the *Arizona Republic* for Oct. 26, 1970.

Admitting a Mistake

In these days the mass media are under massive attacks for "slanting news." Critics of the press have suggested that "press councils" be set up in every city to keep newspapers on the straight and narrow path of "honest reporting." Both the American Society of Newspaper Editors and the National Conference of Editorial Writers have discussed plans of this nature.

On the whole, however, we think it is better to leave the task of straightening out their errors to the newspapers themselves. We have yet to hear a suggestion for a press council that would have the authority to police newspapers without setting up the sort of censorship that is outlawed by the First Amendment to the Constitution.

Last Thursday the Tucson Citizen gave an example of how honest newspapers try to correct their own mistakes. A Citizen reporter, covering the Arizona Town Hall at Grand Canyon earlier in the week, had reported that Governor Williams referred to environmental concerns as "hot air."

In a statement signed by William A. Small Jr., publisher of the Citizen, the newspaper said, "The governor did not use the words 'hot air'—or anything like them—in his speech. They represented the opinions of a Citizen reporter and were attributed to the governor in error in a Citizen story."

Such candid admission of error is rather infrequent in newspapers. Perhaps it should be done more often. For no group of men, no matter how expert and how well-intentioned, can write, print and distribute the equivalent of Tolstoy's "War and Peace" in 24 hours, then tear up the type and do it all over again the next day, without making some mistakes.

The Peoria (Ill.) *Journal Star* ran an editorial, "An Apology to the Lees," June 1, 1968, but to appreciate the impact it is necessary to first read the May 27, 1968 editorial which provoked a reader's letter. That editorial was as follows:

Stop Hoover

The suggestion that the new swimming pool at Peoria High School be named after

Herbert Hoover caught us by surprise. It had never occurred to us that the pool would be called anything but the Peoria High pool.

And the argument of the swimming committee chairman that it should be named for Hoover because he is one of the "few presidents who hasn't been commemorated by a school district structure" just doesn't hold water—not when a simple look reveals that there are 26 other presidents whose names aren't attached to school district property.

And some of those other 26 unhonored names are indeed a match for Hoover—Tyler, Fillmore, Pierce, Arthur, Van Buren, Taft and Harding, for example.

Seriously, though, the Peoria public school system has a nomenclature problem.

Nobody can argue with names like Washington and Jefferson and Lincoln. Nor with the names of the martyrs Garfield and McKinley.

But why do we have schools named after Coolidge and Harrison (we're not sure if it's Benjamin or William Henry) and none named after Ulysses S. Grant, who except for Lincoln was the only Illinoisan to hold the presidency?

And why do we have a school named jointly for James G. Blaine—that "Continental liar from the state of Maine"—and somebody named Sumner? For what is he remembered? Fort Sumner or Sumner's Folly?

How about Northmoor? Is it named after the golf course or the road?

Why has Sterling Avenue been "honored"?

And why is Rolling Acres the only subdivision in town which has been "memorialized"?

Names like Longfellow and Irving, Whittier and Franklin and even Greeley make sense, but what did Robert E. Lee ever do for this country except hurt it?

Why call a school Reservoir for a reservoir that isn't there anymore?

It's hard to kick about the names of local heroes like Loucks, Trewyn, Woodruff, Hines, Kingman, Sipp, and Tyng? It's also hard to defend them, too.

Why do we have a Von Steuben and not a LaFayette?

And why a Webster and no Brittanica?

Why a Columbia and no Vinlandia? *And why a White and no Black?*

The name of Peoria High itself is a problem. Half the people in town call the place Central.

And the name of Manual High is outdated, too. It ought to be modernized. How does Hydramatic High sound?

Yes, we do have problems and the School Board ought to be careful before they jump at the name Hoover.

Depressing, isn't it?

The reader's letter appeared June 1 and was as follows:

Lee Remark Offensive

It is my hope that your rather satirical editorial of Monday, May 27th was written completely in jest. However, this being true, it was still in poor taste. The remark concerning Robert E. Lee was especially offensive and it should either be explained or an apology made.—E. C. Murphy, 1227 W. Barker.

Editor's Note: See today's editorial.

Simultaneously, in an adjoining column, appeared this editorial:

An Apology to the Lees

". . . what did Robert E. Lee ever do for this country except hurt it?"

We asked this question in an editorial this week which made fun of some of the names which have been hung on Peoria's public schools. A letter in today's forum expresses the hope that our bit of satire was written completely in jest and suggests that we either explain or make an apology for the remark about Lee.

First, we will try to explain why we haven't got much use for Robert E. Lee.

What he did for the United States of America is a matter of detailed history. For 36 years he was a good soldier, but at the most critical moment in American history he declined Abraham Lincoln's call to command our nation's armies and instead led armies against our nation.

Lee was a good general, but eventually his armies lost. He was a good loser, a man of high personal character, genuine humility, and selflessness. As an example to other southerners, he applied for amnesty but our government never gave it to him.

Lee was a traitor of the highest order, but because he was sorry some romantic historians have seen fit to forgive him. They stress his generalship at Second Bull Run and Chancellorsville. They minimize his treason.

We can not and should not minimize it. Certainly not today when a new breed of "copperheads" would lead some to think that the high personal character, genuine humility, and selflessness involved in burning a draft card is somewhat honorable.

For touching a match to a draft card today, a man may be sent to jail. For doing what Lee did today a general would be stood against a wall and shot. Lee instead turned over his sword and retired to a college presidency.

That, more or less, is why we bothered to pick on Robert E. Lee.

However, an apology is in order. Not to those who honor the memory of Robert E. Lee, but to those who honor the memory of John Lee, the 19th century Peoria politician for whom Lee School was actually named.

Just because part of the man's name was Lee doesn't make him all bad.

STRAIGHTENING THE RECORD

Some editorials perform the same function as a question and answer column. Often this is in direct response to a reader's inquiry; other times it is in recognition of widespread ignorance or misconceptions regarding a matter. The following letter appeared in the Chicago *Sun-Times* for Feb. 21, 1953 and raised a point about which public housing authorities have tried to inform the public for more than a quarter century, up to and including the present.

Public Housing 'Tax'

The people have a right to know how much tax was lost to the city by the socialization of Chicago's transportation system. We also have a right to know how much tax would be paid by housing projects if they were privately owned. Taking federal money and paying it to cities in lieu of taxes is the same as taking money out of one pocket and putting it in another. We would be money ahead if this phony procedure were stopped. It requires a lot of bookkeeping and hundreds of payrollers all over the country.

Now we must make up this tax loss by a 10 per cent hike in real estate taxes. Every time a politician kills a large public taxpayer, he is simply cutting his own throat. We don't need a Communist Party to wreck us. The scheme works well through our politicians.

BELLIGERENT TAXPAYER

The editorial was run simultaneously on the same page as follows:

Public Housing Pays Its Way

A check for $312,669.86 was turned over to the county treasurer by the Chicago Housing Authority this week. This was in lieu of taxes on 16 low-rent housing developments for municipal services during 1951.

Public housing by law is exempt from real estate taxes based on property value. But it pays in 10 per cent of rent left after paying for heat, gas and electricity.

How does that compare with tax payments? The 1951 "service charge" amounts to THREE TIMES the amount of taxes the county formerly collected from the private owners of sites on which the housing developments now stand.

Broken down into a per-tenant basis, each family of public housing is paying about $40 a year to local taxing bodies. Families in the same low-income bracket living in private housing pay through their landlords about $19, it is estimated.

Paste this in your hat and have it ready for reference next time an anti-public-housing arguer says public housing makes your real estate taxes higher. Actually it helps make them lower.

Summary: Public housing more than pays its own way.

The following editorial, from the same newspaper of Dec. 13, 1970, also tackled a common misconception.

Superficiality and Suburbia

In his Thursday press conference, the President was asked whether the federal government would use its leverage to promote integrated housing in the suburbs. "I believe that forced integration in the suburbs is not in the national interest," he said.

Aside from raising the political "Southern strategy" to the level of national policy, the statement is further appalling because it implies that the President has a 1950 view of Suburbia: vine-covered cottages, white picket fences, all the problems of the cities answered by escape.

In 1970, between 30 and 35 per cent of Americans are suburbanites, and they are beset with problems—blight, inadequate transportation, pollution, crime, debt and inflation and lack of public services. In Massachusetts, more citizens below poverty level live in the suburbs than in the cities.

Integration of the suburbs—by persuasion if possible, by laws if not—is in the national interest. George W. Romney, secretary of housing and urban development, is working along these lines. Business needs integration to meet growing labor demands; socially minded planners seek to stop the trend toward the black city choked by a white suburban noose.

If Mr. Nixon wishes to play politics with white suburban voters—with whom he did well in 1968—well and good. But he at least owes the nation some better indication that he understands suburban problems than a patronizing, offhand remark.

Summary: President Nixon doesn't know what a modern suburb is like.

Another much misrepresented situation involves the Aid to Dependent Children program. Some lawmakers and others seem to think that there exists an army of unwed mothers who deliberately produce as many bastards as they can for the welfare checks, and that the drain on the treasury has become unendurable. The Burlington (Iowa) *Hawk-Eye* tried to counteract ignorance and prejudice with facts in the following editorial March 1, 1961.

Who's Being Punished?

He was a cuddly-perfectly-formed baby with soft, downy curls—but he was a mistake. His parents were not married.

Should helpless children like him be blamed for the mistakes of their parents? If passed, a bill before the Iowa state legislature would do just that. This bill would prohibit a mother from receiving Aid to Dependent Children benefits on her second illegitimate birth.

Legislators seem to think that ADC benefits, too leniently doled out, might subsidize illegitimacy. That if a mother makes a mistake, she does not have to worry. The state will take care of them.

But few unwed mothers think that far ahead: A report to the governor of Virginia recently stated that unwed mothers ". . . have adhered to no moral absolutes; neither did they pause to debate the consequences of their behavior."

Furthermore, the United States Department of Health, Education and Welfare reports that the greatest majority, 87 per cent, of unwed mothers, do not go to ADC for assistance. In Des Moines county itself, fewer than 10 per cent of the 67 ADC cases are unwed mothers.

The conniving unwed mother who considers possible consequences such as the availability of ADC funds, first would consider easier ways out such as preventing the birth altogether or leaving the child on a doorstep.

If an unwed mother gets no support, she may have to send her child to an orphanage. Either way the taxpayers pay for the child's support.

When the mother is willing to keep her child with public aid, the state should be willing to provide that assistance. How much better for the child to have at least one person who is sufficiently considerate of the child to go to ADC for help.

But most important of all is the fate of the child who may have the ability to invent a cancer vaccine or a passenger plane to the moon. The most innocent should not have to suffer the worst consequences.

Summary: The false belief that ADC is a deliberate and expensive fraud is harmful to innocent chlidren and all society.

The Salt Lake *Tribune* for March 12, 1969 reprinted the following editorial from the Denver *Post*. It makes the same point as the preceding Burlington piece.

'Welfare Plot Against Taxpayer' Falls Flat

To hear some people talk, one might assume that welfare mothers are, at the least, a bunch of schemers whose chief goal in life is to find a way to win public handouts.

We won't go into the question of how inadequate and unattractive those welfare payments are. What intrigues us at the moment is a set of figures supplied by the Denver Welfare Department concerning 1968.

In the Aid to Dependent Children (ADC) program there were 2,002 cases added in Denver during 1968. But there were 2,508 cases discontinued. That scarcely fits the critical picture of people scheming for a handout.

Now it's true that some of those discontinued cases may have shifted into some other category of welfare. But 633 of them were for reasons of employment: nearly one-fourth.

We wouldn't want to sugar-coat the picture. The number of people drawing ADC is growing. It is costing more. But possibly it is pertinent to point out that a lot of people go off welfare. A goodly number did so because they were able to go to work. With the work incentive program now in effect, as of Jan. 1, the number should rise in 1969.

We hope the statistic surprises a few people, namely those who think all welfare is a plot against the taxpayer.

Summary: Same as for the preceding editorial.

EVALUATING HISTORY

The usual practice, when an important new historical discovery is announced, is to leave its evaluation to experts, including those on the paper's own staff or available to it. Editorial comment may be merely to direct attention to the new development. More likely the occasion will inspire some editorial writer with a flair for witty or sagacious remarks to utilize his talent. An example is the following from the New York *Times* for Jan. 6, 1972.

Do Not Open Before 2014

The Republic will undoubtedly stand the suspense of the court-ordered postponement until 2014 of the publication of President Warren G. Harding's love letters to Mrs. Carrie Phillips. Most historians, though personally and professionally disappointed, will probably agree with the conclusion of one of their number that the matter "will not be a shadow across the rest of my life."

But have President Harding's heirs considered the risk inherent in the new timing? In the Age of Aquarius, an indiscretion of this nature would be assured maximum understanding, perhaps even admiration. But given the cyclical nature of national attitudes toward the affairs of Eros, who is to say that neo-Victorianism may not again be in the saddle in the second decade of the 21st century?

Summary: Maybe there'd be less shock over the Harding love letters today than in 2014.

The new historical fact or theory may be used to score a point as regards a contemporary problem. That is what the Atlanta *Journal and Constitution* did Jan. 24, 1971.

Robin and the Poor

PEOPLE INCLINED to hero-worshiping have suffered a jolt. A retired history master in England says that years of research have led him to refute the Robin Hood saga.

Not only does he claim that the real Robin Hood was a noble thrown out of his manor for revolting against Henry II, that he never wore Lincoln green and operated miles from Sherwood Forest—but the researcher had the audacity to question whether Robin Hood gave anything to the poor.

Rob the rich? Yes.

Give to the poor? Probably not.

We don't know how Robin Hood or the noble, Alfred de Hunterden, would want to be remembered today.

But we suspect that the poor would still prefer a hand up rather than a hand out.

. . . Which requires far more money for payrolls, money for training, money for education and an abundant supply of patience and understanding.

Summary: Maybe Robin Hood didn't give to the poor of his day but those of our day would rather have jobs than gifts.

When the event on which new evidence is produced is of such recent origin as to influence current thought and action, more serious comment is called for. Even so the style can be quippish as in the following from the Penn Hills (Pa.) *Progress* of Jan. 6, 1971.

Hurrah for Ike!

Recently released Anglo American chiefs of staff documents from 1945 allegedly have placed the blame on the late General Dwight Eisenhower for the fall of Berlin to the Russian Army at the end of the war.

The same information was revealed several years ago by World War II author Cornelius Ryan in his book about the collapse of the Third Reich and the fall of Berlin, "The Last Battle."

Ryan and these recently released documents agree that Eisenhower, over the objection of Winston Churchill and Field Marshall Montgomery, convinced President Roosevelt to let the Russians have Berlin. His reason was that the city at that point in the war had no military significance.

He had another reason, an even more important one; that taking Berlin was possible only at the price of 100,000 Allied casualties. Ike was wrong. The Russians suf-

fered 200,000 casualties capturing this "political" target.

In other words, Ike is to blame for some 200,000 Americans surviving World War II because he let the Russians have the "privilege" of taking Berlin. Regardless of the problems caused by the cold war and a divided Berlin for the past 25 years, we can't imagine General Eisenhower ever making a sounder decision in his long and distinguished military career.

Summary: Ike deserves credit for letting the Russians capture Berlin.

A universal moral, if that is what it is, is drawn by the Chicago *Daily News* in its editorial of April 30, 1972.

Beauty and the Brownings

Anthony Burgess, in a New York Times piece, reminds us that Elizabeth Barrett did not really look like Norma Shearer; that she was an invalid and "an involuntary junkie souped up to the eyes with laudanum and morphine," and that an American writer described her at 48—only eight years after Robert Browning wooed her—as a "crooked, dried-up old woman with a horrible mouth."

Young Browning would have passionately and earnestly disputed the brash American. Six years Elizabeth's junior, Robert (as Burgess says) "swore all his life that Elizabeth was beautiful," and indeed spent the 28 years after her death in polishing and repolishing her ikon.

It raises once more a question that has been much raised lately by the new generation: What is beauty? And we know that they and Browning have a lot on their side: It is in the eye of the beholder, and it does have more important dimensions than color and contour.

The young people go about in blue jeans and shirts and sweaters and sandals and beads, and their hair flies in the wind, and you can see the pimple on a girl's cheek.

Yet they do not appear to be starving for beauty, finding it in one another, and in a lot of places where their elders never thought to look. We rather think they would understand Robert and Elizabeth Browning without any help from Hollywood.

Summary: Definitions of beauty change from the days of Browning to the present.

There was no doubt about the intent of the following editorial from the same newspaper's edition of March 15, 1971.

Citizen Lee

Virginia's Sen. Harry F. Byrd Jr. has discovered that the Union never did restore citizenship to Gen. Robert E. Lee, commander of the Confederate forces, and he thinks it's time justice was done. Byrd says Lee signed a required oath of allegiance after the Civil War ended, but somehow it never reached President Andrew Johnson.

It shouldn't be hard to get the two-thirds vote needed in Senate and House to pass Byrd's resolution. Resentment against the gentlemanly insurgent should have vanished long ago. And alas for Lee, citizenship won't have much practical advantage. It's too late for him to vote anywhere unless it's in Chicago.

Summary: Robert E. Lee could ghost vote here.

GIVING ASSURANCE

The Denver *Post* handled a situation which is not too uncommon: circulation of a rumor. During World War II the official American governmental policy was to discourage rumor clinics which several newspapers established with the laudable purpose of aiding the war effort by exposing lies. It was felt that to repeat a rumor, even to deny it, gave it currency. This was true especially if the matter involved humor or discredited some prominent person. It is not to belittle the reality of the horror of modern warfare to recognize that there are many war atrocity stories which are "old standbys," cropping up periodically through many decades or even centuries. One of the mildest is the stamp collection of a prisoner of war. He presumably writes a letter home in which he requests his family to steam the stamp off the envelope

for his stamp collection. Even though they know he has no such collection, his relatives do as requested. Underneath the stamp they discover a message, usually that the prisoner has had his tongue cut out. The story is absurd if for no other reason than that prisoners' mail do not require stamps. Nevertheless, the tale has been spread at least since the Franco-Prussian War of 1870. If the reader is interested in the subject there are several fascinating books on it. Among the best are *Atrocity Propaganda, 1914-17* (Yale University, 1941) by James Morgan Read; *The Affairs of Dame Rumor* (Rinehart, 1948) by David J. Jacobson; *The Psychology of Rumor* (Henry Holt, 1947) by Gordon W. Allport and Leo Postman; and *Propaganda Analysis* (Row, Peterson, 1959) by Alexander L. George.

The Denver *Post's* editorial appeared July 29, 1967.

The Dangers of Rumor Passing

Responsible newspapers know that when they acknowledge a rumor there is some likelihood it may be given more credence than it deserves. When the rumor is ugly and vicious they know they must be particularly cautious about reporting it.

Such a rumor circulated in the Denver area during the past several weeks. By last weekend, the news department of The Post was receiving an average of 20 telephone calls a day, many of them suggesting that The Post was "covering up" for a number of reasons. All of them asked why the newspaper had not printed "the story."

There were several versions but the most persistent was that a young white boy had been mutilated and murdered by two or more Negroes in the restroom of a Denver drive-in theater.

Sometimes there were vague hints as to the youth's identity, the name and location of the theater, the hospital where he had been taken, the clues which police were following up. In these instances it usually was a "friend of a friend" who knew the inside facts.

But in not a single case was a caller able to supply the name of the informant who could identify any specific aspects of this extraordinarily cruel and bizarre story. Nor was The Post's trained reporting staff able to come up with a single fact which would support the story, or any part of it.

Because of the increasing volume of inquiries, however, the decision was made to report the rumor. It was felt not only that our readers deserved to know the newspaper was functioning as it should but also that a full account might help break the dangerous chain reaction the rumor had set off.

Apparently this happened. At least since the story was published in Sunday's editions, the calls have virtually ceased. But we are left with the feeling that it was far too easy to spread such a rumor; perhaps the more sensationally evil and poisonous, the easier to spread.

Do people prefer not to have certain malignant gossip discredited? Would they rather believe it than be shown it is groundless? We think not many people. But the experience of the past few weeks has demonstrated that enough people are willing links in the rumor chain that the person who really sets out to start something "big" has little trouble.

We have, of course, no proof, but the current story had the earmarks of a well-organized plant. The Negro-white aspect would easily feed the national feeling of unrest, even in a relatively calm community like Denver. It's not unlikely, we feel, the rumor was started here to agitate racial trouble. Experiences of other cities with similar stories seem to bear this out.

Denverites—all Americans, in fact—have a special responsibility in these incendiary times to be skeptical of casual reports that seem tainted with prejudice. Given our experience with this one, it is not difficult to recognize their potential danger to a community.

Summary: The story of the murder of a white boy by Negroes was a vicious rumor.

A common charge against the news media is that they deliberately suppress important information which would cast aspersions upon public officials or others. There is no doubt that a considerable amount of official wrongdoing goes unreported but almost always this is because of secrecy or censorship by mayors, governors, presidents and others. Attempts of the Nixon administration to prevent publication of the Pentagon Papers, the exposés of the My Lai and similar massacres in Vietnam despite the strong efforts made to cover up, the bean-spilling by Jack Anderson as regards duplicity in White House diplomacy during the India-Pakistan war, and many similar incidents have made the public aware of the existence of the perpetual warfare that goes on between the press and government. It is discouraging to professional journalists to note the continual scapegoating of the news media for bad news and the perpetuation of the hush hush rumors. Likewise, it is discouraging to note the reappearance of lies that presumably had once been laid to rest. The Grand Rapids (Mich.) *Press* addressed itself to one such situation involving its community as revealed in the following editorial from its issue of Aug. 16, 1962.

Old Prejudices Die Hard

A Grand Rapids businessman has received in the mail a circular bearing this heading: "Flouridation, the Crime Against All Civilization, written by Rev. Lyle F. Sheen, Pastor St. Malachy's Parish, Geneseo, Illinois." Since it is so typical of the excessive statements made by foes of fluoridation there is no need here to go into its contents, except that part which has particular reference to this community.

"Scientists worthy of the name insist that fluoridation of drinking water can shorten life by ten years," Rev. Sheen writes. "Why are the vital statistics of Grand Rapids, Mich., so carefully covered up? Why do newspapers refuse to print material that carries any real argument against fluoridation?"

This must rank with the worst nonsense the anti-fluoridation forces have come up with so far. First, we know of no authority who has contended that fluoridation shortens life by so much as 10 minutes, let alone 10 years. Every scientific study made by U.S. Public Health officials and others who have investigated the subject without bias indicates that adding fluorines to drinking water has no harmful effects.

Grand Rapids' vital statistics tend to bear this out. And no attempt ever has been made here to cover up these statistics. They are available to anyone sincerely interested in the facts and they have been published in The Press. However, several years ago an old fluoridation foe, a Dr. Miller of Nebraska, misread the figures, confused those for Kent County with Grand Rapids, and failed to note that deaths from certain diseases that had been reported separately were being reported under a single category as deaths due to heart disease. He leaped to the wild conclusion that heart disease deaths had jumped markedly in Grand Rapids, attributed this to fluoridation, and published his "findings."

Dr. Miller has been answered effectively and frequently all over the country, but his followers cling tenaciously to their prejudices. One of those, of course, is that their views never are printed in newspapers. The interested person has only to consult the files of newspapers in cities where the fluoridation fight is hot to learn that this isn't so. Invariably both sides get heard. The battle has waned to nothing in Grand Rapids for the reason that local residents long ago satisfied themselves that fluoridation is safe and that it reduces tooth cavities by as much as 65 per cent in persons who have been "brought up" on fluoridated water. The facts are on the record for anyone really interested in getting at them.

Summary: The old hoax regarding this town's experience with flouridation is circulating again and should be spiked immediately.

In recent years there has been a phenominal growth of columns devoted to reader service. They have such names as "Action Line," "Quest," "Watchem,"

"Sound-Off," and similar ones, to indicate that their editors investigate complaints and requests for information from readers. The flourishing of this journalistic service does not diminish the power of the editorial page to endorse and explain, putting the paper's prestige behind a movement or proposal. In fact, any newspaper which commands respect is going to receive calls for help and advice. Sometimes it is not necessary to go into details in a situation. Rather, all that is required is for the paper to give assurance. It places its reputation for responsibility behind a person or thing. In effect it tells its readers, "It's o.k. We vouch for it. Don't worry." That was the spirit of the following editorial which appeared in the Westwood Hills (Calif.) *Press* for Aug. 21, 1958.

Urban Renewal Survey

After a week's delay, a comprehensive survey of the West Los Angeles Urban Renewal district was under way this Monday. This is a necessary survey. It is one designed to determine the problems of the residents and to inform both renters and property owners about ways they can get assistance on any problem they might have.

The survey is under the direction of the West Area Welfare Planning Council, which prevailed upon Mayor Norris Poulson to authorize such an undertaking. The council contends that urban renewal done well can have a very positive effect—and a very good one—on the community, but that detailed information from the people is needed in an urban renewel district beforehand.

Already, opposition has started against this survey. The opposition is in the form of a telephone campaign and doorbell ringing. The reason for the opposition is unclear, although such words as "constitutional rights" are being used. (This phrase, "constitutional rights," is often used by confused people seeking to confuse issues.)

Actually, there is, of course, no violation of constitutional rights whatsoever in this survey. The survey was initiated by an agency of the community, and it will be asking for information to be given completely voluntarily. When an interviewer comes to the door of a resident, the resident does not have to answer the questions asked. That should be understood by everyone.

But the interviewers—there will be 12 of them working both days and evenings—need the information they will be asking for. And the residents to whom the questions are addressed should willingly, honestly and forthrightly answer the questions.

A resident might ask, "But why should I answer questions put to me by a stranger about my income, my property and other personal matters?"

The reason is this: If the survey is to provide solid information upon which constructive proposals on urban renewal can be made—proposals that will benefit every resident within the district—it must accurately reflect the community.

And the only way it can do that is for residents to give candid, accurate answers to the surveyors, and give them willingly in the spirit of cooperation.

Everyone should accept the interviewers for what they are—members of an organization that is trying to assist them, and to get to the bottom of the problems of the community.

Summary: The housing poll underway is legitimate and should benefit our community.

OBITUARIES

The last service that a newspaper performs for anyone is his death notice. Most obituary editorials follow the rule of not saying anything bad about the dead if it can be helped. They are written only about persons whose importance means that they will be missed by many and the effects of their lifetime activities will continue after their deaths.

It is difficult to avoid being trite and hackneyed while writing the straight obituary editorial, the one which merely summarizes the deceased person's achievements and praises his laudable traits. To

do otherwise would incur the wrath of even the subject's enemies as they would feel that good taste requires letting a person's evil aspects rest with his bones while his good qualities live on. "If you can't find something good to say, don't say anything," would be the advice of probably the overwhelming majority of readers who have been conditioned by traditional impeccable adherence to the say-only-good journalistic rule in practice.

Here is an orthodox obituary editorial about a person of local prominence from a 1971 edition of the Indianapolis *Star.*

Lionel F. Artis

The death of Lionel F. Artis at the age of 75 terminates a life of almost unbelievably broad and deep service to this community.

In terms of vocation he had two careers, as executive secretary of the old Senate Avenue YMCA and as manager for 25 years of the Lockefield Gardens public housing facility. In both jobs he served effectively and with distinction.

But his real career was as an unpaid volunteer in a wide variety of organizations and projects directed toward betterment of the community. There is only a hint of the extent of these activities in the fact that he had been a board member in 23 civic and community organizations.

Mr. Artis was not just a sitting board member. He never joined any board or project with any purpose but to make the powerful contribution for which his talents equipped him. Every work he undertook felt the impact of his bubbling energy and his comprehension of community situations and needs.

He was congenitally cheerful and optimistic, and his face was scarcely known without a heartwarming smile. Yet he was a realist who faced up to problems and situations as they were, and strove to make things as he wished they might be.

He was not so preoccupied with the community as to neglect the broader scene. His work as a volunteer with the YMCA reached into the national and international spheres.

The example he set as a Negro leader and his devotion to the cause of Negro advancement lent immeasurable impetus and strength to that cause.

During his lifetime Mr. Artis received many honors in recognition of the dedication and effectiveness of his works. The results of those works will live long after him.

Summary: He was a hard worker for good causes.

Celebrities usually get lavish send-offs by the newspapers in the communities where they were hero-worshipped. In one way or another the editorial writer is expected to say that a great loss has been sustained, that the departed long will be remembered, and that his good works will live after him. Here is how the Atlanta *Journal* did it for its longtime political leader. The editorial appeared in its issue of Jan. 22, 1971.

Richard B. Russell

The death of Sen. Richard Brevard Russell Jr. leaves a void in the state and in the nation which will not be filled within the foreseeable future.

He was a giant of a man whose influence shaped and molded national policy, particularly in the vital and all-encompassing fields of money and defense.

At his death he was chairman of the Senate Appropriations Committee as well as president pro tem of the Senate. Prior to that he had been chairman of the Senate Armed Services Committee since 1951.

He was the friend of presidents from both political parties. His influence and support were eagerly sought by whoever happened to reside in the White House.

It is characteristic of the man that although he was a life-long Democrat, on matters of national interest he did not hold to a narrow and partisan view. His outlook was too broad to be so constricted. And he threw his support to whatever he thought in the best interests of the nation as a whole.

"I'm a reactionary when times are good," he said in 1963. "In a depression I'm a liberal."

Sen. Russell's potential stature was indicated when he first entered politics. Going to the Georgia House of Representatives in 1921 at the age of 23, he was designated speaker pro tem in 1923 and was elected speaker four years later.

When his father, the late Chief Justice of the Georgia Supreme Court, Richard B. Russell Sr., swore him in as governor of the state in 1931, he was the second youngest governor in Georgia history.

He went to Washington as a U.S. Senator in 1933 and there he remained until his death.

Without seeking the nomination, in 1948 Sen. Russell received 263 votes in Democratic convention balloting for a presidential candidate. Four years later he did actively seek the prize, but the second ballot was his high point and he was not to receive it.

Indicative of the esteem in which he was held, he headed a 1951 Senate investigation of the explosive issue of President Truman's firing Gen. of the Army Douglas MacArthur, and in 1963 was appointed to the Warren Commission which investigated the assassination of President Kennedy.

Throughout his Senate career, Sen. Russell reflected glory and honor upon his native state.

Sen. Russell's accomplishments brought him worldwide fame and renown. At home this is remembered with pride, but at home the senator is remembered for other things. He is remembered for his devotion to his family and to the family home, which was his home at the time of his death, and for the care he took of his family's burying ground near this home. He is remembered at home for his personal charm and rare, dry wit, qualities which he did not trouble to project to the nation and world, saving them for those he knew. He is remembered at home for his pride in his state and in his people who helped develop it from the beginning. He is remembered here for his clean taste for simple things. He is remembered as the father of the University System of Georgia, for he was the governor who organized the system when he reorganized the state, bringing order out of chaos in which separate institutions fought each other for appropriations. In this chaos there was no possibility for growth or quality.

So will he be remembered by the many Georgians who brushed against him or came within his range. He will be remembered also for his adherence to what he considered to be right, and what he was taught was right as a youth. He believed in the Constitution as interpreted prior to the presidency of Franklin D. Roosevelt and he did not change his opinions here, though he must have known that modern historians might judge him harshly on this point. In this as in other things he was consistent to the end.

Summary: He helped put Georgia on the map.

The Green Bay (Wis.) *Press-Gazette* of Sept. 3, 1970 did more than summarize Vince Lombardi's career. In addition, it evaluated it critically and passed strong laudatory judgment.

The Living Lombardi Legend

The untimely death of Vince Lombardi in the prime of his career as a professional football coach and business administrator takes from the sports scene one of its most dynamic and colorful personalities.

Although his death was not unexpected because of the well-founded but unofficial reports of his deteriorating physical condition following two operations, it still came as a shock. Those who have followed Mr. Lombardi's career certainly felt that here was a man of indomitable will who just would not be felled by a physical ailment. And yet his final illness came with devastating and relentless suddenness and to a man who had so prized physical fitness in himself as well as others.

The details of Mr. Lombardi's success in his chosen vocation are well enough known to require no detailed repetition here. Above and beyond that record, however, was the motivating force, the man's philosophy, which must be equally remembered for its impact on those around him as well as those who did not directly come within that sphere. That philosophy centered on man's

striving for perfection within himself. Mr. Lombardi saw failures along the road toward that goal as prods to success, but he recognized success as having its own built-in obstacles toward the effort and dedication necessary to prevent backsliding.

Mr. Lombardi was a hard task-master on the football field because he saw no other way to win. He could understand human failures while demanding perfection. He often was less critical when failures occurred than when success was achieved through less than the complete use of an individual's talents whose complete fulfillment he saw as an obligation. The one human failure he could not forgive was shirking from dedication to reach a goal, even one which seemed beyond human reach.

"Football teaches that work and sacrifice, perseverance and competitiveness, selflessness and respect for authority are the things one must possess if he is to achieve," he frequently said. He saw those qualities also as necessary in man's day-to-day life and as national goals. In evaluating today's national problems he said that "the struggle America faces today is a struggle for the hearts and souls and minds of men" in that "we must walk the tightrope between the consent we must receive and the control we must exert" in accepting the exercise of authority rather than its condemnation.

It was during his coaching tenure in Green Bay that Mr. Lombardi put to the test his belief that loyalty, teamwork, Spartanism with sacrifices and what he called "heart power, not hate power" were the touchstones to success. The result: in nine seasons as head coach, Mr. Lombardi led the Packers to five league championships and two Super Bowl championships. What is sometimes forgotten about him in those successes in football is that he also participated as a leader in many fund-raising efforts for charitable, health and educational organizations. He brought to such participation the same all-out effort which marked his coaching genius.

Green Bay has good reason to be thankful to Mr. Lombardi for taking the Packers from the bottom of the NFL to the heights which may never be matched again by any team in the continuity of their success. In turn, Green Bay provided him with a glittering opportunity to put into practice all of the tenets of his philosophy which he had shaped during his many years as a high school, college and professional coach, primarily as an assistant.

A legend in life, Mr. Lombardi will go down in the history of professional football as one of its greatest coaches and administrators. Just as significant will be the influence he had beyond the football field in his constant emphasis on and the need for man to exercise to the fullest the virtues of loyalty, effort, dedication, appreciation for the dignity of the individual and respect for authority properly and validly exercised.

The man has died but the Lombardi legend will live.

Summary: He practiced what he preached to his players and became a legend, first living and now dead.

It is not always easy to predict the fickleness of fortune in the future, meaning what it will do to the memory of the person under observation. The New York *Times* April 7, 1970 stressed Igor Stravinsky's historic contribution and forecast that his greatness would continue to be recognized.

Greatest of Composers

By common consent, Igor Stravinsky was the greatest living composer. He was the last of the heroic group that flourished in the early part of the century—a group that included such composers as Bela Bartok, Sergei Prokofieff, Arnold Schoenberg, Anton Webern, Ralph Vaughan Williams. All of them helped shape the course of music. But of them all there was, in the period from about 1910 to 1940, no shaper like Stravinsky. After his "Petrouchka" of 1911 and his "Sacre du Printemps" of 1913, music could no longer be the same.

For decades one could hear in world music echoes of the famous polytonal chord in "Petrouchka" and the savage rhythmic innovations of "Le Sacre." What Wagner's "Tristan and Isolde" was to the last half of the nineteenth century, "Le Sacre du Printemps" was to the first third of the twentieth. No

composer, not even the great ones of the period, could escape its influence. Then came Stravinsky's neoclassic period, and again he was the leader in a new kind of musical thought.

In recent years, world music has shifted somewhat from Stravinsky's concepts. That was to be expected, for every age has its own esthetic. Stravinsky himself embraced the Schoenberg-Webern dodecaphonic theories toward the end of his life. But his greatest work had come earlier. What Stravinsky always will represent in music are craft, technique, logic, proportion, rhythm. Above all, rhythm.

One of the most personal and idiosyncratic of all composers, a creator with unusual intellectual strength, an orchestra technician *par excellence,* he was in his day the most modern of the moderns. The man himself was like his music—terse, pithy, possessed of a steel-trap mind and a tart tongue. His witty, often malicious *apercus* make delightful reading. Stravinsky was a seminal figure, and that alone attests to his strength and assures his immortality. No minor composer in history has ever put his mark on the age. Only the major ones do.

Summary: An all-time great now and forever.

On the other hand, the New York *Herald Tribune* was not quite so sure when it ran the following editorial May 21, 1946. A quarter century later Tarkington's fame has not endured, but that does not alter the fact that he made an impact during his lifetime.

Booth Tarkington

It would be idle to dispute about the exact degree of literary eminence attained by Booth Tarkington. Judgments on contemporaries are seldom close to the mark. But it is safe to guess that certain of his books will outrank a host of solemn and tendentious volumes for the simple reason that they portray the essential truth of a typical and particular scene.

He considered himself simply as a professional writer, and he turned out a great many books for the market of unequal value and interest. But in the course of his career he earned the gratitude of millions and achieved first-rate importance by catching a phase of American life and investing it with a charm that has only mellowed as time's passage added a nostalgic quality. His greatest contribution was to write vividly of childhood and youth, not oppressed by the great cares, the tragic twists of personality and environment, that give "social significance," but living the minor epics appropriate to their years in happy homes.

The ideal Tarkington milieu might be described as "Middle American"—the America of the Midwest, of the middle classes, of middling people who were seldom very bad or very good, very bright or extremely stupid, seldom doomed to the greatest tragedies or destined to experience the most exalted ecstasies. It was an adolescent America, poised for an irresponsible moment on the threshold of the harsh demands of maturity, and to a generation accustomed to a sterner atmosphere it may seem a little dull, a little unreal. But there it was and here it is, to the life, in these pages. Booth Tarkington clothed it with the magic of small, homely things, the sights and scents and sounds of the decent, sane way of life so many Americans have known. Therein lies greatness.

If Mr. Tarkington's tales of "Middle America" won him affection, his personal courage in his long fight against blindness and his refusal to submit to affliction earned deep respect. He was alert to his civic responsibilities, but he did not attempt to discharge them by using his books as vehicles for propaganda. His conception of his labor was more modest—and wiser and truer. In all, he was a gallant gentleman, a good American and a fine artist to whom the nation owes much.

Summary: He held a literary mirror up to Middle America.

There is no greater test of greatness than that provided by time when it proves one has been right in both arguing the ways things should go and in predicting what probably would happen. If you guess right you're recognized as having been a genius; if subsequent events indicate you were wrong, you may be recalled for some fine qualities, or as a good loser.

Nobody ever specialized more in predictions nor had a better success average during his lifetime than H. G. Wells, and it was that aspect of his career, with emphasis on the portents for the future it involved, that the St. Louis *Post-Dispatch* emphasized in its Aug. 14, 1946 editorial as follows:

A Legacy of Clairvoyance

Modern man, as H. G. Wells often said, is engaged in a race between education and disaster. The great British novelist and historian died yesterday in London at the age of 79. How nearly disaster had won the race before Wells relinquished the role of interested spectator could be realized only by one who had shared with him his twilight years in a blitzed and robot bombed London.

Wells was a man obsessed by the future. As early as 1908, the year before Bleriot flew across the English Channel, he had anticipated in his novels both aerial warfare and the atomic bomb. In 1933 he predicted World War II, set the date within a few months of the actual opening of hostilities and included war between the United States and Japan in his provision.

The legacy of clairvoyance left by H. G. Wells goes far beyond our own day. He saw the disintegration of western civilization ahead, the decay of cities, the breakdown of law. In the "rugged individualism" of men, in their pride, arrogance, egotism and vanity he saw ahead a time of war, pestilence and famine, when nomadic bands would roam the earth, grubbing a meager sustenance from the roots in the ground.

Yet the Wellsian vision of "The Shape of Things to Come" was not without hope. Disaster will win the first lap, said Wells, but man is able to learn—the hard way. By 1965, he predicted, the first shadowy outlines of the World State would appear and by 1978 world government would have become a fact. Within a half a century after that the rebuilding of our cities would be well under way.

This was H. G. Wells's outline of the history of the future. Perhaps it is as well that he cannot live to see whether and to what extent it comes to pass.

Summary: H. G. Wells predicted correctly many times and left a legacy of future predictions.

The following is an off-beat editorial which seems quite consistent with the career of a leading comedian. It appeared in the Chicago *Daily Tribune* for March 14, 1971.

Oh, for Another Harold Lloyd

It has been a long time since we went to the movies with the relish that we did back when Harold Lloyd was in his prime. His initials stood for Hearty Laughter or Healthy Laughter, and his death on Monday at the age of 77 comes at a time when the world is suffering from a drouth of both kinds.

Today's humor, such as it is, is likely to be contrived. It suffers either from too much inhibition or from too conscious an effort to be uninhibited. Much of the laughter we hear on television is produced by a sound track. Famous old campus humor magazines are withering away, unable to find either writers or readers in sufficient number. The times are such, we often hear, that there is no room for humor, nothing to joke about.

One of Harold Lloyd's greatest assets was his ability to laugh at himself and to inspire others to do likewise. This is perhaps what is most conspicuously missing today. Everybody is so wound up in his own problems and his own causes that laughter is viewed as some kind of sacrilege, or something to be enjoyed only at somebody else's expense. Those who tell us that today's problems are too serious to allow for laughter seem to forget that the Lloyd movies thrived not only in the placid 1920s but also during the Depression of the 1930s, which was a painful time even by today's standards.

Harold Lloyd's humor may not have helped to create prosperity [except for himself], but it certainly made the times more tolerable for many. It might be able to do the same today.

Summary: We need another Harold Lloyd to make us laugh at ourselves today.

Further evidence that it is possible to avoid the somber and macabre in obituary editorial writing was provided by the St. Louis *Post-Dispatch* in its issue of Oct. 12, 1956 which stressed the relevance of what it had to say to the ordinary reader.

Clarence Birdseye, Ladies' Man

Making 30 or 40 or 50 million dollars does not draw as much attention now as it did in the days of J. P. Morgan and Andrew Carnegie. Prosperity has become too common, it seems, to make news except in the campaigning season. But how a man came by his money still makes a difference.

So we note the passing of Clarence Birdseye, a good Gloucesterman and friend of anybody willing to join him in tracking down a whale off Cape Ann. He became interested in this sport, good for a long boat-ride, in his days as a fur trader and missionary with Dr. Wilfred Grenfell along the Labrador coast. It was then that he also got his idea for freezing foods, the idea which made him wealthy and which, considered from the day-in-, day-out angle, probably is working a bigger change in American life than is the H-bomb.

There are, no doubt, many women—and some men—who still give long hours to cooking as an art. But Clarence Birdseye did more than the inventor of the tin can to make cooking, in its utilitarian aspect, a matter of minutes. Gone are the days when food had to be cleaned and carefully prepared for pot or pan. Recite your menu for the day or the week, and the grocer will produce it ready-frozen—anything from biscuits to stew. And you can have strawberries in a snow-storm.

This is why women have become such good bridge players and why department store sales continue to rise. And it is why the weary wage-earner, no matter how the cartoonists draw him, does not have to wait hours for dinner. If the unions won the 40-hour week for men, then Clarence Birdseye repealed the rule which held that woman's work is never done. And what may yet come of this we hesitate to say.

Since he gave women more time to spend with their children, we may have fewer delinquents. Since he gave them more time for the Lady Voters League and the precinct meetings, we may—by and by—have a woman in the presidency. Oh, Birdseye started things moving—just like the man who invented the wheel.

Summary: The man affected our eating habits and possibly had widespread influence.

Not all obituaries are eulogies. In death labor leaders generally remain as unpopular as they were in life in journalistic publishing circles. The Denver *Post* for Nov. 22, 1952 did its best to find something good to say about its subject, but the general effect was that the man was a failure.

Death of a Conservative

In the nearly three decades of growth and turbulence that the late William Green led the American Federation of Labor as its president he steered it down a conservative path away from the political radicalism of European unionism. He was unspectacularly successful.

Following Samuel Gompers as A. F. of L. chieftain, Bill Green also followed with hardly any deviation the Gompers principles of trade unionism-organization of workers on a craft rather than an industry-wide basis. But Bill Green lived in tougher times than did his mentor Gompers. Gompers had only the working man and the employer to consider; Bill Green had John L. Lewis and the surging force of industrial unionism unleashed by the new deal magna charta for labor, the Wagner act. And in coping with the organization of unskilled and skilled workers into mass unions as started by Lewis and carried on by the late Philip Murray, Bill Green failed.

It was his tragic failure. If there was anything Bill Green abhorred it was a house divided in American labor. Labor's house, of course, is divided as a result of the bitterest and biggest struggle large-scale unionism has ever experienced.

The schism of labor came because of the A. F. of L.'s devotion to the principle of craft organization, a principle which the C.I.O. unionists consider outmoded by the development of mass production which utilizes a working force inferior in skills, superior in numbers.

Failing to prevent the schism, Bill Green devoted without great success, his energy to heal the breach and end the dualism of labor. His greatest success, a pyrrhic victory, was getting the Lewis miners' union back into the fold for a short time.

Bill Green was essentially a middle-of-the-roader, an administrator of traditional policy rather than an innovator of new policy. He never held the power of a Lewis or a Murray either in his union or in political affairs. But his skill at the art of compromise kept him in the forefront of the American labor movement. He would not compromise with the C.I.O. because he knew that in compromise the A.F. of L. principles of craft organization would be lost. His successor must face the internal struggle which Bill Green held down and decide whether the nation's largest labor organization can continue its present course or fade away from it into the catch-all unionism promoted by the C.I.O.

Summary: The times caught up with and passed Bill Green.

There is no mistaking the author's defiance of tradition in the Evanston (Ill.) *Daily News-Index*'s editorial for Nov. 20, 1936.

An Imperialist Dies . . .

Rudyard Kipling was a jingoist, a chauvinist and an egoist. He invented the phrase, "the white man's burden" and taught that "east is east and west is west and ne'er the twain shall meet." He was typical of the British Empire at its very worst and did perhaps more than any other person who ever lived to foment racial and international hatred.

Because Olie Speaks and others were able to write catchy tunes to which many of Kipling's poems can be sung easily, his rhymes are better known than those of most other writers of recent years. Among his short stories there are many which are well written, and there is no denying that he presented an authentic picture of the life of the British Tommy in India during the early days of imperialistic conquest there.

* * *

Kipling's Anglophobia was demonstrated in his attitude toward the United States. During the last decade of the 19th century he made a trip across the North American continent of which he wrote in his "From Sea to Sea." Among my notes I find the following which I wrote upon reading that book several years ago:

"It seems at first thought that there must be something ailing with a man who turns from the natural wonders of Yellowstone to swap tales of warfare and militarism with a government trooper. . . . Kipling's patriotism is chauvinistic. It is bred on militarism and barbarism. Brittania should rule, not only the waves but the land and air as well. He scoffs at the American who boasts of his own country and sings his national songs vociferously. Kipling's loyalty is subtle and surreptitious. To the American who has read his latest poem about 'Uncle Sam' it is insidious."

* * *

Arriving at San Francisco Kipling surveyed the fortifications of the bay, ignoring completely the beauties of the Golden Gate. At Yellowstone he met and hobnobbed with Indian fighters and soldiers, finding his chief delight in a former Tommy Atkins. For Chicago he had nothing but ridicule. Try as hard as he could he found nothing from California to New York of which he approved.

Nor did he change much with the years. Everywhere he went it was the military that interested him and the extent to which the so-called inferior races and nationalities were being subjugated and made to appreciate the blessings of Anglo-Saxon civilization. Even in his crabby old age, as mentioned, he talked about Uncle Sam as a rapacious old rascal for believing England should pay back a reasonable share of what was loaned her from this side of the Atlantic during the World war.

* * *

At the time of his death Rudyard Kipling was fortunately sort of an anachronism. The era of conquest over, or almost so, as far as Great Britain was concerned, there wasn't much call for the kind of stuff Kipling used to turn out. His attempts to revive interest in a principle which would put the Union Jack on every flag staff, on the occasion of the silver jubilee of George and Mary, fell lamentably flat. The newer generation of Britishers just didn't understand what the old man was driving at.

Rudyard Kipling was truly the product of his times. Now he is gone, and let it be hoped his times also are gone with him.

Summary: An imperialist is dead. Good.

It's fun to write that way just as much as it must have been fun for Dorothy Parker to quip, "How can they tell?" when informed that Calvin Coolidge was dead. The "say no evil of the dead" rule just should not apply when the person's influence will continue to be felt long after his death. The classic editorial of this type, probably the most-quoted obituary of any kind, was that which William Allen White wrote for the Emporia (Kans.) *Gazette* following the death in December, 1925 of Frank Munsey who bought and killed more newspapers than any other person.

Frank Munsey, the great publisher, is dead. Frank Munsey contributed to the journalism of his day the great talent of a meat packer, the morals of a moneychanger and the manners of an undertaker. He and his kind have about succeeded in transforming a once great profession into an eight percent security. May he rest in trust!

By absolute contrast, the following editorial which appeared in all the *Post* Publications in suburban Minneapolis Dec. 17, 1970 was an unusual and touching tribute to one who was still very much alive in the memories of his longtime colleagues.

Almost One Year Since 'Sonny' Died

Anyone who has lost a loved one, relative or friend by death around the holiday season realizes that the usual Christmas joy also carries some sadness through memories of that person.

That's pretty much the way Post Publishing owners and employees feel at this time of the year, because it was almost a year ago that executive editor H. O. Sonnesyn died at North Memorial hospital.

Today, in fact, marks one year right to the day that Sonny showed up for work for the last time in his life. He died on Saturday, Dec. 20, and people at The Post are grateful that their last exposure to Sonny was a memorable one, because for some strange reason, he spent the better part of Thursday, Dec. 18 visiting with most of his fellow workers, teasing and joking in his usual manner.

The holiday season naturally is the big item at this time of year, but there are many at The Post who will also set aside at least a few moments every Dec. 20 to pay respect to a man who had so much to do with shaping their lives.

We are convinced Sonny was probably the best known individual in the northwest suburban area, especially at the statewide level. His many years as editor of Post Papers singled him out as a very unique man. He was regarded as "Mr. Robbinsdale" and guided Post Papers through the years of growing pains, when suburbs around here expanded from open fields to thriving communities.

When he was alive, Sonny looked forward to the holiday season as much as anyone, but there never was any celebrating on his part when New Year's Eve rolled around, because it marked the anniversary of his mother's death. And now, Sonny's widow, Marge, will solemnly mark Dec. 20 as the first anniversary of her husband's death.

Rest assured, our thoughts and prayers will be with her.

Summary: We still miss him after a year.

VIII

Helping the Community

In everyone's life there comes a time when he would like to see "a nice editorial" in his favorite newspaper. Perhaps that time is when he is named chairman of the United Charities drive or when he becomes fund raiser for the local cancer or heart or multiple sclerosis or some other committee; or perhaps it is when he promotes a home talent theatrical or a lecture series or he is master of ceremonies at the annual Brotherhood Week banquet. Possibly his urge to ask the editor to "put in a good word" comes when he is membership chairman for the Chamber of Commerce, or maybe when he's the coach of the high school basketball team which seems on its way to a championship.

"DUTY" EDITORIALS

The causes, campaigns, christenings and the like for which editorial support may be solicited are seemingly limitless. There is hardly a week or a day that has not been proclaimed by a president or governor or mayor or some other dignitary as suitable for contemplating or memorializing some person, place or event. It takes only a cursory glance at one's junk mail to reveal that there has been a prodigious proliferation of worthy causes in recent years.

The "duty" or "ceremonial" or "puff" or "booster" editorial (to use only the respectable terms by which they are known in newsrooms) is "an occupational disease in newspapering" according to Anson H. Smith, Jr., Boston *Globe* editorial writer, in his contribution to a Spring, 1968 *Masthead* symposium on the subject. Much as he and the other participants agree that they would like to avoid this type of assignment, all admitted it was impossible. Editors of large metropolitan newspapers find it easier to say "no" and some representatives of small and medium-sized city dailies even defend the "duty" editorial or at least give strong rationalizations for its prevalence. Harry Boyd of the Cedar Rapids (Iowa) *Gazette* wrote what many believe: "It wastes less time and energy to write something than to explain why you won't, or didn't."

Boyd continued by way of defense: "Moreover, we never can be sure that the duty pieces are more a waste of space than what we'd write otherwise. At least some who read the duty editorial are genuinely pleased by it. Many of the others think it was nice of us to write it. The rest don't read it anyway, as soon as they find out what it is—which is quickly." Boyd concluded: "On the whole, I think the standard duty editorial, much as they may sound alike, are desirable if not necessary in a relatively small community like ours. They nearly always bring favorable comments, which is more than can be said of a lot of the stuff we write. And they save readers the effort of expressing sentiments they share themselves but too often don't get around to voicing."

An even stronger statement on behalf of the booster editorial was written by Kenneth Rystrom, editor of the editorial page of the Vancouver (Wash.) *Columbian,* in an article, "Provincialism As a Vested Interest," in the Spring, 1970 *Masthead.* He wrote:

> This provincialism isn't all bad. We take pride in the city, the state and the region in which we live. We want them to be admired. Because of this dedication to our communities, newspapers contribute as much as anyone toward making our communities better places in which to live. An editorial writer who isn't interested in helping to improve the city and the state in which he lives ought to move elsewhere or give up editorial writing.

Reminiscent of the revivalist who answered the criticism that his results were not lasting by saying a bath doesn't last either is the remark of Parker Kent, associate editor of the Calgary (Alberta) *Herald:* "If they are thoughtful and well done, such editorials exercise a useful influence. People may know beforehand everything you have to say but it is essential that they be reminded of what they know and be re-infused with good intention," to which Fred Panwitt of the Chicago *Daily News* adds: "Just because we get tired of writing pieces that we tend to categorize as 'duty' doesn't mean the audience is sick of reading them."

Good or bad, the "duty" editorial, or whatever you want to call it, is here to stay. Bob Heck of the Rockford (Ill.) *Morning Star and Register-Republic* stated the inevitable conclusion: "If a newspaper is to fulfill its community service role, the duty editorial, by whatever name it masquerades, is essential."

So how do you go about getting them written? Thomas E. Noyes says his paper, the Washington *Evening Star,* assigns such pieces to a stylist, "one less devoted to the search for ultimate truth than to the nimble juxtaposition of words." The Boston *Globe* feels the only workable rule is "be as original as possible." James E. Jacobson, editorial page editor of the Birmingham (Ala.) *News,* says of the task to find something stirring to say about Fire Prevention Week: "That's where creativity surfaces." When he ran the editorial page of the Pittsburgh *Post-Gazette,* John Lofton confessed he used to "politely ask one or the other of the junior men on the page if they will be so kind as to do a piece on the United Fund, Brotherhood Week or whatever it is," on the theory that "the senior men have already done their stint at such things." Nobody, however, was penalized for pleading inability to fulfill the assignment.

The point is that everyone has perhaps one good Support the Red Cross or Remember Mother's Day editorial in him. It's trying to write the second such piece that is difficult. So there's the temptation merely to rewrite the publicity material and that strangely enough, usually satisfies the solicitor of the editorial mention.

A typical banal editorial pat on the back is the following from the Dallas *Morning News* of Jan. 20, 1954.

Planned Parenthood

For nearly two decades the Planned Parenthood Federation, which maintains a modern clinic at 3620 Maple, has been helping Dallas parents. It has given marriage and premarital counseling and has referred to private physicians many persons in need of medical treatment. It has helped some married couples to overcome sterility and has enabled others to have babies "by choice and not by chance."

This Dallas center, one of more than five hundred of its kind over the country, had more than two thousand clinical visits last year. It has the cooperation of some of the city's leading physicians and has helped to give special training to medical students and nurses. Especially effective in work among Mexicans and Negroes, it hopes to establish soon a branch in West Dallas.

Now the federation is engaged in its annual fund-raising drive. With Mrs. Larry Hart as campaign chairman, it seeks $15,000 to carry on its welfare work for 1954. Those who visit the center and see the essential work it is doing will realize that it is one of Dallas' more important social agencies and will want to help support and expand its activities.

Even worse is this one from the Mason City (Iowa) *Globe-Gazette* of March 12, 1955.

For Our Mentally Ill

In every section of the country increased attention is being paid to assistance for the mentally ill. Since this is a development more recent than expansion of care for the physically ill it has farther to go before comparably adequate facilities are provided.

States are taking a new look at the type of hospitalization which they provide for mental cases and in a majority of instances surveys show much to be desired in buildings, equipment, in physicians and in trained attendants.

Growth in population and pressures of life, which a larger proportion find difficulty in meeting, make expansion of mental institutions necessary.

At the same time new methods of treatment have promise if facilities are made available to physicians skilled in treating mental ailments.

That this newspaper could do better if it felt like it was demonstrated just a few days earlier, March 7, 1955, in an editorial in support of one of the few agencies that even the newspapers with the strictest taboo lists exempt when requests to come to the rescue with an editorial helping hand are received. This editorial is strong because it localizes its appeal.

Red Cross Stands Ready When Disaster Strikes

If any organization can be said to constitute a symbol of man's compassion for his fellow man and an impelling willingness to go to his help, that organization is the American Red Cross.

In the whole gamut of man's misfortunes, be it flood, epidemic, tornado or other disaster, the Red Cross has always stood ready to mobilize a mighty battalion of helpers to give effective aid.

We who live in Cerro Gordo County and surrounding counties have been fortunate in that we have had few disasters. But we have experienced enough to learn how effective and helpful the Red Cross can be.

An example of this came last summer when an area in the west part of the city was flooded. In this disaster the Red Cross demonstrated that it is more than a symbol. It became the vehicle through which all of us could give help.

The Red Cross, because it had trained personnel, provided the leadership whereby emergency and rehabilitation assistance was given to some 30 families in the flooded section of the city.

The relief for those 30 families cost close to $5,000 and covered such basic needs as clothing, food, household furnishings, repair of electrical appliances, the repair of flood damaged houses and medical needs.

In times of such disaster most of us are stirred with an impulse to help. Had the call come to us for contributions the night water was pouring into these homes most of us, feeling fortunate that our own homes were dry, would gladly have responded.

But raising the funds then would not have provided immediate emergency assistance. The help had to reach the flood victims instantly.

The Red Cross was ready with money already on hand. Funds for this program were provided by the national Red Cross organization from monies collected in the last fund drive a year ago.

The help the affected families received was a gift from the American people who gave because they had faith and trust that the Red Cross could make their gifts to disaster victims most effective.

Mason City's experience must be multiplied a hundred, perhaps a thousand times, to give the whole Red Cross picture in this one field of human help.

The story of how the organization went to the help of other flood victims in Iowa last summer is an epic in itself. In Sioux City, Des Moines, Fort Dodge and other communities hundreds of families were evacuated from their homes, served meals, given clothing and shelter and then helped in the rehabilitation of their homes.

The total cost to the Red Cross of this giant service to alleviate human suffering in Iowa was $147,428.

These are indeed vital contributions to man's welfare, but they constitute but one phase of the Red Cross program that touches the lives of all of us in one manner or another.

Surely, in the light of such performance, all of us will want to make a contribution to keep the Red Cross ever ready to meet such emergencies.

Who knows?

We could be the ones who will benefit the most in the coming year.—E.A.N.

By contrast, the localization of the following editorial seems fictitious. Possibly this was a canned piece with only the figures in paragraph two and the name in the sixth paragraph changed to make it applicable to the particular circulation area. The rest of the piece conceivably could be run without change anywhere else. It is to conjecture how many readers reached the last two paragraphs with their direct appeal. The editorial appeared in the Park Forest (Ill.) *Star* for April 15, 1971.

Crusade Under Way

Appropriately enough, because spring is the time of renewal and rebirth, the American Cancer society has kicked off its annual Crusade to help eradicate this most dreaded disease of mankind.

The goal for the society's South Suburban unit, which is headed by William V. Rosenquist of Commonwealth Edison company, is $108,500. The unit serves 52 suburban areas south and southwest of Chicago, including Crete and Monee townships, with a total population of more than 700,000.

In 1913, when the ACS first opened its doors, cancer patients felt shunned and doomed. The word "cancer" was rarely printed or mentioned in public. Cancer research held little interest or promise for most scientists or physicians.

Today, thanks in large measure to the work of the ACS, these attitudes and situations have changed completely. Knowledge and experience have shown that cancer often can be cured if treated promptly and properly, and further breakthroughs are anticipated. This has revolutionized the approach to the cancer problem. Today one out of three persons in the United States afflicted with cancer is being saved, and about half could be saved under optimum circumstances.

One of the most important of these circumstances, insofar as the Cancer society is concerned, is obtaining the necessary funds for research and for public education in recognizing common danger signals and in taking appropriate action.

During April, the peak of the Crusade, hundreds of volunteer workers in the South Suburban unit will visit door-to-door, distributing literature containing life-saving facts about cancer. At the same time the unit will be soliciting contributions to the society's work.

The theme of the Crusade is, "We Want to Wipe Out Cancer in Your Lifetime." Saving lives starts with the individual himself. This first step can be a substantial contribution to the 1971 American Cancer Society Crusade.

When the publicity man for the worthy cause hasn't done the editorial writer's work for him, a lazy way is to skim through an annual report or similar document and make complimentary remarks about what seem to be the highlights. Since the writer has predetermined that his editorial is to be laudatory, he makes no attempt at critical analysis. He merely seeks topics about which to make banal remarks. The following from the Birmingham (Ala.) *News* for Oct. 2, 1958 is a perfect example of this kind of slipshod research and writing.

Health Council
Strengthens Community

The Health Council of Birmingham and Jefferson County has just completed three years of good work in helping to raise standards and strengthen the health of the people of this community. It is seeking to bring about the orderly development of a well-balanced and adequate community health program. As is explained in its annual report for 1957-58, the council does this primarily through organization and coordination rather than by giving direct service. Its activities are closely related to those of other groups engaged in planning for health, welfare and recreation in Jefferson County.

One of the council's notable achievements has been its after-care program for state mental hospital patients. As the retiring chairman, Dr. John W. Simpson, pointed out at the recent annual meeting, this program is making it possible for selected patients in state hospitals to be placed in Jefferson County homes and trained for jobs by the State Rehabilitation Service. We heartily agree with the advisory committee for this program in its statement that "the value and significance of having a preson leave a mental hospital to return to the future life of the community will be worth the time, effort and money expended to make this possible."

The council's committee on nutrition conducted a Better Breakfast Campaign in September, aimed at helping to educate the public to the importance of improving breakfast eating habits.

The year saw the organization of a lay advisory committee to the Jefferson County Board of Health "to seek special counsel in highly technical matters and to seek broad public interest and support on matters of great importance to the public health."

The problem of caring for the needy sick of the community received the attention of the council's indigent medical care committee.

The council is doing valuable work for the people of Jefferson County, helping materially to bring better health for many of our citizens. Officers and members of the council and its several committees are to be warmly commended for their efforts.

Comment

Only by inference is the conclusion of the first sentence substantiated in the editorial to follow. What standards? How was the health strengthened? What do these words mean? "orderly development," "well-balanced," "adequate"? It does no good to refer the reader to a report. This is a lazy shirking of responsibility. How is "organization and coordination" beneficial? What specifically is being done?

This paragraph merely states an objective and labels a program. It imparts no knowledge or understanding. The editorial writer merely accepts a doctor's word that it is good. So it is good.

The Better Breakfast Campaign was an advertising stunt originated and paid for by General Foods and managed by a Chicago public relations firm. Object was to get people to eat more cereals.

What does the quotation mean specifically?

What was done?

Just a vacuous pat on the back. For what?

Examples do exist to prove that it is possible for an ingenious writer to avoid triteness. The following editorial from the Chicago *Sun-Times* for Nov. 14, 1971 used description and narration as attention-getters. This short piece is not monotonous.

It Takes More Than Cookies

One marvelous morning, a little incandescent lamp of a girl waited at the breakfast table for a principal day in her still-brief life. It was the day of her investiture as a Brownie Scout, and though investiture was a full handful of hours away, she sat crisply in her new uniform, tie tied, beanie on top, proud, smiling around the missing teeth. And then she crisply spilled her milk, all across her lap, and above and beyond her lap and on the tie, and lordy, how she cried.

That morning was a while ago, and she is an experienced Brownie now, and will become a Girl Scout, full-fledged and sophisticated, like her sister before her. She will become an example, too, for the sister who still is a tagalong, and she will become a woman, and the scouting will help with that just as it helped the patient mother who cleaned away the spilled milk that marvelous morning.

Memories are precious, and scouting builds them. When the parents, neighbors and friends of the 46,622 Chicago Girl Scouts ring your doorbell today, as they plan to do between 12:30 and 4 p.m., help them. The goal is $110,000.

Girl Scouts can't grow on cookies alone.

Summary: The title states it.

The same newspaper, April 20, 1971, personalized its appeal on behalf of a special occasion.

If He Asks, Tell Him

This is Earth Week.

The next time someone says to you, "Well, what can I do about the problems of the environment?" tell him. Tell him to use biodegradable laundry soaps instead of detergent; to turn off the light when he doesn't need it; to buy products in refundable containers, soda pop, for example; to pick up litter no matter who dropped it; to use natural predators instead of DDT.

Tell him to store food in reusable, washable containers; to return coat hangers to the cleaners; to carry his own tote bag to the store; to plant trees, which absorb carbon dioxide and produce oxygen; to report abandoned vehicles; to organize a drive for scrap iron, paper, bottles, and you name it; to think about riding a bike.

Tell your friend he can buy a small car and use non-leaded gasoline; can report air pollution to authorities; can use a live Christmas tree and replant it after the holidays; can contribute to ecology groups; can study the issues concerning the environment and pollution; can take a quick instead of a protracted shower when water is short; can boycott products overly packaged.

Tell him to give outgrown clothes to charity; to put a litter bag in car and boat; to use his garbage can instead of the kitchen sink garbage disposal unit; to plant grass instead of putting down cement or asphalt. Tell him to teach his children these things and to think more of quality of life instead of standard of living. Tell him all these things. And then tell him—without being too goody-goody about it—that you're trying to do these things and wish he'd pass the word.

Summary: Every citizen can do plenty to help save the environment.

The following is a well-constructed and logical postmortem editorial following a special occasion. It is from the Philadelphia *Inquirer* for May 28, 1971.

A Grand Night for Walking

Just about everybody in the happy throng of thousands who turned out for the "Take a Walk" on Walnut street Wednesday night seemed to be having a good time—and that was the objective.

The success of this affair should, at the very least, inspire more like it. Periodic evening walk parties, perhaps in various sections of the center-city business district on a rotating schedule, well might prove to be not only immensely popular but a catalyst for healthy competition in generating new ideas for enlivening the downtown area after day-time business hours.

Beyond that, the Walnut Walk could open eyes to attractive possibilities in giving some of our streets back to pedestrians on a more or less permanent basis.

No doubt the novelty of strolling on a street usually jammed with automobiles was a large factor in drawing crowds to the seven blocks on Walnut west of Broad after the traffic was detoured at 6:30. But the festive air and party atmosphere proved something else: Philadelphians can have as much fun as anybody when the setting is right, the weather is cooperative, and people usually in too much of a hurry even to say hello to passersby have the time and the inclination to get to know one another.

Neighborhood block parties are a Philadelphia tradition, and a delightful one, but they have always been primarily what the name implies: neighborhood affairs. Centercity block parties that can bring everybody together, and offer shopping opportunities as well for those who are so inclined, give a new and pleasant twist to the old tradition. Let's have more nights like that.

Summary: Let's repeat the Take a Walk experiment.

The writer of the following editorial for the Indianapolis *Star* creates the impression of deep sincerity. He seems to be a fan of the sport he is advertising and to be eager to do it even if the whole affair is a mercenary enterprise.

Canoe Regatta

It can hardly be denied that one of man's greatest accomplishments was the discovery he could "ride" on water.

From the raft, or the hollowed-out log perhaps, to modern day ocean liners, freighters and giant tankers stretches a fascinating history covering every conceivable variety of craft, hand-propelled, or driven by the wind or by power.

One of the earliest, most beautiful, most practical and still widely used of man's floating conveyances is the canoe. In the Western Hemisphere the canoe, in birch-bark form, was brought to a pinnacle of perfection by American Indians who depended on it for fishing, hunting, trapping and mobility.

Essentially the same elegant vessel, employing other modes of construction, is in common use today for all kinds of sporting purposes, and the canoe is likely to remain a favorite, among those who love boats, because of its graceful lines, light weight, portability, and the ease with which it can be made to shoot through the water once its handling has been mastered.

Canoe lovers and experts, and even outright novices for whom the canoe may still be a "tippy" craft, will have the chance to savor the delights of canoeing, or to test their skills in more challenging aspects of the sport, during the Hoosier Canoe Club's eighth annual Fall Creek Regatta to be held Saturday and Sunday, Oct. 2 and 3.

There will be 1,000-meter sprints, slaloms, 5 and 10-mile races, a 10-mile voyageur medley and other events for experienced canoeists and also shorter "fledgling" races involving a novice class known as the Metropolitan Division.

All events are open to non-members as well as to members of the club. The 10-mile racecourse, which includes sections of rapids, will run from the 71st Street bridge over Fall Creek, near Fort Benjamin Harrison, to East Fall Creek Parkway, one block east of Keystone Avenue, where race headquarters will be located. Official entry forms and complete information on the regatta may be had by writing to: Hoosier Canoe Regatta, 3626 Thorncrest Drive, Clermont, Ind., 46119.

Spectators will find the events easily seen from the extensive parkways along Fall Creek Boulevard, which are also good picnic grounds and vantage points from which to enjoy the fall colors that are likely to be in full view by the time of the regatta.

The affair should be pretty to watch, fun to take part in, a chance to catch a glimpse of one of the accomplishments of the past differing not greatly from its beginnings eons ago.

Summary: The forthcoming festival will be great fun.

PAYOLA AND PRIZES

Most of those who seek editorial support for what they consider a worthy cause are humble supplicants, pleading for attention on the merits of their requests. Some others, however, are would-be customers, willing or eager to provide compensation for the space they are able to grab.

William Brooks, Jr. of the Minneapolis *Star* led off a symposium on "Should Editorial Writers Accept Gifts?" in the Spring, 1960 *Masthead* with a blunt, "In the first place, why not be honest and use the proper word? Payola is bribery, or a bribe, depending on how the word is used."

Few others who contributed to the symposium or to a subsequent one on "Does It Begin With a Cigar?" in the Fall, 1965 *Masthead,* were so vehement. All recognized the danger of being indoctrinated or brainwashed if they were the recipients of lavish entertainment by either a public or private host. On the other hand, it was the concensus that highly qualified editorial writers have the moral stamina to maintain objectivity despite the hospitality and any feeling of social indebtedness it created.

The importance of editorial writers' seeing something of the world cannot be denied. Only a comparatively few of the larger papers can adhere consistently to a strict pay-as-you-go policy. So they allow their staff men to accept invitations from foreign governments to visit their nations, usually in parties with other editorial writers, and they are represented on junkets paid for by their own government, to inspect military establishments or to visit battlefields. They take inspection cruises and they go on inaugural flights as the guests of private aviation companies.

All this is freeloading on a much grander scale than the luncheon, cocktail party or dinner that is almost routine and which often is accepted because it is possible to repay it in kind. Some newspapers have strict rules forbidding their editorial employes, mostly in the newsroom, from accepting gifts at Christmas or on other occasions. Sometimes it is stipulated that a reporter must return any present that costs more than a certain amount, possibly the price of a fifth of whisky. Sports writers today mostly have their expenses paid by their offices rather than by the managements of the teams they accompany on trips. Usually, however, they are allowed to accept season passes to games just as the music and drama critics go free to entertainments and the book editors do not have to pay for review copies of best sellers.

To be avoided is the reputation as a moocher, an habitual frequenter of affairs where there are "free eats" and possibly favors for guests. Also, and more important, there is the Caesar's wife principle— the avoidance of the appearance of evil, evil in this case meaning undue influence on an editorial writer's judgment. Old timers scoff at the suggestion that their integrity can be bought cheaply, and there probably is no better way to summarize than with the words of Robert H. Estabrook, then Washington *Post* associate editor, used: "The only real guide is a sense of propriety." Donald L. Breed, editor and publisher of the Freeport (Ill.) *Journal-Standard,* facetiously sounded the plight of the small town writer in the following verse:

'Well, If They're Good Seats . . .'

I never got bourbon,
(Once I got nuts,
And once I got a penknife,
One that still cuts.)
I never got Scotch,
To make me tight,
(Once I got a desk set,
But the pen won't write.)
No crooks endeavor
To woo me as friend,
I send nothing back,
There's nothing to send.
(True, at Christmas
When people are trimming trees;
The dry mat company

Sends me cheese.)
But oh, dear Saint Nick
Don't seduce a fella
With second row seats
For "Fiorello!"

BOOSTING AND DEFENDING

Any newspaper naturally boosts the community which it serves. Any other attitude would be inconceivable as the best interests of all are intermingled. There have been many examples of how to promote civic spirit throughout this book. A paper which lives up to its responsibility is vigilant in guarding the home town's reputation and in seeing to it that the reputation continues to be deserved. It not only reports chicanery as it surfaces but it assumes the initiative in exposing it.

Throughout the entire history of the United States the "bigger and better" psychology has been a significant factor. More hysterically stated at some times than at others, the yardstick of success nevertheless always has been growth. This year's gross national product must be above last year's and the same for income, personal and public alike, and population. Some cities still complain if the official census reveals they have been exaggerating in their own estimates. The idea is that boom days must never end, the frontier must keep expanding, new goals must be set before old ones are reached. The rip snorting, he-man, up-and-at-'em mythology has been widespread and it has been perpetuated by McGuffey readers, Horatio Alger and Rover Boys fiction, Longfellow's poems, happy-ending plays and movies, self-help magazines and books, get-rich-quick projects, and in many other ways.

Few American newspaper editorial pages today are gung-ho, whooping it up for progress. Overwhelmingly conservative in their economic and political outlooks, they are more sober than in the past in their appraisals of schemes for civic improvement.

They may even be occasionally critical of The Establishment and cautious about adopting its enthusiasms. What follows is a good example of restrained hurrahing. The author almost seems to be arguing with himself trying to determine whether the occasion is one for unmixed jubilation. The result is a reasoned appraisal. It is from the Toronto *Globe and Mail* for May 30, 1968.

The Challenge of Bigness

Because of a natural human tendency to invest round numbers with special significance, we may expect to witness next month some kind of official salute to Metro Toronto as its population passes the 2 million mark. There is something to be said for making an occasion of it, if it prompts the area's leaders and citizens to take their bearings rather than drift aimlessly on the tide of rising population.

Bigness is not an unqualified blessing for a city, yet the dominant feeling is likely to be one of pride at the pace of our growth and at the thought that so many people from all over the world have chosen to make their homes here. It has all happened much more rapidly than even the best-informed among us imagined. Former Metro Chairman Frederick Gardiner said in 1953 that Toronto might reach the 2 million mark by 1973, but it has taken 15 years, not 20.

Canada's population has also been rising rapidly, but the urban share has expanded. Ten years ago, the Metro area population of 1,400,000 represented about 9 per cent of Canada's 16,500,000; today it stands close to 10 per cent.

What does great size give us? On the credit side we can point to the economic strength to generate wealth and a relatively high level of income; a number of cultural activities, such as theatre, ballet and symphony orchestra which could not flourish to the same degree in a smaller centre; the influences of two universities; first-rate hospitals; three daily newspapers; a vast range of shopping facilities and other services.

One might be tempted to mention expressways and the rapid transit system—and yet these are not really big city advantages.

They are, rather, among the facilities on which big cities must spend much of their wealth simply to make urban life tolerable. They almost belong on the debit side with air and water pollution, traffic jams, the high crime rate, the loss of tranquility and parkland, the erosion of individual identity and the consequent paradox of loneliness in a crowd.

From time to time, as civic leaders have looked over the disadvantages of life in a large city, there have been suggestions that we might achieve the best of all possible worlds by deliberately cutting off growth at some predetermined level. There is some doubt about the practicality of the idea, however, and in any case it smacks of retreat from problems which could be made to yield in the face of intelligent planning.

In all probability, then, Metro Toronto, and the arc of heavy population that reaches around the shores of Lake Ontario on either side, will continue to burgeon. There are many larger cities in the world and there is much we can learn from them.

There is vulnerability in our size. (Pictures of mountains of garbage in the heart of Paris following a general strike illustrate how perilously close we urban dwellers run to choking on our own refuse.) But there are also reasons for moving with optimism and confidence toward our third million. The optimism and confidence could be enhanced, of course, if more of our 2 million souls accepted the challenge of leadership which a great city presents.

Summary: Let's not cheer too loudly because we now number 2 million.

When some necessary improvement is in jeopardy, the newspaper should be expected to come to the rescue. Donald Breed did exactly that when the town took it for granted that the proper authorities in Washington would consider its needs to be so self-evident it didn't have to continue its agitation. When their failure to make a nuisance of themselves resulted in an adverse decision, Breed and his fellowtownsmen were aghast. Their indignation is evident in the following "sputtery" editorial from the Aug. 21, 1959 Freeport (Ill.) *Journal-Standard*.

Flood Control Is a 'Must'

Flood control for Freeport, on the basis of a combined dike and bypass, has received a temporary setback through inability of Congress to allocate $10,000 for immediate restudy of the project. Nevertheless, flood control remains a very live item on the unfinished business of this community.

The project must be kept constantly before all authorities responsible for ultimately carrying it out. The real need of Freeport and the adverse experience and losses of former years must be made the material of a convincing presentation.

It is a remarkable fact that officers in the Army Corps of Engineers have repeatedly spoken of a "renewal of interest" in flood control for Freeport. The fact is there has never been any lapse of interest. What has lapsed has been the continuous presentation of our case. That must not occur again.

It is true that projects of this type have come to have a bad name with members of Congress, and a generally "bad press" throughout the country as "pork barrel" spending.

The correct and only way to combat the prejudice is to demonstrate the genuine need, the economic advantage to the immediate community and to a wider public.

The factual presentation of our case should be vigorous rather than apologetic, and supported by evidence of a local determination to obtain whatever rights are ours under the law which authorizes federal participation in such projects.

If we have rights here, frequently presented but never pressed, we should press them.

It is fortunate that budget hearings start in September, in the course of which inclusion of the $10,000 item in next year's appropriations can be urged.

Rep. Leo E. Allen has promised to make every effort to see that this item, a small one, is approved. Approval will be only a beginning of a long process. But the process has been too often started and interrupted in the past. Interest has never been passive; it has always been active. But the expression of that interest may have been too polite in former years. There is a time for everything, and the time for mere politeness is over.

The state has already put itself on record as willing to cooperate in a state-federal-local project. The city administration, the chamber of commerce and local industries are equally committed. From now on effort should not be interrupted.

Summary: We do too want that study.

Next comes an example of an editorial writer's getting out of his ivory tower to do the reporting for the news side in advance of and as preparation for institutional comment on the editorial page. The editorial writer is Albert W. Bates of the Orange Coast (Calif.) *Daily Pilot*. As the result of a personal tour and interviews with a score or more authorities, Bates wrote a full page illustrated feature, "Political Threat to Our Water," for the June 14, 1971 edition of his paper. Three days later he editorialized as follows:

Water in Jeopardy

For the arid southwestern part of the United States, no subject and no project can have more importance than the water supply. Obviously, without water no other aspect of life can go on.

California as a state, and Southern California in particular, have been farsighted in keeping the flow of potable water ahead of population growth and need.

The aqueducts, dams, hydroelectric power plants and irrigation projects which make up the system both within and outside the state stand as models.

Within California, the system has greatly reduced nature's own form of pollution—devastating floods which destroy lives, homes and the land itself.

But now one of the last phases of the State Water Project—and one of its most vital—is in jeopardy. It is the Peripheral Canal planned to carry fresh water down

the eastern border of the Sacramento-San Joaquin Delta. After years of study from every conceivable angle—agricultural science, engineering, ecology, hydrography, to name some—the canal was chosen as the solution.

It would provide fresh water to feed the agriculture of the Delta, constitute a dam against salt water intrusion from San Francisco Bay, protect homing fish on their spawning runs, and finally move to Southern California to help relieve the salinity developing in water from the Colorado River.

Five years ago there was no opposition. But then the industries with more than a hundred plants lining the coast of Contra Costa County had second thoughts. Under fire as polluters of the river system and San Francisco Bay, they saw the fresh water from northern California as a means to flush their pollutants.

State law does not recognize this as a legitimate use of precious fresh water. Nevertheless, the industries set out to win that water away from Delta agriculture and Southern California by defeating the Peripheral Canal project. They organized the Contra Costa County Water District. That district uses hundreds of thousands of dollars each year in a campaign seemingly aimed at dividing the California delegation in Congress and thereby blocking a federal 50-50 participation in the canal project.

Rep. Wayne N. Aspinall, D-Colo., chairman of the House Appropriations Committee, has told the California congressional delegation, "Get your own house in order before you ask Congress to appropriate the $120 million federal share."

The leader of the northern forces is Rep. Jerome R. Waldie, D-Antioch, who seems bent on making sure the delegation remains divided.

If this tactic defeats the canal project, the water will be sent westward, not to Southern California.

If he succeeds, the state would have to go it alone for the total $240 million bill. The cost would eventually be repaid by water users, but the state-federal partnership is needed now to get the canal built.

Southern Californians, and the central Californians also adversely affected, should join in a strong protest to Congress.

Summary: Because of greedy water polluters, we may lose $120 million federal money for the Peripheral Canal.

Among the favorable letters received in response to this editorial were ones from the state senator from the area, a member of the Senate Water Resources and Natural Resources and Wildlife committee, and the general manager of the Metropolitan Water District of Southern California who said it was the first time a Southern California newspaper had exposed the political shenanigans so clearly. It is congratulations of that sort which make the job of pounding out editorials seem worthwhile.

When civic pride is injured the loyal local newspaper is indignant along with everyone else. In a position to say so, it does as, for example, the Pittsburgh *Press* did Oct. 15, 1971.

Our Bucs Are No Bums

Whether the Pittsburgh Pirates win or lose the 1971 World Series, one thing is now clear: Our Bucs are no bums.

After the Pirates had lost the first two games to favored Baltimore, many sports writers questioned whether the Bucs even belonged on the same field with the Orioles —let alone appear in the same world-championship series with them.

Take, for instance, the esteemed Mr. Arthur Daley of the New York Times, the only sports writer ever to win a Pulitzer Prize.

After Baltimore had trounced the Bucs in the second game, Mr. Daley labeled the 1971 World Series as "strictly a bargain-basement offering that lost most of its zest and sparkle because the Orioles seem so utterly superior to the Pirates."

"*Although euthanasia is not a practice that merits approval,*" he added, "*this World Series may present an exception. It might even be an act of kindness for the Baltimores to put the poor devils out of their misery as swiftly as possible. Like four straight, eh?*"

But for haunting hyperbole one would have to turn to that highly touted sports pundit from Los Angeles, Mr. Jim Murray.

"This World Series," he wrote after Game 2, "is no longer a contest, it's an atrocity. It's the Germans marching through Belgium, the interrogation room at the Gestapo. It's as one sided as a Russian trial . . . Pittsburgh should ask where they go to surrender.

"*It (the World Series) should rank with such other great contests of history as the St. Valentine's massacre, the yellow-fever epidemic and the bombing of Rotterdam.*

"To enjoy it, you'd have to be the kind of person who goes to orphanage fires or sits at washed-out railroad bridges with a camera.

"Like the elephant, the Pirates are going home to die. . . . The situation is not only desperate, it's terminal."

      *   *   *

The very day this Homeric prose appeared in print, the Pirates upended the "super" Orioles. And they haven't stopped winning since.

The Series now stands 3 to 2 in favor of Pittsburgh. And by now the Pirates have outhit, outfielded, outpitched and outhustled those awesome Orioles.

The world championship, of course, won't be decided until this week end. But even if the Orioles manage to overhaul the Pirates (a horrible thought), the Bucs have demonstrated that they are no pushovers . . . and that even guys who hit nothing more than typewriter keys can be caught away off base.

Beat 'em, Bucs!

Summary: You fellows popped off too soon.

The series' outcome was a Pirates' victory, 4 games to 3, but the city's enjoyment was marred by news reporting, mostly by the Associated Press, that the celebration became an orgy with uncontrolled violence and "displays of public lovemaking, nudity and drinking." In an article, "Pittsburgh's

Ephemeral 'Riot,'" in the *Columbia Journalism Review* for January/February 1972, an editorial writer for the Pittsburgh *Post-Gazette*, Ralph Z. Hallow, revealed that the accounts, given sensational play in newspapers all over the world, were gross exaggerations.

CRUSADING

They give prizes—Pulitzer, Sigma Delta Chi and others—for courage shown in editorial stands which defy powerful interests or community prejudices. Usually these brave editorials accompany or follow news or feature articles and possibly also cartoons and other illustrative material. No better example exists than the case of the Santa Barbara (Calif.) *News-Press* which won the Pulitzer prize for 1961 when its 85-year-old editor and publisher, Thomas More Storke, was the first American journalist of importance to attack the then-thriving John Birch Society. The prize winning editorial appeared Feb. 26, 1961 as follows:

The John Birch Society

During recent weeks, the News-Press has sought to enlighten its readers about a semi-secret organization called the John Birch Society. . . .

First, let there be no mistake about this: Communism must be opposed vigorously. Its gains throughout vast areas of the world are shocking. Every American must be alert for Red infiltration. But that does not lead logically to the conclusion that to fight communism at home we must throw democratic principles and methods into the ashcan and adopt the techniques of the Communists themselves, as the John Birch leaders would have us do.

The News-Press condemns the destructive campaign of hate and vilification that the John Birch Society is waging against national leaders who deserve our respect and confidence.

How can anyone follow a leader absurd enough to call former President Eisenhower "a dedicated, conscious agent of the Communist conspiracy"? Those are the words of the national leader of the John Birch Society, Robert Welch, in a manuscript entitled "The Politician," of which photostatic copies are available.

The News-Press condemns the dictatorial undemocratic structure of the society.

The News-Press condemns the tactics that have brought anonymous telephone calls of denunciation to Santa Barbarans in reecnt weeks from members of the John Birch Society or their sympathizers. Among victims of such cowardly diatribes have been educational leaders, including faculty members of the University of California at Santa Barbara, and even ministers of the gospel.

The News-Press condemns the pressures on wealthy residents, who fear and abhor communism, to contribute money to an organization whose leader has said that "for reasons you will understand, there can be no accounting of funds. . . ."

The News-Press challenges members of the society to come into the open and admit membership. . . .

The John Birch Society already has done a grave disservice to Santa Barbara by arousing suspicions and mutual distrust among men of good will. The organization's adherents, sincere in their opposition to communism, do not seem to understand the dangers of the totalitarian dynamite with which they are tampering.

And if they believe that in being challenged they have grounds for suit—let them sue. The News-Press would welcome a suit as a means of shedding more light on the John Birch Society.

Summary: The John Birch Society is a menace and it can sue and be damned.

The Milwaukee *Journal* did not win a prize for its July 23, 1955 editorial but it captured the admiration of jouralistic colleagues for its courage. The *Journal* obviously was ahead of its times and almost two decades later this fact may be difficult to realize. Nevertheless, the editorial was several weeks in the making and publication was postponed because of differences of opinion among executives. Expecting a considerable outcry, the paper was surprised and, in fact, chagrined when it received only two letters, one pro and one con, after the piece's appearance. At a National Conference of Editorial Writers critique session, every participant agreed that his paper would not have emulated the *Journal*.

Exploding World Population

The population of the world is growing at the rate of about 90,000 a day! According to United Nations estimates, it will increase by at least 500 million in the next 25 years and perhaps by as much as 1.2 billion.

In the last 50 years the population of the United States has doubled, and since 1950 it has grown by almost 13.5 million. The baby boom puts pressure on our school system, and increased longevity presents acute new social problems involving our older folk. But as yet our bountiful harvests assure that none need go hungry, although the decrease in other resources is causing concern.

It is in other parts of the world, however, that exploding population is a force as powerful as that of the hydrogen bomb. In underdeveloped countries like India, China, Egypt and Puerto Rico and lands of limited area like Japan, population is increasing beyond all efforts to increase food supplies and provide profitable work. The UN food and agriculture organization, which has itself done an excellent job of increasing food supplies, estimates that for every undernourished person in the world before World War II there are now almost two.

The answer is some means to keep the birth rate within bounds.

This is the goal of the Planned Parenthood Federation of America. Its concern is the control of fertility, which involves both preventing conception for parents who want no more children and encouraging conception for those who suffer from sterility. Since 1948 the federation has supported 21 research projects—eight of which are continuing. The purpose is to understand the reproductive process better and specifically to develop a simple, cheap, dependable method of preventing conception without permanently affecting a woman's ability to bear children.

Perhaps the most hopeful research is with the lithesperm weed that grows in the Rockies. The Shoeshone Indians believed that its roots, when eaten by women, caused sterility for several days. Animal experiments now give promising confirmation, leading the federation to believe that if the substances that influence fertility can be extracted or produced synthetically, a cheap antifertility pill may be produced for widespread distribution.

The conviction that people in population pressed areas would accept such a pill is supported by the overwhelming response of Japanese women to the more dangerous reliance on abortion as a means of birth control when abortions were legalized after the war.

The consequences of overpopulation are appalling. Yet, as Harvard gynecologist Dr. John Rock points out, not more than 500 American scientists are directly engaged in studying fertility control, at a cost of half a million dollars a year.

By contrast, 145,000 American scientists and engineers are principally concerned with the problem of atomic energy. Known funds at their disposal are about two billion dollars a year.

"If we could muster about one-thousandth of this amount to finance the study of human reproduction," says Dr. Rock, "we could assuredly obtain the greatest aid ever discovered to the happiness and security of individual families—indeed of mankind. This would avert man's self-destruction by starvation and war. If it is discovered soon, the H-bomb need never fall."

Summary: We must practice birth control.

In 1960 religion was an issue in the presidential campaign. Sen. John F. Kennedy was not the victim of such vicious attacks as had been directed against Gov. Alfred E. Smith, the first Roman Catholic ever to be nominated for the presidency, in 1928; but he went to great pains to reassure non-

Catholics that he would not take orders from the Vatican or promote narrow church views. It was quite a blow, in the midst of the campaign, for Catholic bishops in Puerto Rico to become involved in their local elections, ordering their parishioners to oppose the incumbent government. In a series of 20 editorials, William J. Dorvillier challenged the clerics and won a Pulitzer prize for the San Juan (P.I.) *Star*. The first of the editorials was as follows:

The Pastoral Letter

The Catholic bishops who signed the pastoral letter forbidding Catholics from voting for the Popular Democratic Party have transgressed grievously against the people of Puerto Rico, against their country and against the Catholic Church.

Archbishop James P. Davis, Bishops James McManus and Luis Aponte Martinez have sinned against the people by making it mandatory that they equate their religious faith with their democratic political convictions.

The bishops have sinned against their country by making Puerto Rico the helpless pawn for bigots to use for their political ends, and to injure the Catholic Church in the national campaign.

They have sinned against the Church by making it a temporary synonym for bitterness and hatred, instead of love, among a people who know how to keep their worship and their politics separated.

The bishops have all the rights of citizens to express political opinions and to urge support for their chosen candidates. But they have no right to use their religion and the weight of spiritual sanctions to intimidate faithful Catholics in the exercise of their franchise at the polls.

This pastoral letter is more than an indiscretion. It is an action devoid of any virtue because it so obviously is a result of long and thoughtful premeditation.

Because this pastoral letter is indefensible and inexpiable as an affront to a people who have built a model democracy, we hope Pope John XXIII will transfer the bishops to posts outside Puerto Rico and that they will be replaced by representatives of Catholicism who recognize the indispensability of the principle of separation of church and state in a democracy.

Summary: The Catholic bishops are misusing their religious powers.

When you've "stuck your neck out" and demonstrated bravery throughout a long fight, you may consider yourself justified in crowing a bit in the event you are justified. That is what the Toledo *Blade* did July 17, 1964 in an editorial which, however, stressed the serious aspects of the situation and not primarily the paper's vindication.

'A Mockery of Justice'

After almost a decade in the Ohio Penitentiary, Dr. Sam Sheppard, convicted in Cleveland for the murder of his wife in one of the most sensational cases in the history of American crime lore, is now held to have been denied his federal constitutional rights by a trial that U.S. District Judge Carl A. Weinman describes as "a mockery of justice." Whether this will lead to freedom or a new trial for Dr. Sheppard is, of course, still uncertain.

But The Blade, whose Dec. 22, 1954, editorial "Free Press And Fair Trial" helped gain for it the Ohio Bar Association's first journalism award for outstanding contributions to the administration of justice, considers it significant that the sensational treatment of the case by Cleveland newspapers which our editorial scored was one of the major factors in Judge Weinman's decision to grant Dr. Sheppard a writ of habeas corpus.

In 1954, we wrote: "The hue and cry raised in Cleveland newspapers after Marilyn Sheppard was found murdered could not help but inflame public opinion even as it pointed the finger of suspicion. One of the papers, which virtually demanded the arrest of Dr. Sheppard, almost had a vested interest in his conviction." We said then that "during the long-drawn-out trial the Cleveland papers, and a good many others, treated it like a Roman holiday. With a man's life at stake, they competed with one another in whipping evidence up into one sensation after another."

Judge Weinman, in his decision, writes that "If ever there was a trial by newspaper, this is a perfect example." One Cleveland newspaper, he said, "took upon itself the role of accuser, judge, and jury." And prominent among actions he said violated Dr. Sheppard's constitutional rights was the failure of the trial judge to grant a change of venue or a continuance due to the great amount of publicity.

This has been an amazing case from the start, bizarre in its nature and tangled in the legal maneuvering arising from it. And the finish is not in sight, although after years of fruitless appeals, up and down the legal ladder through state and federal court systems, and motions on all sorts of grounds, Dr. Sheppard's counsel finally found a legal key that turned.

Whatever happens, there can be no really satisfying outcome to this case in which the first court chapter was written in an atmosphere that the Ohio Supreme Court, though it upheld Dr. Sheppard's conviction, labeled that of a "'Roman holiday' for the news media."

Should Dr. Sheppard win freedom and there is no new trial, this would not remove the shadow attached to his name as an acquittal by a jury would have done if that had been the result of a fairer trial in the first place.

Should he be tried again, the state would face all the difficulties inherent in presenting a case now 10 years old and the verdict would still provoke controversy. An acquitted Dr. Sheppard would still have spent over nine years in prison that could not be recaptured. For the state and the public there would be left hanging the question of who did murder Marilyn Sheppard, and the trail would be cold indeed to follow now.

Should Judge Weinman not be upheld, his findings on the conduct of Dr. Sheppard's trial and the atmosphere in which it took place will still suggest strongly that our system of justice did not work in the Sheppard case as it should. Especially for those concerned with the delicate balance between the constitutional rights of a free press and those of an accused to a fair trial, Judge Weinman's decision would remain a most unhappy footnote.

For this clouded situation an abuse of freedom of the press is in large part responsible.

In his autobiography, a Cleveland editor did not hesitate to take credit for himself and for his newspaper for the role played in getting Dr. Sheppard to trial. He justified it as a service to the community and its enforcement of law to overcome what the editor was convinced was a conspiracy to defeat the ends of justice.

Newspapers and their editors do have to take risks in trying to fulfill their professional responsibilities to their communities. But The Blade still thinks, as it did in 1954, that "a fair trial, involving the age-old struggle of the individual against all-powerful government, is the most basic, the most essential of all human rights."

We do not believe that the rights of a free press are paramount to that of a fair trial, even though an editor sometimes yields to the temptation to act as if he were the savior of the law or the instrument of divine retribution.

Summary: Recalling the Cleveland paper's behavior, the court decision in the Sheppard case is correct.

Pulitzer prize judges study exhibits presented by contestants or in their behalf. Except for an additional section which included a miscellany of editorials on other subjects, what follows is the entire presentation by which John Strohmeyer of the Bethlehem *Globe-Times* won the Pulitzer prize for editorial writing in 1972.

Editorial Writing Exhibit

Events dealing with this exhibit began on the night of Aug. 5, 1970, when Bethlehem, Pa., experienced its first outburst of gang violence arising from racial tensions.

The Protection Neighborhood Youth Center, which is in the shadows of the stacks of Bethlehem Steel, was strafed and firebombed. One bullet killed a 14-year-old black girl and another seriously wounded a 16-year-old Puerto Rican boy.

The city was outraged by the incident. Much of the blame was directed at Robert Thompson, a bearded, long-haired high school English teacher who as a volunteer youth worker organized the youth center to serve the city's growing youthful Puerto Rican population. While a similar volunteer recreation center organized by Thompson had been operating usefully in another part of the city for four years, it made little difference. Police viewed Thompson as a radical who abetted troublemakers. Others began talking openly about his political views, freely branding him a communist.

The sudden change in the mood of the city polarized police, youth, and much of the community in a way Bethlehem never experienced before. City Council ordered the youth center—a city-owned building—closed and bars were placed across the doorway and windows. Responding to pressures about him, Bethlehem Mayor H. Gordon Payrow ordered police to get tough if youngsters persisted in congregating on sidewalks. The result was almost nightly jostling between police and militant youth.

Confrontations grew into club-swinging melees behind the stands and in the alleys after night football games. One night, police swept up five young Puerto Ricans, whom they termed the troublemakers, and beat them inside the police station, as a story documented with photographs of injuries and an eye-witness account of a policeman would later show. When the Human Relations director investigated rumors, he was fired and his report suppressed.

Inevitably, there would be a showdown and one occurred on Thanksgiving Eve, 1970. Police and youth battled in the street following a call to investigate a barroom brawl. Twenty persons were rounded up and arrested. One of them was Robert Thompson, booked, jailed for the night, and charged with conspiracy.

It is necessary to include this editorial position, published Nov. 30, 1970, to put the 1971 exhibit in perspective:

Destroying the Peacemakers

The Thanksgiving morning barroom fracas and the mass arrest of 21 persons in the near-riot constitute a matter of only the gravest concern.

* * *

We now see the rising militance of disaffected youth on one hand and the resort to blunter measures by police on the other. It is bad enough that two already hostile camps harden some more, but the tragic aspect is that police are losing the distinctions between the troublemakers and the peacemakers.

* * *

The humiliating arrest of Robert Thompson, a respected youth advisor, for the reasons stated is a sad turn. An honors English teacher at Freedom High who spends nearly all of his spare hours working with youngsters at Illick's Mill, Thompson is one of few in the city who lives and feels the problems of youth. He has been the one person with a finger in the dike while appealing within the established system for help in a deteriorating situation.

* * *

It is a tribute to his dedication that Thompson left his bed in the middle of the night in an attempt to cool off the confrontation developing in the area of the Ale House in the early hours of Thanksgiving morning. But as far as police are concerned, he was part of the problem. They herded him among 21 others into a paddy wagon for a night in jail and an arrest for unlawful assembly, conspiracy and disorderly conduct. A ranking officer conceded that Thompson tried to mediate in the ruckus. When asked why he was arrested, he replied, "Well, he was there."

* * *

The actions of Patrolman John Stein, who handed in his badge at the spot rather than participate in the arrests, is a far more vivid repudiation of such police shotgun tactics than any words of outrage.

* * *

It is not our intent to minimize the incendiary matters in the air that night. Coming so soon after a robbery and stabbing in another section of the South Side earlier in the night, the Ale House incident had all the signs of organized trouble. Yet, it is fully as important for police not to overreact as it is for them to capture the lawbreakers. Instead of resorting to hard police work to apprehend the real troublemakers and press the case against them to the hilt, police simply made a sweep.

*   *   *

The Thanksgiving morning incident is bound to set off new polarizations and cause more side-choosing in the community at large. Meanwhile, very little beyond words is happening to get at the root of the problem.

*   *   *

In a letter published elsewhere on this page, Prof. Victor Valenzuela of Lehigh University asks the crucial question: while frictions grow between the increasingly sadistic young and the increasingly irritated society, what is this city and its leaders doing to analyze the problem and bring forth the remedy? Strangely, this is the same question Robert Thompson asked two years ago, one year ago, and as recently as last month.

Early in January, 1971, the *Globe-Times* printed Patrolman John Stein's personal account of why he quit the force. He told of the agony of a city split by hostile camps, of police inviting confrontations with "Pork Chops," and of the police station beatings in which the head of the police department made it a point to appear and personally bloody the skull of one of the young Puerto Ricans. Photographs and hospital records documented his account.

In an editorial published Jan. 18, 1971, John Strohmeyer put forth the paper's position:

Remove Stigma

A councilmanic investigation of events centering around the "brutality" incident of Sept. 25 at the Bethlehem School District Stadium and later in police headquarters is long overdue. Yet, the necessity for such scrutiny should never have arisen.

*   *   *

Last week's revelations by ex-patrolman John A. Stein must finally strip away a layering of contradictions and begrudging admissions by police and city officials which have eaten into the very fabric of community social relations in past months.

*   *   *

As an early reaction, certain officials have objected to this "new light" without an adequate advance warning and time to prepare further explanations.

*   *   *

The fact is that nothing has been revealed which has not been common knowledge within the police and administration circles for months. But the police reports of what transpired inside the station on the night of Sept. 25, when five young defendants were roughed up, have not been made part of the public record to this day. Meanwhile, neither the mayor nor council saw fit to explain the stunning contradiction in which the top police tried to cover up the incidents by stating they knew nothing of the beatings one day and then meekly accepting the findings of the Human Relations Commission the next day by admitting certain incidents had occurred and that verbal reprimand had been issued.

*   *   *

Now with former officer Stein's eye-witness account of what happened that night, more scurrying for cover is again evident.

*   *   *

John A. Stein came to Bethlehem a "new model" policeman — intelligent, educated, idealistic and yet practical enough to participate in the department's own reorganization. His gradual disillusionment and eventual solitary stand for what can only be considered minimal standards of investigation and discipline point a sorry finger at police moral leadership.

*   *   *

Any organization under constant public criticism cannot be expected to operate effectively and, sadly, the nation's police have borne much of the brunt in recent battles for social change.

❖ ❖ ❖

Bethlehem, too, has changed much in recent years and police here have been shocked and dismayed to suddenly find themselves the objects of scorn. But just as much of this universal disrespect is unconscionable, the violent enforcement of seemingly more proper attitudes is dangerously reactive.

❖ ❖ ❖

Besides creating Bethlehem's credibility gap, a head in the sand attitude by the Bethlehem police has permitted abrasions to grow into a full-scale alienation of many young people. It would have taken little time and training to recognize that certain police responses heighten the problem instead of lessening it. Provocations to retributive violence by juveniles yelling obscenities is immature and hardly meets professional police standards.

❖ ❖ ❖

Acknowledgment that these standards were not met that night of Sept. 25 might early have cooled tensions and mistrust which finally culminated in the senseless events of Thanksgiving morning.

❖ ❖ ❖

The new decade has commenced on a hopeful note. Council's budget, with the mayor's provision for professional youth workers and staffing of youth centers, points a community commitment to a cooperative direction.

❖ ❖ ❖

Yet, the taint of the old will remain until the clouds lift from the contradictions that characterize the police actions following the night of Sept. 25. Only when all the facts are laid out and we get down to the real stock taking can we remove this stigma which hobbles honest police work and stifles the climate of goodwill.

When City Council refused to investigate the police beatings, an editorial challenged as follows:

Whitewash

The vote of confidence passed by City Council to reaffirm its faith in the Bethlehem Police force is about as meaningless as a vote for motherhood. It was an obvious attempt to apply a coat of whitewash on important issues raised by the concerns of former policeman John Stein.

❖ ❖ ❖

Ex-officer Stein, who served on the force two and a half years, might have found it easier to step out silently and concentrate on his studies at Lehigh, where he is completing his fourth year. However, the cover-up of the role of high police officials in the station house beatings and the growing needless alienation between police and youth compelled him to state his views and risk the scorn of many of his former colleagues.

❖ ❖ ❖

Only Councilmen William J. P. Collins and Walter Dealtrey seemed to understand the issues raised by Stein's account: (1) How could a departmental hearing which recommended a verbal reprimand really deal with the matter when, as it now develops, Public Safety Director Irvin Good was seen swinging at one of the youths corralled in the police station on the night of Sept. 25. Was Good identified as a participant, and, if so, was he supposed to reprimand himself? (2) There have been many police arrests but few cases ever get to the prosecution stage: Why? As Councilman Collins asked, "I would like to know whether any of these alleged criminals have been given a license to commit crime."

❖ ❖ ❖

Council's blindness to these concerns was best expressed in the long harangue delivered by Councilman Ray Dietz who attempted to impugn the motives of John Stein, the Globe-Times, and apparently anyone else who would dare to question the operations of the Bethlehem police force. It never occurred to him that the motivations might have been public interest. Instead of recognizing his own public duty to clear the stigma, he chose to pour on platitudes about his pride in the police force. In the words of Mark Twain, Councilman Dietz showed only he would rather be popular than right.

❖ ❖ ❖

A more proper way to "stand behind our police" is to ensure a responsible administration, to correct those abuses of police procedure which are letting so many arrest cases slip away, and to set standards for the vast majority of city policemen who want to do their duty above reproach.

❖ ❖ ❖

By voting not to clear the air, City Council indicated that it either doubts its own ability to muster "a calm and serious approach" to the truth, or it is so certain of the outcome of an investigation that it fears the revelations.

—Jan. 21, 1971

Mrs. James Caskey, Action Line editor of the *Globe-Times,* helped start a legal defense fund to help Thompson meet expenses of a trial. Some prominent people opposed such a community effort. To which the next editorial responded:

Lessening the Inequity

At the close of Wesley United Methodist Church's six-part panel discussion, "The Street Scene: Youth In Bethlehem," Dr. Charles Chaffee, retired Bethlehem Area School District superintendent, expressed reservations concerning the recommendations drawn up by the 19 panelists who participated in the programs. The response he received showed that others shared his beliefs.

❖ ❖ ❖

Among other suggestions, Dr. Chaffee urged "caution" when referring to proposals calling for the establishment of an area legal defense fund, and the support of the newly founded Lehigh Valley Bail Fund, Inc.

❖ ❖ ❖

He asked if anyone believed that a magistrate will hold a person over for court, and if the courts would take action against that person, unless sufficient evidence suggests that the party in question committed a crime.

❖ ❖ ❖

One point Dr. Chaffee apparently overlooked is that the basic assumption underlying our legal system states a man is innocent until proven guilty. Neither arrest nor arraignment establishes guilt or innocence, only the trial itself. Thus, until a verdict is pronounced, we are dealing with an innocent man.

❖ ❖ ❖

That innocent man is guaranteed the right to proper legal defense, and does not have to spend the time pending his trial in jail if he can meet the financial requirements of bail.

❖ ❖ ❖

For many citizens in this immediate area and the country as a whole, however, both bail and proper legal defense are luxuries. Whether the barriers be economic or educational these people are denied the rights of due process of law. Because of inability to finance bail, they are forced to sit in jail or prison, having been convicted of no crime, while others accused of the same or even worse crimes are able to pay bail and go free. The difference is in the pocketbook.

❖ ❖ ❖

The same is true for legal defense. For many, retaining a private attorney, no matter what the caliber, is totally unfeasible. They are forced to turn to the over-worked, under-staffed—and often inefficient—public defender's office. Again, another person accused of a similar or worse crime but with more economic resources available is able to retain a more effective attorney and perhaps win a more favorable verdict.

❖ ❖ ❖

To balance the inequities, concerned citizens in both Bethlehem and the nation are forming bail funds and legal defense funds. These non-profit organizations are established behind the premise of equal justice for all. They provide bail and assist in obtaining creditable defense for those unable to afford these items themselves. Without such groups, the noble ideal "equal justice for all" remains the biting reality of "justice for the wealthy and pot-luck for the poor."

—March 17, 1971

Impact: More than $4500 was raised. The fund covered all legal fees for Thompson, a Lehigh University scholarship student, and several others.

On June 7, 1971, the case against Thompson and most of the other defendants was thrown out of court, but even the judge compounded the injustice. Our editorial stated:

Badly Bungled

Judge Michael Franciosa had some harsh words to say about the defendants as he threw out the charges against them in the now lamentable Ale House case this week. It is too bad that the judge spoke with such a lack of distinction. He had good grounds to be distressed, but his blasts should have been leveled first against the ineptness of the police and the district attorney.

❄   ❄   ❄

Serious misjudgments started when Bethlehem police swept 21 persons off the street after the Thanksgiving Eve barroom fracas. Among those thrown into jail was Robert Thompson, then an honors English teacher at Freedom High and now a full time youth worker. Thompson was called out of bed during the height of the melee to try to cool off the militant youths outside the South Side barroom. However, police made no distinction between the troublemakers and peacemakers. Officer John Stein deemed the seizures so outrageous that he handed in his badge and quit on the spot.

❄   ❄   ❄

The ineptness was compounded in the all-night grilling and conferences at which District Attorney Charles Spaziani personally appeared for consultations. Bethlehem police insist the district attorney called the shots on the charges while Spaziani insists it was a police decision. Nevertheless, youth worker Thompson et al. were arrested for unlawful assembly and conspiracy, charges more appropriate for those plotting the overthrow of government than participating in a common barroom fracas. Yet, in expressing his distress that the men before him had to be freed because evidence did not sustain the charges, Judge Franciosa refused to even obliquely suggest that the district attorney's office bungled badly for bringing such a poorly mis-cast case into court.

❄   ❄   ❄

Finally, the judge himself added to the considerable errors in his tongue-lashing of all eight defendants as he threw the case out of court. He lumped Thompson, the city's most enlightened youth worker, and all others together and applied an even coat of tar on all of them. Again, in the judge's mind there were no distinctions between the troublemakers and the peacemakers when in fact each of the eight defendants had individual reasons for being at the scene. And each had a different purpose.

❄   ❄   ❄

It was merciful perhaps, that Thompson and the other defendants never did get a chance to present their case. This spared Mayor Payrow the embarrassment of trying to explain a puzzling ambiguity that still lingers. At the hearing in December, Patrolman James Doyle testified he saw Thompson at the scene pointing his finger at Mayor Payrow's face and exclaiming, "You'll pay for this!" In the trial this week, Doyle did not have Thompson pointing a finger but simply "hollering something." Even the reduced version is inconsistent with Thompson's low-key character. Yet this accusation is bound to stand in the public mind even though the mayor publicly said shortly after the melee that he didn't remember seeing Thompson, a person who served in his boy scout troop and later emerged as the foremost supporter and worker in the mayor's youth programs. Fair play demands that the air be cleared of this contradiction.

❄   ❄   ❄

Meanwhile, the whole case will go down as a sad chapter in Bethlehem history in which misjudgments, over-reaction and undoubtedly political grandstanding almost shattered a city trying to deal with common frictions. But there are heartening aspects too. Bethlehem police have instituted changes in outlook and procedure which stress preventative work and caution on over-reaction. Thompson and a crew of others trained for this specific duty now work with youth on the streets. But perhaps most heartening of all is that many citizens sensed the injustice in the Ale House mass arrests and came forth to put up bail money and later a defense fund. This was civic outrage expressed in the most constructive manner.

                 ✪   ✪   ✪

It was a hard lesson. Bethlehem is a wiser and a more sensitive city. And it has managed to preserve the loyalties of the Bob Thompsons despite ample cause for distress over the handling of the Ale House cases.
June 10, 1971

In addition to the foregoing, John Strohmeyer wrote about a dozen other editorials on related matters in this troubled period. They were an important factor, we believe, in influencing the following events that brought the city through its first racial flareup:

1. The Protection Neighborhood Youth Center reopened with the city's blessing. The building was refurbished, it was staffed by youth workers selected from the neighborhood and trained by the recreation department, and it operates today as something of an unstructured youth center within an Establishment administration.

2. Robert Thompson took a leave of absence from the school district to work full time with alienated youth as a detached staff member of the Family Counseling Service.

3. The Bethlehem Police Department, under Mayor Payrow's direction, took steps to correct areas of friction. It began to hold its own classes on minority problems and under a project strongly urged by *Globe-Times* editorials it funded two full-time policemen (unarmed) to work in community relations to spot potential trouble and to head it off.

4. The churches, in another program, warmly advocated by the *Globe-Times,* sponsored three trained street workers. The school district hired a Spanish-speaking teacher to help start programs for youngsters with difficulties adjusting to the English language.

5. Bethlehem enjoyed a quiet summer.

6. On Jan. 18, 1972, Robert Thompson was picked as Bethlehem's Outstanding Young Man of the Year, an annual honor awarded at a civic function sponsored by the Junior Chamber of Commerce. Among those to offer his congratulations was Mayor Payrow, recipient of the first such honor 21 years ago. Thompson was nominated by a panel of community leaders with the tribute: "He more than any of us felt the problems."

HOLIDAYS

No writing assignment of any kind results in greater use of platitudes, outworn figures of speech, too familiar quotations, and other devices for being banal and ineffective than the ordinary newspaper holiday editorial. This is not a purposeful situation; rather, an inevitable one. Nothing is more difficult to compose than one's second editorial on the same holiday, and it is not easy to be original or imaginative even when making one's first effort.

The most famous of all holiday editorials is, without serious rival, that which Francis P. Church wrote in 1897 for the New York *Sun.* It was a reply to a child whose father had suggested that she write to it to ask:

Is There a Santa Claus?

We take pleasure in answering at once and thus prominently the communication below, expressing at the same time our great gratification that its faithful author is numbered among the friends of The Sun:

"Dear Editor:
I am 8 years old.
Some of my little friends say there is no Santa Claus.
Papa says 'If you see it in The Sun it's so.'
Please tell me the truth, is there a Santa Claus?

Virginia O'Hanlon
115 West 95th Street"

Virginia, your little friends are wrong. They have been affected by the skepticism of a skeptical age. They do not believe except what they see. They think that nothing can be which is not comprehensible by their little minds. All minds, Virginia, whether they be men's or children's, are little. In this great universe of ours man is a mere insect, an ant, in his intellect, as compared with the boundless world about him, as measured by the intelligence capable of grasping the whole of truth and knowledge.

Yes, Virginia, there is a Santa Claus. He exists as certainly as love and generosity and devotion exist, and you know that they abound and give to your life its highest beauty and joy. Alas! how dreary would be the world if there were no Santa Claus! It would be as dreary as if there were no Virginias. There would be no childlike faith then, no poetry, no romance to make tolerable this existence. We should have no enjoyment, except in sense and sight. The eternal light with which childhood fills the world would be extinguished.

Not believe in Santa Claus! You might as well not believe in fairies! You might get your papa to hire men to watch in all the chimneys on Christmas Eve to catch Santa Claus, but even if they did not see Santa Claus coming down, what would that prove? Nobody sees Santa Claus, but that is no sign that there is no Santa Claus. The most real things in the world are those that neither children nor men can see. Did you ever see fairies dancing on the lawn? Of course not, but that's no proof that they are not there. Nobody can conceive or imagine all the wonders there are unseen and unseeable in the world.

You tear apart the baby's rattle and see what makes the noise inside, but there is a veil covering the unseen world which not the strongest man, nor even the united strength of all the strongest men that ever lived, could tear apart. Only faith, fancy, poetry, love, romance, can push aside that curtain and view and picture the supernal beauty and glory beyond. Is it all real? Ah, Virginia, in all this world there is nothing else real and abiding.

No Santa Claus! Thank God he lives, and he lives forever. A thousand years from now, Virginia, nay, ten times ten thousand years from now, he will continue to make glad the heart of childhood.

Of the multitudinous other pieces that have been written upon this maudlin display, none is more pertinent to this study than the following from the Louisville *Courier-Journal* for Dec. 27, 1936.

No Name On His Stocking

That perennial Christmas favorite, the *New York Sun* editorial, *Is There a Santa Claus?* has been dusted off for use by newspapers which still believe their readers will respond to a heart-throb. One of them, the *Edmonson News*, appends the signature, "CHARLES DANA." Thus is anonymity ungratefully rewarded.

FRANCIS P. CHURCH wrote *The Sun's* great Christmas editorial, and there are those who know details of CHURCH's career. But no one knows what else he ever wrote, although his products may have been of the finest caliber. That is the inevitable penalty—if penalty it is—of editorial writing. The individual shrinks; the world widens.

Who remembers as many as half a dozen great editorials and their writers? Editors, yes, but not authors of editorials.

The editorial has its effect upon the thought, as intended, but its title rarely remains with the reader. Even the subject matter grows cold with the passing of the days—like the grass of the field which today is and tomorrow is cast into the oven.

It is the newspaper which reaps the credit, if any, for great or attention-claiming editorials, which is as it should be. Even though the editor waxes great in other fields or his own, few know his products if his name is not signed. Who knows anything of what WILLIAM CULLEN BRYANT, HORACE GREELEY, NOAH WEBSTER, WALT WHITMAN, WILLIAM DEAN HOWELLS, THACKERAY, DICKENS or BARRIE wrote for their newspapers?

Personal journalism, even in its hey-day, was recognized as not an end in itself. One of its greatest exponents, HENRY WATTERSON, wrote in these columns:

> There is a power greater than this (personal journalism), and that is the power of the brave, earnest and thoroughly equipped mind which forgets itself, and goes in to accomplish results, not in its own exaltation, but for purposes cherished beyond its exterior belongings . . .

In other words, if you want a "by-line," start reporting the ham-and-eggers in the prize ring.

If FRANK CHURCH, whose "boss" is credited with his famous editorial, were alive today he might answer VIRGINIA O'HANLON by saying: "Yes, there is a *Santa Claus*, VIRGINIA, but not for editorial writers."

Some editorial writers use the occasion of the year-end holidays to philosophize for the benefit of what they must consider a serious body of readers. The New York *Times* probably has the wherewithal to obtain the best possible talent for every occasion. It's Dec. 24, 1971 editorial was typical.

God Rest Ye Merry . . .

It is probably just as well that Christmas comes but once a year. People are capable of dispensing and absorbing just so much good cheer, and by a Gresham's Law of its own, the real thing can easily be driven out of circulation by a synthetic product generated by canned caroling, Santa Clauses standing on the sidewalks and even outsize doctors' bills bearing Christmas seals on the envelope.

The displacement might not matter much were it not for the fact that the genuine product, never in long supply, has grown scarcer in these years of affluence, enlightenment and rising expectations. Or does it only seem so because cheer these days is not only apologetic and easily subverted but plainly unfashionable? It is considered naive, square—something hardly to be countenanced in a sophisticated salon.

The prevailing cheerlessness is explained by some in terms of Attica, Bangladesh, the recession, the Nixon Court and other such deplorable aspects of the year's news. But it is greatly to be doubted that, except where the recession has hit home, any of these are enough to produce a pervasive melancholia in the general population.

And even if they were, it is hard to see why the world would be less given to Christmas cheer this year than it was in any of the 1,970 years of the Christian era that preceded it. If social consciousness is the touchstone, why was anyone in his right mind cheerful even in that golden afternoon at the turn of the century, when the world was calm on the surface but racism was still unconcealed and violent, when labor was beaten down and children worked in coal mines, when woman's place was either in the kitchen or the sweatshop?

The world is not appreciably happier for the social advances made since then, because people do not care much about where the human race has been but only where it is at the moment and why it isn't further along. That is how progress is made. But since perfection is forever elusive, frustration grows with each advance, and if it is good cheer that one seeks, he had better seek it in himself, for he will not find it in progress—either in laws and movements which invariably stop short of achieving the miracles he hopes for, or in new political heroes, whose feet inevitably turn out to be made of clay.

The good cheer of Christmas—the real thing—now, as always, is extremely personal, a flickering but ancient hope in the heart of man that has nothing to do with buying and selling or social progress or politics. Cutting through the wrappings to this core of the day, we wish our readers, personally and individually, a Merry Christmas tomorrow, and many more to come.

Until its untimely end in 1966 the rival New York *Herald Tribune* used to compete in seriousness on such occasions, as the following Jan. 1, 1943 editorial illustrates.

A New Year Comes

The great wheel has turned again; that small drop of matter upon its vast, invisible rim, that little and spinning ball we call the earth, has completed another circuit through the soulless and empty passages of space; while in the streets at midnight last night the cowbells and tin horns and whistles celebrated this cosmic and at the same time largely irrelevant event with their minuscule clamor. A new year has been ushered in.

In a way it means nothing. The earth has wheeled through a myriad of journeys around a sun which is itself drifting through the enormous depths of chaos; there is no beginning or end to any of them; a new year is always starting at every point in the endless path, and the moment we happen to have selected for this observance is purely arbitrary and accidental.

In a sense the new year is meaningless. It is the intervention of astronomy into the tight-woven and continuous web of human affairs. It has no significance for either; it has no actual existence in the cold, impersonal reaches of space, neither does it mark any real division in the tense issues of life and death, of love and battle, in which humanity is engaged. Yet in another sense it means a great deal for both.

The new year is a recognition of man's dependence upon the empty forces—the motions of stars and planets, the operation of gravity, the interaction of the seasons—by which he is bound; it also marks his magnificent and presumptuous insistence upon imposing on these inhuman powers his own sense of order, of logic and of fitness. There is no sign-post in the heavens marking the end of the final hour of the twelfth month of the year; mankind consequently has set up one of its own, and blows its own tin whistles, however tinny their sound in the great reaches of interstellar space, to announce the genuine importance of that achievement.

It is important. It means that the idea of order and fitness can be, in some measure, imposed upon the dark and primitive tides which surge through and around our existence.

Each New Year's Day is an announcement, not only that man has achieved a certain understanding of, and therefore a conquest over, the immense motions of the planets, but that he can understand and conquer the many other mysterious forces in himself and in his environment, reducing them as well to a similar order and logic.

This year finds millions of men and women locked in a terrestrial struggle—in which many must yet die, must suffer bereavement and loss and injury—directed fundamentally toward that end. It is a war waged to set up the fixed signposts of decency and peace and order in human relations which the primeval chaos failed to supply. It is a war which a year ago was being lost, which today—however little we can pierce the future or foretell the length and agony of the road—is beginning to be won.

A tin whistle, sometimes, is a nobler and a braver instrument than all the sonorous trumpets of eternity.

Lucky is the editorial writer who can find an appropriate local news peg to use as a text, or at least a pretext, for a slightly different Christmas editorial. The Chattanooga *Times* was able to do so Dec. 24, 1971 as follows:

The Best Gift of All

What could be a more precious gift at Christmastide, or at any other time, for that matter, than that of life itself?

Of such nature was the act in which firemen, policemen and rescue squad members participated Tuesday in rescuing five-months-old Roslyn Gaines from a burning apartment in the Boone-Hysinger Homes. Quite literally they returned her to the land of the living through expert resuscitation measures.

Police Lt. Bernard Gloster, a chance by-passer as the fire broke out, radioed for assistance and then attempted to go into the apartment himself. He was driven back by heat and smoke. Firefighting equipment was on the scene quickly, and Firemen Roy Creasman and Ronnie Wendt donned masks to search the rooms for the infant. Once she was found and brought outside, Fireman David Brown began to apply mouth-to-mouth resuscitation. On the trip to the hospital he and Gene Glaze of the rescue squad managed to restore her heartbeat by massage.

All in a day's work? Perhaps in a sense, because it was what the men are trained to do. But the circumstances demonstrated extraordinary ability and devotion to duty by all those involved. And what a day it was in the life of tiny Roslyn Gaines.

Many holidays and anniversaries, especially patriotic ones, provoke historical resumés and comparisons with contemporary situations. These must be carefully handled so as not to be merely encyclopedic. The following from the Patterson (N.J.) *News* of Nov. 25, 1970 is soporific, almost completely lacking in originality

A Day for Thanksgiving

It would be a rare person, indeed, and one to be pitied, who cannot find cause for giving thanks. The blessings are there and the purpose of the Thanksgiving holiday is to bring them to mind and reaffirm in all of us a spirit of gratitude.

Few improvements in the lot of mankind have ever evolved without strife, or convulsive upheavals even though some wars have not brought the benefits for which they were fought.

Our Revolutionary War guaranteed the independence which enabled a free people to build the greatest nation on earth, a country where there has been and still is opportunity for all and where life is better than under any other flag. The Civil War, with its pain and death, preserved the union and made possible great gains in human welfare.

Our modern wars have been thrust upon us by those who would enslave peoples and by those who murdered millions in race hatred.

These wars did not bring the hoped-for lasting world peace but they did deliver things for which to be thankful.

We must be grateful for life, for sustenance of life, for our families, for our friends, for our opportunities. If we each were to put our troubles in our own bag, throw our bags in with those of others, and if it became a matter of choice, we would usually take our own bag back.

The United States has problems but the bright side of the ledger is fuller than the dark side and we can offer thanks in advance for the good which we can hope will come out of our present troubles.

The Pilgrim fathers observed the first Thanksgiving in October 1621 to give thanks for a bountiful harvest. Another Thanksgiving day was observed in the summer of 1623 at the end of a drought.

President George Washington assigned Thursday, Nov. 26, 1789 "to be devoted by the people of these states to the service of that great and glorious Being. . . ." After that, various states and sections had days of thanksgiving but the next official national recognition was given by President Lincoln when he proclaimed the last Thursday in November 1863 "as the day of thanksgiving and praise to our beneficent Father who dwelleth in the heavens. . . ."

Historians do not generally recognize an earlier proclamation by President Lincoln because it dealt chiefly with thanks for victories in the Civil War.

Some travelers observed two official Thanksgivings in 1939 when President Roosevelt, to extend the Christmas shopping season, advanced the holiday one week. Some states did not go along with the President and celebrated on the usual date and this custom is once again observed.

We do have many things to be thankful for as individuals, as a nation, as inhabitants of the Earth, so almost universally we will say thanks with prayer that we live in a blessed land.

The following, which appeared in the Fort Wayne (Ind.) *Journal-Gazette* for Nov. 26, 1970, had the virtue of being brief but that's about all that can be said for it. The profound thoughts turn out on analysis not to be so profound at all, just boringly commonplace. Play semanticist and substitute "blab" for every virtue word, line after line. You'll not have much left.

Happy Thanksgiving

What an experience it would be, if those of us who are celebrating Thanksgiving today, could be transported back through time and actually see at first hand the Thanksgiving celebration of the Pilgrim Fathers and Mothers at Plymouth, Mass., in 1621.

What a remarkable little group of men and women they were. How the future years have respected them!

They knew the meaning of hardship. They had the courage to rise above it.

We hope they always will keep their honored place in our history and that we shall always try to be like them.

On this Thanksgiving today in 1970, do we have the clear vision to see what our America is like?

Do many people get a distorted view of their country and its contemporary civilization?

Are we properly grateful for what we have and what we shall be able to attain in the years immediately before us?

We have faults, but we have virtues.

We have poverty, but we have wealth.

We have illiteracy, but we have knowledge.

Do we overstress the shortcomings, and understress the positive achievements?

What would the Pilgrim Fathers think of the progress which we have made since their time on this continent? They could hardly believe it.

And sometimes we—of this generation—do not seem to believe it either.

We must give thanks to God for what we have attained. We must add to it.

We must increase our energy, our aspirations and our faith.

We must strive in the days ahead of us for peace, for justice, for nobility of spirit.

That it is possible to express sentiment without becoming sentimental and to be original while using a strictly orthodox style was excellently demonstrated by the Baltimore *Sun* for Nov. 24, 1961.

Thanksgiving

Mrs. Klein was low in spirit as she told her first-graders, as in so many years past, to draw a picture of something for which they are thankful. She thought once again of how little to be thankful for these particular children, the mixed offerings of a progressively deteriorating neighborhood, actually had. She wondered what she herself in her lonely state would have drawn, if the assignment were hers.

From her long experience as a teacher Mrs. Klein knew that when it came time to show the papers, most of the class would have drawn pictures of turkeys or of bountifully laden Thanksgiving tables. That was what the majority believed was expected of them. She also knew with certainty that Janey would draw a picture labeled "Mother," because Janey's mother would have expected it of her. As for Robert, he would draw a battleship because he was always drawing battleships (although his explanation would be as plausible as ever: battleships protect us and so they are something to be thankful for).

What took Mrs. Klein aback was Douglas's picture. Douglas she looked upon as her true child of misery, so scrubby and forlorn, and so likely to be found close in her shadow as they went outside for recess. Douglas's drawing was simply this:

A hand obviously, but whose hand? The class had its own ideas, seemingly captivated by the abstract and surprising image. "I think, Teacher, that it must be the hand of God that brings us food," said one.

"A farmer," said another, "because they grow the turkeys."

"It looks more like a policeman, and they protect us."

"So do the battleship men." (This from Robert.)

"No, not a policeman; the crossing guard lady who helps us across the street."

"Mothers help children most of all." (Jane, of course.)

"It's Uncle Sam, Mrs. Klein. I remember a hand in the paper like that once, taking some children into a school."

"I think," said Lavinia, who was always so serious and final, "that it is supposed to be all the hands that help us, only Douglas could only draw one of them."

Mrs. Klein had almost forgotten Douglas in her pleasure at finding the class so responsive. He looked embarrassed now, and unwilling to explain to the class. When she had the others at work on their numbering, she bent over his desk, seeing again the raveled sweater against the dirty neck, and asked whose hand it was. Douglas barely mumbled, "It's yours, Teacher."

Back at her desk Mrs. Klein thought of how she must have taken Douglas by the hand from time to time. She often did that with the children, and Douglas was usually standing silently by. But that it should have meant so much. Perhaps, she reflected, this was her Thanksgiving, and everybody's Thanksgiving. Not the material things given unto us, but the chance in whatever small way to give something to others.

SEASONS

The New York *Times* is in a class by itself for its short editorials on the seasons, almost month by month. They vary, some being highly descriptive, some scientific, some historical or poetic, but all have the same flavor of creativeness. Here are a few examples of the *Times* original seasons editorial features.

The Year's High Noon

Summer comes, with the solstice, tomorrow. We are now in the midst of the year's longest spans of daylight, though by the end of the week they will have begun to shrink again toward autumn and October. A late spring made everything hurry into June, and now July is just ahead of us.

But we enter summer with the natural world well in order. There will be a new moon on Tuesday. Venus is the morning star. The zodiacal sign changes from the Twins to the Crab. The Little Bear stands on his tail in the northern sky at evening, and the Big Bear is high overhead. The brook in the meadow still burbles, not yet shrunken with summer, and the river flows as deliberately as time itself.

Wild roses still bloom at the pasture's edge. First cutting of hay is baled and stowed and the meadow is green with new growth. Field corn reaches for the sun. Garden peas fatten pod, lettuce heads, strawberries ripen. Summer, and the house wrens bubbles with morning song, the wood thrush sings to the warm evening. Slow dusk is freckled with fireflies, prickled with mosquitos. Dawn is gauzed with mist over the lake, fragrant with the smell of mountain pines. Noon begins to simmer and quiver with the shrilling of the cicada.

The countryman now has time to catch a quick breath between hayfield and cornfield, the city man and his family have time to take a vacation. Suddenly we all are aware that summer passes, even as winter, and that the year's high noon cannot last forever.

June 20, 1971

The Fall

The color comes, creeping down from the north in slow waves of gold and crimson in birch and maple, and for a little while we marvel at the sweep of beauty, cherish the spectacle of a single tree. The totality of change, of a green world gone and a dazzled, emblazoned world taking its place, is almost beyond belief. Then comes rain and wind, and the ultimate meaning of fall is at hand.

Autumn is a calendar season, but fall is the time when the color comes swirling down from the treetops. Day before yesterday the rising sun lit a vast bonfire in the maples, and at noon the light beneath them was so golden it shimmered. Yesterday it rained. Today the maples stand half naked against the clearing sky and the incredible wealth of beaten gold is on the ground beneath them. Fall has come, the fall of the leaves.

Color persists, but except in the oaks it is in tatters and remnants. And the oaks, with their deep reds and purples and leathery browns, only emphasize the fall. Birches stand slim against the hillsides. Elms are a row of witches' brooms.

On the ground the fallen leaves are restless, skittering at the roadsides, drifting into the fence corners, free as the wind itself. But their colors already begin to fade. Their brief glory is gone. Winter will quiet them, mat them, leach them, make the fall a meaningful part of the year, the whole.

—Oct. 25, 1964

Change

Old weather lore says only that March will be windy, choosing not to prophesy even from week to week. But of one thing we may be sure—March not only brings change but is change. You see it, you hear it, you feel it.

A March day that starts with a snow squall may turn to rain before noon and become mild as May and sunny as June by three o'clock. A March week that begins with a thaw that could bring violets to bloom by Friday may switch to brittle cold and ice again by Tuesday evening; and what will happen by week's end is anybody's guess. But the trend is there, the trend toward April, toward spring. You see it now in the color of the red-osiers and the willows.

You hear change beside any brook. Those fortunate enough to live beside a brook can almost gauge the temperature, morning, evening and night, by the brook's chatter and song. A day of melt back in the woods and on the hilltops makes the brook sing of April well into the night. The lakes are still hostaged to winter, but the rivers have broken their bonds and the crunch of floes tells of the break-up of February far upstream.

You feel the change in the air. The March wind lacks the fang of January. It isn't a warm wind, but it isn't fresh out of Saskatchewan. And on a sunny afternoon when the wind is calm you can feel the change in the very sunlight. You remember that gentle touch. That, you know, is the way spring feels. It may vanish with a passing cloud, but it will come again.

—March 14, 1971

April Dawn

Dawn comes surprisingly early, with sunrise just before 5:00. It is a misty dawn. Not fog, but mist, which begins to lift before sunrise but lingers like the most filmy folds of gauze for the first rays to glint and gleam through, especially over the river in the valley and the lake at the foot of the mountain.

Trees and bushes are gemmed with the night's heavy dew. First leaves have begun to appear, a green haze in the woodland's lower story. Above, in the treetops, is the pastel promise of summer's green canopy. Now it is the greenish yellow blossoms of the elms, the crimson of the red maple's buds and flowers, the blush of buds on the white-bolled birches. There is little green yet in the treetops, but it will spread up from the pastures and the meadows and the brooksides, from the understory bushes. The green will rise like the night's mist, even from the bloodroot leaves at the woodland's border and the anemones, their leaves made twice as green by the whiteness of their bloom. April's early blossoms are the promise of the flowery floods of May.

Promises too are the first-light songs of the awakening birds. Cardinals, with their clear, loud whistling. Robins with their old, familiar songs only slightly varied, one singer to another. Orioles, thrashers, tanagers, grosbeaks—the treetops echo and the mist makes it sound like a chorus in a vast auditorium. Nearby is the sudden burst and rapid trill of a house wren, the clear, high trill of a field sparrow. All welcoming sunrise, another day. All promising tomorrow, and May, and June and the coming of summer.

—April 23, 1972

A more orthodox or conventional handling of April is the following from the Minneapolis *Tribune* for April 19, 1970.

On the Question of April

Without T. S. Eliot, spring essayists would have no one to quote when they call April the cruelest month, and without the Internal Revenue Service there would be one less subject to make bad jokes about. Although not unequivocally in favor of April, we hold the view that it is something better than the wasteland time of year.

Tax collectors, like draft boards and meter maids and other modern amenities, are only a manifestation of democratic self-rule. And certainly one ought to applaud such efforts at bureaucratic friendliness as the invitation received the other day by an acquaintance to come in and see the Internal Revenue people. "We will make our review of your records as brief and as pleasant as we can," said the notice. The fact that the law requires the taxpayer to appear was not touched upon until the last paragraph and even then, discreetly.

But April is more than income-tax deadlines. Only the dour would say that it is also a reminder that real estate taxes come due next month. Others, we among them, are cheered by the disappearance of the last traces of snow, worried that summer may bring a lengthening of miniskirts, delighted with April rain and sunshine alike, and hopeful that it is not too late to prevent in later years the silent springs predicted by Rachel Carson.

April makes no distinctions. It can be enjoyed by elitist or majoritarian, Southern strategist or Northern liberal. That lyric line of Robert Browning's—"The lark's on the wing"—would have to be updated to include hawks and doves. Even though all's not quite right with the world, on balance we approve of April.

The beginner may think these are filler editorials and not difficult to write. He'll know better after he has tried to do it himself. The practice will be excellent for him.

IX

Special Fields

1. Politics
2. Education
3. Labor
4. Crime

Unless it occurs locally a world series or championship prize fight or similarly important sports event will be ignored by most editorial pages. Fans hardly would respect the opinions of an editorial writing generalist; they have become conditioned for more than a generation to turn to the sports pages for analytical comment and criticism by experts whom they take great delight in second guessing as they do umpires, referees, coaches and managers.

There are other special audiences for which the editorial page is not the primary source of intellectual provocation or leadership; and the trend is growing to limit the range of topics with which the formal editorial page writers must concern themselves. The cause is the tremendous aggravation of social problems and of human knowledge in many fields which require high-grade expert knowledge and specialist treatment. No editorial jack-of-all-trades can cope with the complexity of modernity and few newspapers can come anywhere close to affording employment of a sufficient number of scholars to handle the assignments.

There is no topic or field of interest completely taboo to the editorial writer. However, he increasingly restricts himself to pointing out the general effects of an event rather than attempting a critical appraisal. For instance, if the local football team wins a conference championship, the formal editorial writer will offer congratulations, perhaps refresh readers' memories of the fact that the team's rise to high calibre began with the hiring of a particular coach or some change in facilities. He will not become detailed about techniques, tactics or strategy on the playing field. The same for new developments in science, religion, medical research, public health measures, pollution control, city planning, sharp changes in the business or financial world and many, many other areas. Experts, often with the title of editor, expound knowledgeably on such matters in other parts of the paper. Some of them have become authorities in their fields, respected by those whose activities they report and criticize. This is not to say that the editorial page cannot contribute to public understanding of any important matter. The editorial, however, is written by laymen for laymen and the time is past when such service is sufficient for the deeply concerned.

Today's social, economic and political problems are too many and too complex for generalists. More expertise and consequently more specialization is essential in any field one can mention, including editorial interpretation of contemporary affairs in a journalistic publication.

Another example: editorial page readers could not expect to find a discussion there of transubstantiation—whether the communion bread and wine actually change into the flesh and blood of Jesus Christ or are merely symbolic. However, if any church announces a change in its orthodoxy as regards this or some similar vital issue, one would expect the editorial writer to explain what it might mean in terms of membership, influence, and activities in the community as a whole. If, as now seems likely, American astronauts and Soviet cosmonauts frolic together in space, there will be plenty written about the technical achievement and its forecast for further scientific experimentation. Such speculative analysis will appear on pages other than the editorial which doubtless will confine itself to the political consequences of the event.

To repeat, there is no field which the editorial writer must avoid, despite the growth of specialists whose writings appear in other parts of the paper. There is, on the other hand, hardly a field left in which these specialists do not offer competition to the editorial writer in commanding the interested reader's attention. There are still some important fields in which the formal editorial writer can range at will while ignoring the fact that he is not alone in them. Among the most important of these fields are politics, education, labor and crime. Even though there are political editors and columnists, education editors, labor reporters and crime reporters, the average editorial writer operates as though he were ignorant of their existence. There are other fields in the same category, but consideration of these four should suffice to serve the purpose of this exposition. There is not a city or town, no matter what its size, that is not fertile soil for news and editorial opinion in these four areas. For the foreseeable future, it would seem the formal editorial writer will continue to

operate as though he were expert in these fields, possibly consulting other members of the total force somewhat more than in the past but without surrendering any prerogatives or admitting any disability to operate as though enjoying a journalistic monopoly.

POLITICS

When he was mayor of Waukegan, Ill., Robert Coulson, later an Illinois state senator, wrote an article, "Let's Not Get Out the Vote," which appeared in *Harper's* for July, 1955. In essence he advised his constituents and everyone else to stay away from the polls unless they had familiarized themselves sufficiently with the issues and candidates to cast an intelligent vote. An heretical attitude, one which Robert and Leona Rienow developed in an article, "Should People Be Dragged to the Polls?" in the *Saturday Review* for July 30, 1960.

It would be refreshing to come across a newspaper editorial reflecting this iconoclastic viewpoint, if for no other reason than to offset the monotony of the appeals to patriotism and pleas to support democracy which almost all election eve editorials contain. This is not tantamount to recommending that people not vote. Certainly there is no intention of suggesting that the franchise should be deprived anyone. Possibly whatever value that expression of the viewpoint would have would be in the form of shock treatment to arouse indolent citizens from their lethargic neglect of their civic responsibilities.

A prime function of a free press is to stimulate interest in and provide guidance in how to exercise good citizenship. All democratic institutions, notably the schools and the news media, should be dedicated to that purpose. Hence the task of motivating people politically is a year-round one, and trying at the last minute to shame those who have resisted previous attempts to interest them into going to the polls is futile and probably not in the interest of good government. An ignorant vote, in other words, may be worse than no vote.

What follows is a very wishy-washy appeal to voters to educate themselves on candidates and issues. It is from the Las Vegas (Nev.) *Sun* for Aug. 27, 1950.

Elective Officers All Important

As election time rolls around, the emphasis is often placed on key political offices—high state positions or local positions, which are generally in the public eye.

Offices of Governor, United States Senator, Congressman, and on the local level, Sheriff, District Attorney and perhaps state legislators receive a lot of the voter's attention.

There are dozens of other official offices, however, that should require the voter's careful analysis. Too often, some of the minor offices are overlooked, yet they are important to the voter because many of these officials will be making decisions of major concern to the voter.

An office may seem insignificant in the light of the greater responsibility attached to higher office, but no position which involves the welfare of the public is insignificant.

It behooves every voter to make some attempt to look into the background of candidates for the so-called lesser offices. Voting for a candidate merely because the name might sound good, or his name is in a certain position on the ballot is no better than not voting at all—in fact it is not as good.

The Southern Nevada Memorial Hospital Board, Regents of the State University, Public Administrator, Constable, Trustee of the School Board are all offices that might fit into this category, yet each one is of vital importance to the voter.

Try to check the backgrounds of the men or women you select for all offices, but above all, don't forget that any elected official should be chosen for his honesty, integrity, and ability.

Everything that the author of the preceding editorial wrote is, of course, true. The editorial, however, provides no help whatever by way of solving the problem of voter ignorance. It is more the responsibility of the news department than the editorial writers to tackle that situation and such an effort is usually made. Through news stories covering the activities of candidates, by biographical sketches and interviews with rivals on the issues, the attempt is made to give at least thumbnail sketches for the benefit of potential voters. The practice is widespread of presenting questionnaires to candidates to obtain their stands on important issues. Newspapers do this on their own initiative, and they also take cognizance of similar efforts by the League of Women Voters, Americans for Democratic Action, labor unions, business groups and others.

This fact gathering is for the purpose of acquainting readers with a modicum of what they should know about comparatively minor offices. Regular news coverage of the campaigns for president, congressman, mayor or other high offices, plus interviews and reports of position papers originating with the candidates' public relations offices, mean that the most important races are covered fairly adequately. Despite reforms there still is the long ballot containing the names of candidates for a sizable list of offices other than those which command major attention. Many, perhaps most voters have never even heard of some of the offices, much less of the rival candidates. Efforts to reduce the number of elective offices have shortened the ballots in some localities but proposals to do so are opposed by many who argue that in a democracy the people should be given the opportunity to make as many choices of officeholders as possible. Practically, well-organized political machines benefit by the long ballot because of the number of voters who vote the straight ticket when confronted with the choices between sets of unfamiliar names for offices of lesser importance, at the bottom of their paper ballots or the voting machines. Split voting is definitely on the increase for major offices. In 1968, for instance, Arkansas reelected a Democrat to the United States Senate and a Republican as governor and then gave its electoral votes to the presidential candidate of a third party. Similar amazing results are reported with increasing frequency in all elections. Old party loyalties are loosening and the independent voter is growing in importance.

For this development many explanations are forthcoming: the strengthening of civil service protection of government employes against dependence on political patronage; the diminution of ethnic or nationality ties despite the efforts of political parties to keep them alive; the increase in literacy and the amount of schooling voters possess; the decline in the importance of the precinct captain in the everyday lives of citizens in need of help and a reduction in the social importance of political headquarters and of political rallies, parades, picnics and similar form of entertainment. Modern life is so complicated that many institutions have been weakened in their influence on the present generation. These include importantly, the family, church, school and the political party.

The editorial page's role in preparing voters for intelligent behavior includes the endorsement of candidates together with explanations of the preferences shown. This usually runs a fortnight or so before election day, in time for the recipients to make use of the accolades in their campaigns, and it should be based on research into the qualifications of rivals for the same public offices. At a general election there may be hundreds or even thousands of contests within the circulation area of a metropolitan newspaper. It is utterly impossible to give reportorial coverage to these contests: for representatives in the state legislature from perhaps 25 districts; for congressmen from about half as many districts; for county superintendent of schools, assessors, auditors, sanitary district and forest preserve district trustees, park board commissioners, school board members, coroners, sheriffs, a multitude of judges and clerks and maybe even constables and justices of the peace. Newspapers try to give brief sketches of most of the candidates, but the data usually given are birthplace, education, occupation, marital status, military service and possibly religion. There just isn't room to describe every candidate's stand on the issues or to give his platform, not to mention any "behind the scenes" information to provide a realistic picture of what kind of person he really is. The information available to voters falls far short of what any employer wants before he hires someone. Voting is an act of helping to hire public servants and it is done without adequate screening.

When a reader asked, "Why do you endorse candidates for public office?" Albert W. Bates, editorial page editor, responded in the Orange Coast (Calif.) *Daily Pilot* as follows:

> Many people go to the polls without knowing the candidates well enough to vote on them—or don't go to the polls at all, for the same reason. We feel these readers are open to reasoned suggestions. We know the candidates both personally and from their records because we think this is part of our job. We share our special knowledge with our readers when we carefully exercise our privilege to suggest that a given candidate is best qualified for the job he seeks. We also are careful to see that our editorial opinions, expressed on the editorial page, do not influence our reporting of the campaign —or any other news—in our news columns.

Similarly, Richard B. Childs, editor of the editorial page of the Flint (Mich.) *Journal*, contributed this statement to a symposium on "Candidate Endorsements—Who, When and Why?" in the Summer, 1968 *Masthead*:

> In keeping with the conviction of the Flint *Journal* that a newspaper has an obligation not only to present the news as completely, accurately and impartially as

possible, but also to express its opinions and judgments on matters of concern to the public, this newspaper will publish its preferences for certain candidates in the Nov. 8 election.

Our endorsements will be based strictly on our judgments of how well the candidates are suited to serve the community in comparison with their opponents.

In some instances, we will recommend a vote for a candidate whose qualifications will not be all that could be desired but who, we believe, would be a better public official than his rival.

More extensive and informative was what Creed C. Black, editor, wrote in his signed column in the Philadelphia *Inquirer* for Oct. 25, 1970.

Here's Why—and How— We Indorse

By Creed C. Black
Editor of The Inquirer

When a man gets to be my age," Mr. Dooley once told his friend Hennessy, "he ducks political meetin's, an' r-reads th' papers and weighs th' ividence an' th' argymints—pro-argymints an' con-argymints—an' makes up his mind ca'mly, an' votes th' Dimmycratic ticket."

An editor's life would be simpler if newspapers made their political indorsements as automatically as Mr. Dooley made up his mind.

And there was a time in American journalism when that was the way they did it. In the age of the "party press," newspapers played the role of political organs with no pretense of fairness or balance.

A few, regrettably, still operate in that hoary tradition. But their number is dwindling. Over the years, most publishers and editors have come to realize that blind partisanship not only makes skeptics of readers but dilutes a newspaper's influence with the politicians as well.

* * *

Here on *The Inquirer* as on other Knight newspapers, we are guided by a code laid down by John S. Knight which says in part:

"We have no entangling alliances. We are not beholden to any political party, faction or special interest."

Those, incidentally, are the only political guidelines a Knight editor gets. This means that the buck for the editorial positions *The Inquirer* takes—including its election indorsements—stops at the editor's desk.

It does not mean, however, that these are just one man's opinions.

In considering this year's statewide races in Pennsylvania and New Jersey, for example, we invited the candidates in for a frank discussion with a group of our editors. Joining me in those sessions were Harold Wiegand, George Wilson and Herbert Harrigan of the editorial page staff, executive editor John McMullan, political writer Gene Harris, and on some occasions city editor Bob Greenberg.

Each member of this group was asked to submit his judgment individually, so abundant advice was available at decision time.

* * *

Predictably, the ultimate decisions—to indorse Hugh Scott and Nelson Gross for the Senate and neither candidate in the Pennsylvania governor's race—did not please all our readers.

Some have quite naturally disputed our choices, some have accused us of a cop-out for not indorsing either Ray Broderick or Milton Shapp, and one phone caller objected to the notion that we would dare try to tell HIM how to vote at all.

So why do we indorse?

Because we believe that one of the duties of a newspaper is to "audit" government affairs and share the resulting information and opinions with its readers. We further believe that the readers look to their newspaper for such information and opinion in political affairs just as they do in other fields ranging from finance to fashions to football.

We make no claim to infallibility, and we are not trying to pick winners as though we were handicappers. We are simply saying that on the basis of our audit here is a man we can recommend. And if we don't feel we can recommend anyone, we say that, too.

Our role is not to cast a vote but simply to add to the sum of knowledge and judgments the voter himself takes into the polling place.

It's inevitable that playing this role as an independent newspaper will produce some strong differences of opinion. But that, as some sage observed, is what makes horse races possible, marriages risky, and democracy work.

Black suggested the manner in which decisions are reached. Practice differs. In some chain operations, in presidential elections, votes are cast by the editors of member papers and the results bind them all. In other instances, there is considerable or even absolute local autonomy. On single ownership papers the publisher has the last word and the amount of voice others possess is his to determine. When there is consultation, usually involved are the editor, managing editor, editorial page editor, city editor and political editor, at least. In 1964, a symposium in the Spring, 1965 *Masthead* revealed, many publishers wrote their own endorsement editorials after their editors expressed strong opposition to Barry Goldwater. That year, for the first and only time during this century, a Democratic candidate for president received the support of more daily newspapers than his Republican opponent, the count being 41 to 34 percent. Usually the Democratic candidate receives the support of only about 15 percent and most of them are in the South where the Democratic leaders may not be too enthusiastic about their party's candidate. They remain Democratic only because of their congressional seniority which gives them control of most important committees. In 1972 about 95 percent of all papers which endorsed favored President Nixon over Senator McGovern. The solid South became Republican instead of Democratic and that included the newspapers.

The victories of many Democratic candidates, from Franklin Delano Roosevelt to the present, despite the opposition of a sizable segment of the press, makes the eagerness with which candidates seek newspaper endorsements seem excessive. Sometimes it almost appears in local elections that the support of a newspaper constitutes "the kiss of death." Such voter independence probably is an indication of a healthy democracy, but it is injurious to the morale of members of a newspaper's staff when endorsements are given officeholders whom the reporters have been exposing as incompetent or worse. In 1971 when all four Chicago newspapers endorsed Richard J. Daley for reelection as mayor, 88 editorial staff members of the *Daily News* and 61 members of the *Sun-Times* editorial departments bought space in their own newspapers to express their contrary opinions, based on what they had learned as newsgatherers.

An anonymous midwestern daily editorial page editor began his contribution to the Spring, 1965 *Masthead* symposium, "Our newspaper dealt with the presidential endorsement with a 'three-one punch'—that is, three years of supporting programs and policies of progress and one year of reaction."

A typical endorsement editorial was the following in the Buffalo *Evening News* of Oct. 29, 1969.

Ryan: The Right Man for Sheriff

The contest for Erie County sheriff has shaped up as perhaps the closest county race in Tuesday's election—in large part no doubt because of the glamour attaching to the highly-publicized marijuana and narcotics raids led by the Democratic challenger. Yet we believe any fair accounting will establish that the Republican-Liberal incumbent, Thomas W. Ryan, is far better equipped than his Democratic-Conservative rival, Chief Michael A. Amico of the Buffalo Police Narcotics Bureau, to handle the responsibilities of this important office.

Sheriff Ryan not only was a brilliant Buffalo police officer, rising to the rank of inspector, but he has served much more broadly in a series of high-level executive posts in both government and industry, including 7½ years as first director of the State Division of Safety.

His grasp of his duties is sound and perceptive. While he is amply aware of the seriousness of the drug problem, he points out that there is more to the Sheriff's Department than "arresting college students and reaping big headlines," and turning it into a "gigantic narcotics unit" with "a deputy hiding behind every bush on every college campus."

The sheriff has wide-ranging criminal and civil responsibilities, including management of the county jail, that require broad administrative ability and insight. He must, in Mr. Ryan's words, "recognize priorities, he has to have perspective, he has to know how to make an organization tick, he has to be budget conscious."

While both candidates display awareness of the need to modernize county law enforcement, we feel Sheriff Ryan has a superior sense of the constructive possibilities for advancing area police co-ordination. And he has shown a talent for working co-operatively, not abrasively, with the many town and village police agencies with which his office must maintain close contact. In spite of our high regard for the work of Chief Amico, we fear his rather flamboyant approach as indicated in the campaign might result in building up the sheriff's office as a competing rather than co-operating county law enforcement unit.

In short, Sheriff Ryan is a well-qualified incumbent who knows what he is about and who has completed nearly a year of successful performance in the post. If voters ever had reason to keep the right man in the right job, we believe they do in this case.

What do you do when you discover you made a mistake? Calvin Mayne discussed "The Unendorsement of a Candidate" in the Spring, 1970 *Masthead*. The answer: you just admit your error and give your reasons and hope it's not too late. In the case of a candidate for the Rochester city council, it worked and the *Times-Union* received credit.

It's not only newspaper endorsements that come in for adverse criticism, both within and without the office; the same is true of the ratings that politically-minded organizations give candidates. The Chicago *Daily Tribune* ran an effective editorial on this subject Feb. 15, 1972 as follows:

Propaganda By the Score

The League of Women Voters, which once styled itself as an objective and independent champion of the public good, has announced its annual ratings of the members of Congress. Senators Percy and Stevenson so pleased the league that they received scores of 100 per cent. Rep. Philip M. Crane [R., Ill.] and Sen. Barry Goldwater [R., Ariz.] were not so pleasing. They both received a rating of zero.

To the average voter trying to figure out how well his congressman or senator performed for him during the year, such scorekeeping must seem startling. Were Mr. Percy and Mr. Stevenson such paragons that they were perfect in everything they did? Are Mr. Crane and Mr. Goldwater so evil or incompetent that they merit nothing better than a zero?

Of course not. The league's scores have nothing to do with ability, diligence, integrity, or other things which might interest the electorate. Instead, the scores indicate how the senator or congressman voted on issues important to the league and how close he or she came to the league's activist liberal philosophy.

To reward the "good" and punish the "bad" senator or congressman, the league structures its rating system in such a way that the difference between the "bad" and the "good" is made to seem one of night and day—hence the absolute scores of 100 per cent and zero.

This propagandizing is useless to the voter. Worse, the League of Women Voters is not the only culprit. As *Tribune* columnist Willard Edwards noted recently, this heavy-handed stuff is practiced by groups all over the political spectrum. Big labor's lobbying organizations do it, as does the liberal Americans for Democratic Action. Another practitioner is the American Conservative Union, which deals harshly with anyone who veers from its ultraconservative principles. In its annual ratings, only two of Illinois' 11 Republican congressmen merited 100 per cent. The others, most of them men with solid conservative reputations, received scores ranging from 22 to 79 per cent. The low scores were attributed to a couple of "bad" votes on issues which were "weighted" for special emphasis by the A. C. U. scorekeepers.

"These ratings ignore such vital factors as the member's industry, his influence in committees, his ability to get things done," Mr. Edwards said. "They fail to supply the voter with the information he really wants—'has his representative in Congress fought to protect the interests of his constituents?'"

However bewildered he is by this rating system, the voter is not stupid. The ratings may say little about the individual congressmen, but they tell the voter a great deal about the organization compiling the scores. One thing they may tell him is that the organization and its propaganda had best be ignored.

Summary: Ratings of congressmen by private groups must be judged by the groups' purposes.

Often endorsement is all that a newspaper does for a candidate. This is especially true of metropolitan newspapers regarding the multitude of minor offices to be voted upon. On the other hand, in major races it is customary to enter into the campaign debate, once it heats up, mostly in support of the favored candidate. Sometimes this can be done by brief reaffirmation of faith as in the following from the New York *Times* of Oct. 26, 1970.

Voice of Courage

A nation starved for political leadership heard last night the moving voice of a public official determined to keep freedom from being assassinated by the ruthless night riders of the political right. The voice was that of Senator Charles E. Goodell explain-

ing—extemporaneously and eloquently—why he does not intend to submit to the acts with which Vice President Agnew and other Administration hatchet men are attempting to cut short not only his own political career but all independence and progressivism in the Republican party.

Over the years this newspaper has endorsed many candidates of whom we are exteremly proud, but Mr. Goodell's courageous declaration last night puts him at the very forefront of our list. New Yorkers can vote for him next week with a sense that their votes represent contributions to an America that remembers what America is all about, not a land sunk in fear, hate and selfish advantage.

A typical sober analysis of campaign oratory was the following from the Chicago *Daily News* for Sept. 18, 1964.

Backward with Barry

Sen. Barry Goldwater's campaign speeches in the South are heavily larded with a topic dear to the Southern heart—state's rights. One can almost hear the echoes of the guns at Shiloh and Antietam in the charges that the federal government in Washington must be curbed if the country is to survive.

The growth of centralism is undeniably a valid issue, and the trend in that direction worries many people in places other than the South. But the Goldwater proposals for reversing that trend go so far beyond the usual expressions of concern that they would, if put into effect, make for a revolution in mid-20th Century America.

In Montgomery, Ala., Goldwater drew a picture of a government with the President and Congress stripped of virtually all powers except those in the areas of foreign relations, defense, and the general welfare. The states would reign supreme within their borders, accepting a share of the federal income tax take, but spending the money as they pleased without any "interference" from Washington.

This is the kind of talk state officials in Alabama, Mississippi, and adjacent states like to hear. The federals are always meddling in one way or another, and especially in their insistence that contracts, aid for higher education, and grants-in-aid be administered equally without regard to color of skin. It would be so much simpler if Washington would just fork over the money and let the local politicians run the show in their own way.

But the Goldwater view glosses over or omits entirely some fundamental questions. For example, are the Southern states, in receiving "a share of the income taxes collected from them" to get that and no more? If so, the South had better desert Goldwater fast. Nearly every Southern state receives far more from the federal government than it sends to Washington. It is industrial states like Illinois that chronically run a deficit, pouring extra taxes into the Treasury for Mississippi and Alabama to draw on.

And why shouldn't the central government keep a close check on federal money spent within the state? Uniformity in such matters as highway construction would be reason enough to set federal standards. Guarantees that money collected from all the people goes to benefit all the people impartially are also needed—and especially in the South.

Goldwater is speaking in terms of conditions that haven't existed since the Civil War when he puts such stress on states' rights. Does he really want to turn the clock back, and undermine the federal authority that far? Or is he merely feeding the prejudices of the South in order to button up a few electoral votes?

During the same campaign the Evansville (Ind.) *Press* came up with facts and figures to refute what it believed to be misinformation. The editorial was published Aug. 19, 1964.

Goldwater Way Off Beam in Charges of Defense Lag

If any American has lost sleep over recent talk of holes in our defense system, he should be reassured by the statistics of Defense Secretary McNamara.

In long-range missiles (ICBM) we are ahead of the Russians 800 to 200, according to McNamara. In Polaris-type submarine missiles we lead 256 to 142 and ours are by far superior. In long-range bombers, which are the specific subject of recent dispute, our edge is even greater—1100 to 100, or 1100 to 250 if you count Soviet bombers able to reach only a fringe of the United States.

As to Senator Goldwater's fear that U.S. deliverable nuclear capacity may be cut down by 90 per cent in the next decade, Secretary McNamara answers:

"Our strategic forces are and will remain in the 1960's and 1970's sufficient to insure the destruction of both the Soviet Union and Communist China under the worst imaginable circumstances accompanying the outbreak of war. There should be no doubt about this in the mind of any American. There is none in the minds of our enemies."

Senator Goldwater himself is author of a statement, two years ago, which, in our opinion, applies accurately to the present situation. We quote from his book, "Why Not Victory?":

"During the presidential campaign of 1960 the absurd charge was made by Mr. Kennedy and others that America had become—or was in danger of becoming—a second-rate military power. Any comparison of over-all American strength with over-all Soviet strength reveals that the U.S. was not only superior, but so superior both in present weapons and in the development of new ones that our advantage promises to be a permanent part of the U.S.-Soviet relations for the foreseeable future."

Events proved both the bomber gap and the missile gap to be phony. Current implications that our guard has been let down, or is going to be let down, may be filed away in the same envelope.

These observations are not intended to discount Barry Goldwater as a candidate for President. A man should be judged on his total program, balancing the good with the bad, and the campaign barely has started. But we would say he comes on the far short end of this particular argument.

A visit by a candidate to the newspaper's circulation territory is always the occasion for editorial comment. Horance G. Davis,

Jr., won the Pulitzer prize for editorial writing in 1971 for a series of editorials in the Gainesville (Fla.) *Sun* in opposition to the actions and candidacy for reelection of Gov. Claude Kirk. The following was typical of the hard-hitting campaign. This piece was published Aug. 3, 1970.

Do You, Governor Kirk?

Governor Claude Kirk is due in Gainesville today, and we want to pose a question.

Does he want re-election so badly that he will pull a George Wallace and split Florida's people asunder?

It is a fair question, we think, because of Governor Kirk's racial posture of the past few months. Early this year, he sought extension of the deadline for school desegregation. This was not unreasonable.

But what followed was contemptible. He descended into Manatee County, twice suspended the School Board to keep it from implementing court orders, and caused a confrontation with U.S. marshals—almost to the point of violence. Under threat of contempt of court and $10,000 daily fine, Governor Kirk retreated while muttering "victory" all the while.

Victory for whom? Certainly not law and order.

The governor's latest binge concerns private schools. He attacked the U.S. Revenue Service for removing their tax exemptions. Governor Kirk conveniently ignores that the IRS ruling clearly applies only to segregation academies.

Does Kirk approve of federal tax exemptions to schools created to avoid integration? "I don't know of any school that is actually doing what you're saying," he replied.

We can give some tips.

● While he's in Alachua County today, Governor Kirk might chat with County Commissioner Ralph Cellon, whose Rolling Green Academy out Alachua way was founded after school integration in February, has 100 students, a faculty of seven, and tuition of $450.

● He might also look into the explosive expansion of the Heritage Christian School out on North 34th Street, which intruded on public school property to recruit students who had the necessary $575.

● He might ask about the embryonic Oak Hall Preparatory School founded by Dr. Billy Brashear and Dr. Harry L. Walker, open to all "without regard to race, creed or color"—with $1,100 tuition, of course.

These are not monumental and hardly worth pressing. More important is the state of Claude Kirk's mind. And we desire to address him directly.

Back in 1964 when passions ran hot, you said this, Governor Kirk: "I believe in equality before the law and equality of opportunity . . . We must put to an end the cultivated feeling of minorities and recognize that we are all Americans."

Back in 1967, you told the Saturday Evening Post: "I'm not one of those red-necked governors like Lester Maddox . . . I'm the only good guy in the South."

Later, when invited to a segregation conference in Alabama, you said: "We here in Florida . . . cannot join in attempts to subvert or delay the law of the land as interpreted by the Supreme Court."

The important thing, Governor Kirk, is whether you have abandoned these high ideals and cast your political lot on the side of bigotry.

Do you, Governor Kirk, think so little of your people?

Most campaign editorials, as in the illustrations so far given, stress the issues and the stands of the rival candidates regarding them. Sometimes the tactics employed to get votes require attention, as the Chicago *Sun-Times* believed when it published the following editorial Oct. 30, 1970.

Campaign Without Winners

The campaign which President Nixon and some of his colleagues have run has disturbed even some Republicans. New York's Mayor John V. Lindsay put it well: "When the President and his lieutenants tell us to be afraid, when they pretend that respected candidates condone violence—as though Weathermen were running in this election—they are deserting the essential principles of both country and party."

The fright-campaign theme Lindsay assails is exemplified by a full-page advertisement in today's Sun-Times which uses quotes out of context. Its message is that Democrats encourage, excuse and forgive violence, that is, make the streets unsafe. This is demagoguery of the worst rank. The ad was accepted in the spirit of free speech, a privilege its sponsors abuse.

In speech after speech Mr. Nixon and others have suggested that voting against Democrats will wipe away poverty, racial hatred, the war, recession and inflation. Vote, says the President, against the Democrat who "has given encouragement to, has condoned lawlessness and violence and permissiveness.

In brief, the President has reverted to the venom of his pre-White House days. He would lull the people into thinking America's terrible problems can be cured simply by voting Republican. Meantime, Mr. Nixon— and the corps of experts and writers he and Vice President Agnew have hired—tell us nothing of what is to be done about these problems. The President remains silent in the face of calls of leadership from his Commission on Campus Unrest and from the United States Civil Rights Commission.

Only two years ago Mr. Nixon said he would bring us together, partly through encouraging tolerance, by, as he put it, leading all of us in lowering our voices. Only two years ago the Republicans came into office partly because their then chairman, Ray Bliss, converted the faithful to the dictum, let no Republican speak ill of another.

Now the President has permitted a slashing attack on the incumbent GOP senator from New York, Charles E. Goodell, who is up for election Tuesday. Goodell, it has been made clear by Agnew and others, failed to support Mr. Nixon on too many crucial issues. Mr. Nixon chooses to ignore history: The health of the two-party system lies in each party's being a coalition of all sorts of interests and viewpoints.

The Republicans may carry the Senate on Tuesday. But it now seems that because of the campaign Mr. Nixon has encouraged, he will be faced with a bitter and hostile opposition. Opposition he had when he took office, yes, but it was not bitter or hostile.

We hope it is not so, because we pray for a successful President no matter who he is. But we fear Mr. Nixon's campaign this autumn marks his downfall with Congress. That body already is Democratic and now it is likely he will be faced by an embittered and truculent opposition.

In campaigning as he has, Mr. Nixon has ignored his primary job, that of leading and governing the nation. He must of course be a good head of his party. But his engaging in the crassest of partisan politics— the below-the-belt attacks on opponents instead of just stumping for his allies—has been an appeal to the worst in voters, not the best. As Lindsay also put it: "This is one of the few campaigns in memory in which men apparently seek not merely to defeat their opponents but literally to eliminate them from our public life."

Anyone's hindsight always is better than his foresight, and editorial writers are no exceptions to the rule. After the people have spoken on election day everything becomes clear. Whereas it was uncertain the day before what would appeal to this or that element of the population, once the votes are counted it becomes instantly possible to state exactly what issues influenced whom, why and how much. Maybe so, but a little more modesty might be in the public interest. If the editorial writer is so smart the day after election so that he knows exactly how to interpret the outcome why could he not have given everyone the benefit of his wisdom the day before the polls opened? To write, "The voters rejected this" or "They obviously favored that" is just foolhardy second guessing with hardly any evidence to support it. A typical editorial in the orthodox vein, just short of "We told you so" in spirit appeared in the Milwaukee *Journal* for Nov. 4, 1970.

Lucey's Solid Victory

Wisconsin voted decisively Tuesday for the politics of affirmation in the state government. Both the solid success of Governor-Elect Patrick Lucey and the stunning legislative victories in support of him mark the overthrow of the politics of negation and reaction that held sway until now, not in Gov. Knowles' office but in the controlling powers of the last two Legislatures.

Oddly, the voters appear to have decided that the kind of moderation and progressiveness that Knowles has stood for was more likely to come from the Democrat Lucey than from Knowles' intended Republican successor, Jack Olson. This was the thinking, apparently, much more than about party loyalties and a personality contest.

The big switch coming just at this time is historic, because Lucey is the first Wisconsin governor-elect to have a certain minimum of four years in office ahead of him. He won't have to start campaigning for re-election by next spring. He will have an unprecedented opportunity to make his program work. And he will be able within the term to dominate the appointive offices. If he doesn't come a bad cropper, he could thus establish his party more firmly than it ever has been.

The big switch coming just at this time may well be historic for the central city of Milwaukee and its metropolis, too. For Lucey's comprehension of the special gravity of metropolitan problems is distinctly fuller and more promising than Olson's appeared to be. If he can make his leadership effective, the prospects for fiscal justice and metropolitan solutions are suddenly bright.

If Lucey had been saddled with continuing Republican control in both houses of the Legislature, his personal victory would have had far less meaning. With astonishing forcefulness, however, voters swept away the power of Assembly Speaker Harold Froehlich and consigned his remaining right wing cohorts to the back seats. From a 48% minority position in the Assembly, Democrats seized 19 GOP seats for a full two-thrids majority.

This is what can put a Lucey administration in business. It is the big triumph and accomplishment. For a new speaker co-operative with Lucey will, through his appointing power, give support to the executive in the powerful joint finance committee most particularly. While the GOP still has the Senate majority, the Democrats gained there, too, enough to put pressure on re-

sponsible members of the majority not to obstruct sound legislation. The Senate may check Lucey but probably will not block and frustrate him in reasonable goals.

Wisconsin has opted for progressive state government. It has signed up for a potentially productive new administration.

Chicago Today made a penetrating analysis of campaign tactics, the effects of which were measurable. The following editorial appeared in its issue of Nov. 5, 1970.

Why the Vote Pitch Fails

One of the leading casualties in Tuesday's election was not a candidate or a party, but an idea. It was the belief, cherished by many political experts, that the voter is essentially a kind of robot. If you press the right buttons, he can't help but vote the way you want.

The idea may be repellent, but is not quite as absurd as it sounds. After all, if heavy advertising can sell products, why shouldn't it sell candidates too? The same impulses seem to be in play: the voter's [or the customer's] desires, fears, feelings of insecurity. If skillful commercials can direct these impulses toward the result the advertiser wants it hardly matters whether he's advertising a new detergent or a new candidate, right?

Wrong. Logical as the theory may seem, it didn't work Tuesday. It doesn't even seem to work in reverse, so that the candidates with the heaviest advertising always lose. One such candidate will win, another won't, and the pattern doesn't seem to have much to do with the hard sell one way or the other.

In Illinois, the big TV pitch seemed to backfire. The spot commercials for Senator Ralph Smith and Sheriff Joe Woods, which by implication accused their opponents of all kinds of unlikely things, helped substantially to defeat Smith and Woods. [Incidentally, a word of grateful praise is due here to WGN-TV, which refused to run quickie campaign commercials. On Channel 9, a candidate had to appear for more than 5 minutes on a non-news show or he didn't appear at all—a policy that we hope will be standard thruout the nation by 1972.]

The same lack of pattern resulted from the campaign forays by President Nixon and Vice President Agnew. Maybe they helped, maybe they didn't; in any case the results certainly didn't measure up to the effort. In particular, Mr. Agnew's performance as a name-calling virtuoso won a lot more applause than it won votes.

If our own feelings are a clue, voters not only are unimpressed by a big-money, high-pressure campaign of this kind; they resent it. They do not like to be treated as objects, so many voting units to be wound up and activated by the big spenders. And that's just fine with us.

The manipulators, tho, won't believe it. Rather than admitting that formulas don't work on the voter, they'll try to figure out where this particular formula went wrong. And we can bet they'll be back two years from now—this time with a sure-fire campaign strategy, a knockout winner, a pitch that the voters will just have to buy.

Most election postmortem editorials are according to formula or formulas. Among the possible themes are: "Our man has won and everything's now going to be better" or "We think the better man lost but we must now all support the people's choice and pray that he will do better than we had thought." Perhaps the most overused word in such prosaic effusions is "unity." All of a sudden, after months of wrangling, peace and prosperity seem to depend on the extent to which differences can be forgotten in a hurry. Most such bilge is printed for sensible readers to ignore because of the difficulty of thinking up anything else to say. Here is an example of a remarkably successful editorial which included most of what everyone else said, in repetition of what they had written previously, but which looked both to the historic past and to the future to provide perspective. The fact that this editorial has "held up" since its appearance Nov. 4, 1964 in the Hartford (Conn.) *Courant* is proof of its skillfulness. The readers of this book will be spared an example of the "peace in our times" effusions with which most editorial writers acclaimed Lyndon Baines Johnson's election to end the war in Vietnam—pronto. It would be an excellent exercise in humility for authors of political editorials to review their past efforts, especially their predictions during and after the votes were counted. It might inspire them to be a bit more cautious and it might make them not sound so much as though they possessed all-seeing eyes. Here's the Hartford editorial.

America Makes Its Choice

This unusual, vaguely unsatisfying, and often dirty campaign has brought forth one redeeming, cleansing, value in its outcome. In past years the extreme right has often cried out in frustration, as the Republican Party lost election after election, that the reason was that Republican candidates merely said, "Me too," to the Democratic Party's lead. In Senator Goldwater's own words, what the country wanted was a choice, not an echo.

We have now had that choice. Yesterday the American people gave their answer—resoundingly. Senator Goldwater was defeated by a heavier margin than any supposedly me-too candidate.

At times during the campaign, to be sure, the issue seemed clouded. In the first place Senator Goldwater, as he faced the reality of the voters' wishes, fuzzed up the image that had made him the darling of his adherents. As recently as in 1963 he had written, "I think Social Security should be voluntary." But at the Hershey unity conference last August he changed this by 180 degrees: "And let me also repeat—for perhaps the millionth time, lest there be no doubt in anyone's mind—that I support the Social Security system and I want to see it strengthened." As the campaign went on it became hard to tell, from the Senator's words, just where he stood on any issue. Still, few of us had any doubt where he really stood, in either foreign or domestic policy.

Then again the alternative offered by President Johnson was neither as strong nor as clear as it might have been. He was the effective politician, no doubt. Here was the great compromiser who could soften hurts, lessen differences, and get bills passed. Yet here was a man whose "private lack of ethic," as Dean Sayre put it last summer, left many of us with concern.

This was less a matter of Bobby Baker or Walter Jenkins than of a free-wheeling attitude that showed through the substance of what Mr. Johnson did. One could see it in the inconsistency of retaining ownership of those broadcasting properties, while holding an office that sits in ultimate judgment on T.V. and radio. With this went an incessant razzle-dazzle campaign, of which Hartford had its sample in an hour of handshaking in a few downtown blocks before a campaign speech. Had Mr. Johnson tended to the business of government more, and politicked around the country less, he would not only have presented himself as a candidate of responsible dignity, but might have solidified his own appeal to conscientious voters.

* * *

For all that, yesterday's verdict appears to leave no alibi. The choice was as clear as yesterday's answer was unmistakable. The radical right that in 1964 took over the party may cry treason. But it had the candidate of its choice, and its own men, backed by true believers who worked with fire in their eyes and hope in their hearts, ran the campaign. Is everybody out of step but the faction that was beaten yesterday? Hardly. Yesterday's defeat did not follow because Republicans deserted the party. At San Francisco, last July, the party had left them. It did so when it shouted down and trampled on the Scrantons, Rockefellers, and Romneys, and then proudly flew high the flag of extremism.

Thus yesterday's re-election of President Johnson was less a mandate for some shapeless, cliche-ridden Great Society than a vote for conservatism in its real sense. As the dictionary says, conservatism is "the disposition and tendency to preserve what is established; opposition to change." What yes-

terday's vote showed was that American people want to conserve those advantages they have won through all those busy years, from the Depression to World War II and Korea, and through all the changes since.

* * *

One can see the meaning of all this if one looks backward down through the corridors of time. Since it first contested an election in 1856 the Republican Party has won 16, the Democratic Party only 11, of all the 27 elections held through 1960. But it is significant that half those G.O.P. victories were won before 1900. Beginning with the 1900 election, and up until yesterday's, the score in this century has been equal: eight victories for the Republicans, eight for the Democrats. Yesterday made it nine. But again there is a sharp dividing line—the year 1932. In the first 32 years of the 20th century there were only two Democratic victories, by one man—Woodrow Wilson. Since 1932 there have been but two Republican victories, by one man—Dwight Eisenhower.

If this means anything, it means that in the last generation the G.O.P. has not incarnated the hopes and desires of the great center grouping of the American people. It was not thus in the G.O.P.'s great days. The Republican Party began as a crusader, spearheading a morally outraged nation's will to free those black, native-born Americans who were slaves. From that the Republican Party went on to do other things that the people wanted done. It was the party that saved the Union. In the days after the Civil War it gave everybody material good—free land for the farmer, a tariff for industry in a country that remained a debtor nation until World War I, and a full dinner pail for labor.

* * *

This party of doers of the national will was also the party that wrote the first civil-service laws, passed the anti-trust laws, brought the robber barons of railroading under control, led the American nation to its place on the world stage, and pioneered the beginnings of international peace and justice.

There will come a time when the Republican Party—or if like the Whig Party it fails, some successor—will again seize the ball of national destiny from the opposition. But it will do so by getting things done, not by opposing them, or by longing for days that are no more.

Today no one can see when, or how, this will happen. But the Republican Party must again be taken over by those in its ranks who understand the modern world, and want to steer a sensible, realistic course through it. Today it may look as though the G.O.P. were a wreck, with the radical right in charge of the wreckage. Let it be noted that the radical right took control of the party legitimately and honestly, by dedication and hard work. Those who wish to return the party to its great tradition must work as hard to win it back. Today is none too soon to begin.

More orthodox were the three editorials with which the Chicago *Tribune* summarized its reactions Nov. 9, 1972. They illustrate journalistic joy, sorrow and hope, as follows:

Mr. Nixon's Mandate

If any President in history could claim to have won a mandate from the people, it is Mr. Nixon. He has won reelection with the greatest percentage and numerical majority of the popular vote on record, greater even than Franklin Roosevelt's at the peak of his power. And while some voters may simply have regarded Mr. Nixon as the lesser of the available evils, the size of his majority, in the midst of an astonishing binge of ticket-splitting, suggests that most people really voted in favor of Mr. Nixon and his record.

But if there is a mandate, what is it? First and foremost, it is to follow thru with the negotiations which have led the people to think that peace in Viet Nam—and an honorable peace—is "at hand." Such a peace means not only extricating American forces from the war, but doing so under conditions that will not lead to the Communist enslavement of nations that want to be free and to whose freedom we have committed ourselves. If the negotiations are going as well as the administration has eagerly allowed us to think, then such a peace should indeed be at hand, and Mr. Nixon will have been justified in delaying final agreement until all

of the kinks are ironed out. If not, Mr. McGovern's charges of politics and deceit will begin to assume some credibility.

The second mandate is to win a more decisive victory against inflation than can now be expected against Hanoi. With Europe now wallowing in its own inflation, we now have a real chance to regain at least some of the trading advantage which we have lost. The problem is to bring this about without committing the United States to permanent economic controls and taxes which stifle the profit incentive that is essential to our economic productivity. This means Mr. Nixon will have to continue fighting off political would-be Houdinis with sleight-of-hand solutions that sound good on the floor of Congress but don't work.

With these mandates go lesser obligations which there will be a temptation to overlook but which must be met if the Nixon administration is to achieve the place in history which, in many respects, it deserves. We're thinking mainly of those involving public confidence. Like Caesar's wife, the administration must avoid not only the existence of scandal but the appearance of scandal.

Watergate, for example, was a trivial issue until the administration made it into a bigger one by seeming to cover up. It must be pursued honestly and openly. Administration reticence has led to the appearance of scandal in such things as the Russian wheat deals even tho we've seen no proof that it exists. Finally and most importantly, the administration must become a champion of the freedom of the press which is being nibbled at to an alarming extent by various government agencies. Unless the press is as free to expose incompetence and corruption in all levels of government, without fear of harassment, as Vice Presidents are (and should be) to criticize the press, there will not be the full confidence which the administration should seek.

Fooling Enough of the People

You can't fool all of the people all of the time, but it seems you can fool them long enough to get elected. That is what Daniel Walker managed to do in defeating Gov. Richard Ogilvie.

With his roadshow of magic tricks and theatrics, Mr. Walker posed as all things to all people. Yet things which please downstate conservatives don't generally please lakefront liberals, as both groups are likely to learn. Probably the most bitterly disappointed will be those foolish Republican conservatives who voted against Mr. Ogilvie because of the state income tax. They will soon find they voted for a man who wants to tax them even more, as Mr. Walker has demonstrated in his statements on "a more progressive" income tax.

Daniel Walker's success poses two serious problems for Illinois. One concerns his ability to govern. Neither party has strong control of either house in the legislature, and the hostility of one toward the other is surpassed only by their mutual hostility to Mr. Walker. His lieutenant governor, Neil Hartigan, is a man who vigorously disagrees with many of Mr. Walker's positions and who will not hesitate to make his disagreement known.

It may well be that the wag was right who said: "If Walker is elected, the state will be run by the Illinois Supreme Court."

The other problem is what will happen to the many good programs Mr. Ogilvie has undertaken. He planned a comprehensive effort to tackle Chicago's transportation problems on an area-wide basis. Mr. Walker's transportation program amounted to little more than his opposition to the proposed Crosstown Expressway.

Mr. Ogilvie set in motion a plan to bring about property tax relief thru federal revenue sharing. Mr. Walker's reaction was to denounce the whole effort as a "gimmick" and a "fraud." Judicial reform, correctional rehabilitation, mental health, and the other improvements Mr. Ogilvie was working on must not go down the drain.

The ticket-splitting which contributed to Mr. Walker's election is supposed to reflect voter intelligence. Yet the dumping of Gov. Ogilvie strikes us as the opposite. We hope that Mr. Walker will prove more realistic and reliable in office than he has been as a candidate.

Mr. Carey Deserved It

However much the inept and irascible Edward V. Hanrahan deserved to lose the race for state's attorney, Bernard Carey overwhelmingly deserved to win it. Seldom does a man of his stature, ability, and integrity even become involved in Cook County politics, and to have one finally triumph is a matter for rejoicing. We are particularly pleased to see that he received the support of voters of every ideological persuasion. His victory was a blow for good government and not merely a liberal crusade.

Working with U.S. Atty. James Thompson, Mr. Carey should assure good government to this county. The last time the Republicans held both of these offices was from 1956 to 1960, but they failed to take advantage of that opportunity for reform. Mr. Carey and Mr. Thompson have already demonstrated that they will not fail.

Mayor Daley has much to lament in the election of a skillful Republican as state's attorney, but we think, in political terms, he is better off. With his arrogance, his divisiveness, and the hostility he generated in the black community, a reelected Edward Hanrahan would have proved a disaster for the Democrats.

Our only complaint about Mr. Carey's election is that the large numbers of blacks and liberals who turned out for him were also responsible for the election of Daniel Walker as governor.

Where the dividing list exists between politics and government is almost impossible to determine. Politicians are conscious of the fact they must stand for reelection every day of the year. The perceptive newsman can be excused for seeking a political motivation behind virtually every act of every elected officeholder.

Sam Reynolds of the Missoula (Mont.) *Missoulian* provides a first-class example of what happens when you keep a close watch on what your representatives do. During his campaign for Congress, the former Missoula Mayor Richard Shoup came out strongly against the supersonic transport (SST). Western Montana is strong on environmental protection. March 18, 1971 Shoup voted against the SST appropriation but in May, when it was attempted to revive the project, Shoup was absent during the vote. Reynolds thinks this editorial, nailing lies, was too long "but deservedly so." It had considerable impact. It appeared in the paper's issue of May 23, 1971 as follows:

Shoup's Tangled Web

SHOUP STILL OPPOSES SST

WASHINGTON (AP)—Rep. Richard G. Shoup, R-Mont., said Tuesday he remains opposed to the SST although he missed a vote on an appropriation for the supersonic transport plane last Wednesday.

Shoup said committee work prevented him from voting when the fund bill was approved by the House last week, but he was paired with an absentee who favored the SST.

"I voted against the SST March 18 and I have not changed my position," he told a reporter.

Shoup said if he had been present Wednesday he would have voted against the SST amendment.

The Congressional Record lists Shoup as not voting and paired with Rep. Wiley Mayne, R-Iowa.

That story appeared in last Wednesday's Missoulian. It agrees with what Rep. Dick Shoup told us the afternoon before, when he called The Missoulian from Washington.

We believe it is wide of the truth, and that the congressman thinks he can play games with the truth because he is so far away.

SHOUP: Committee work prevented him from voting May 12 when the SST bill was before the House. He told The Missoulian that the committee (the Interstate and Foreign Commerce Committee—the only committee Shoup belongs to) that week was busy with the investigation of CBS and with working out a railroad strike settlement bill, and that such work kept him busy.

RESPONSE: Perhaps committee work did keep him busy. Yet of the 43 members of the Interstate and Foreign Commerce Committee, 41 were on the floor of the House and voted on the question of SST funding. The massive majority of Shoup's committee was not too busy to vote.

SHOUP: He was paired with another absentee who favored the SST, Rep. Wiley Mayne, R-Iowa.

RESPONSE: Rep. Mayne voted *against* funding the SST last year, and voted *against* it twice in March of this year. We called Mayne's office last week and talked to Jack Watson, Mayne's administrative assistant. "He (Mayne) is definitely against the SST," Watson said. Mayne was busy with Judiciary Committee work when the vote was taken, but "he would have been consistent and would have opposed" the SST had he been on the floor when the SST vote came up, Watson said.

SHOUP: The Congressional Record lists Shoup as not voting and paired with Rep. Mayne.

RESPONSE: That is true, but deceptive. The record lists 15 pairs of representatives either "for" or "against" the SST. Under separate title, "Until Further Notice" is the entry "Mr. Shoup with Mr. Mayne." The record does not specify how either Shoup or Mayne stood on the SST.

Shoup's insinuation that he was paired with a pro-SST man appears to be simply false. Mayne's consistently anti-SST record, his anti-SST words on the floor of the House last March (See Congressional Record—House, March 18, 1971, page H 1726), and the ready assurances of his assistant that Mayne still opposes the SST, all indicate that if there was a pro- and anti-SST pair, it was with Shoup, not Mayne, in the pro-SST role. You cannot pair two people who take the same stand on an issue. It would make a very odd couple.

Shoup also told The Missoulian that he didn't realize the SST was such a hot issue that people here would get heavily worked up about it. We'll let that incredible naivete stand on its own merit.

Why should the congressman squirm and snarl the truth? We suspect the truth is that he was put under pressure from the Nixon administration to switch from his anti-SST stand in March to a pro-SST stand, that he realized it would be politically harmful to do that, and so he simply absented himself from the SST vote on purpose as a way to compromise a difficult position.

If that's so, why didn't he simply say so, face the criticism, and be done? Why did he try to spin this tangled web of nonsense that only makes him look worse and worse?

He'll have to answer that. We suggest that from now on he level with his constituents.

The sequel to the editorial is this: when Shoup told a University of Montana School of Journalism class that he had been "crucified," Reynolds included the following short comment in his June 13, 1971 Sunday wrap-up editorial:

Rep. Dick Shoup said in Missoula last week that he was "crucified" because he missed the vote on reviving the supersonic transport project.

It's a question of semantics. While there is a similarity, nevertheless there also remains a difference between being crucified and being nailed.

EDUCATION

When they handle educational topics editorial writers think and sound like the parents that most of them are. Just as they want teachers to tell them whether their youngsters are above or below average, near the top or the bottom of their class, so they evaluate the performance of the school system by comparative statistical yardsticks. How do our children's scores on tests compare with national averages? Are our teachers paid more or less than their counterparts in cities of comparable size? Do enough of them possess advanced academic degrees? Do we get enough merit scholarships? Win enough national prizes? How about the proportion of applicants from here that are accepted by prestigious colleges? And so on—the great game of statistical averages and scores which has been encouraged by teachers' colleges and schools of education for well over a generation. We group or "track" children on the basis of their supposed innate capacities as revealed by Stanford-Binet, Wais, Wisc, Goodenough, SCAT, and other standard tests. Fortunately the infallability of these sadistic practices is being challenged today by black and other parents who are weary of having their sons and daughters put into "dummy" classes because they are considered inferior on the basis of so-called intelligence tests which were devised to estimate the factual knowledge of children reared in entirely different environments. Los Angeles and some other cities already have outlawed the use of these tests which have distorted pedagogical values for a half century. The New York *Times* pointed out the absurdity of the testing-conscious mind in its issue of June 23, 1972.

Dumbbell Test

The story of two Hunter College staff members who flunked their civil service examinations because they could not lift a 25-pound bar bell over their heads with one hand is a classic illustration of the continuing abuse of the testing process. One of the victims is an audiovisual technician who never has had any trouble working and moving her projectors; the other is a graphic artist and audiovisual adviser who, to the best of anybody's knowledge, is not required to lift anything much heavier than a pencil or a file card.

The test the two women were obliged to take to gain civil service status and retain their jobs also included running an obstacle course. While municipal bureaucracy abounds in obstacle courses, they are rarely of the kind that require physical agility to surmount.

The explanation by civil service spokesmen that surveys show lifting of heavy objects to be a requirement in many jobs merely clinches the argument against letting a bureaucracy determine its own testing process. The bureaucratic tendency is to standardize, with the result that, in this instance, women whose main asset is creactivity must compete with furniture movers. Moreover, a predominantly male bureaucracy will set predominantly male standards.

By keeping out persons with special and appropriate talents, such hurdles discredit the testing process. They play into the hands of those who, in the mistaken belief that quality controls are undemocratic, oppose all testing. Standards are best protected when the tests are geared with the greatest possible precision to the qualities needed for the particular job or activity.

Testmakers who fail to comprehend this necessity should be notified that they have flunked their own basic test and should be reassigned to less sensitive duties, even if they can pass the weight-lifting requirement.

Suggested readings for the editorial writer interested in this subject include *The Tyranny of Testing* (Crowell-Collier, 1962) by Banesh Hoffmann; *The Brain Watchers* (Random, 1962) by Martin L. Gross and *They Shall Not Pass* (William Morrow, 1963) by Hillel Black of the New York *Times.*

Since the organized labor-led political fight to establish them over a century ago, the public schools always have been the objects of stormy debate and the happy hunting grounds for propagandists of every complexion. The old Latin School concept of education for an elite, ladies and gentlemen, went by the board early in the history of American public school education which has been touted as an egalitarian institution basic to the well-being of American democracy. No tests are held at periodic intervals, as in most other countries, to determine who can continue his schooling, with the poor rote learners and bad memorizers being weeded out even more ruthlessly than they are punished by American school administrators by various types of segregation. Many American colleges maintain entrance requirements with heavy emphasis on the traditional classical background. This is in part because of the stipulations by Andrew Carnegie and some other philanthropists that they maintain such standards in order to continue to qualify to receive the financial support. Still, the public high school has steadily become more than the so-called college of the people. Within a generation at least two more years of tax-supported education will be widely available in junior and community colleges, and the proportion of young people who take advantage of the opportunity seems bound to accelerate. There has been no increase in school dropouts despite the amount of maudlin reporting on the subject. Actually, whereas in 1900 only 6.4 percent of the age group finished high school, by 1940 the proportion had passed 50 percent; in 1960 it was nearly 65 percent and today it is about 75 percent. In many fields a college degree means no more today than a high school diploma did a generation ago. It is a necessary credential for many jobs in business as well as in the professions. At the time one-fourth of the American adult population still is functionally illiterate, meaning unable to read comprehensively beyond the fourth grade level.

The original impetus for free public schooling in this country was economic, to permit the underprivileged the opportunity to acquire skills so as to be able to compete with their better-heeled peers. After World War I the vocational education movement received great support from some segments of American industry eager to encourage the schools to train apprentices for industry. Since then the development of automation and a fast changing technology has made most of the old manual training and shop courses obsolete, but the girls continue to learn typing, shorthand, and bookkeeping, often with the cooperation of local businesses.

The most commonly heard complaint by both dropouts and those who struggle along to obtain the work slip in the form of a diploma is that much of the curriculum is not relevant to present-day problems. Basically the high school course of study has scarcely changed at all during the past half century. The student takes English for four years, thus devoting 25 percent of his time to it. The course is heavily weighted with critical analysis of literature, very light on writing skills. Composition work continues to be what are called themes, which have no counterpart whatever in everyday life. Another 25 percent of the time is devoted to foreign language, with living languages gradually replacing Latin but with the emphasis on reading knowledge rather than speaking or even writing ability, none of which the majority will ever have a chance to test anyway. The example of the military in wartime—that it is possible to teach the practical use of even obscure dialects when use is to be made soon of the skill—has been completely ignored by modern educators at all levels. Though lightened somewhat the foreign language hurdle remains for anyone seeking the Ph.D degree.

A third quarter of the average high school student's time is devoted to mathematics and science, and since the Russians beat the Americans initially in the race into space by lauching sputnik in 1956, the emphasis on these subjects has accelerated. Possibly there has been a slackening of the pace in the past few years when the shock and subsequent fear and the sense of shame wore off and especially when the market became glutted with engineers. Still, the problem of the teen-ager who is not mechanically inclined remains. High school courses emphasize laboratory and technical training with slight attention to the meaning or significance of scientific knowledge throughout the centuries. As Prof. Robert Havighurst, famous University of Chicago professor of education, has pointed out, the average person goes through life never having to use any of the mathematical knowledge he was given after the eighth or possibly the sixth grade. Nevertheless, it is deemed essential that everyone know how to work problems in algebra and geometry and possibly also trigonometry and calculus, and to do simple experiments in the chemistry and physics laboratories to get the results which the instructors know are the correct ones. Students with a talent or interest in any branch of science may find the regimentation a dis-

couragement rather than an opportunity to nurture their interest.

The fourth quarter of the high school students' time is devoted to history: ancient, medieval, modern and American, and he is expected to memorize names and dates and the provisions of treaties and the main battles of wars from the dawn of man to the present. Well, not quite the present. To avoid hearing from patriotic and other groups it is safe to stop the instruction short of the past decade or maybe earlier. As a prominent north Chicago suburban superintendent once explained, "The children will come face to face with reality soon enough. It is our function to protect them from emotional disturbance." That means avoiding the controversial in the classroom, another way of saying the contemporary and important. Modern kids know much more about what's going on in the world than their parents did at their age, but they have learned it from television, news magazines and in other ways rather than in the classroom. Now that they are voting at 18, it is fortunate that these alternative ways of learning exist.

The preceding paragraphs have touched on some fundamental issues which should be but seldom are of importance to editorial writers. They sin more by their acts of omission than by those of commission in this field. Usually they support efforts to get more money out of the federal government or state legislature for use of the local schools, and they endorse local referenda to allow increases in the tax rate so as to raise more money to meet the needs of an expanding school population. When it comes to the really important issues, however, they almost unanimously cop out. And maybe it's a good thing that they do because there is so much conflict today, so many reports and books with which anyone should be familiar before taking part in the debate, that the all-purpose editorial writer may be performing a public service by keeping his mouth shut, or rather by keeping his typewriter silent on matters about which he knows too little.

Still, there is the game of averages already mentioned. The concept so prevalent throughout American life that expenditure of money can solve anything permeates editorial thinking in this as in other fields. All sorts of "crash" programs get support to find the cause of this or that disease, end poverty, make the streets safe, put a stop to sin and wickedness and, to get back to the subject, make our children smart. The point of all this sermonizing has been that the most important educational problems cannot be tackled in terms of percentages or percentiles, or even in terms of dollars and cents. Certainly a school building obviously in need of repairs must be fixed up. There must be playground facilities and equality in the equipment provided schools in all sections of the community. Discrimi-nation is a proper subject for editorial comment. Photographers can take pictures of broken down plumbing and reporters can note the absence of textbooks, dictionaries, maps and similar teaching tools. Editorial writers can raise cain about such bad conditions.

When it comes to editorials on educational as distinguished from school matters, it is not easy to find good examples. In fact, it is virtually impossible to do so. A wide open opportunity exists for some editorial writer to become expert in this field. If he were to acquire the necessary background, however, his talent probably would be better utilized as an education editor or columnist or feature writer. The following is an honest effort to raise some pertinent educational issues. It appeared in the Arlington Heights (Ill.) *Herald* for Nov. 29, 1956.

Are Today's Pupils Intellectual Robots?

That we must have funds to pay decent wages to teachers; that we must be able to afford adequate school buildings and facilities for growing pupil populations; that we must find an equitable source of revenue readily available to schools; these are certainly legitimate topics for serious examinations.

But our emphasis on problems of school finance may have placed us in danger of evaluating all school needs chiefly in terms of dollars.

There is evidence to support the accusation we have forgotten the schools' basic function:

To develop educated, cultivated human beings, intellectually equipped to face a world of transition and change with new ideas and an ability to meet, intelligently and creatively, the challenge of new times.

About school buildings, health, lunches, civic responsibility, kindness, good humor, spontaneity—we have nothing to learn from the school of the past.

But about reading with ease and understanding the best that has been thought and said

Comment

Well structured introductory paragraphs. They make the subject matter of the editorial clear.

in the world—of THAT we do have much to learn.

Books in 'Baby Talk'

The basic skill of reading itself has become so acute a problem that it prompted a national best seller on the subject.

And concerned educators now charge that elementary schools are placing before their pupils reading material that is merely pre-digested baby talk, too often the only kind of literature thought appropriate for children of today.

Perhaps it IS true that, for the first time in history, Americans see their children getting less EDUCATION than they got themselves.

Not too many years ago, the fifth or sixth grade student was exposed to healthy helpings of Byron, Coleridge, Defoe, deQuincey, Dickens, Emerson, Fielding, Hawthorne, Hazlitt, Dr. Johnson, Jefferson, Shakespeare, Shelley, Swift, Thoreau, Swift, Longfellow, Cooper, Poe, Oliver Wendell Holmes, Irving, Goethe.

This was Rudolf Flesch's *Why Johnny Can't Read* (Harper, 1955), one of the first attacks on Dick and Jane nonsense that words must be considered as gestalt entities and the existence of syllables and of phonetics should be ignored. Cockeyed theories of this sort have poured out of schools of education. Many originate with candidates for doctoral degrees who must discover some new angle or gimmick or theory with which to impress an examining committee. If the candidate passes he qualifies to become an administrator and usually cannot resist the temptation to put his original theories into practice on the job. School boards, made up mostly of pennypinching businessmen with no understanding whatever of educational problems, are impressed by the apparent erudition of their superintendent. Result: the administrators have taken over and the classroom educators are just hired help who resist as best they can the brainstorms of their nonacademic superiors. Their social status, especially in the small town, is lower than that of most other public employes, including the unskilled. They are expected to devote their entire lives to their professions and are expected to be leaders in community activities, singing in the choirs, teaching Sunday School classes, leading scout troops and marching in Memorial Day parades. Their moral standards must be higher than those of the children's parents.

The fifth or sixth grader today finds most of these names strange. He's more familiar with "Josie's Home Run" by Ruth G. Plowhead or "A Midnight Lion Hunt" by Three Boy Scouts. He's sure to know Fletcher D. Slater, Nora Burglon, Gertrude Robinson, Gladys M. Wick, Sanford Tousey, or J. Walker McSpadden.

Hollow Log to Pentagon

It is ironic that in the days of the one-room school houses and the hollow log there was greater emphasis on really intellectual development than in today's vast, Pentagon-like educational institutions.

High schools are not immune from such criticism either.

Colleges and universities are expressing concern at the growing inability of high school

Modern college students who went through the elementary and secondary schools since World War II find it difficult to believe that this is true. But it was and the author still has the Elson reading books which he used to prove it. In those days you learned to read, not by learning machines or other gadgets but simply by reading, and you did it orally before all your fellow students and you did not resent it when the teacher helped you with your pronunciation or diction. Somehow the literature produced by the authors here listed was understandable. Many elders today recall that the only acquaintance they ever had with Homer and other masters was before they became teen-agers.

graduates to read intelligently, express themselves concisely or indicate any capabilities for original thought.

A professor recently put his class to a test. For an hour, he lectured absurd exaggerations and falsehoods, but not one student questioned or protested what the professor said. The only sound was the docile scratching of obedient pens transposing what might well have been a "party" line.

Have our schools hatched for us a generation of intellectual automatons?

Teacher training institutions have emphasized guidance, individual adjustment and understanding—and yet have failed even here?

Last week, a human relations expert told a group of prospective teachers that bias and prejudice are unwittingly being drummed into the minds of school children.

And from the president of Illinois Institute of Technology last week came this report: declining attention given mathematics in high schools may cause America to lose its scientific supremacy. The president explained that a poor background in mathematics was responsible for the largest percentage of rejections at Illinois Tech. Blamed were outdated mathematics programs, poorly trained teachers, and uninteresting and meaningless instruction methods in the schools.

Man's Future at Stake

Every citizen must be concerned with the intellectual vacuum confronting our schools; there is no other single aspect of our social structure more vital to the continued expansion of an enlightened, democratic society.

Man's future welfare and development, the progress of organized society, the security of a free world—none of these will be finally determined by salary or tax revenue or assessment. Their fates rest in a marketplace of ideas.

If we are not equipped to compete equally in this exchange of ideas, we are not going to win a permanent place in the world of the future, a world of change and challenge.

Can our children of today meet that challenge of tomorrow?

Possibly this was a piece of deliberate nonsense by Alfred Jay Nock, often used in such experiments but really no worse than a great deal of the gobbledegook that is encountered in many areas today. Every journalist should be required to read, "Ralph Waldo Emerson, Thou Shouldst Be Living at This Hour," a talk by Wallace Carroll, editor and publisher of the Winston-Salem *Journal and Sentinel* to the New England Society of Newspaper Editors at Cambridge, Mass. Dec. 6, 1969. It was condensed in the June, 1970 *Nieman Reports*.

What teacher training institutions have done is to stress how to teach with little concern for what is to be taught; methodology and theoretical courses, often containing identical material, are a joke on any campus.

The specialist feels everyone should have an interest in his field. Full opportunity should be provided for all with the talent and interest but the attempt to make everyone into a scientist after sputnik was absurd. What is meant by scientific supremacy? Science is international and there are no secrets among scientists. It's impossible to keep them.

The writer is not sure of himself as he gropes for words to express his inchoate ideas. He knows something is wrong but is not well enough versed in the field to know what it is. His attempt to arouse thought is commendable but his editorial falls far short of clarifying much of anything.

We aren't too sure.

And that is the gravest indictment of all.

Many editorials on education, or more properly school subjects, are written by prejudiced and/or uninformed writers. The following from the *Wall Street Journal* of Aug. 4, 1960 is one of the worst ever written.

The Myth They Won't Let Die

Federal aid for school buildings is the No. 1 item on the Republican platform's agenda for education. It is also the No. 1 Democratic education promise.

Now this insistence on Federal aid and Federal nosing around can only be attributed to one of two factors: either the two parties believe that there is a great public demand for Federal aid and thus great political dividends to be gained in proposing it. Or the makers of the platforms haven't taken the time to add 1 and 2.

For all one has to do is add 1 and 2 to see how untrue the myth is that the nation's schools are falling apart and can only be saved by the vast power and money in Washington.

This newspaper has long known it for a political myth. Hardly a week goes by that local units of government—whether state, city, county or school district—do not announce the successful sale or the offering of bond issues for schools. The total for the nation runs into hundreds of millions of dollars a year, all raised by taxes voted by the public on themselves. Here and there a place has fallen a bit behind the average—but, as everyone knows—in order to reach an average, some must be above and some below.

It was the "average" Federal aiders pointed to with dismay a decade ago. And it was the average that, 10 years ago, led the nation's communities to embark on the greatest school building program any like period in America has yet seen.

Well, then, what is the average today? The U.S. Chamber of Commerce has dug into the figures of the Federal Office of Education, and the results should astonish the politicians, if they would only look. The figures show

Comment

"Nosing around" suggests the tone of what is to follow.

As federal income taxes to pay for the killing skyrocketed, taxpayers struck back in the only way they could. Disregarding the fact that the federal government is to blame for their plight they reject most school bond or tax increase proposals with the result that many schools suffer by reducing the length of the school year or operating with insufficient teachers and supplies.

Gross inequalities always have existed. In 1950, when this editorial was written, Alaska spent $585.10 per pupil which represented 3.2 percent of personal income devoted to education. In New York the expenditure was $585 or 3.7 percent. At the other extreme Alabama spent $217 per pupil or 3.8 percent. South Carolina spent $223 or 4.5 percent. What these figures show is that the poorer states try just as hard as the wealthy states but the taxable real estate isn't so valuable. In 1970 the California Supreme Court ruled the local property tax revenue plan, district by district, is inequitable and probably started a trend toward equalizing the cost of schooling in a migratory age when it is as important to someone who has children in Michigan that the children of another in Mississippi be educated as well.

It is the United States Office of Education. The age of buildings does not prove there are enough of them, a point the Chamber of Commerce and the editorial writer overlook. The overwhelming evidence provided by national education organizations, representing teachers, parents, school

that current class room "shortages" are the lowest in the past quarter century. Half the classrooms now in use have been built since World War II. Government surveys, the Chamber reports, indicate that less than 15% of the nation's school districts have used up their resources, or reached their legal borrowing limits.

Whereas the public was told that only Washington could do the job of meeting the growing school population, the communities not only met the so-called "crisis" but went far beyond it. From 1950 through 1959 pupil enrollments increased by 10.2 million—but enough schoolrooms were built to take care of 16.8 million youngsters. Not only that; the school districts also employed enough new teachers so that the average number of pupils per teacher dropped from 26 to 25—though the public was led to believe that teachers were leaving the school systems in droves.

None of this is meant to argue that there is still not room for improvement. But it is meant to argue that there is no need now and that there never was a need for Uncle Sam to take over the nation's schools.

For the myth that the schools are in a bad way persists. It may be, as we said in the beginning, that the two parties simply haven't taken the time to add 1 and 2 to find out that Federal aid isn't needed.

Or it may be, as we also suggested, that the Republicans and the Democrats in power believe that the public wants the long arm of Federal aid reaching into every school district in the land. But if they believe that, then they ought to ask themselves a question:

If the nation's people wanted Washington to build the schools, why then did the people themselves build so well to prevent it?

boards, administrators and others, has been that classrooms are overcrowded, facilities inadequate and unequal, and teachers in short supply and underpaid.

No authority is given for these figures which are diametrically inconsistent with those from all other reputable sources.

A red herring. Nobody is proposing that Uncle Sam take over the nation's schools although educators generally agree that there should be national standards with federal supervision of how federal funds are used.

The language becomes hysterical and the thinking is illogical. It sounds like Marie Antoinette or George III.

Few editorials in any field are worse than those that are written to blame society's present-day ills on the schools. If the argument was that the schools neglect to encourage students to study and participate in civic affairs, including politics, the argument might make sense. However, the angry attacks on the schools are from exactly the opposite point of view. The schools are charged with deliberately undermining American virtues, allowing subversive teachers to indoctrinate tender minds, using un-American textbooks and so on and on and on. It's been going on for many years and the list of scholarly martryrs include some of the most outstanding scholars of the times. They have been investigated, tried, humiliated, demoted, dismissed, their writings blacklisted, their government jobs cancelled. In our generation, among the most famous victims of such red baiting and witch hunting have been Scott Nearing, Corliss Lamont, Bertrand Russell, Harold Rugg, Charles A. Beard, Linus Pauling, Owen Lattimore, Robert Oppenheimer, Robert Morss Lovett and many, many more. Teachers wish that they possessed the ability to impress their students to anywhere near the extent that the vigilantes contend they do. Many a potential first-class teacher has been discouraged from entering the profession because of the necessity to be constantly on the alert to protect his academic freedom and other democratic rights. Newspapermen can understand how unpleasant it is to be scapegoated so often that it detracts from the best professional performance. Who wants to submit himself to such indignities when there are other, mostly more remunerative, ways to exercise his talent?

The following editorial from the Columbia (S.C.) *State* of Feb. 23, 1968 is a typical attempt to explain the bad state of the world by pointing to the campuses.

Impetuous and Immature

One aspect of the matter of dissent in America hasn't yet been fully explored; namely, the fact that the vast majority of today's dissenters are under the age of 30.

Magazines, newspapers, TV interviewers and the like simply fawn upon spokesmen for the dissenting crowd in America. Yet those spokesmen are sometimes only 30 years old, or 23 or perhaps 27. Since when is the "wisdom" of young people to be sought after rather than the wisdom of our elders?

Oh, it's all very well to say that today's youngsters are more "committed" than their parents were, a generation ago. But such talk is nonsense. Young people, since the beginning of the world, have been restless, rebellious, "know-it-all," and often rude.

Our mistake lies in having paid so much attention to such rebelliousness. We have, quite literally, fawned upon our children—as though they were the source and fount of all wordly knowledge.

They aren't. And the sooner older people realize this, the better. Some of our children, both Negro and white, are burning down America; and while it's important to realize that most of the furor and ferment comes from a relatively small group, still we're busy asking them what their reasons are, instead of slapping some sense into their heads or, at the least, some discipline into their behavior.

In the Old World, in Europe, children are expected to study while they're in school, and

Comment

Youth has always been rebellious. Today's dissenters, disgusted with the world, say they don't trust anyone over 30.

"Fawn" is a smear word and the statement is a gross exaggeration. No content analysis of the media would substantiate it, but if the statement of the lead paragraph were correct, it would seem the journalistic media should investigate. Since this editorial was written the voting age has been lowered to 18 and in 1972 the campaign headquarters of most candidates all over the country were run by young people, no longer just errand runners.

The insinuation is that youth has committed some great offense yet all that is charged is strong interest in current affairs.
That word "fawn" again. What does it mean? Too much love?

While their elders are burning down Southeast Asia to set the example. Most arson against minority groups is committed by whites and the victims are blacks or other minorities that have moved into better homes.

In what countries does this occur? Ones that we admire? Until recently American students were to respect their elders. Those who don't are shipped, or denied further funds for their schooling. In some countries, children who take part in street demonstrations, either for or against the government, are properly thrashed by their parents.

All of us love children, of course. They give us some hope of immortality. But they weren't born with wisdom, and at age 23, they aren't yet ready to pontificate on civil rights, the war in Vietnam, or much of anything else. We all appreciate the fact that they're interested in such subjects; but we aren't prepared to accept their judgments, proposals or (bless us) their ultimatums.

Older Americans may be mistaken in some of the things that they do. Young Americans, though, have got to learn that Molotov cocktails and shouting obscenities are not arguments; they're the products of youth and rebellion.

"Ye who listen with credulity to the whispers of fancy," sang Samuel Johnson," and pursue with eagerness the phantoms of hope; who expect that age will perform the promises of youth, and that the deficiencies of the present day will be supplied by the morrow, attend to history."

Dr. Johnson knew, as those of us who are mature now know, that young people always expect too much. Today, they call themselves dissenters; but really, they're mostly dreamers —which may be all right, provided they don't become destroyers as well.

lackadaisical whereas students in other parts of the world, including Latin America, were in the vanguard of political movements. The thrashings, if they happened, didn't do any good and they may have been ordered or forbidden by a Fuhrer. During the past few years no American demonstrations have compared in intensity with those at the Universities of Paris, Tokyo, Mexico and other places.

Life apparently begins at 40, or maybe the author of this editorial would say 60 with wisdom really the monopoly of octogenarians. This creates visions of long-bearded patriarchs sitting in their tents and giving orders to obsequious young subjects. It's pathetic.

The criminal syndicate of adults is more expert at the use of Molotov cocktails and other murderous weapons and no young person knows how to use swear words better than some of our recent presidents.

Most rebels who led worthwhile movements in the past were young, including most American Revolutionary War heroes.

No wonder so many people lack confidence in old timers over 30 who created the mess the world is now in and go into tizzies at suggestions for change.

In 1952 Louis LaCoss of the St. Louis *Globe-Democrat* won the Pulitzer prize for his editorial of Aug. 6, 1951. Twenty years later, after the television quiz show scandals, Bobby Baker, Billie Sol Estes, many exposés of crookedness involving wrestling, horse racing, basketball and other sports, and almost daily exposés of skulduggery in almost any field imaginable, it is difficult to understand the impact of this editorial or, especially, of the events which were the occasion for it. Actually this editorial was very iconoclastic inasmuch as the public's protests were loud and almost unanimously in condemnation of the guilty cadets. West

Point had been held up as a symbol of all the virtues that made America great, and so it was a shock to the national ego for clay feet to be exposed and for evidence to be forthcoming to indicate the military academy never had deserved its reputation which thereupon was revealed as being a myth. Some of the disgraced young men changed their names to escape the social and economic punishment they drew.

Low State of Public Morals

The discharge of 90 West Point cadets for cheating at examinations is only one facet of the many-sided problem of moral disintegration nationally that is causing many to wonder whether America is going down the path of decay that caused the Roman Empire to fall.

The West Pointers were dishonest. They cheated. Some did so because they couldn't play football and keep up with their studies.

The excuse of the athletes accents the abnormality of thinking in many institutions of higher education as to the part sports should play in college life. The necessity of having a good team, to assure big revenues to build a bigger stadium to make more money, has led many of our colleges into the evil device of buying players, of competing in the open market for a star halfback. Some colleges have recognized the error and have de-emphasized sports, as should be done.

At West Point the incentive was a bit different because Uncle Sam foots the bills there, but there was the incentive for the individual to "make" a team that was tops or near it in the nation. So, if practice on the field intervened, cheat a little and make the necessary grades.

What happened at West Point reflects a present distorted attitude toward old-fashioned honesty and integrity that ⎰revails not only in our schools but in America's social and political life.

When 90 West Point cadets stray from paths of honesty, when nauseous revelations are made of the bribing of college basketball teams, when too many youths of both sexes flout the laws of chastity and decency —when these derelictions of the youths of our lands are toted up, there comes a time for sober questioning among the adults.

Where does the fault lie? In the home? Perhaps. In the school? In part. In the churches? In part.

But in the main the fault lies in the nebulous field of public morals and spirituality which was so highly cultivated by the founding fathers and which of late has been so scantily tilled. Among too many of us the accepted premise is that anything is fair unless we are caught; that each of us is entitled to something for nothing; that the world owes us a living; that an honest day's pay is almost unethical; that gypping the other fellow before he gyps you is the only policy that pays off.

The level of public morals is low. Unfortunately, the good example is not set in Washington. The President is victimized by his friends, but a false sense of loyalty prevents him from moving forthright against them. His reluctance condones wrongdoing. Leadership in both parties is weak, because it is consistently attuned to the next election, not to what is best for the public welfare. In fact, public morals are low because politics at all levels is played at a historic low.

The time is here for moral regeneration. West Point is just one item in the sad chronology. The Roman Empire fell, not because it was overwhelmed from without but because it decayed from within. If this is an appeal for a return to the day-by-day practice of old-time religion, and respect for God's moral law, so be it. When the moral fabric of a nation begins to unravel, it is time to do some patching before the entire garment is gone. The cause and effect of this deterioration nationally will be issues in next year's presidential campaign.

The last two paragraphs of this piece have the cart before the horse. The newspaper was not friendly to President Truman and so scapegoated him. Was the low level of morality in Washington the cause or the result of the situation in general? The South Carolina editor blamed youth; the Missouri editor blamed politicians. Obviously a much more penetrating scholarly analysis is needed.

The extent to which public opinion had been modified was provided when the Air Force scandal broke more than a decade later. The following from the Chicago *Daily Tribune* of Jan. 26, 1955 illustrates the change.

Cheating

The number of cheaters on examinations at the Air Force academy is placed as high as 100, 29 of whom already have resigned. Meanwhile, a survey by Columbia university has disclosed that about half of the students at 99 colleges admitted cheating.

Rep. Samuel Stratton, a New York Democrat, has rushed in to say that because many of the Air Force cheaters were members of the football squad, professionalism in college and service academy football is to blame.

The last big scandal of this sort was in 1951, when 90 West Pointers almost half of them members of the Army football team, were expelled. That was the year of Harry Truman, Gen. Vaughan, mink coats for White House secretaries, gift freezers, and wholesale corruption in the internal revenue service.

Within the last year we have had Bobby Baker, Billie Sol Estes, and other examples of fast-buck artists in or on the periphery of public life.

Is it possible Congressman Stratton has put his emphasis in the wrong place and that the corruption of people in public life to whom the young might look for example has had something to do with the decline of ethical standards?

Sometimes editorial writers can see through the scapegoating of others, especially politicians whose stock in trade often is to blame everything on their opponents. The following from the Chicago *Sun-Times* of Dec. 12, 1951 was a commendable attempt to expose bigotry and promote common sense.

Emphasis on Athletics

Many mixed-up Americans seem to have an idea that a university that turns out winning athletic teams is doing its full duty toward developing good Americans. And that, conversely, there must be something suspicious about any university not particularly interested in athletics.

This rah-rah, country club attitude recently found its way into the Congressional Record. Rep. Harold Velde (R-Pekin) declaimed:

"It occurs to me that ever since the famous Alonzo Stagg left the University of Chicago as its head coach and the athletic program was relegated to a practical nullity, left-wing and pseudo-liberal teaching and thinking has flourished."

Velde has been making a lot of noise in Congress about what kind of teaching is going on at the University of Chicago and Roosevelt College (which doesn't even have a campus, unless Grant Park can be so re-

garded). He has been terribly concerned whether the morals and patriotism of their students have been corrupted by the "latitude and liberalism" allowed at those institutions.

In his own district, Bradley University did exactly what Velde prescribes for colleges. It put emphasis on athletics. In fact, it put so much that a court has denounced Bradley overemphasis on athletics as responsible for the "moral debasement" of some of the players.

In passing judgment on three former Bradley University basketball players who were involved in the big college fix scandal, Judge Streit of New York said:

"The defendants at the bar were corrupted and demoralized by a system which set athletic success above education."

Their contact with Bradley University, said the judge, left the students with "visible moral blemishes."

It seems to us that Rep. Velde should be more concerned about Bradley University than a couple of universities that do not accent athletics. Especially since Velde reports in a biographical sketch in the Congressional Directory that he has two children who are students at Bradley.

LABOR

"Have you ever seen a prolabor editorial?" the author asked students for 30 years and professional editorial writers who belong to the National Conference of Editorial Writers since 1950 when he joined the prestigious group.

"Yes," finally answered Lauren Soth, Pulitzer prize winning editor of the editorial page of the Des Moines *Register and Tribune*. "I have written them." He continued:

But in recent years we and many other papers have had more articles critical of labor unions, I think, than ever before. The reason for this is that the big labor unions are as monopolistic, as restrictive, as much "establishment" as the big corporations. They are all hanging onto what they have and resisting any change in technology that might upset their empires.

Labor unions, particularly the craft unions, have been about the worst hindrances to fair employment. The heavy vote for George Wallace in the state of Michigan reflects the labor union racial bias.

The bosses of labor union empires even have resisted union organization in some fields, such as agricultural workers in Louisiana, Texas and other areas.

I think that is why most people who are liberal minded no longer regard support for labor unions as liberal."

Another way of putting it is that organized labor has become one of the principal props of the Cold War.

Chagrin over the present state of American organized labor was expressed by the *Christian Science Monitor* Dec. 5, 1967 as follows:

Challenge for Labor

Labor leadership in the United States is still struggling to maintain effective contact with the rank and file.

With growing affluence, the blue-collar union member often reacts like some of the less enlightened among middle-class Americans to such matters as tax increases, antipoverty drives, and larger work opportunities for Negroes. Simultaneously Walter Reuther accuses the AFL-CIO leadership under George Meany's long presidency of losing its progressive dynamism.

Workers have been moving to the suburbs, enjoying $10,000-a-year incomes, sending their kids to college—all very worthwhile. But they have developed a stake in the status quo which has meant that, in the recent mayoralty elections in Cleveland and Gary, the white workers voted in large majorities for the non-Negro candidate. And this though the union leaders had urged the workers to forswear racism.

After the elections, AFL-CIO President Meany declared "American voters have rejected racism as a political issue. This defeat of prejudice at the polls is a most important and encouraging development." Which sounds fine, but labor in working-

class districts voted for the opposition—though not entirely for racial reasons.

In Cleveland, for instance, Carl Stokes, the Negro candidate, managed to win more than 20 per cent of the votes in many white districts—except in working-class areas, where he won only 10 per cent. Leaders realize that the task of bridge-building between whites and blacks is still seriously incomplete in the labor movement.

A similar problem faces British trade unionism. Labour government officials in London pass antiracist laws and set worthy standards for welcoming West Indians and Pakistanis into British factories. Then at local union headquarters the nonwhites have to fight hard to win apprenticeship openings.

Other gaps have appeared between the leaders and the rank and file in America and Britain. Lucrative wage agreements negotiated by union leadership are frequently upset—as insufficiently beneficial—by the rank and file. This type of dispute accounted for one-seventh of all strikes handled by federal mediators this year. In London an eight-week wildcat dock strike has only just been settled, after seriously damaging Britain's export drive.

The AFL-CIO chieftains, meeting in Miami Beach, face a continuing challenge to maintain a dynamic brand of leadership, to avoid complacency and the status quo, in short, to keep abreast of the smart young men of the rank and file.

Summary: The rank-and-file of labor is becoming too smug.

It was not always so. Since colonial days to the immediate past, labor was the decided underdog in American social, economic and political life. Whatever affluence it enjoys today came as the result of hard struggle. Nobody ever gave labor anything. Every gain came after years of fighting followed by more years of effort to preserve what had been won. Throughout most of the time, the press of the nation was virtually unanimously antilabor. It is difficult if not impossible to mention anything which today is recognized as having been a labor victory that received the support of an appreciable proportion of the nation's newspapers. The press opposed Woodrow Wilson's New Freedom. It shared the hatred of the economic royalists for Franklin Delano Roosevelt's New Deal. It had no use for Harry S. Truman's Fair Deal and little enthusiasm for John F. Kennedy's New Frontier. It didn't even understand Lyndon B. Johnson's Great Society for which it probably should be forgiven as neither did anyone else. The extent to which yesterday's radicalism becomes today's orthodoxy, with the attendant moral that the circumstances should teach tolerance and openmindedness, was presented capably by the Salt Lake *Tribune* for June 24, 1969 in the following editorial:

Of Time and the Militant

Demands by today's militants seem far out to defenders of the status quo. But some of the "impossible" goals will probably be accepted fact in the not too distant future. The observation is prompted by announcement that private papers of the prosecutor at the trial of Chicago's Haymarket rioters are being offered for sale by a New York dealer.

On the night of May 4, 1886, police attempted to break up a workers' meeting in Haymarket Square. Someone threw a dynamite bomb at the police and officers and workers exchanged pistol shots. When order was restored seven policemen were dead and 70 wounded while the demonstrators suffered two dead and 12 wounded.

Eight men were indicted for the killings, some of them charged as accessories to the murders even though they had not even been present the night of the killings. Public animosity against the workers was high and one Chicago newspaper declared: "They attempted to destroy society. Society must destroy them."

Of the eight society did indeed destroy four by hanging. One committed suicide by placing a small dynamite cap in his mouth and setting it off. Three were pardoned by the governor.

What cause was the meeting in Haymarket Square called to promote? Was it overthrow of capitalism? Was it the repudiation of the Constitution? Was it denouncing high taxes? Not at all. The workers had assembled in Haymarket Square that fateful May night in support of the eight-hour day!

Summary: What seemed radical yesterday may seem conservative today.

The author of the following editorial in the Frederick (Md.) *News* for Dec. 1, 1951 probably wasn't aware of how far out his thinking had become by comparison with only a decade and a half earlier.

The Search for Security

The amazing growth of life insurance in the last fifteen years has been one of the less publicized and more spectacular phases of the universal search for security and ease in old age.

In 1935, life insurance in effect was just 100 billion dollars. By the end of 1952, the manager of the insurance department of the United States Chamber of Commerce figures insurance in effect will reach 300 billion. That is at the rate of two thousand dollars for every man, woman and child in the United States.

However, that is only half the story. The same informant figures that by the end of next year, government insurance in force will be even

Comment

Minor matter: "last" means there is no more; correct form here would be "past." Superlatives as "amazing growth," "spectacular phases," and "universal search for security" are a clue to the writer's immaturity. When you understand your subject you don't have to fall back on bromides.

Averages are deceptive. Every man, woman and child does not have $2,000 insurance. Some Daddy Warbucks probably has several million dollars worth to bring the average up when millions who have none are counted.

"Half the story" is trite and quite obviously inaccurate given the figures that are used.

more, a figure of 325 billion. That includes life insurance in force under the Social Security Act, the Veterans Administration, the Railroad Retirement Act and the Civil Service provision.

The outstanding growth of government insurance was presented as a sign that socialization of insurance was progressing at an alarming rate. However, growth of public and private insurance have gone hand in hand. Both have benefited from the fact that the national income has trebled in the same time, that life expectancy has been stretched by twenty years, and that people are more willing to provide for themselves out of their own earnings than to become public charges in their old-age.

A more characteristic editorial handling of a vital labor matter was the following editorial from the Niles (Ohio) *Times* of Aug. 19, 1959.

Landrum-Griffin Passes

The unexpected adoption of the Landrum-Griffin "tough" labor reform bill by a vote of 229 to 201 is a demonstration of the innate conservatism of the American people. Even zealous advocates of the measure had privately given up hope of passage, although predicting a close vote. The vote stands in striking contrast to the admitted fact that labor union political activity had been the major factor in electing last November what was prematurely termed a "liberal, pro-labor" Congress.

But the truth is that the people are more conservative than their Congress and the Congress is more conservative than the liberal pundits of the press and radio have reported.

On the non-teller vote on the Landrum-Griffin bill, the supporting majority was 15. But when the roll call vote placing each legislator on record was called, the majority actually rose to 28.

Like all other great events, the victory arose naturally from an inexorably developing conservative trend ever since the supposedly "liberal" Congress started last January. The public demand for a "sound dollar," the fast growing opposition to "inflationary" measures, and for fiscal and budgetary soundness, resis-

What is astounding here is the acceptance of social security. When it was up for a final vote in Congress it was called socialistic and it was argued that private insurance companies would be ruined. Desperate publicity efforts to defeat the measure included pictures of pretty girls wearing dog tags which it was claimed would happen if the bill were passed. Everyone would get a number and this, it was argued, was horrendous. The roorback came too late for rebuttal. In time it was pointed out that everyone already had plenty of numbers: telephone, house, bank account, driver's license, voter registration, and many more, and democracy seemed somehow to survive the phenomenon. The fact that the viciousness which characterized the attacks on the social security law had disappeared by 1951 was, indeed, phenomenal. Since then the only debates on the subject have concerned how to extend it.

Comment

What happened was that when the numerous liberal congressmen, mostly from the West, got to Washington, they were confronted with the realities of party discipline. They either followed the leaders or they were penalized by bad committee appointments and in other ways.

The leadership never was beholden to any but the interests responsible for their election.

tance to public power and other socialistic pretensions—all showed up first in the switch by the Democratic congressional leaders from a "liberal" giveaway policy to what those leaders termed a "moderate or middle-of-the-road" handling of pieces of legislation.

Behind all this—as careful analyses by observers here sum it up—was the tapping of the residual conservatism at the grass roots. Conservatives, haltingly before last fall's election and alerted and alarmed after the election, swelled a growing movement of political action among segments of American business.

Next, President Eisenhower—with an ameliorated situation at the White House after Sherman Adams left—began to find himself. His forthright TV speech calling for passage of the Landrum-Griffin bill on August 6 served as a tonic to the accumulating political action of the grass roots. The consequent mail to Congressmen was tremendous.

Then Senator McClellan's labor rackets crusade—at first only against corruption, then widening to include a bill of rights for union members—laid much of the groundwork; so that, when on the eve of the voting, McClellan called over from the Senate for passage of the Landrum-Griffin bill, he swayed many votes. Also, GOP House Leader Halleck worked wonders in rounding up Republicans (he lost only 17 out of 153).

All this in the face of the massive lobby of the labor oligarchy, working around the clock in the Capital. Heavy-set men, easily identifiable as labor lobbyists, roved the corridors of hotels on the Hill (where many solons live), knocking on doors early and late. One lobbyist was heard to say, poking his finger in the face of a Congressman, "Listen, you, this is it. You'll do this or else." And without effect, for this grim fact stares us in the face, as a warning for the future, that the fight isn't yet over: 122 out of 184 Democrats who voted against the Landrum-Griffin bill on Thursday took labor money in the last election.

The crusade for labor reform enjoys early endorsement from one of the great idols of the labor movement, Supreme Court Justice Brandeis, who, seeking to protect many years ago the nascent union movement, nevertheless feared unions might eventually acquire too much power and misuse it. He said in this connection, "Absolute power leads to excesses."

Throughout the attempt is to create the bandwagon effect: there is a strong conservative trend.

Who are the "observers here" who did the careful analysis? It's news that Niles, Ohio is the seat of such learned activities.

Subsequent events have shown how fictitious this attempt to create a conservative trend was.

Landrum-Griffin was promoted as a prolabor measure, to protect the rank-and-file. It required little or nothing by way of fiscal accountancy that large unions hadn't been doing for a long time. This editorial reveals that the bill actually was intended as antilabor, to at least discipline the unions. In other words, much of the argument for the bill was hypocritical and is now confessed.

This is an exaggeration of the pressure tactics used. Since Big Labor had little or nothing to lose, it didn't pay much attention to the bill by comparison with its strong support for the Wagner Act and its fight against Taft-Hartley.

"Heavy-set men, easily identifiable as labor lobbyists" is thoroughly absurd. The traditional cartoonist's caricature of a lobbyist is a fat businessman with dollar signs on his vest. No lobbyist, however, is so crude any more. This kind of behavior went out with the covered wagon.

A very strained and unclear quotation, applicable to many situations.

Hard as they may try to disguise it, a majority of American newspapers still espouse the Old Deal economic philosophy: what's good for General Motors is good for everybody else. The trickle-down aid-to-business philosophy of pre-FDR days never has been abandoned by the Establishment which includes most of the owners of newspapers. Prime the pump from the top through aid to commercial establishments and financial institutions and prosperity will be shared with those lower down on the economic ladder. By contrast the New Deal concept was to increase purchasing power at the bottom so that prosperity would spread upward, not downward. A recent reaffirmation of the old philosophy was the following editorial in the Baltimore *Sun* for Sept. 25, 1971.

Profit Rates

Profits are a target for certain politicians, union leaders and consumer advocates, who make a point of saying that profits must be controlled, along with wages and prices, during Phase Two after the freeze ends. The freeze order itself has been condemned because it didn't freeze profits. But economists know that the matter isn't nearly that simple. Businessmen and investors know that the general level of profits is abnormally low. Anyone who stops to look at the facts can readily see that profits are an integral part of the economic system which provides productive jobs for men and women and which pays a major part of the taxes by which government operates.

Perhaps this is all too elementary to be repeated. Yet nearly every day the specter of swollen profits is raised by somebody, and more often than not by somebody who should know better. And as *The Wall Street Journal* noted the other day, if labor's argument for "controls" over profits ever gets anywhere it could slow down or even prevent a return to stable prosperity. In practice, moreover, the price freeze and the wage-price controls set up thereafter will restrain profits, severely in the case of corporations which agreed to large wage increases shortly before the mid-August freeze.

"Ironically," as the *Journal* said, "the chief uncertainty the worker faces is whether or not his employer will operate profitably. A reasonable record of profitability is essential to preservation of the employee's job and the wages it provides."

Profits have not risen during inflation as have wages and prices. After-tax corporate profits in 1970 are placed at $41.2 billion as compared with $49.9 billion in 1966. The U.S. Chamber of Commerce has pointed out that in 1970 business profits as a percentage of the gross national product were at the lowest level since 1938. Business profits during the past year averaged 2.3 cents per dollar of sales, the lowest in more than 15 years. Between 1965 and the second quarter of 1971 the share of the national income for employee compensation went up from 69.8 per cent to 75.8 per cent; in the same period the share for after-tax profits went down from 8.2 per cent to 5.3 per cent.

Labor leaders and others who are attacking profits now could more usefully be arguing for the fair rates of profits which will bring about greater employment. Further, an argument should be made for more competition in business, both as to commerce within the United States and as to world markets; competition whets efficiency as it restrains profits. One of the factors in the inflation still plaguing this country has been the ability of powerful unions to push up wages beyond the gains justified by increased productivity. Restraints on the misuse of economic power by big unions and big corporations could be more effective in preserving competition, moreover, than rhetorical attacks, of the kind we have been seeing, on profits.

Mild support for labor's viewpoint was contained in the following editorial which appeared in the Milwaukee *Journal* for April 12, 1972.

Hit at Excess Profits

The Nixon administration's struggle to cope with inflation is facing another critical test. A government survey shows that more than 20% of the nation's biggest businesses —far more than originally believed—seem to be increasing their profit margins improperly under the federal price control system.

This is precisely what critics like AFL-CIO Chief George Meany have been contending. When Meany recently quit the Pay Board in a huff, he charged that the American people were being victimized by lax control of prices and profits, while being "squeezed in the paychecks." Now the government is indicating with its own data that Meany was partly right—not in fruitlessly storming off the Pay Board, but in worrying about excessive profit margins.

For revealing what appear to be specific violations, the government deserves credit. It is also to be commended for threatening court action to roll back prices that cannot be justified. The measure of the system's effectiveness and credibility, however, will be whether tough talk is backed by robust action. Meany and millions of others will be watching.

Labor Day editorials mostly are for the purpose of informing workingmen that they are fortunate to live in a capitalistic society which makes it possible for them to enjoy the highest standard of living of any labor force in the world. By inference, any discontented laborer lacks gratitude or understanding. A typical editorial, which followed this formula, was the following from the Chicago *Sun-Times* of Sept. 2, 1968.

Labor Day Capitalists

Persons old enough to remember the Great Depression of the 30s are often seized with nostalgia for the good old days when, it seems, $50 a week went further than $125 a week today. The National Industrial Conference Board has produced statistics to support this.

A family of four with an income of $3,000 in 1939 paid only $30 in federal taxes. That left $2,970 to spend. Coffee was 13 cents a pound, butter 22 cents, ham 18 cents and eggs 19 cents a dozen.

Today a similar family needs an income of $8,417 to have the same purchasing power. Income taxes and social security take $1,084 and inflation $4,363. That leaves $2,970 in 1939 dollars.

The family that earned $5,000 in 1939 would need $14,282 to stay even; the family of $10,000 would need $29,629.

Those who established their families after World War II might be interested in these figures: A family earning $3,000 in 1949 needs $4,643 today to stay even. The $5,000 income of 1949 must be $7,661, the 10,000 income must have risen to $15,022 and the $25,000 income to $37,727.

There is a bright side of the picture that can be noted on this Labor Day.

In 1939, $30 a week was considered a fair wage.

In 1949, the average weekly pay of an industrial production worker was $50.24, or $1.27½ cents for a 39.4-hour week.

Today the weekly pay is $108.20, or $2.84 for a 38.1-hour week.

Wages have more than doubled, more than keeping up with taxes and inflation.

One big reason: automation and improved machines have increased the productivity of each worker. These new tools have been made possible by greater investment of capital. Much of this capital, through the purchase of common stocks, has come from workers themselves, who thus become capitalists.

Americans who celebrate Labor Day today also celebrate the American free enterprise system that has made this nation's workers the most prosperous of all time.

Despite the sympathy which may ooze on Labor Day, once the holiday is over, it would be smart for labor to recognize and keep its proper place. That means realizing that its betters should be allowed to function without hindrance. The following editorial from the Chicago *Daily Tribune* of March 5, 1954 is typical of this sort of reasoning.

Trustees Should Be Trustees

The term of John Doherty as a Chicago school trustee expires in May. Mr. Doherty, who is international representative of the United Steelworkers union, CIO, said that he hadn't given thought to the matter of his reappointment but felt that the important thing was that his group continue to have representation on the board.

That, unfortunately, is the reason, and so far as we know the only important reason, why Mr. Doherty should not be reappointed.

As a board member he has usually displayed good sense in discussions. But his principal interest, and that also of Trustee Haggerty, the AFL board member, has been as a partisan of the thousands of unionized employees of the board—few of whom, incidentally are CIO members.

The school board is an employer with many thousands of employees. When labor unions demand representation on the board what they really demand is that the unions move a couple of their spokesmen over to the management side of the bargaining table. That is incompatible with the obligations of any trustee.

It isn't any reply to his objection to say that labor leaders have as much right to sit on school boards as businessmen do. That is self-evident, but always with the proviso that both regard themselves as trustees running the schools for the pupils, and not as spokesmen of either unions or business. President Traynor is a former officer of Swift & Company, but he isn't on the board to sell hams, or to speak for business in general. He regards his trusteeship as a public trust, not as a brief for special interests.

There is a lot of ability in union leadership, and it should be used in public office. Unfortunately, too many union leaders who take public jobs regard themselves, as Mr. Doherty made clear that he does, as special pleaders for unions rather than as citizens impartially serving all the public.

The persistent efforts of die-hard Old Dealers to undo the prolabor measures passed in New Deal days have been demonstrated in many ways, none more importantly than in the attempt to vitiate the effect of the National Labor Relations (Wagner) Act by means of so-called right-to-work laws which 19 states at least adopted before Congress in 1965 repealed Section 14B of the Taft-Hartley Act which

permitted them. The St. Louis *Post-Dispatch* tersely summarized the arguments against such laws as follows:

A Right-to-Work law does not in fact protect anybody's right to work. Such measures are not sponsored by workers. A Right-to-Work law prohibits the closed shop, union shop or other union security arrangements or contracts, even if a large majority of employees favors them.

It weakens unions, but it also restricts collective bargaining, and tends to substitute individual bargaining instead.

It is difficult to see how state laws weakening unions generally could protect their members from mishandling union funds or rigged elections and undemocratic practices or "sweetheart" contracts.

About the strongest prolabor editorial on the subject was that which the Boise (Idaho) *Sunday Statesman* ran Oct. 8, 1961.

Craft unions, able to command comparably higher wages, retain dignity and responsibility. In Idaho, non-craft unions already are making progress, and probably generating part of the 'right-to-work' conversation as underpaid workers search for union help. This has been the history of union organization—workers have been driven to seek help from unions when their incomes were substandard. This will continue to be the history of union effort.

It is at once evident that not a single interested supporter of the 'right-to-work' idea lives on an income slightly above a dollar an hour. Most of them long since have "had it made". . . .

Idaho doesn't need a "right-to-work"-for-nothing law or that kind of a reputation.

More typical was the following editorial from the Chicago *Daily News* of March 4, 1957.

Free Indiana

The Indiana legislature upheld that state's growing reputation as a citadel of individual freedom when it passed a law forbidding compulsory union membership. It outlaws "union

Comment

At the time Indiana was represented by two of the most conservative senators in the United States Senate, Homer E. Capehart and William E. Jenner, and was still the stronghold of Ku Klux Klan-

shop" contracts in which all employes must pay dues to the union or be discharged.

The unions have conducted bitter fights against such laws. In so doing, they discard the case for individual freedom which they made for so many years in battling to get the "yellow dog" contract outlawed. This was a device in which newly hired workers were required to agree either to join no union or one approved by the employer.

The argument most often heard for the union shop is that the "free rider," who benefits from the union's activities, should be compelled to help support it. This seems to us superficial. It is as unsound as saying that because the church and the PTA work for the good of the whole neighborhood that all should be taxed to finance them.

The additional fact is that a large part of union dues is spent for political and economic propaganda, publications and other activities which might be violently contrary to an individual's own convictions.

Some candid union leaders have admitted that their zeal for the union shop stems from the desire to increase the economic and political power of the unions. To take a contrary position, as Indiana has done, is not to deny the value of the labor unions, but only to assert that they must continue to prove themselves worthy of voluntary support.

ism in the North. Only the editorial writer seemed aware of any growing reputation or would interpret the passage of such a bill as being evidence of it.

Yellow dog contracts were outlawed by the Norris-LaGuardia Anti-Injunction Act in 1932. The nomination of a North Carolina federal circuit court judge, John J. Parker, to the United States Supreme Court by President Hoover was not confirmed by the Senate because Judge Parker had upheld such contracts.

The analogy is fallacious. In the first place, church property is scandalously tax exempt and so, of course, are schools. PTA dues and church contributions are deductible from federal income taxes. More importantly, the choices suggested are not comparable. One does not have to belong to a church but all but a small minority must work for a living.

Corrupt practices and labor laws forbid use of union funds for political purposes. After a vicious attempt to catch Sidney Hillman of the Amalgamated Clothing Workers and a founder of the New York American Labor Party, in violation of the law, further attempts to entrap unionists were abandoned. Voluntary fund raising drives are conducted to support the AFL-CIO Committee on Political Education but no dues are used. Union officers are elected democratically under the supervision of the National Labor Relations Board if necessary.

This is pious gobbledegook to disguise the motivation which is: turn the clock back to the glorious '20s of Coolidge Prosperity.

The value of open shop laws to business was demonstrated by the following typical editorial from the Indianapolis *Star* of Dec. 3, 1957.

Come To Indiana!

Lockheed Aircraft Corporation wants its employes to have individual choice in the matter of joining a labor organization. The State of Indiana would like to have some additional industry.

May we suggest that the two get together?

Indiana's Right-to-Work law, like most others in the nation is being tested on the question of the agency shop. However, the

basic philosophy behind the Hoosier statute is the idea that a man can choose his own union, and support it at his discretion. It may be that the United States Supreme Court will uphold the Sixth District Federal Court of Appeals which said that an agency shop is unlawful in Indiana.

As a growing member of an important industry, Lockheed will almost certainly expand. When it does, Indiana leaders in business and government might suggest that this is an ideal location for future operations.

On two important questions that often control the location of industry, Indiana and Lockheed have a lot in common.

A well-balanced appraisal was the following Cleveland *Press* editorial:

Too Much Law in Labor Negotiations

If sponsors can collect enough signatures for a referendum, there'll be a proposal on the ballot next fall forbidding compulsory union membership.

Some states already have a law or constitutional amendment of this sort.

These are popularly known as "right to work" laws, although the name has been in dispute, and Ohio backers are casting around for a better title.

But whatever it's called, the effect of the bill would be to forbid labor and management from negotiating agreements in which employees would have to join unions.

If this proposal actually gets on the ballot, the Press expects to oppose it—for two major reasons.

First, and most important, labor relations work out best when there's a minimum of government interference.

Secondly, this proposal has already been offered in the Legislature, and failed.

The Legislature is the right place for decisions on bills such as this one.

If the backers of every proposal turned down by the Legislature went running to the people, it would lead to hopeless confusion.

Public policy should be to encourage labor and management to handle their problems on their own, without a lot of coaching from the outside.

The inevitable result of too much law in labor negotiations is that both employers and employees fall into the habit of leaning much too heavily on government.

Furthermore, it would give legislators a handy excuse for ducking every hot potato, since they could argue the issue would be offered directly to the people anyway.

Theoretical acceptance of the importance of the workingman, even support of specific legislation is one thing. Taking labor's side in a strike situation is something else again. Since the first walkout in the New World, that of the Boston bakers in 1741, labor has had to contend with a hostile public opinion "when the chips are down" as they are in a strike situation. Long before a tieup of transportation or communication facilities or an interference with electrical or other power became so catastrophic as it unquestionably is today, the public, with editorial writers agreeing, generally has resented any interferences with the everyday lives of city dwellers. And the tendency always has been to blame labor, no matter what the grievance. In fact, it is rare that labor's side of any dispute receives much publicity. And no editorial ever says in essence: "Go to it, labor. The boss is a stinker. Go get him!"

The teachers' strike about which the following editorial appeared in the May 26, 1972 Chicago *Sun-Times* was not for the purpose of improving pay scales or working conditions. Rather, it was against the violation by the Chicago Board of Education of gains contained in the contract signed almost a year earlier, a fact which it is impossible to learn from this typical editorial. At the time the Chicago schools again were being threatened with the loss of millions of dollars of federal funds because of misuse and, ironically, the Illinois legislature was passing a bill to give $30 million to parochial schools despite an Illinois Supreme Court decision saying it was an unconstitutional act. The $30 million was almost exactly what the Chicago school board needed to live up to its contract obligations with the teacheres and to avoid ending the school year a fortnight ahead of time. This editorial is thoroughly dishonest both because of what it says and because of what it ignores.

Selling Out the Schools

The Chicago Teachers Union and the Board of Education have scratched each other's backs and there will be no teacher strike for now. But before there is any light-hearted dancing in the streets, let it be understood that the so-called settlement is just a pseudo-event that postpones and compounds the present financial crisis.

On the surface, it may appear that the board conceded very little for the right to reopen the schools. The teachers union had demanded restoration of 11 days cut from the end of the present term and of 4,536 jobs scheduled to be eliminated in September. It settled for a June cutback of five days, with six days to be cut in December, and accepted the board's pledge that the jobs would be restored if the money becomes available.

In reality, however, the board caved in. Instead of standing behind budgetary decisions that stem from the facts of a whopping financial deficit, the board in effect agreed that such decisions are subject to union approval whatever the financial situation.

The 11-day early closing was a reasonable if not optimum means of saving money. To renege on that decision by splitting the 11 days between June and December merely postpones the day of reckoning, and does so on the union's terms. Surely, there is no guarantee now that the union will not, in December, insist on again postponing the closing on threat of strike.

By the same token, the union is quite likely to insist on restoration of all those 4,536 jobs, whether the General Assembly furnishes the money for them or not. To restore the jobs would cost the board $45 million, which could represent another 24 days of early closing in December, which in turn could generate another union fuss, ad infinitum.

The so-called settlement of the present crisis solved nothing decisively except the postponement of a planned strike. The net result beyond this was a further loss of credibility all around.

The problems of the Chicago school system are complex, but the amount of money available defines the limits within which the union and board must work. To meet problems within such limits requires not bluster but cooperation toward solutions that benefit children.

Sadly, the Chicago Teachers Union appears to have gotten out of touch with the children, while the School Board appears to have sold out to the union. We would hope that the CTU membership, half of which voted against a strike, can get its union back on the proper track, and we look forward to changes in the board and its method of operation.

Nothing rebounds to organized labor's discredit more than any outbreak of violence during a demonstration or strike. Almost a half century ago a Senate committee of which Sen. Robert M. LaFollette, Jr., of Wisconsin was chairman, exposed the extent to which spies and provocateurs were used by business and the existence of lucrative agencies, the principal one headed by Pearl Bergoff, to supply strike breakers or scabs, as the laboring man called them. Seldom has a court action or impartial investigation proved that violence during strikes was the fault of labor. In fact, quite the contrary has been the case from the days of the Molly McGuires and Knights of Labor and the Pinkerton detectives to the present. The 1937 Memorial Day massacre before the Republic Steel Company plant in South Chicago was an instance. Ten unarmed parading strikers were shot in the back and killed and hundreds were injured. Newsreel pictures of police brutality were shown privately by the American Civil Liberties Union and made available to Paul Y. Anderson of the St. Louis *Post-Dispatch* by the LaFollette committee. They were, however, officially banned from theaters in Chicago and suburbs. An overflow protest meeting in the Civic Theater featured Carl Sandburg, Paul Douglas, Robert Morss Lovett and many other personages of similar stature. Meyer Levin wrote a novel, *Citizens*, about it. If he had used real names today his book would be called an example of New Journalism.

What follows is a typical "labor is always to blame" editorial from the Memphis *Commercial-Appeal* of May 3, 1972.

A Black Eye for Labor

The construction workers who turned to violence in Memphis Monday disgraced themselves, their union and their cause. Whatever the merits of their complaint against the local chapter of Associated General Contractors may be, there was no excuse for the vandalism and other violations of the law.

Some of the blame rests on the Memphis Building & Construction Trades Council. Although it called for a peaceful protest, the union does not seem to have taken all the precautions it could have to minimize the possibility of violence.

What may have started as an honest labor demonstration for most of the 3,000 union members who gathered at the union headquarters quickly got out of control when the workers reached the AGC offices. Innocent persons could easily have been hurt. A piece of cement was thrown through a window and hit a secretary's desk. Fortunately she wasn't sitting at it.

Later a private guard for a union contractor was beaten at a construction site at Memphis State University. What was gained? Nothing but a black eye for the labor movement.

The great majority of the workers did not join in the violence, but they also share the blame for not keeping others from doing it. Those workers who were arrested should be prosecuted promptly. They are adults, not boys on a lark, and they should be held responsible for their actions.

Officials of the union admitted that they lost control of the members Monday. They promised more orderly demonstrations in the future. But the disturbances yesterday showed either that the promises were not supported by adequate planning or that the officials couldn't handle the job of controlling a large number of men in an emotionally tense situation.

There are better ways for a union to express disagreement with management than by mass turnouts at construction sites. The local officials might think about recent comments by Hunter Wharton, general president of the Operating Engineers (AFL-CIO)

In criticizing the pressure tactics of the construction unions, Wharton said, ". . . if we were to take stock we would soon find that our employer-employe relationship and our public image are wanting and need new directions." He called for less muscle and more professionalism in negotiations.

Demonstrations such as the one in Memphis are really confessions of failure—that labor and management haven't made the system work. The negotiators should try a little harder.

If the commercial press were to take the side of labor, the editorials would take cognizance of the complaints cited in the following from the Sept. 1, 1966 *Machinist*, publication of the International Association of Machinists and Aerospace Workers, AFL-CIO.

Public Interest?

During the long airline strike, hundreds of editorials appeared in the commercial press urging Congress and/or President Johnson to order the men back to work.

Although the strike was won and the airlines are flying again, the newspapers are still crying for legislation that would apply to strikes in any important industry. So far, we have come across only one (1) editorial in an English language newspaper in the United States that had the nerve to suggest that forcing Americans to work against their will might be unconstitutional.

The *News and Sentinel* of Colebrook, N.H. (Circ. 2,200, weekly)—by its own tell—has never been pro-union. It has disagreed bitterly with labor's position in the number of strikes. But, the *News and Sentinel* editorial continued:

"The airline strike, somehow, has brought home some truths all along the line. We have been troubled from the beginning by the assumption on the part of just about everybody that the President, or the Congress, can simply order the striking machinists back to work. There is still something in the Constitution, we are quite sure, prohibiting involuntary servitude."

The *News and Sentinel* is right, of course (see above). But the daily newspapers ignore the constitution. In the public interest, they are willing to force men to work for the profit of others.

The Constitution gives the Government ample authority to protect the nation's health and safety. But Congress has no authority to suspend anyone's freedom because of "public interest." If the Constitution does suspend American liberties whenever it is in the public interest, the right to strike won't be the only right suspended.

Someone could make a good case that it would be in the public interest if this nation were better informed about the issues that cause strikes. There is ample evidence that some commercial newspapers and magazines are misusing the right of free press.

Life magazine, for the worst example, is failing the public interest when it blathers, as it did last week, that the airline settlement "struck fires of anarchy and avarice among other workers whose contracts are due to expire soon."

The airline strike was anything but anarchy. For 43 days, 35,400 IAM members walked the picket lines in 231 cities without incident. They conducted a peaceful strike for legal objectives.

The $40,000 a year editors of *Life* magazine have no standing to write about the "avarice" of wage earners trying to raise families on $100 to $140 a week, take-home.

There was nothing in *Life* magazine about the issues that caused the airline strike. There is little or nothing in many of the newspapers about uncontrolled rents, uncontrolled grocery prices, uncontrolled clothing prices that are causing discontent.

If the "public interest" is going to be the test of American liberties, someone is bound to suggest that the test be applied first to the right of free press. We hope it will never come to that.

The 1955 Pulitzer prize for editorial writing went to Royce Howes of the Detroit *Free Press* for his attempt July 26, 1954 to give a complete and fair appraisal of a work stoppage in the automobile capital. One wonders where the news side of the newspaper had been all the time, making the editorial writers feel it was necessary to write this sort of piece which, it would seem, should come under the heading of factual reporting under the direction of the city desk. Apparently this was an instance in which one department of a newspaper stepped in after another department fell down on a job, and it won fine commendation for doing so.

In auto shops the strip which frames the insides of your car's windows is called garnish molding. Screws hold it in place, and of course there must be holes for the screws.

How many of these holes can reasonably be drilled in eight hours by Dodge assembly line men was the seed of the disagreement which last week made almost 45,000 Chrysler Corp. workers idle and payless.

The insignificance of the little hole in contrast to the immensity of loss to all whom the strike touched reminds of nothing so much as the old nursery rhyme that tells how what began with the loss of a horseshoe nail ended with the loss of a kingdom.

The question we want to examine here is whether Detroit can afford that kind of cause-and-effect sequence.

We are not thinking of just the pay which the strike cost Chrysler workers who participated or whose jobs stopped temporarily because of the strike. Nor are we considering primarily the cost to the corporation in production and dislocation. And while we are not forgetting all the merchants of goods and services whose cash registers rang up less money because so many were out of work, that isn't the cause of our primary concern, either.

How the Strike Began

What troubles us most gravely is the long-term damage to Detroit as a place to prosper, whether you are a production worker, management man or merchant. Accumulatively, affairs such as last week's strike hurt Detroit's reputation. And when its reputation goes, hope of an ever-building prosperity goes with it.

Industries do not like to locate, or even continue, in a place where the trivial can cost so much. Workmen don't like to establish where instability is so great that a triviality can cost them a week's pay or more.

We would not attempt to allocate the degrees of responsibility for the Chrysler Corp. stoppage last week.

Nor do we contend that either union or management should have shrugged off everything as trivial that occurred between the disagreement over drilling little holes and the idling of nearly 45,000.

After all, between loss of the horseshoe nail and loss of the kingdom events became increasingly less trivial. So with the progress of the dispute at Dodge.

What happened was this, and here we relate the company's story and then the Dodge Local's version.

Until June 28, there were 26 men installing garnish moldings. Each accomplished the entire process. The molding was adjusted, clamped in place, holes drilled, screws driven and clamp removed by the individual men.

A New Installation Process

On that day, following an efficiency study, engineers changed the operation. A man did just one thing in the installation process. Those who fitted didn't clamp, those who clamped didn't drill, and so on.

One thing this did was to enable a man to work more or less in place as the car passed him. Formerly he rode down the line in the car and walked as much as 100 feet back to resume his station. In time, it was anticipated, the new way would reduce the garnish molding crew to 18 men and permit transfer of the other eight to new work.

The system according to the engineers, has been for some time in almost all—and perhaps all—other auto plants. They say it involves no speedup, but a greater production efficiency.

Under this plan at Dodge, four men were assigned the drilling job. July 12, one of them was warned he was not keeping pace and was causing other drillers to lose position. The next day he was sent home, and the three other drillers were warned that they were not keeping up to standard. At the same time, extra drillers were assigned. July 14, the drillers again lost position, extra

ones were added and supervisors demonstrated how the job could be done without losing position. But the next day the other three original drillers lost position so rapidly that they fell 15 cars behind.

They were sent home and warned that they would be discharged if their work wasn't satisfactory when they came back. This brought a resentment among other workers, the line became jammed, it had to be shut down and 5000 men were sent home.

The next day two of the drillers returned, failed to turn in the work required of them and were fired. That was a Friday. Nearly 100 men didn't return from lunch, the line had to be stopped once more and the next Monday the strike was called—so improperly, it now turns out, that it had no legality in the eyes of not only management but of the UAW.

Officials of the Dodge local say that with the change of procedure in the matter of garnish molding there was no chance for a "rest break" possible formerly because a man could get his immediate job done by working fast and finishing it in less than the required time. Now, the local says the next job is constantly waiting and a 10-minute relief can be had only when the foreman grants it.

75 Cars an Hour

No time study, says the union, has been made, though in early July a grievance was filed and such a study requested. The management asked that the study be postponed 30 days to give men opportunity to accustom themselves to the new system. That would be necessary, it was explained, to determine actually what the method should call for in work output.

What has happened, says the local, is that production line manpower is set up to handle an even flow of 75 cars an hour, but frequently must handle 85 cars an hour. This occurs, it was explained, because unavoidable stoppages of the line (breakdowns, absence of materials, etc.) are compensated for by increasing speed so that the day's output averages 75 cars an hour.

The local's version of the discharge of the two men, which touched off the strike, par-

244 / *Principles of Editorial Writing*

allels that of the company—except that the company says the firing was "for deliberate refusal to put out a fair day's work and refusing to do what they were told."

First the matter of how and by whom the holes, five in each molding, were to be drilled. Then two men fired. After that close to 45,000 idled.

We don't think very many people will see any necessity for the drastic consequence of so little. Nor do we think when the cause is analyzed it can do anything but bring harm to the whole city.

We remarked that we would not attempt to assess degrees of responsibility—not exact degrees.

Harm to Whole City

But it seems apparent that the Dodge local was anything but free of fault. In fact that much was ruled Friday when the parent UAW ordered the strike called off and said that the vote under which it was called was improper.

Under UAW rules a strike vote must be taken on a specific grievance, and any subsequent strike actually called can only relate to that grievance. The vote taken several months ago under which the Dodge local's leadership acted concerned a matter having nothing to do with how a garnish molding shall be installed.

Perhaps management let dissatisfaction run too far and get out of hand. It seems to us there could have, for instance, been a tentative time study. Its results need not have been that final, but at least some guidance might be had from it and the workers who thought there should be one somewhat mollified.

The UAW, at the international level, might have been better advised had it stepped in sooner instead of giving the Dodge local so much time to work its way out of an untenable position.

In any event, somewhere there should have been more statesmanship, more regard for proper procedure and more sense of proportion. No such blow to the whole economy of Detroit should be struck over such a microscopic issue.

The weakness and danger in the union position, as we see it, is that it endeavors to assume management prerogatives in trying to say how a plant shall be run; what production methods shall be employed; how much patience must be shown employees who cannot or will not do the same job which has been demonstrated as reasonable elsewhere.

Management Should Manage

Names need not be named, but anyone casually acquainted with Detroit's latter day industrial picture knows that just such relinquishment of management function have been a prominent part in the departure from this region of certain industries, and the abolishment of thousands of jobs forever.

It is the condition which drives industry from a place. It is prominent among the reasons why some industries have not been able to meet the challenge of competition.

What labor shall receive in wages, what hours it will work, what benefits it will receive are properly matters for the union in collective bargaining. So are working conditions free from avoidable hazard to safety. Other items proper to union bargaining can be named.

But assumption of the right to manage is not one of them, and assumption of that right is inevitably destructive. It can only lead to fewer jobs.

Firm retention by management of the right to manage, on the other hand, makes more jobs. The plants where work is steady and employment high are those where management—even at the cost of riding out strikes—has kept a firm grip on its right to say how things shall be done and what standards those who ask employment will be expected to meet.

What the Strike Reflects

We believe that realization of this fact of life is extremely essential to Detroit.

Ours is a tremendous industrial city. Its might and prosperity rest on the payrolls of industry in very great part. There is every reason to believe that unless unnecessary discouragements to industrial growth are presented it will attract more industrial wealth, offer more jobs and increased security.

But what is reflected in the strike and compelled shutdown which put almost 45,000 men and women on the street is a definite and emphatic discouragement. Such exhibitions can turn enterprise from Detroit despite a great many factors here which normally would attract it—as they have attracted it in the past.

Our purpose in discussing the incident of the Dodge strike is not to castigate any individuals or groups as such. But we do believe it represents something which Detroit can ill afford. And our interest in this city's welfare requires that we cite to Free Press readers the implications and the portents involved.

What they point to is something neither Detroit nor any other community can afford if its people and its institutions want to maintain a competitive position—and we are thinking of men and women who must compete for jobs just as much as we are of industries which compete for markets.

Finally, a clue to the attitude of newspaper management regarding labor unions was contained in the following piece which appeared in the Minneapolis Morning *Tribune* for Aug. 7, 1962.

To Our Readers

We are happy and relieved to resume publication today of the Minneapolis Tribune and the Minneapolis Star, after an interruption of 116 days caused by a strike of our drivers, mailers, printers, stereotypers and pressmen.

We are restoring normal Tribune, Star and Sunday Tribune service to readers and advertisers throughout the Upper Midwest just as quickly as possible.

As we said on April 12, the day the strike began, we believe the strike was tragic and unnecessary. We have continued to believe that the issues between the company and the striking unions could and should have been resolved through normal bargaining procedures—and, if agreement could not be reached in that manner through binding arbitration by an outside third party.

The strike issues of new methods, equipment and manpower, as well as wages and employe benefits, have now, fortunately, been settled. How much better it would have been, however, if at least the key issues could have been settled by arbitration—as the company repeatedly offered—thereby shortening or avoiding altogether any interruption in publication.

When the welfare of a great city and region of the country is so clearly jeopardized, we believe there is an almost paramount obligation on both management and labor to avoid a strike. The public interest is clearly involved whenever so many people's access to the news, as well as so much business activity, is so sharply curtailed.

The cost of the strike to the reading public in terms of late or unavailable information, as well as inconvenience, has been very considerable. In addition, thousands of advertisers, large and small, have lost many millions of dollars of sales; and these lost sales, in turn, have resulted in less general business activity than otherwise would have been the case throughout the Upper Midwest this spring and summer. Our employees who did not report for work lost more than $3 million in pay. Our 13,000 carrier salesmen and other distributors lost more than $1.4 million as a result of the strike. Almost everyone was affected in one or more ways.

Now, however, the strike is over, and we would like to express our gratitude to many people. . . . to the hundreds of employees who continued to report for duty at the Star and Tribune throughout the strike period, and whose work helped make it possible for us to get back into operation so quickly;

. . . to the federal and state mediators and conciliators who met in an unending series of negotiations and conferences;

. . . to Gov. Anderson and Mayor Naftalin who, when requested by the Twin Cities local of the American Newspaper Guild, gave generously of their time and talents to help settle the dispute;

. . . to the business community and to the advertisers normally served by the serious difficulties caused by the interrupted publication of the two newspapers; and above all, to the reading public, who were a remarkably patient victim of the strike.

Now we are again devoting full energies to publishing the best newspapers of which we are capable, for the people of Minneapolis and the Upper Midwest.

It is certainly good to be back.

John Cowles, President
Joyce A. Swan, Publisher

CRIME

Most newspapers display precious little intelligence in their editorializing on crime, or in their news coverage either for that matter. Not that the often heard charge that crime news encourages lawbreaking has any validity, or that either playing down or ignoring antisociability or playing up every court conviction would make any difference. What is to be regretted is the journalistic failure to provide greater leadership in educating the public away from superstitions and unscientific notions regarding the nature of criminal behavior and the way to correct or control it. The college graduate who has taken a good course in criminology could write, or at least think rings around most of the veterans who pontificate in an intellectual vacuum.

"Back your police" so that "law and order" can be maintained and we can all be "safe in the streets," howl the shallow thinkers and the knee jerk mentalities. Perfectly understandable this concern, and thoroughly laudable the snappy slogans. But rapes, muggings, and other offenses, major and minor, are not going to be eliminated by any display of bumper stickers or billboards. Nor will the rate of the most serious offenses, including homicide, be seriously affected by any increase, however large, in the size of the police force, either afoot, on horseback, or in squad cars. Conversely, in most if not all situations, the police do not deserve credit for any decline in lawbreaking, nor is it their fault when the opposite is the case.

Here is a typical editorial linking an unsolved murder to the alleged inadequate size of the police force. It appeared in the Chicago *Sun-Times* for Sept. 1, 1957.

No Policemen on the Beat

On the night that Judith Mae Anderson disappeared and went to her death, not one policeman was walking a beat in the Austin police district where she lived.

There was only one policeman on a three-wheel, radio-equipped motorcycle, the modern way to patrol an area.

The district has a population of 143,985—more than the City of Peoria. It embraces six square miles. Under ordinary circumstances there would have been as many as 18 men walking beats. There would have been five men on three-wheel bikes. There would have been four squad cars on patrol. (There were three). There would have been in all, 34 men on duty at the police station and in the area. (There were only 13).

Why was the district undermanned?

The major reason: withdrawal of men from Austin and all other police districts for assign-

Comment

The girl left a girl friend's home late at night to take a bus to her home a few miles away. She was not seen again alive. Her dismembered body was discovered when it floated ashore in three barrels. It was revealed that she, with her girl friend, made a habit of soliciting rides, often with strange men. No policeman would have been likely to detect an oncoming murder. The victim in this case, as in two other murders which occurred in Chicago about the same time—one involving two Grimes sisters and the other two brothers and a boy friend—were all teen-agers out after dark alone.

This editorial was a laudable attempt to alert the smug white northsiders to the bad situation on

ment to special details needed to patrol areas where racial tension exists.

Eight policemen had been withdrawn from Austin Station's middle watch for use in areas far from Austin. In addition, more than the normal number of policemen were off duty. Several had time coming because they had worked overtime when the district was made shorthanded by reassignment of other men to race details.

Virtually every district in Chicago is similarly overworked and undermanned because 287 men presently are assigned each day to such areas as Calumet Park and Trumbull Park, where white racists have used violence against Negro citizens.

These incidents may seem far away and of little personal concern to the good citizens of Austin and other residential neighborhoods where the crime rate is below average and racial understanding and tolerance is seemingly only an academic matter.

But a lack of police protection in their own neighborhoods results from the behavior of such hoodlums as those who attacked a picnic of Negroes in Calumet Park and touched off a riot July 28. Austinites may read dispassionately about the long-simmering situation at Trumbull Park Homes without realizing that their own sons and daughters are receiving less protection than they should because troublemakers in that area have drawn away from the Austin district the policemen who usually patrol its streets and alleys.

No one knows, of course, whether Judy may have escaped death if the normal number of policemen had been on duty the night she disappeared. Some residents of the area reported they heard screams. If a policeman had been nearby and heard the screams, and had investigated, tragedy might have been averted. The absence of just one policeman could have been responsible for Judy's death.

Experts on crime prevention tell us that the more policemen on duty in the neighborhoods of the city, the fewer crimes there will be. Last month, New York declared war on juvenile crime and put all of its 23,000 police personnel on around-the-clock emergency duty, crime dropped sharply.

the south side where bigots were interfering with the attempt of Negroes to move into a public housing project. The fact that the Anderson murder might not have been prevented if all the policemen assigned to duty in Trumbull Park had been in Rogers Park instead doesn't diminish the praiseworthy intent; but the argument is still miserably weak.

The editorial loses some of its effectiveness because it is so repetitious. It would have had more impact if it had been about half as long.

To be really safe every one of us should have a body guard. And who would watch them?

If such experts exist they should be identified and quoted precisely. The New York episode caused a reign of terror which embittered young people and had no lasting effect.

New York has only twice the population of Chicago and only half again as much territory. But it has three times as many policemen.

Two appropriate steps to fight the slaughter of our innocents suggest themselves.

One, the community must unite against sowers of racial trouble; a good start is the stiff charge filed against 11 of those arrested after the Calumet Park disturbances. They menaced the entire community, not just Calumet.

Two, the community needs more policemen and better administration of police personnel. The 2,000 policemen added within recent months were not enough.

There should be as many policemen on the force as are necessary to patrol every street in the city *constantly* after dark.

This is emotional language, not calm and deliberative.

It's just too too smug to argue: double the size of the police force and cut the incidence of crime in half. This is an intellectual cop-out and an avoidance of the real causes of criminal behavior. There will be no progress as long as this sort of panacea-chasing advocacy persists as the only solution.

During the five year period, 1965 to 1970, 71 percent of the 2,819 homicides reported in Chicago were committed by relatives, friends or acquaintances of the victims. More than 76 percent of the murders involved altercations, with domestic quarrels leading the list (397). Fewer than 12 percent involved felonious assaults (robbery or burglary) and just 2 percent were listed as underworld crimes. A black man was ten times as likely to be murdered as a white man, and a black woman twice as likely to be murdered as a white man. Virtually no murders of white women occurred.

The foregoing facts indicate how far off base many raucous editorial appeals to declare war on the Mafia, protect ourselves from parolees and curb the freedoms of minority groups are—just about 100 percent at variance from the facts.

In recent years there have been several news stories from different parts of the country telling of bystanders who failed to come to the assistance of persons being victimized by muggers, robbers, or other lawbreakers. The alibi, "I didn't want to get involved," became a scornful gag line for professional comedians. Editorially the New York *Times* demonstrated perceptive

originality in the following editorial which it ran Jan. 7, 1972.

Surrender on 42d Street

The recent episode of a small-time bank robber, cornered on 42d Street near Times Square by two brave and conscientious bank employes but "set free" by a hostile crowd of hoodlums, puts the spotlight on an untenable situation. The fact that a criminal could be chased for more than two blocks in broad daylight in a busy and notoriously crime-prone area without encountering a police officer, can only lead the ordinary citizen to reconsider the wisdom of walking there at all.

The region, once celebrated as the Great White Way, has virtually been abandoned to sleazy peep shows, petty thieves, pimps, panhandlers and loiterers in search of the unwary and unprotected. Yet, the area is clearly part of the city's lifeline of offices, hotels and theaters. If tourists as well as New Yorkers feel that they cannot go to Times Square in safety, the city will increasingly be looked on as a place to stay away from.

When the two bank employes had to surrender to a menacing mob, they gave convincing proof that the 42d Street jungle is unbelievably deficient in protection by both uniformed and plainclothes police—even at

2 P.M. on a weekday. Unless effective—and permanent—measures are taken, the law-abiding citizen's only sensible response will be to shun the area. For the city to allow this to happen would truly be the Broadway Follies of 1972.

Policemen presumably feel they are handicapped by the United States Supreme Court decisions protecting the civil liberties of suspects, including the necessity of warning them against making statements which might be used against them and advising them of their right to counsel. Electronic surveillance, now a fantastically developed operation, with routine wiretapping already almost crudely old fashioned, no knock laws and third degree measures would be in the interest of law and order, it is contended. Just how widespread these undemocratic and sadistic ideas are held by rank-and-file policemen is uncertain. Some loudmouth spokesmen do voice them as similarly dangerous beliefs and the editorial outcry against them is by no means as loud as should be expected in a nation dedicated to the proposition that all men are created equal and so on.

The following from the Penn Hills (Pa.) *Progress* of Feb. 17, 1971, is unusual because of the point of view, although unfortunately verbose in its expression.

Use of 'Reasonable Force' Provision Too Ambiguous

The laws in Pennsylvania governing the handling and discharge of fire arms for hunting animals apparently are more specific than laws governing the use of firearms by police officers when enforcing the law on people.

Some people in Penn Hills were somewhat chagrined to learn this last week after the shooting incident on Feb. 7 when two police officers fatally shot down a fleeing car theft suspect.

There is little doubt at this point that what these officers did was legal. Pennsylvania law specifically empowers an officer to use such extraordinary means in halting a fleeing felony suspect. The concern, and it is a legitimate one, is over the moral issue involved. Is a stolen car worth a man's life?

A coroner's inquest scheduled today (Wednesday) will deal with the legalities involved and there isn't much doubt what the verdict will be, justifiable homicide. In defense of the policemen involved, there also will be those who will argue that had the car theft suspect not fled he would be alive now.

That undoubtedly is true. But was indiscretion in attempting to escape sufficient cause to shoot him down? That's an answer that a coroner's jury isn't equipped to answer.

The Penn Hills police chief has assured the community that members of the Penn Hills force are adequately trained in the handling and use of firearms. He also discloses that at least once a year the entire force undergoes in-service training on arrest and search and seizure procedures, during which the laws governing the use of force in making arrests is thoroughly reviewed.

We don't doubt for a moment this is true. We do, however, doubt the effectiveness of a law on such a grave matter that leaves far too much up to individual, split-second judgment. Pennsylvania law imposes on all police officers the obligation to consider the degree of force necessary in making an arrest. It becomes ambiguous, however, when it adds that a policeman is "privileged to use reasonable force," but "not privileged to use unreasonable force." Apparently no one has defined when force is reasonable and when it is unreasonable.

It's downright frightening to contemplate that men are given guns and the authority to enforce the law on such flimsy, highly interpretative guidelines for the use of those guns.

It is not our intention to add to the burdens that might now weigh heavily on the shoulders of the policemen involved in this incident. Police work is a difficult vocation because it so often is performed in the grey areas of an individual's rights as opposed to the rights of society. Some countries, such as England, have deemed it necessary to arm police only with night sticks in order to protect individual citizens against the possibility of an officer's rash act.

This is not true in America. Sidearms have been the American way since the frontier days, so the gun that hangs from a policemen's hip today is a law and order tradition. Our society, however, has determined that it can accommodate this frontier tradition without condoning frontier justice.

Policemen are armed to enforce the law, but they are not judge, jury, prosecutor and executioner or at least they shouldn't be. The law, however, is dangerously vague on this and deserves a thorough review by our State Legislature before another tragic shooting occurs "in the name of justice."

The self-congratulatory nature of the following editorial from the Chicago *Sun-Times* of Sept. 18, 1951 was justified. The paper did persist until justice was done and a prominent officeholder discredited. Not permanently, however. A decade later Boyle became chief justice of the reorganized Cook County court system. When his name appeared on the ballot, the *Sun Times* endorsed him.

The People Win in the Moretti Case

State's Attorney Boyle has caved in to the overwhelming pressure of public opinion in the Moretti homicide. In asking the chief justice of the criminal court to appoint a special prosecutor to take the case before the grand jury for a second time, Boyle does an about-face.

Two weeks ago, the case was closed as far as he and his assistant, James A. Brown, were concerned. They were satisfied with the decision of the August grand jury which failed by one vote to indict Policeman Michael Moretti for slaying two young men and wounding a third.

But the *Sun-Times* was not satisfied. Our reporters talked to members of the grand jury. A picture of confusion in the grand jury room was developed.

It was apparent that the presentation of evidence had been mishandled—in Moretti's favor. The reason was obvious: Moretti was on Boyle's own police staff. He has political drag. Five other members of his family are also on the public payroll, the *Sun Times* revealed.

In his spree which preceded the killing, Moretti had been in the company of two of Boyle's closest aids. Boyle and his assistant, James A. Brown, rushed the case before the grand jury, allowing Moretti himself to testify, dragged racial prejudice into the case by stressing the fact the main witness against Moretti and his two victims were of Mexican extraction, and generally so discredited witnesses against Moretti that the grand jury never got an accurate picture of the shooting.

Only eleven jurors voted to indict. A majority of 12 votes was needed. One juror was out of the room at the time of the vote. He later told *Sun-Times* reporters he would have voted for an indictment.

On the basis of our findings, this newspaper Sept. 4 demanded the Moretti case be reopened and that a special prosecutor be appointed. We said that we did not presume to pass judgment on Moretti's guilt or innocence but that his guilt or innocence had not been established.

A few days later every other Chicago newspaper followed the *Sun-Times* lead. Public indignation rose.

Monday, the *Sun-Times* revealed that Brown had introduced a false police record at the inquest. He said one of Moretti's victims had been convicted last June for possession of dope. This was not true.

After this latest *Sun-Times* revelation, Boyle gave up.

The people have won a victory and by Boyle's own capitulation he pleads guilty to mishandling the case.

With negligible exceptions newspapers accept the definition of crime implicit in the following quotation from Ramsey Clark, former United States attorney general, and disregard the adverse criticism of the judgment evaluation used. The quotation is from Clark's book, *Crime in America* (Simon & Schuster, 1970).

It is the crimes of poor and powerless people that most enrage and frighten the affluent, comfortable and advantaged majority. Riots, muggings, robbery and rape are loathsome not only because they are inherently irrational and inhumane but because they and their causes are so foreign to the experience of people with power that they are incomprehensible. . . . It is the inhumane and irrational condition of the poor that finally causes some among them to commit such crimes. . . .

The crimes to which we pay the least attention are those committed by people of advantage who have an easier, less offensive, less visible way of doing wrong. Illicit gains from white-collar crime far exceed those of all other crime combined. Crime as practiced among the poor is more dangerous and less profitable.

One corporate price-fixing conspiracy criminally converted more money each year it continued than all of the hundreds of thousands of burglaries, larcenies or thefts in the entire nation during those same years. Reported bank embezzlements, deposits diverted by bank employes, cost 10 times more than bank robberies each year. . . .

Anyone who prattles about born criminals or criminal classes; usually identifiable racially or ethnically, is hard put to explain a Bobby Baker or a Billie Sol Estes or any political grafter, briber or bribe recipient, the granting of contracts for the expenditure of public funds without competitive bidding, illegal wiretapping and other violations of privacy and civil liberties by law enforcement officers, at the top as well as at the bottom of the hierarchy, price fixing by supposed business competitors, arson against a member of a minority group who moves into a previously segregated neighborhood, cheating on income tax returns, breakups of peaceful demonstrations by hard hats on orders from their WASP employers, chronic prevarication by officeholders from the president down to reporters and others, and many, many more instances of what could be lumped under the blanket heading of white collar crime. Given the ignoramus' definition of crime, plus religious superstition, and you get the following editorial from the *Deseret News* of Jan. 28, 1969, routine for that page.

THE SPIRITUAL CRISIS

How Much Crime Can America Take?

Assuming that it takes five minutes to read this editorial, by the time the reader reaches the end, 24 serious crimes will have been committed somewhere in America.

During this brief period there will be, on the average, one robbery, two aggravated assaults, 10 burglaries, five car thefts, five other larcenies, and a forcible rape.

In the next hour, someone in this country will be murdered.

Take these facts, shocking as they are, and multiply them by the fact that much crime—no one can be sure exactly how much, but knowledgeable observers believe it could very well constitute the bulk of many crimes such as rape—is never reported.

To this equation add the fact that crime in America has been increasing at a rate variously

Comment

Says Ramsey Clark in *Crime in America:*
Most crime is never reported to police. And much crime is inaccurately reported. . . . To the extent that it has been accurately reported, murder occurred less frequently per capita in the United States in the 1960s than during the 1920s and 1930s—and probably, though we do not know, well below the rate during the 19th Century. In 1967, for instance, the murder rate was 14 per cent lower than in 1933. If we knew of all the murders committed in that earlier period, the contrast might be considerably sharper. Certainly our crime statistics generally became substantially more all-inclusive between 1933 and 1967. . . .

Likewise, Dr. Karl Menninger, author of *The Crime of Punishment* (Viking, 1965), denies that there has been any real increase in violent crime and says that the idea behind the "law and order" phrase is self-destructive.

figured at from seven to 10 times as rapidly as the population has been growing.

Finally, take into account that 72 percent of total arrests for serious crimes are youthful offenders, and that each year the proportion grows greater.

All this is why there's a sharp limit to the satisfaction Utahns can take from this week's report that with 313 more arrests in 1968 over 1967, Salt Lake City's crime index is increasing less than that of the nation as a whole. Like the occupants of a rowboat, we can hardly take the position that the leak in the other end of the boat is no concern of ours.

The crime rate also shows that President Nixon was right when, in his inaugural address a week ago, he diagnosed what ails America as being fundamentally a *"crisis of the spirit."*

What is a "crisis of the spirit"? What's a spirit? And, if there is any such thing, why and what do you do about it?

Granted that poor social conditions such as slums, unemployment, and poverty can foster despair and stir up resentments that are all too easy to express in violent, unlawful ways. But how can the increasing crime problem be explained away on this basis when by most objective standards America is growing more prosperous and its prosperity is being more widely shared all the time?

This is the "superior clay" argument, indicating the complete ignorance and indifference of the well-off upper crust. Public welfare rolls are burgeoning as the spread between haves and have-nots grows.

Granted that police forces across the country are under-staffed, under-paid, and over-worked. But isn't this a symptom of America's increasing lawlessness, rather than a cause?

This just isn't so.

And what is "moral fibre"? What the millionaire polluter or tax evader or briber of officeholder lacks perhaps?

Granted, too, that police have been handcuffed and disrespect for the law has been inspired by court decisions that have made it unreasonably difficult to obtain convictions and have freed confessed criminals to rob, rape, and murder again.

Even so, how can any assessment of the growth of crime in America be considered complete without taking into account the rift in the nation's moral fiber?

Just ask FBI Director J. Edgar Hoover, who reports that children who attend Sunday School regularly seldom become involved in juvenile criminal violations. Conversely, of 8,000 youths who appeared before one juvenile court judge,

In their classic, *Studies in Deceit*, Hugh Harthorne and Mark May declared that all organized efforts to teach children to be honest failed. Moral instruction in Sunday schools showed a dismal failure. Children who went to Sunday school tended to be less honest than the average. Gordon Allport, author of *The Nature of Prejudice*, says: "On the average churchgoers and professedly religious people have considerably more prejudice than do non-church goers and nonbelievers. . . . Brotherhood and bigotry are intertwined in all religion."

none had parents who attended church regularly, and only 42 of the youths themselves had attended regularly.

Ask Harold R. McKinnon, San Francisco lawyer who has been a member of that city's police commission. On the basis of his experience in dealing with crime, he concludes that "What we need is a moral revolution. What we need is character, morals, and a way of life that makes crime disreputable."

Or just ask yourself if it isn't common sense that America's overemphasis on material things creates desires exceeding any respect for laws and fundamntal rights . . . that the entertainment media's overemphasis on sensuality and brutality stimulates the weak into excesses . . . that the failure of many parents to provide spiritual and religious training for their children leaves a void that is frequently filled by improper influences.

Crime in America is too big a problem for the task of cleaning it up to be delegated entirely to Congress or the courts or to the police. Rather, it is a task that should be shouldered by each of us as parents and as responsible citizens concerned with guarding this land of ours against the decay that results when men walk in fear of each other.

What is a moral revolution? Crime is a social phenomenon which differs at different times in different places.

Here the writer has a glimmer of understanding of how social goals affect human behavior. Americans are brought up to believe they must compete and succeed by defeating others. The main badge of success is financial gain. This is the capitalistic ethos and our lawlessness is the price for our free enterprise.

This is platitudinous and meaningless.

Presumably a sober analysis which went to the core of the problem was published Oct. 1, 1971 by the Buffalo *Courier-Express.* It is lengthy and the purpose laudable. The frustration which the writer cannot conceal is pathetic. The gist is that a small minority of hoodlums is responsible for lawlessness and that they must be suppressed. The writer suggests his complexity when he recalls the Horatio Alger tradition that the poor underprivileged but honest boy can pull himself up by bootstraps, and he is impatient when the American Civil Liberties Union shows mercy for the losers in the economic rat race who harass those who have chosen the path of righteousness. The writer just doesn't grasp the concept that it's not just a few recalcitrants who, for reasons he cannot understand, deliberately

prefer to be bad. He won't allow himself to suspect that there might be something wrong with the system which creates such a state of mind. His solution is not stated in such godly terms as the Mormon newspaper repeatedly does it, but he has no solution other than more of the same old thing which he admits has broken down. He plays the wrathful Jehovah of the Old Testament!

Mobilizing Against Gang Violence

When children are afraid to go to and from school because they are afraid they will be attacked by gangs en route, or when a youth jumps out a school window to avoid a gang beating, we have reached a deplorable state of affairs. Yet this is the sorry situation in and around several schools in Buffalo—at Clinton Junior High, at Grover Cleveland High, at East High and, to a lesser extent, at other city schools. The violence has frightened the students, disturbed the teachers and staffs and has forced early closing of schools in some instances. No one who has any concern for the welfare of this city can view such a situation with equanimity.

We agree with Dr. Joseph Manch, superintendent of public schools, when he says that this is basically a community problem. He and his department are responsible for what goes on in the schools, of course, and must be held primarily accountable. But this does not relieve parents of their responsibilities.

And certainly it is the community which must accept responsibility for what happens elsewhere, not only among school-age youngsters but among all members of the populace. It is the community which must shoulder the burden. Dr. Manch has issued an open invitation to police, community groups, parents and others to attend a meeting to consider ways of combating the growing problem. Such an undertaking merits widespread support.

* * *

The problem is not confined to Buffalo alone and certainly not to schools alone. Resort to violence seems to have become a way of life for certain segments of our society. It is evident in destructive demonstrations by college students, in the bombing and overturning of school buses by destructive adults who don't like laws or policies in regard to school integration. It is evident, of course, in prison riots and official overreaction to problems which might well have been curbed without bloodshed. It is evident in the bombing of buildings, in the burning of banks, in the destruction of records, in the desecration of flags.

These aberrations get so much attention that they sometimes seem to represent the predominant attitude of American people today, a totally false impression. The predators make up a very small segment of the people, but their activities are so outrageous that they get most of the attention.

Who pays special heed to the millions and millions of Americans who go on day after day doing their jobs, staying out of trouble, being responsible citizens and hoping that they will not be the targets when the violent ones become active? Many of the quiet ones early in their lives were sociologically deprived and economically depressed. Many were products of broken homes or misunderstood youths. It wasn't easy, but they managed to overcome these handicaps without resorting to lawlessness and violence. And frequently they become the victims of the lawless few. When that happens, who raises his voice to defend their constitutional rights, their unalienable rights to life, liberty and the pursuit of happiness? Where is the American Civil Liberties Union when these liberties are being violated by hoodlums who find it easier, and probably more satisfying, to break a head than to hold a job?

There must be a concerted effort everywhere to curb the few who are preying on our society, taking advantage of every facet of the law, every court and administrative decision designed to improve society and using it to tear that society down. It must be a federal action and a state action and a local action.

* * *

No level of government can look to some other level and say: You do something about this! There must be action in Buffalo and in Albany and in all the other cities and all the other capitals. In Buffalo, with special reference to the troubles in the schools, the action should involve not only stepped-up police activity, surely an appropriate task for the city's community peace officers and police cadets, as well as the roving youth patrol, but utilization of all the resources of the community—church groups, parent-teacher associations, the schools themselves. It might even be desirable to organize parents in street patrols, as was done in Britain to protect women from would-be rapists during the blackout of World War II.

The School Department could help, too, by not pushing ahead with any expansion of its busing program to achieve integration. We have no quarrel with the goal of integrated schools, and we are not implying that the incidents of school violence are racial in nature. Nor are we saying that the busing should be stopped. But it does seem to us that, in the existing circumstances, any extension of the busing program might hinder the task of restoring normality to school operations by increasing the possibility of racial friction.

The growing incidence of violence needs to be nipped before it becomes cataclysmic. The hoodlums must be apprehended and punished. The maintenance of law and order is properly a police function, but a community mobilized for action can be a big help.

The author of the following editorial, which appeared in the Miami *Herald* for May 13, 1951, didn't even attempt to understand what's wrong; but he did realize that the problem is international and that excessive chauvinism is a handicap in any attempt to improve local conditions.

We Can Stop Home Variety at Least

HERE ARE two examples of terrorism which are of concern to the American people.

The one is the report of its foreign mission board to the Southern Baptist Convention now in session in Miami.

It recites how terror stalks the Chinese countryside; how Red leaders of the land conduct anti-American activities not only for propaganda purposes but to "eliminate all Chinese not in sympathy with the new government. Mass accusation meetings, trial and executions darken the pages of history. Deeds of terror know no bounds."

The other is in the United States. The Associated Press described it this way:

"An undertone of terror appeared in the graft case of five policemen (New York) with an ugly telephone threat to the prosecutor and the beating up of the brother of his star witness."

Both are patterns. Of the two the home-grown variety is the worse.

It is spawned by official corruption.

It is the tool of the Underworld.

It is the enemy within the gates. Its power to destroy, unless checked by the

law-abiding, will effectively undermine this nation.

In December, 1971, the President's Commission on Federal Statistics reported that crime statistics are inherently inaccurate but failed to adopt the motion of one member that the task of compiling them be taken from the Federal Bureau of Investigation whose *Uniform Crime Reports* have been appearing since 1930. The "so many crimes a minute" type of press release, which the *Deseret News* and most other journalistic media find irresistible, has been the object of adverse criticism by scholars since the inception of the service. So vehement did the attack become that, on the recommendation of an advisory committee from the International Association of Chiefs of Police, the system was revised in 1959. Two editorials to follow will indicate the startling results. The first, from the Denver *Post* for Sept. 5, 1959, complains because the first FBI report under the new system showed the city in a worse light than previously.

Progress on the Crime Front

The latest crime report of the Federal Bureau of Investigation gives a misleading picture of the crime problem in Denver and offers no hint to the progress that was made this year.

In the report, covering a year that ended eight months ago, Denver is ranked 13th among U.S. cities in the number of major crimes per hundred thousand people.

To achieve this rank, however, the city is lumped together with Arapahoe, Adams, Jefferson and Boulder counties. The crime rate for the entire area is no measure of the efficiency of the Denver police.

Denver also has a more thorough crime reporting system than many other cities. Its high ranking may not mean more crime but better record keeping.

The important thing is that the crime rate in Denver has declined since the end of the FBI reporting period on Jan. 1.

For the year to date, there have been 133 fewer crimes in the serious category in Denver than there were during the same period a year ago.

There has also been a substantial reduction in juvenile crime.

The use of a special motorcycle task force to saturate different sections of the city on different nights with police protection this spring, undoubtedly helped to keep the crime rate down.

And the addition of 21 new policemen—half of whom were assigned to patrol beats—may have acted as a crime deterrent.

The police also captured a number of active criminals, who might have swelled the crime totals further if they had not been behind bars.

This is not to say that Denver has no crime problem or that everything necessary to fight crime is now being done.

But the situation is not as bad as the FBI statistics suggest. And progress is being made.

By contrast the Chicago *Daily News* complained editorially Sept. 12, 1959 because Chicago was shown to be better than it deserved.

FBI Confuses Us

It is just possible that Chicago's reputation as a crime-ridden city has suffered a mortal blow. The FBI's new method of accounting drops the Chicago area clear down to 85th place on the list of regions by rate of serious crimes.

In the new tabulations, sizable suburban areas are included in the metropolitan region for which the crime rate is calculated. This results in offsetting Chicago's worst districts with the crime figures from such places as Barrington and Independence Hill, Ind.

The same kind of metropolitan grouping is followed throughout the country. Consequently, the findings become virtually worthless as a measure of crime prevention and law enforcement in a particular city. Hardly any police force has total jurisdiction over any of the areas compared. In every instance, it would be possible to debate the appropriateness of the areas included. This factor, rather than the local habit of law observ-

ance and law enforcement in any given municipality, could determine the findings.

Los Angeles, with a serious crime rate of 2,507.6 per 100,000 population, emerged as the worst in the nation, with Miami second at 2,303.3. Detroit, New York, Baltimore, and such unlikely candidates for ill fame as Topeka, Kans., make the list ahead of Chicago's figure of 943.5.

In the total of 174 metropolitan groupings, Chicago stands very close to the midpoint. For the reasons stated above, we have no idea whether the City of Chicago proper would come out average, or better, or worse.

The persistent attacks on the reliability of the FBI statistics over the years came from about every source possible except the newspapers and news magazines. After about 20 years of it, the indominable J. Edgar Hoover did consent to include the following statement in the *Uniform Crime Reports* which appeared quarterly up to the time of Pearl Harbor and semiannually thereafter.

In publishing the data sent in by chiefs of police in different cities the FBI does not vouch for their accuracy. They are given out as current information which may throw some light on problems of crime and criminal-law enforcement.

Typical of many analyses of the FBI statistics was that which appeared in *The New Yorker* in the spring of 1958. The publication had been shocked by a New York *Times* headline, "Youths Charged With Nearly Half Major Crimes in '57, the FBI Reports." The headline advertised a news account of the most recent FBI report. Said *The New Yorker* in part comment:

If you took a "group of serious crimes classified separately—murder, manslaughter, rape, robbery, aggavated assault, burglary, larceny, and auto theft," the FBI reported, "those under eighteen made up 47.2 per cent of persons arrested for such crimes."

"Separately" to us seemed to mean "singly," or "one by one." We were astonished that JDs [juvenile delinquents] had committed 47.2 per cent of all murders, 47.2 per cent of all aggravated assaults, and the rest. In the next paragraph, though, it developed that "separately" referred to "group of serious crimes," which was to be considered separately from another group of (more, less, equally) serious crimes, not listed. In the group of serious crimes separately considered as a group, the FBI had taken the percentage of persons arrested for each type of crime who were under eighteen, and then averaged all the percentages. Sixty-seven per cent of the persons arrested for auto theft during 1957, for example, were under eighteen. Auto theft is and has always been a typically adolescent crime; adolescents take autos because they are too young to own any themselves or to have driving licenses, and in most cases the autos are found within a week. Thus the 67 per cent figure is not very exciting news. Six percent of the persons arrested for murder were under eighteen. If you average 67 and 6, it is plain that 36.5 per cent of the persons arrested for auto theft and murder, considered separately as a group of serious crimes, were under eighteen. This sounds more ominous; the 36.5 might give the fast reader an impression that one out of every three murders, like one out of every three auto thefts, was committed by a JD. Actually, if you cut burglary—which technically includes breaking into a locked summer house at the shore—larceny, and auto theft off the end of the separately considered group, the JDs come out inconspicuously. For instance, they have been arrested for 9 per cent of all aggravated assaults (which is far too much, of course), but that doesn't make as good a subhead as "nearly half." The facts are disquieting enough; nobody has to improve on them with statistics.

This iconoclastic spirit was slow to spread to the daily newspapers which are prone to play up reports that the local community's crime rate has gone down and to bury any news to the contrary. Editorial writers as well as politicians like to quote good FBI reports, saying. "Now these are not our figures; these are figures compiled by the FBI as a result of an independent and objective study of crime throughout the country." That, of course, is 100 percent wrong, complete nonsense, because all the FBI has are data voluntarily submitted to it by city police departments which can cover up or exaggerate in accordance with local needs. Comparison of any year's figures with those of other years is difficult because the sample of cities submitting reports to the FBI is never the same for two successive years. An introduction of a better records system may result in showing a crime increase, the validity of which is questionable. Police departments sometimes make their communities look better than they deserve by changing charges, so that cars become lost instead of stolen, grand larceny becomes petty larceny and so forth. There are no statistics more unreliable than crime statistics unless they be for church memberships which often include backsliders, some of them almost from the day of infant baptism for the rest of their lives. Some denominations count newly baptized babies as members whereas others do not do so until confirmation or some other rite at puberty. One last warning: the crime statistics do not pretend to be anything except crimes which are reported to police. It is not easy to estimate how many unreported or other offenses there were.

Youthful crime, or juvenile delinquency, probably concerns editorial writers and all others who think of it more than any other aspect of the total problem. No longer is it possible to assert smugly that it's only ghetto kids who shoplift, jackroll, steal cars, engage in sex orgies, violate the narcotics laws and get into trouble in other ways. Well-heeled youngsters from the affluent suburbs are just as defiant of the status quo as their under-privileged counterparts in the inner cities. Many facts and theories are advanced to explain the phenomenon: the changed economic system so that there no longer exists the opportunity to become an independent entrepreneur which means to face a lifetime as an Organization Man; the widespread example of crime, corruption, and irresponsible life patterns on the part of adults; the cheapness of life as the result of atomic warfare and worldwide violence between presumably civilized nations; the frustration which follows failure to persuade policymakers through peaceful means such as by petitions, parades, rallies, demonstrations, strikes and so forth.

All of these and other sociological factors must be considered. What must be guarded against is the easy answer and the scapegoat. Generation after generation there have been attempts to blame the apathy of children on their reading matter—dime novels, romantic folklore mostly about the wild west, exaggerated success stories of the Rover boys type, newspaper comic strips, detective stories which play up violence, science fiction, mystery novels, trashy love stories in pocketbook format, and so on and so on. What follows commits the offense of accepting the single-cause diagnosis of the j.d. problem. It appeared in the Asheville (N.C.) *Times* for Sept. 2, 1954.

The American Crusade Against Crime Comics

The current crusade in the Asheville area against the crime-horror-comic book is geared effectively to the snow-balling national movement to wipe out at least this one contributor to juvenile delinquency. We do not recall any reform campaign, local or nation-wide, which ever had such strong and apparently almost unanimous support behind it. Nearly all the comic book publishers have declared their championship of the cause. The American Legion yesterday pledged its support to the comic book industry's drive to clean up its own mess.

In this community school administrators and teachers, the public library, numerous civic organizations, drug stores, patriotic groups and the newspapers are actively participating in the drive to remove all crime-horror-comic books from the newsstands. The local campaign seems assured of much success since the two companies, which between them handle all comic books distributed in this area, have pledged their full cooperation. But we shall undoubtedly have to contend with crime-comic book "bootleggers."

This American crusade against a strange type of product that is much too typically American, was inspired in part by a book which appeared last April entitled "Seduction of the Innocent." It was written by Dr. Frederic Wertham, the noted psychiatrist and author

Comment

The Institute for Propaganda Analysis would label "snow-balling national movement" an attempt to create a bandwagon effect. This first sentence takes it as proved that these books are a contributing factor; no argument. Citing the American Legion as the final bit of evidence to prove unanimity is presumptuous. In 1958 J. D. Maurice of the Charleston (W. Va.) *Daily Mail* won the Sigma Delta Chi editorial writing prize for his courageous successful fight against a proposal to establish a municipal censorship board and board of review for motion pictures, books, pamphlets, magazines, and other publications. Maurice revealed that by the time his campaign got under way virtually every organization in the city had said "of course not" to the appeal. "Do you believe in smut?" Once the implications of any such first step toward erosion of freedom is pointed out, the pendulum swings in the other direction as it began to do shortly after this Asheville editorial appeared.

There was no doubt about Dr. Wertham's eminence. He saddened his many admirers by his narrow stand in this instance. In fact, his book isn't so shocking as G. Legman's *Love and Death*. The issue is not whether this sort of reading matter is good for children; trash is a waste of time for anyone. The issue is censorship

who had made a seven-year study of comic books and juvenile delinquency.

In that book the author disputed claims then current that "normal" children are not led to crime through reading crime-comic books. Normal children from "secure homes" are affected, Dr. Wertham said, because as long as the crime-comic book exists, there are *"no secure homes."*

Furthermore, charged Dr. Wertham, "while no one says that crime books alone are the cause of juvenile delinquency, it is my opinion without any doubt that crime comics are an important contributing factor and in thousands of cases it is the normal child who is affected."

Let no one confuse this crusade with any which advocate censorship of books on serious subjects. Crime comics are produced for the kid trade and virtually all parents and teachers consider them vicious in their effects on youngsters. This crusade mustn't be slowed down either by the fact that apparently hardly anybody is opposing it.

The fact remains that millions upon millions of these crime comics are circulated throughout America every year. This is a highly profitable enterprise—and many of those who reap the profits are not likely to give them up voluntarily.

Here is the issue. The good ladies of Evanston, Ill. who ran about threatening news dealers and pasting up certificates to show they cooperated confessed to a graduate student reporter that comic books were "just the start." Publicly they said exactly the opposite. In a democracy you either have freedom and faith in people or you don't. To keep up to date in this field the editorial writer should peruse regularly the *Newsletter on Intellectual Freedom,* published monthly by the American Library Association, 50 East Huron Street, Chicago, Ill., 60611, for $5 yearly.

The Miami *Herald* did an effective original job of pointing out a source of juvenile and later adult delinquency much more important than comic books, in the following editorial which appeared Feb. 4, 1965.

"It's OK, Son, Everybody Does It"

When he was six years old, he was with his father when they were caught speeding. His father handed the officer a $5 bill with his driver's license. "It's OK, kid," his father said as they drove off. "Everybody does it."

When he was eight, he was permitted at a family council, presided over by Uncle George, on the surest means to shave points off the income tax return. "It's OK, kid" he said. "Everybody does it."

When he was twelve, he broke his glasses on the way to school. His aunt Francine persuaded the insurance company they had been stolen and they collected $27. "It's OK, kid," she said. "Everybody does it."

When he was fifteen, he made right guard on the high school football team. His coach showed him how to block and at the same time grab the opposing end by the shirt so the official couldn't see it. "It's OK, kid," the coach said. "Everybody does it."

When he was sixteen, he took his first summer job, at the big market. His assignment was to put the over-ripe tomatoes in the bottom of the boxes and good ones on top where they would show. "It's OK, kid," the manager said. "Everybody does it."

When he was eighteen, he and a neighbor applied for the opening at the service academy. Johnny was a marginal student. His neighbor was in the upper three percent of his class, but he coudn't play right guard.

Johnny got the assignment. "It's OK, kid," they told him. "Everybody does it."

When he was nineteen, he was approached by an upper classman who offered the test answers for $3. "It's OK, kid," he said. "Everybody does it."

Johnny was caught and sent home in disgrace.

"How could you do this to your mother and me?" his father said. "You never learned anything like this at." His brother, aunt, and uncle also were shocked.

"The youth of today are failing," said the psychiatrist. "They refuse to determine between right and wrong."

"More than fifty percent of our students are cheats," said the educator. "It's shameful the way young people carry on today."

"The youth of today are setting a pattern that is alarming," said the sociologist.

"We got the bums cleaned out," said the commandant of the academy," and now we can walk tall."

If there's one thing the adult world can't stand, it's a kid who cheats.

And the Indianapolis *Star* used a refreshing editorial short to provide some balance to the raging debate.

When One Thinks of Others

A story in The Star's "Happy News" feature the other day told of a lad at Boys Town, Neb., a home for wayward and homeless boys, whose attitude has been revised by the experience of putting energy into helping other people.

The 17-year-old had been in trouble for shoplifting and vandalism, and by his own admission did not get along well with people. On the advice of a counselor he volunteered for unpaid work as a hospital orderly. After 539 hours of it within a year he had earned a formal commendation for his work, and his school grades had risen from straight Fs to Bs and Cs.

It's an oft-told story. Paying attention to the problems of other people gives anyone a different perspective on his own life.

Until the campaign to abolish capital punishment gathered momentum in the 1960s, most newspapers unashamedly had the "catch 'em and kill 'em" philosophy regarding law enforcement. A brief but typical expression of it was contained in the following editorial which appeared in the Grand Rapids (Mich.) *Herald* for March 19, 1955.

More Sense

Bills offered by two State Senators to shorten the prison terms proscribed for certain minor offenses make considerably more sense than the recent effort to make first degree murderers eligible for parole after 17 years.

Comment

As already pointed out, most murders are committed by relatives of friends of the victims. Murder is not a habit with such people. Of 391 homicides in Chicago in a single year, 94 were committed by members of the victim's family, 144 more by close friend, and an additional 22 by lovers.

The movement to abolish capital punishment gathered momentum as judges and juries progressively refused to inflict it. Of an estimated 15,000 murder convictions in any given year, it was unlikely that more than 50 would end in infliction of the death penalty. At all times throughout this century there have been from a half dozen to a dozen states without capital punishment. Its abolition had no appreciable effect on the crime rates in those states unless it was downward as the result of greater certainty and less severity of punishment.

In an enlightened age, the purpose of prison sentences is the protection of society. Killers must be locked up both to prevent a repetition of their crime and to deter others. Non-violent crimes logically call for shorter terms.

The Gilbert and Sullivan theme, "Let the punishment fit the crime" is a good guide.

Gilbert and Sullivan in *The Mikado* did not endorse but rather ridiculed the slogan which dates from the Mosaic concept of "an eye for an eye and a tooth for a tooth." This philosophy was the basis for the post-revolutionary French code of 1791. Anyone familiar with Dickens' *The Tale of Two Cities* or Hugo's *Les Miserables* knows that earlier French justice was unequal. Two persons convicted of exactly the same offense might receive vastly different sentences depending on the whims of judges and their political views. The new code, however, came into disfavor as it was obviously a "magna charta for the criminal," letting him know exactly the risk he took. More important, when there began to develop a science of criminology it gradually came to be recognized that the precept should be "punishment to fit the criminal."

This was the picture of family murders in 1964 in Chicago, unquestionably a typical situation which should cause editorial writers to reexamine their assumptions in case they conflict.

—Twenty-five husbands killed by their wives.
—Nineteen wives killed by their husbands.
—Four daughters killed by their mothers.
—One son killed by his mother.
—One son killed by his father.
—One father killed by his son.
—One granddaughter killed by her grandmother.
—One stepson killed by his stepfather.
—Two stepfathers killed by their stepdaughters.
—Four brothers killed by their brothers.
—One brother killed by his sister.
—One son-in-law killed by his mother-in-law.
—One mother-in-law killed by her son-in-law.
—Three brothers-in-law killed by their brothers-in-law.
—One sister-in-law killed by her brother-in-law.
—Twenty common-law husbands killed by their common-law wives.
—Three ex-wives killed by their ex-husbands.

The case for the retention of capital punishment was strongly stated by the Chicago *Daily Tribune* Oct. 1, 1953 as follows:

The Death Penalty

A plea for abolition of the "barbarous and useless" death penalty was made by Senator Giovanni Persico, president of the Italian Association of Penal Law, in an address to the sixth international Congress of Penal Law in Rome.

Capital punishment is barbarous in the sense that it has been used by barbarians, but it might equally be called civilized because most of the nations accepted as civilized employ it. It is not useless if it prevents murders. In the nature of things, it is impossible to present statistics showing the number of murders that did not take place because the potential killer feared the death penalty, but there is no doubt that men on trial fear it.

Prison certainly is preferable to the electric chair from the criminal's point of view. Every verdict of a judge or jury that carries the lesser penalty is greeted with rejoicing at the defense counsel table. Many a criminal has bargained with the prosecutor, entering a guilty plea on a promise of a long prison term, for fear that a jury might fix death as the punishment.

To say that the death penalty is useless because criminals don't fear it therefore flies in the face of facts. The only question is whether they fear it at the time a crime is committed. Insane persons and perhaps those who commit crimes of passion may not be deterred by thought of punishment, but the same cannot always be said for professional criminals.

When any nation reaches a stage of civilization where crime is no longer a problem, it may be able to take Senator Persico's advice, abolishing not only the death penalty but all other forms of punishment. Here in the United States we have not reached that stage. We still need every available weapon against crime: efficient police work, prompt and just action by the courts, and punishment that fits crime.

No more sincere or impressive plea against capital punishment has been written than the following editorial which helped the Libertyville (Ill.) *Independent-Register* win the Illinois Press Association award for best all-around newspaper in the state for two successive years. The editorial, written by James McCulla, now with the Milwaukee *Journal*, appeared March 29, 1962.

The Death Penalty

At 12:06 A.M. last Friday one of history's non-entities propelled to center stage for a brief moment by an event of passion, paid the debt society demanded of him.

Vincent Ciucci, a grocer, was executed in the Cook County Jail for the murder of his son, who was one of three Ciucci children as well as Ciucci's wife who died, apparently, during a momentary but horrible episode.

After Ciucci's death, Warden Jack Johnson opened a letter written by the man the jury adjudged a murderer. Ciucci began "Sir, I have just made my peace with God, attended Holy Mass and received Holy Communion."

He went on to claim that the version of what transpired the night his wife and three children were killed, he had given Johnson several years earlier was ". . . the honest-to-God's truth."

He claimed that he was in a bathroom, heard strange sounds in the apartment, found his wife leaving the childrens' room with a rifle in her arms, took the rifle from

his wife, discovered his three children dead and then turned to his wife and emptied the gun into her.

Ciucci, when he wrote that letter, was either:

1. Demented to the point that he believed as true a false tale woven by his troubled mind and therefore not responsible for his final words;

2. A conscious liar;

3. A man innocent of the murder of his children.

We do not claim to be students of the human mind.

But we find it difficult to believe that any man, standing on the threshold of eternity, would tempt the judgement of God with a lie after he had made his "peace with God." What is the percentage in such an act who, unless he no longer has the mental capacity to be human, will not face up to the truth knowing the irrevocability of death and its influence on the condition of the human soul for ever after?

If, in fact, Ciucci was in control of his faculties and realized the awful future that might result from a final lie and if, therefore, he did indeed tell the truth about events of Dec. 5, 1953, then society has committed irretrievable error.

Is it just that the possibility of such error should continue to exist? It is not. Capital punishment should be done away with. Death is final, it can not be reversed. We mock justice when we continue to exact the death penalty.

We doubt the deterrent power of the death penalty. How many killings are the result of deliberate, malicious planning? How many more there must be that result from an act of blind passion which crowds from the mind the quality of rationality.

There have been repeated attempts to do away with the death penalty in Illinois. Many strong and knowledgeable voices urge its cessation. Numbered among them are churchmen, politicians, criminologists, penologists, sociologists, psychiatrists and even the governor.

During the last session of the General Assembly a bill was introduced which would have declared a test moratorium for several years, but it did not become law.

We hope the next session of the Legislature will display greater enlightment than previous sessions and that as a matter of fact, some of our newly elected 31st District people will lend their support to the test moratorium.

Under goading from Joseph D. Lohman, University of Chicago sociologist who first was head of the state parole board and later the successful blue ribbon Democratic candidate for Cook County sheriff, Chicago papers became enlightened regarding some aspects of criminological theory and practice. The following editorial from the Chicago *Sun-Times* of Oct. 30, 1951 reflects the progressive spirit.

Who Turns Robbers Loose?

Five years ago, George Crouse, a young robber, was captured after a series of holdups, sluggings and kidnappings. He was sent to the penitentiary.

Six weeks ago the gates of the prison opened and he was tossed back into society, unreformed and unsupervised. Within a few days he got a revolver and went back to his trade—armed robbery and burglary.

He terrorized young couples—he boasted he liked pretty girls. He stole autos and crashed two of them, one in a hit-run accident. One month from his release he was blasted with a shotgun by a citizen while prowling a house. He died a short time later.

Who was responsible for turning this criminal loose without supervision to terrify women, steal and crash autos and break into homes?

The parole board? No. The parole board knew he was a menace. It ordered him kept in custody as long as possible. The responsibility for freeing this particular gunman must be shared by the politicians who tinkered with the parole law in 1943 and by Judge Harold Ward, who sentenced Crouse in 1946.

Under the system in effect before 1943, a robber received a mandatory sentence of from one year to life. The parole board decided later how long the term should be, depending on the prisoner's past history and how good the chances appeared to be that he could return to society and behave himself. When a man finally was paroled, he had to have a promise of a job by a civilian sponsor and he was checked regularly by a parole agent.

Judge Ward, then a state senator, sponsored the 1943 change in the law. This required that judges set a minimum and maximum time of their own. This newspaper opposed the change. It was supposed to "toughen" the penalties against criminals. Actually, as experience has shown, the law has been a boon to crooks. Take Crouse, for example.

Judge Ward set his sentence at from four to eight years each on four charges at the end of five years and three months, whether the parole board believed he was a good risk or not.

When Crouse first came before the parole board at the end of his minimum four years, the board quickly decided he was a bad risk and ordered that he serve the maximum time—but under Judge Ward's sentence, this maximum was only five years and three months.

So Judge Ward decided, back in 1946, that Crouse would reform in five years. He had no way of knowing that. He took a chance.

The Crouse case is a good example of what Joseph D. Lohman, chairman of the state parole board, means when he charges that there actually is far greater leniency shown by many judges than any parole board ever showed.

In the period from 1943 to 1947 nearly one-third of all those who had to be released from jail unconditionally, like Crouse, wound up in jail again. But less than one-fifth of those paroled committed new offenses.

The parole board is better able to judge how long a man should stay in jail than the judge who passes sentence. As the Schlarman report to Gov. Horner in 1937 stated, we must have "punishment to fit the criminal," not "punishment to fit the crime."

Critics of the present parole board have made a big hullabaloo about the number of paroles it has granted. The number of paroles isn't as important as their subsequent records. During a one-year period, former Gov. Dwight Green's parole board released 695 prisoners. Within the next six months 159, or 22.9 percent, violated their paroles and were sent back to jail. During a comparable, more recent period, Gov. Stevenson's board, under Lohman, released 829 prisoners. But during the next six months only 128, or 15.4 percent went wrong.

The workings of the parole system since 1943 show that with a non-political parole system operated by trained civil service experts—such as recommended in the Schlarman report—fewer such men as Crouse will be released from jail to terrify the citizens than under the present system by which a judge attempts to guess how long it will take to reform a criminal, and too often guesses wrong.

The next session of the legislature must take away from judges their present authority to be foolishly lenient with bad risk criminals as a result of pressure from families, friends or politicians.

Personal Journalism

When James Gordon Bennett, Sr., charged in the New York *Herald* that some other New York editors used their editorial columns to advance their speculative stock operations in Wall Street, Col. James Watson Webb of the New York *Courier and Enquirer* knocked Bennett down on Wall Street and beat him with a cane. When Bennett persisted in his attacks on the "respectable, sixpenny, Wall Street papers," Webb did it again. In the May 10, 1836 issue of the *Herald*, Bennett stated his reaction in part as follows:

> As to intimidating me, or changing my course, the thing cannot be done. Neither Webb nor any other man shall, or can, intimidate me. I tell the honest truth in my paper, and I leave the consequences to God. Could I leave them in better hands? I may be attacked, I may be assailed, I may be killed, I may be murdered, but I never will succumb. I never will abondon the cause of truth, morals, and virtue.

Hardly outdone was Colonel Webb who typically wrote as follows:

> At the request of individuals, under circumstances which forbid us listening to the promptings of our own feelings, we are compelled, for the first time, to soil our columns with an allusion to a beggarly outcast, who daily sends forth a dirty sheet in this city under the title of *The Herald*.

Also disturbed by the new type of journalism represented by Bennett's *Herald* was the New York *Journal of Commerce* which declared:

> That little dirty penny paper, *The Herald*, whose Editor, if he got his desserts, would be horsewhipped every day. . . .

THE GOLDEN ERA

All of this happened in 1836 and is related in *Main Currents in the History of American Journalism* (Houghton Mifflin, 1927) by Willard Grosvenor Bleyer, director of the School of Journalism at the University of Wisconsin during its formative years. What has been quoted was the beginning of the so-called Golden Era of Personal Journalism of which some contemporary editors and journalists often become envious.

Those who in retrospect we respectfully call Giants of the Press were vigorous crusaders for the political and other causes they espoused, and they were ruthless competitors. They frequently explained their high ideals editorially. A few typical examples follow:

James Gordon Bennett Sr. (1796-1872), New York *Herald:*

I go for a general reformation of morals—of manners. I mean to begin a new movement in the progress of civilization and human intellect. I know and feel I shall succeed. Nothing can prevent its success but God Almighty, and he happens to be entirely on my side. Get out of my way, ye drivelling editors and drivelling politicians —"I am the choice of ONE crying in the wilderness, prepare ye the way of the Lord, and make his path straight.". . .

Every great reformer in the world has been objected to as I have been. . . . Zoroaster, Moses, Socrates, Seneca, Luther, were all considered madmen. Why should not I?

I speak on every occasion the words of truth and soberness.

Samuel Bowles (1826-1877), Springfield (Mass.) *Republican:*

Press and pulpit and platform must take on a higher usefulness than they have hitherto. Party must be shoved for some time to come into the background. Every honest, God-fearing man must make the performance of even trivial public duties a question of conscience. A higher, more searching test must be applied to public acts and public men.

Henry J. Raymond (1820-1869), New York *Times*:

The majority of thinkers are indolent. One man in ten thousand does his own cogitation, The press, the country more than the city—the weekly more than the daily does create and rule the prevailing sentiment. Such being the fact, greatly is the need of a more elevated editorial character. Make the press answerable for its emanations as the sources of immense issues for good or ill, and we shall benefit it infinitely more than by depreciating its power. Its propositions would then be more maturely considered; its language more cautiously measured; and its influence more benignly felt. The editorial of an American paper is usually the first warm impression of a fact, set down at white heat. The editorial of the German or English redacteur is generally a sober, elaborate essay, embracing none but mature results of reflection. When we have borrowed a few of these foreign traits, the press may be equal to its mission. They are needed, and are easily had.

Edwin Lawrence Godkin (1831-1902), New York *Evening Post:*

We treat our readers as grown-up men and women who can bear to hear the truth, and know how to reason from it with regard to their own duty, and not as children who have to have pretty stories told to them and fine promises made to them to keep their courage up. . . . A good editorial is the earnest address of an exceptionally able and an exceptionally well informed man to some fifty thousand, more or less, of his fellow citizens. When the world gets to be so intelligent that no man shall be more intelligent than any other man, and no man shall be swayed by his passions and interests, then there will be no need of editorial expressions of opinions, and editorial arguments and appeals will lose their power.

Horace Greeley (1811-1872), New York *Tribune:*

An essential element in the truly literary or scholarly character is a love of the truth for the truth's sake. Nothing but this passion for the dissemination of sound and true views can compensate the editor for his intense and unremitting labor.

He who is not conscious of having first interpreted events, suggested policies, corrected long-standing errors, or thrown forward a more searching light in the path of progress, has ever tasted the luxury of journalism. It is the province of journalism to lead and to lead.

Bleyer characterized Greeley as "the most outstanding example of personal journalism in this country. . . . Greeley was a great editorial propagandist, the greatest possibly that American journalism has ever possessed." Today's converts to the Women's Liberation movement would have been pleased by the following from a characteristic editorial after the first national convention of the Women's Rights movement in 1848 at Seneca Falls, N. Y.

It is easy to be smart, to be droll, to be facetious, in opposition to the demands of these Female Reformers; and, in decrying assumptions so novel and opposed to established habits and usages, a little wit will go a long way. But when a sincere Republican is asked to say in sober earnest what adequate reason he can give for refusing the demand of women to an equal participation with men in political rights, he must answer, None at all.

In the same personal journalism vein was the following which appeared in the New York *World* of Joseph Pulitzer (1847-1911) in 1884 according to Mark Ethridge who credits John Oakes, chief editorial writer of the New York *Times*, with having found it. Ethridge cites it in an article, "The Come-Back of Editorial Pages," in the Summer, 1966 *Masthead.*

> If Grover Cleveland has a whole family of illegitimate children, he would be (more) worthy of the Presidential office than Blaine, the beggar at the feet of railjobbers, the prostitute in the speaker's chair, the lawmaker broken of inland grabs, the representative and agent of corruptionists, monopolists and enemies of the Republic.

Ethridge quoted Oakes as saying that the first authentic editorial page in the United States was in the New York *Aurora* about the beginning of the 19th century. According to Bleyer, James Cheetham was the first editor to print editorials in almost every issue of his paper, *The American Citizen,* which he bought in 1800 and edited until his death in 1809. Many other sources say the distinction should go to Nathan Hale (1784-1863) in the Boston *Daily Advertiser.* Wherever the credit belongs, it is known that the formal newspaper editorial was born very early in the 19th century. "Prior to that," Ethridge wrote,

> . . . editorial expression was largely in pamphlets and broadsides. The editorial began to flower later on in the century when the question of states' rights and slavery began to tear the country apart. There emerged such figures as Greeley, Dana,

Medill of Chicago, Lincoln's original sponsor, William Lloyd Garrison, who may have done as much to create the Civil War as anybody, Henry Watterson of the *Courier-Journal,* Prentice, also of Louisville, who incited a bloody Know-Nothing riot, Halstead of Cincinnati and others of lesser fame. There were special characteristics about these men: They owned, or were major owners of their own papers; they were preeminently editors rather than publishers; and they believed in and practiced personal journalism, a practice which persisted long after their time—in fact, until almost our time.

CRITICIZING COMPETITORS

Times *have* changed. The press has been influenced by the same economic factors that affect all other businesses. That means the trend toward monopoly has been continuous. In 1909 there were approximately 2,600 daily newspapers in the United States; today there are about 1,750. In the meantime the population has doubled once and almost twice. Perhaps the fact that in a one-newspaper or at least single ownership situation, a great deal of psychic energy is preserved. Instead of calling one's competitor names for his views on contemporary affairs and for his journalistic behavior, it is possible to vent the same amount of spleen on non-journalistic rascals, of whom there are quite a few. Before going completely modern, however, let us take a few more nostalgic moments to recall the fun editorial writers had a century ago. Here are a few examples:

In 1888 the New York *World* said of Charles A. Dana (1819-1897) of the New York *Sun:*

> The statements are malicious lies, about what may be expected of Charles Ananias Dana. A mendacious blackguard who, not content with four months of virulent lying about a candidate for the Presidency . . . is capable of any distortion. The revival of the St. Louis affair . . . is worthy of an assaulter of women and a mortgaged broken-

down calumniator in the last agonies of humiliation. . . . The public will judge this as it has judged his other acts of cowardice, malice, and mendacity.

In the New York *Post,* and its weekly supplement, *The Nation,* Godkin thundered against the yellow journalism of Joseph Pulitzer's *World* and William Randolph Hearst's *Journal* which were competing with each other in sensationalizing the situation in Cuba and helping to bring on the Spanish-American War. A mosaic of his editorial opinions in February and March, 1898 follow:

> The admirable conduct of the government officials in Washington renders the course of the sensational press in this city more shameful by contrast. Nothing so disgraceful as the behavior of two of these newspapers this week has been known in the history of American journalism. Gross misrepresentation of the facts, deliberate invention of tales calculated to excite the public, and wanton recklessness in the construction of headlines which even outdid these intentions have combined to make of the issues of the most widely circulated newspapers firebrands scattered broadcast throughout the country. . . . It is a crying shame that men should work such mischief simply in order to sell more papers.
> The reason why such journals lie is that it pays to lie, or in other words, this is the very reason for which they are silly and scandalous and indecent. They supply a want of a demoralized public. Moreover, such journals are almost always in favor of war, because war affords unusual opportunities for lying and sensation. That war involves much suffering and losses, does not matter. Their business is not to promote public happiness or morality, but to "sell the papers."

Meaning the *Sun* and *Herald,* which were keeping the *Tribune* off the newsstands, Horace Greeley denounced "the immoral and degrading Police Reports . . . which have been allowed to disgrace the columns of many of our leading Penny Papers." In an editorial on the manner in which a mur-

der case had been handled by the sensational newspapers, Greeley wrote:

> The avidity with which all the particulars attending this horrid butchery, the murderer's trial, execution and the confessions, real or manufactured, said to have fallen from his lips, have been collected, published and read, evinces no less a depraved appetite in the community, than a most unprincipled and reckless disregard of consequences on the part of those who are willing—nay eager, for the sake of private gain, to poison the fountains of public intelligence, and fan into destroying flames the hellish passions which now slumber in the bosom of Society. We weigh well our words when we say that the moral guilt incurred, and the violent hurt inflicted upon social order and individual happiness by those who have thus spread out the loathsome details of this most damning deed, are tenfold greater than those of the wretched miscreant himself.

Now, to go modern. Contrast the following editorial which makes very much the same complaint and which appeared in the Milwaukee *Journal* for Aug. 15, 1946.

Crime and the Press

Newspapers of the United States have often been criticized for printing news of crime. It has been contended by some that the nation would be better off if crimes were not reported at all.

Newspapers have rightly insisted that these criticisms are unwarranted. They have maintained that only a nation fully informed in all respects can meet its problems. They have pointed out that if newspapers did not report crimes and show what happens to criminals, the incidence of crime would increase, because the war on crime would lose its vigor.

News of crime, properly presented, accomplishes a vital social purpose. The critics, however, have ample reason to deplore the sensationalization which is practiced today by even some of the better papers, and which is carried to definitely anti-social extremes by others.

The handling of the Heirens case by the Chicago newspapers was an example to which the critics may point. There was no need to dramatize the life history of a young man who, sane or insane, found pleasure in killing. Such exploitation of a sordid case, though it may thrill the unthinking reader, will not contribute toward a healthy public mind.

Not to report crimes at all would leave the nation helpless to meet one of its grimmest problems. But to raise the individual criminal and his exploits to the level of national phenomena, adding detail to inconsequential detail in a frenzied race to see how low the printed word can go, can only be detrimental.

It is time for editors, individually and in their associations, to re-examine their responsibility for constructive handling of crime news. Pandering to morbid curiosity is wrong.

Mostly today mention of a competitor or of any other newspaper, in fact, is avoided in editorials as in news stories. To some this seems a childish policy but the temptation to do otherwise just doesn't arise very often. In a strategic position to needle the downtown press are community and suburban newspapers for whom it is easier to stay virtuous. What follows is a typical editorial dressing down that appeared in the Chicago community newspaper, the *North Side Sunday Star*, for April 18, 1948. The editorial oozes sincerity. Leo Lerner, editor and publisher who undoubtedly wrote it, was a longtime leader of liberal causes. His style here is loose, more suitable for his signed column, but the sober analysis he gives to the situation cannot fail to impress anyone who reads it. It is the deep feeling of the author that makes this an effective piece of writing.

Let's Use Our Heads, Not Our Headlines

One of the things we've learned in the newspaper business is that there are 2 sides to every story. Let's remember this is America, where no person is guilty until proved guilty.

Our heartfelt sympathy goes to the bereaved family of beautiful 17-year-old Joanne Sweeney, 1410 Farragut, who was struck and killed by a car loaded with teensters at Touhy and Western, on Tuesday. This newspaper does not condone reckless driving nor speeding. The tragedy was a terrible one, make no mistake about that.

However, the flamboyant treatment given the accident by the daily newspapers, led by the Hearst press, has practically crucified these boys in advance.

Maybe these lads weren't trying to show off. Any driver will attest to the swerving caused by trolley tracks or jostling of an elbow. But if it were you, and you saw big scary, red streamers saying, "Hunt 5 in 'Show-Off' Girl Killing" and others equally terrible, would you dare to give yourself up? Many adults have run away from accidents too. What can we expect from frightened youngsters who are being made more frightened by the newspaper hysteria?

Are the daily newspapers actually trying to find the youths, or just trying to sell newspapers? We feel it's the latter.

Whatever the motive, neither the press nor the police has a right to prejudge the case! Who really knows the facts?

In the interest of fair play for both the family of the dead girl and the boys in the auto, this newspaper is offering its services.

If youths, or any friends of theirs who have knowledge of who they are, will contact Frank Boege, editorial director of this newspaper, at BUckingham 7500 or BRiargate 7100, the resources of our 22 papers will assure them of a fair trial. We will help to obtain a competent defense attorney and do whatever is necessary to see to it that the boys are treated with an American sense of fairness. We are certain that the Sweeney family wants the boys treated fairly and justly.

In the interest of a better community, we want to see that justice is done. But justice means equal treatment to everyone!

By contrast the following editorial is an outstanding example of rationalization, a defense which doesn't square with many of the known facts. It appeared in the Chicago *Daily Tribune* for Jan. 30, 1957.

What Makes a Newspaper

What makes a newspaper is news, and contrary to the hopes and advice of a good many people who do not work on newspapers, it is irrelevant that it be "good" news. The Grimes murders are in point.

A number of the characters who have been drawn into the investigation are among the most depraved people that can be found in this or any other ctiy. The reputations of the two victims have been blackened, on what basis of truth it is impossible to tell at the moment. It is hard to judge verity when most of the witnesses are congenital liars.

But these stories have been news, and as the records of our circulation department show, more vital news than inaugurations or the world series. The interest cannot be laid to the disclosures of depravity. The murders are a matter of deep concern to parents throughout Chicagoland, who cannot feel sure of the safety of their own children until the crime is solved.

This kind of story imposes a special duty on newspapers, gives special urgency to their obligation to seek the truth. We have suspected, and we grow more certain as time passes, that some of the statements given in this case, and printed in our pages, have been untrue. But this has been the evidence as it was developed by the authorities charged with the duty of finding the killers, and it was our readers' rights to know what they were doing.

This duty of checking and discarding the obviously false, of presenting only the evidence that seems tenable in the circumstances, imposes special strains on even a good news staff. In our news department in recent days there were no scenes suitable for the TV cameras, no ruffled hair, no waving of papers, no shouts of "Stop the presses!" But the news team worked smoothly to turn up one exclusive development after another and with the cooperation of our mechanical and circulation departments, to give these stories, the most important of which were obtained several hours after midnight, to our readers.

If these men didn't get excited, they didn't get much sleep, either, the city editor, day city editor and their assistants, the rewrite men,

Comment

The Grimes sisters, teen-agers, were last seen alive about 11:30 P.M. en route home from a movie. Almost a month later their nude bodies were discovered in a country road ditch about 35 miles away. The coroner's verdict was that they died the night they disappeared and froze to death, even though the temperature never was below freezing during the time they were missing. The main evidence was a toxicologist's report that their stomachs contained food they had eaten for dinner that night. Strangely, there were no traces of popcorn they were seen eating during the movie. The dinner food would have been digested by 1 A.M. The girls had been raped. Because many of the questions asked the girls' mother at the inquest were leading, this author and a prominent Chicago radio commentator tried to find the tape recording of the testimony. We were rebuffed everywhere except at one station where we discovered the tape had been split to cut out what we wanted. The official transcript also was edited. So a circus worker who had been arrested and had reenacted events of the month the girls were gone and, in minute detail, the murder itself, was released and was extradited to Florida where he was tried for an offense almost identical to the Grimes case. The case was used to discredit Sheriff Joseph D. Lohman who was not popular with the Democratic machine which had been compelled to run him as a blue ribbon candidate after a huge scandal. The Republicans were delighted and so was the Back-of-the-Yards Council whose reputation was otherwise injured. Its director was the brother of the administrative assistant to the cardinal. So disgraceful was the cooperation the Chicago papers gave the whitewashers that the Washington *Star* sent Edward Prina to investigate. The results of his efforts were included in a full-page article, "Murder Won't Out," in the April 25, 1957 issue of the paper. By that time the city's interest had lagged. The *Tribune's* attempt to exculpate itself, and with it all of its competitors, is in almost complete disregard of the important aspects of the case.

They probably all got time-and-a-half overtime pay. If not, they should unionize the *Tribune* plant.

reporters and photographers, and copy editors, worked without regard to their normal shifts.

And when these jobs were finished, often in the small hours of the morning, there remained the task of printing and distributing the papers. Mechanical and circulation department employes stayed on the job many hours after they were scheduled to go home. As an example of their accomplishments, the supposed confession in the case didn't become available until 4 A.M. Sunday, yet by the unorthodox device of printing hundreds of thousands of supplements to papers that were already in the hands of distributors, the story got to most of our readers in Chicago and suburbs that same morning.

We take no pleasure in seeing our circulation mount on a story as sordid as this one, but we are proud that in matters of vital concern to themselves and their children, the people of Chicago turn to THE TRIBUNE for the news.

The only sane comment on all of this would be a vulgar remark.

The last paragraph of the following editorial was weak but what preceded it was a careful documenting of the case that the author, Creed C. Black, had against the publication. This editorial appeared in the Nashville *Tennessean* for Aug. 18, 1955.

Opinions Made to Order

The editorial policies of the *Tennessee Farm Bureau News* for several years have been puzzling to a majority of the members of the Tennessee Farm Bureau Federation. But the August issue really offers them a piece of material to scratch their heads about.

Presented on the back page as a full-page editorial is a series of cleverly phrased questions on the social, economic, and political questions of the day. For each question there is a set of three answers, also cleverly phrased.

The editor of the *Farm Bureau News* advises that the questions and the answers are for suggested use in county meetings of Tennessee Farm Bureau leaders for discussion of organizational policies for next year.

He offers some conclusions on policy that may prove rather startling to Tennessee farmers in the year 1955. The price support program for farm products, for example, is dubbed as an example of "state monopoly capitalism." Public ownership of electric plants is identified likewise. But the worst label of all is reserved for the graduated income tax.

That wicked device of government for paying the bill for services to all the people is bluntly labelled "socialism-communism." In the same category is lumped the tax on land or real property. Outlined in bright red is the Farm Bureau editor's statement fixing the "socialism-communism" label on the graduated income tax and the real property tax. Only pale pink is necessary to highlight his identification of publicly-owned electric plants, meaning such things as TVA.

But this is not all. The *News* editor has some further opinions he believes will be of help in guiding county Farm Bureau leaders in arriving at policies of the organization for next year.

It is "state monopoly capitalism," he says, when some of the interest rates are set by government. This means, of course, that interest rates for loans made by Production Credit, drought loans, land bank loans, rural electrification loans, and loans to farm cooperatives—all now fixed by agencies of government—merit the pink high-light treatment. And, just to be consistent, if it's bad for the government to regulate interest rates in these fields, certainly it has no business making such loans.

All in all, the editor of the *Farm Bureau News* has done a very clever job of outlining to the Farm Bureau members how he thinks they ought to feel on such issues as TVA, farm price supports, federal support of farm credit, continuation of low interest REA loans; and the graduated income tax.

It will be interesting to see if he and Mr. Tom Hitch, the state Farm Bureau president, can persuade the members of Tennessee's largest farm organization to accept their opinions on these subjects.

Like the members of a family who stop quarreling when a third party tries to intervene, the collective press strikes back at criticism which could include any or all newspapers. Spokesman in this instance was the weekly trade journal, *Publishers' Auxiliary,* which ran the following in its issue of June 19, 1954.

O'Neil Mistakes Realism for 'Communistic Influence'

James F. O'Neil, publisher of the American Legion Magazine, says "too many of the wrong kind of people have moved into journalism" and are exerting a harmful influence against the best interests of the country.

Mr. O'Neil mentioned the danger of interpretive reporting which "force-fed propaganda" to the public rather than honest, objective news.

His attitude results from confusion. He mistakes honest, mature, thorough digging by trained specialists with "collectivist" propaganda.

A calm look at the American press today—weeklies and dailies of all circulation categories—hardly shows the Communistic influences he reports.

Perhaps he is so shaken by the Daily Worker he sees reflections of it in every paper he reads. Perhaps he believes ignoring day-to-day events will remove them.

Just what does Mr. O'Neil want? Constant jubilant shouting about the glories of America? Daily reassurances that this nation has gone as far as it ever will in its progress?

His thinking then is much like that of a man in the last century. He wanted the patent office closed because everything had been invented.

Political reporting, like other reporting, requires deep analysis. Major problems must be shown from all sides for the enlightenment of the reader.

Bland, shallow reporting won't explain much less than remove any issues.

Mr. O'Neil apparently thinks weighty, informative, heavily backgrounded material which leaves comic-strip devotees in the dark is subversive.

Unfortunately, problems of the world cannot be solved while chatting over a cup of coffee.

The American press and its army of writers has covered local, national and international strife. Preponderantly it has emphasized the success of the democratic processes of this country.

The press of the nation is not selling Communism to the American people; the people don't want it.

Probably the editors at whom the following was aimed never saw it, but it is a good example of journalistic indignation and it did readers of the San Francisco *Examiner* good to read it, March 19, 1971.

Dishonest Editing

Justice William O. Douglas of the U.S. Supreme Court has not been a favorite of this newspaper. Despite our feelings about his opinions and rulings—both public and private—we are indignant over recent Soviet editors' selective use of quotations from his published works.

Ignoring accepted international rules regarding publication, the editors of the propagandist Russian magazine USA have taken remarks from one of Douglas's books, "Points of Rebellion," and twisted them completely out of context.

To put it plainly, the Soviet editors have tried to present Justice Douglas as an apologist for their cause and an advocate of Communist ideology.

Nothing could be further from the truth. Although Justice Douglas's comments may reflect an ultra-libertarian approach to present day problems, he is not an ideological Communist.

The immediate dupes in this case are workers within the USSR who receive information only as it is edited and offered to them.

Those editors who deliberately falsify foreign published works however are the worst fools; in their duplicity—in the long run of history—they are only fooling themselves.

The call for self-discipline contained in the following editorial from the New York *Times* of Sept. 17, 1970, was directed mainly against the electronics media, but it served the purpose of proving that there is an ethical sense in some journalistic offices.

No Place to Cry

Within a few minutes, on a recent evening, three television channels presented these three episodes:

An elderly man who, knowing his daughter to be aboard, had seen the Alitalia jet break in two at Kennedy airport, responded in near-hysteria when a reporter asked him: "How did you feel?"

A little girl among the passengers hijacked by Palestinian guerrillas was asked on arriving in New York whether she had been scared, and then: "Are you ever going to fly on a plane again?"

Still dealing with the returned hostages, a cameraman's voice was heard harshly chiding one of his targets for trying to move away and hide. Then, suddenly, a sobbing woman's face swam into focus.

Newspaper and television reporters alike are often guilty of insensitivity to human grief crying out for the comfort of privacy. Pursuit by camera is more objectionable than unfeeling questions by reporters only because the victim is so frequently unable to simply turn away and remain silent.

If the right to cry in privacy has been omitted from the Bill of Rights, it may be because the framers of the Constitution believed that human compassion would be sufficiently strong to give tears a place to hide.

The almost-dead type of editorial, illustrated earlier in this chapter as characteristic of newspaper warfare of a century ago, is revived occasionally when some editor reaches the emotional boiling point. Such happened in the case of the following editorial which appeared in the Chicago *Sun-Times* May 24, 1951.

A Barefaced Lie

The Chicago Herald-American on Tuesday front-paged a picture of a sobbing, heartbroken, 11-year-old boy named Roger carrying the body of his dog, killed by an auto. The caption under it said:

"Roger's sorrow parallels that felt by a child whose pet has been stolen and carved up for vivisection. Bill pending in Illinois legislature would foster such base thefts and multiply children's grief."

This is a barefaced, contemptible lie. The editors of the Herald-American ought to be ashamed of such irresponsible journalism.

Comment

For many years before the death of William Randolph Hearst Sr., there was hardly a day that some Hearst paper was not engaged in an anti-vivisection campaign. Inspiration was Irene Castle McLaughlin, who operated Orphans of the Storm, an animal shelter, at Deerfield, Ill. and was a close friend of Hearst's mistress, Marion Davies.

It is an attempt to deceive children. It is an attempt to make children believe that members of the legislature want to break children's hearts by taking their pets from them. It is an attempt to make children believe doctors and scientists are cruel and heartless.

None of these things are true and the editors of the Herald-American know they aren't true. They are slavishly following a whim of their big boss, William Randolph Hearst, who long ago fell for the hysterical lies of antivivisectionists.

Here is the truth about the so-called "dog bill":

The bill actually would discourage the theft of pets for sale to medical laboratories. It provides that only unclaimed, unwanted stray dogs—who would be put to death anyway—be turned over to medical schools and laboratories to be used to find new ways to benefit humanity. There are many safeguards to insure return of pets that are lost.

Once the researchers have an assured supply of unwanted dogs, the necessity to buy dogs from outside sources—some of which may be "dognapers"—will be ended.

As for the Hearst charge that dogs are tortured, anyone who has visited Chicago laboratories knows better. Men of science who are looking for ways to ease human suffering—and incidentally find ways to cure dogs of disease, too—are not the brutes that Herald-American would have children believe.

Antivivisectionists have considerable nuisance value for medical schools. They frequently go to court against university administrators. They ignore the fact that they probably profit constantly, through the consumption of medicines and medical practices, as the result of animal experimentation.

A CONTEMPORARY EPISODE

As would seem fitting, viewing the situation with historical perspective, the contemporary editorial debate concerning busing of school children to achieve racial integration has matched the Richmond papers, *Times-Dispatch* and *News-Leader,* now under the same ownership, against the Washington *Post* and New York *Times.* Despite the name calling the Confederates' attack is comparatively mild and the northern reply is dignified.

A typical exchange began when the *Times-Dispatch* Feb. 13, 1972 used the following as the second part of a two-part editorial, the first part of which, entitled, "Needed: A Leader . . . ," called for support for President Nixon and others in their opposition to busing.

. . . And Fairness

Lack of leadership is not the antibusing crusade's only problem. It suffers, too, as a result of the despicable double standards that some influential commentators apply in sanctimoniously analyzing the issue.

Consider, for example, the bald hypocrisy of The New York Times. Recently, that newspaper editorially applauded the Richmond school consolidation decision of U.S. District Judge Robert R. Merhige Jr., a decision calling for the busing of large numbers of children, prescribing quotas designed to achieve racial balance in public schools and ordering the racial composition of each school's faculty to reflect, generally, the racial composition of the total faculty of the entire consolidated system.

Now, if the Times considers busing and racial quotas desirable for Richmond area schools, it surely considers busing and racial quotas desirable for New York City schools, right? Wrong. When a special study commission proposed such integration devices for New York last week, the Times objected. Controversial and unrealistic, the Times called the proposals, adding:

The key to the proposed approach is to create a strict ethnic balance that approximates the racial pattern of total pupil population. In New York City, where the white enrollment now constitutes less than 40 per cent, this would mean that a white minority of roughly that proportion would have to be maintained in every school. Such a redistribution could be accomplished only by either transporting large numbers of white children into the presently predominantly black schools or by phasing out all schools in such areas. Both approaches would run into massive opposition on the part of black as well as white parents.

Equally questionable is the commission's proposal to bring about an ethnic balance among each system's teachers and administrators to reflect the racial profile of the total population. We have long urged effective measures to train and recruit greater numbers of educators among the minorities, along with elimination of licensing procedures which result in racial discrimination. But to impose a relatively rigid ethnic balance is to mandate a quota system with its inherent discriminatory and divisive consequences.

Well, *trot out the cliches*: It depends on whose ox is being gored, the shoe is on the other foot, what's sauce for the goose is sauce for the gander, turn about is fair

play and tit for tat. Obviously, the Times has no strong convictions about busing and racial quotas. It favors busing and quotas for the South but not, perish the thought, for Fun City. Unfortunately, many of the nation's decision-makers read, and possibly often heed, the Times. If it ignores the contradiction in its views, they may ignore the contradiction too. And the antibusing crusade will suffer.

The New York *Times'* reply appeared Feb. 25, 1972 as follows:

Busing—Facts and Fiction

A newspaper in Richmond, Va., ignoring the facts and deliberately distorting the record, has charged The Times with "hypocrisy" in our editorial position on school-desegregation busing. Central to the charge is the allegation that The Times applies a double standard to integration South and North.

A factual restatement of our position may not persuade the segregationists of the Richmond journal to give its readers a more accurate and truthful appraisal than they have yet seen fit to present; but the general confusion over school desegregation, and particularly the President's Southern strategy on the busing issue, warrant in any case a straightforward recapitulation.

Officially maintained segregation—whether by explicit force of law or as a result of behind-the-scenes manipulation—is unconstitutional. A variety of devices is available to eliminate it, and busing is merely one of these. It has been ordered and applied, as Senator Walter F. Mondale underscored in his courageous speech last week, far more sparingly than has been suggested by the widespread political exploitation of this emotion-charged issue.

Segregation resulting from housing patterns, though not considered unconstitutional as presently interpreted by the Supreme Court, is nevertheless also undesirable and should be reduced whenever possible. We have held this view regardless of where segregation occurs. In New York City and its suburbs. The Times has supported a variety of efforts, including rezoning, construction of schools in locations favorable to integration, and busing as well as the elimination of bureaucratic procedures which have hampered the more effective integration of teaching staffs.

It is sheer distortion to depict busing as the devil's instrument, when more than 18 million children daily go to school by bus, not including the millions who use public transportation. But we consider undesirable —as does the Supreme Court—the long-distance busing of young children, in Richmond, Va., as well as in Richmond, New York.

Similarly, we do not believe that creation of a rigid racial balance of enrollments or imposition of fixed quotas for the teaching staff are desirable or required by law. The placement of pupils, in order to be educationally sound, must consider such factors as the benefits derived when a minority of disadvantaged youngsters is integrated with a majority of children from more favored homes—rather than vice versa.

We have never suggested that school integration is easy to achieve, particularly so long as old racial injustices and the continuing gap between poverty and affluence breed suspicion, hostility and fear. No miracle can cure America's historic affliction overnight, and we expect no such magic anywhere, North or South. But it may well be that our consistent support of integration, and of constructive and reasonable measures to move closer to its attainment, angers those advocates of segregation (in Richmond and elsewhere) who falsely try to make it appear that we preach a simplistic "all or nothing" line precisely because they want "nothing" to triumph.

Not all of the polemics have been so gentlemanly—or rather, so ladylike, inasmuch as many of the Richmond editorials were composed by Mrs. Ann Merriman. The biggest furor occurred after the *News-Leader* published a full-page Open Letter to the Supreme Court of the United States July 22, 1970 and urged readers to express agreement by signing a coupon which the paper said would be forwarded to the court. The editorial, "An Appeal to the Court,"

which accompanied the advertisement, was as follows:

An Appeal to the Court

On the page opposite today, this newspaper appeals publicly to the Supreme Court of the United States to make explicit "the right of a parent to have his children educated in the public schools of his choice." We are asking Richmond area residents to sign the open letter, and to return it to us at Box 1-H, Richmond 23201, by August 7. Signed letters will be forwarded to the Supreme Court. Copies of the open letter, together with copies of this page, will be available Thursday free of charge in the main lobby of Richmond Newspapers, Inc. Copies will be sent to the President, the Vice President, the Cabinet, all members of Congress, every governor, and every member of the Federal judiciary. Copies also will be sent to syndicated columnists and major daily newspapers. It is our hope that other newspapers will undertake similar projects.

Perhaps this letter is a forlorn endeavor. Surely no one who signs it should expect it to accomplish any miracles. Nor by this letter do we suggest, or countenance, defiance of the law. But freedom of choice is a defensible doctrine. It stands firmly in the tradition of American liberty. We believe the Supreme Court ought to know that under freedom of choice, integration has gone forward in Richmond's schools—albeit at its own insistent pace. We believe the Supreme Court ought to know that under freedom of choice, the high quality of education in Richmond's schools has been maintained. And we believe the Supreme Court ought to know that the people of the Richmond area support liberty—for all races—and oppose force.

The Supreme Court should be informed about these things, because the Supreme Court has wrought the Orwellian changes in pupil assignments in the past 16 years. Only the Supreme Court can call a halt to further manipulation of the nation's school children. No matter what the decision in the Richmond case, Federal District Judge Robert R. Merhige, Jr., ultimately will be bound by decisions on school integration handed down by the Supreme Court. Until the Supreme Court clarifies the contradictory and confusing points in many Federal court decisions, it would be imprudent for Judge Merhige to act hastily in the Richmond case. Pending such a clarifying decision from the Supreme Court—expected this fall—Judge Merhige should delay his ruling in the Richmond case, and reinstate the City's freedom-of-choice plan.

The South has been to Appomattox before. It has experienced adversity and defeat; it knows the name of the game. But no hardship visited on Richmond by the egalitarians—not even the relegation of freedom of choice to the legal ash heap—will warrant retaliation against children, black or white. Richmond area parents want the best possible education for their children; they do not want incipient race war in the public schools. Those parents understand that unlike claims for equal treatment, demands for compulsory association are neither legitimate nor truthful. They remain convinced that reason will prevail. And they sincerely hope that through full airing of the arguments, the Supreme Court will turn away from the anti-rational Procustean theories that threaten to tear the social fabric of this nation apart.

In an editorial, "A Time for Sanity," Aug. 4, 1970, television station WWBT, Channel 12, called the petition, "a morally bad thing. Courts of this land should not be asked to respond to pressure. Courts are based on law. Only Heaven knows what would happen to our system of government with the three separate and equal branches if our courts were to be influenced and coerced by a massive mailing from well-meaning citizens rather than by a judicious rendering of decisions based on law."

WRVA radio editorialized July 31, 1970, "The busing issue is going to ultimately have to be decided by the Supreme Court and we doubt that the decision is going to be swayed by bales of newspaper tear sheets from the 'Daily Thunderstorm' or by the number or stature of those who choose to intervene."

A succinct statement of the viewpoint of those who considered the action of the Richmond paper to be unwise was the following from a small local weekly in the Richmond area, the *Metropolitan Observer,* which printed the following editorial Aug. 5, 1970.

Giving a False Hope

A local daily newspaper has seen fit to use what we believe is a dangerously un-American propaganda tool that is not only contemptuous of our form of government, but is misleading in that it gives the participants the hope they are accomplishing something.

We refer to "An Open Letter to the Supreme Court of the United States."

Not that we disagree with its contents. Far from it, we DO agree with most of what is said in the letter.

But these are our objections:

Thousands of sincere and concerned Richmonders are avidly signing and distributing these letters in the misguided belief that they will influence a decision on the school situation favorable to their viewpoints.

Nothing could be further from the truth.

Courts should not, and we hope to heaven never will, be coerced or influenced by public pressure, right or wrong.

Any court that would even read such coercive appeals would be contemptible to every concept of true unbiased and legalistic justice.

Should that newspaper really wish to influence the decision, why don't they go about in the American way? Hire legal talent to intervene before the Court to present in a constitutional way arguments that would present an honest and legal influence upon the Court.

Undaunted, the *News-Leader* answered its critics Aug. 10, 1970 as follows:

By Way of Rebuttal . . .

In recent days, local broadcast media have criticized this newspaper for its publication of the Open Letter to the Supreme Court. It is being said that we are: (1) arousing false hopes; (2) attempting to pressure the Supreme Court; (3) criticizing Judge Merhige unfairly; and (4) engaging in an un-American propaganda campaign.

In ordinary circumstances, we would let this criticism pass without comment, for any rebuttal necessarily takes on defensive overtones. Other media in the community have every right to criticize THE NEWS LEADER if they disagree with this newspaper's policies, but, in the course of this recent criticism, a number of statements have been made that beg for clarification.

From the beginning, this newspaper made it clear that no one should entertain false hopes that signed Open Letters would accomplish miracles. Nonetheless, no governmental institution can remain remote from the will of the people, not even the Supreme Court of the United States. Courts were created to interpret the law, and that law is established through the will of the people. It is a matter of record that the law of the land, on any given day, is what nine men on the high court say it is.

Surely the nine men who ultimately will determine the future of this city's schools should be made aware of how the people of Richmond feel. Like all Americans, Richmonders have the right under the First Amendment to petition the government at any time for a redress of their grievances, and that government includes the tribunal that will decide the future of their children. The Supreme Court, as Mr. Dooley noted, does follow the election returns.

It has been said that the people should express their wishes to their congressmen and Senators in Washington. That suggestion certainly raises false hopes. The will of Congress, opposing compulsory busing for the sake of integration, was made explicit in the 1964 Civil Rights Act and, more recently, in the Whitten Amendments, but the courts continue to ignore this expression of congressional intent. Congressman William C. Cramer of Florida drafted the anti-busing provision in the 1964 Civil Rights Act, and that provision flatly prohibits forced busing. "I know what the law says because I wrote it," he says, "The

courts, however, have chosen to ignore the Cramer anti-busing law." Those who oppose compulsory busing, then, must look to the courts, not to Congress, for relief.

Another critic stated that integration has been the law of the land since 1954. Indeed, no. In *Brown v. Board of Education,* the Supreme Court ruled that no child could be denied admittance to a school by reason of his race. At that time, the court did not order integration; it merely prohibited segregation by law. In subsequent years, the high court has ordered desegregation and unitary school systems, but it has remained vague on the issue of *de facto* racial imbalances resulting from residential living patterns, as in Richmond. It never has demanded forced busing. Meanwhile, Federal District and Circuit Courts continue to hand down contradictory rulings that serve only to confuse.

Still another critic seems to think that this newspaper has criticized Judge Robert Merhige unfairly. We have criticized Judge Merhige in the past for his rulings in other cases, but the closest we have come to criticizing his actions in the city's school case was to express astonishment at his suggestion that the city might consider consolidation of school districts with Henrico and Chesterfield Counties [July 8]. On Friday, Judge Merhige himself expressed amazement that the city school board had taken his suggestion so seriously that the board was seeking to enjoin the counties as co-defendants. "It's one thing to sit down and talk with folks," he said, "but it's another thing to drag them into court."

Because we believe that the people of Richmond, and readers outside Richmond, have a right to make their views on compulsory busing known, this newspaper has offered them an opportunity to register their opinions. To date, more than 30,000 of them have responded. In our view, the Open Letter does not constitute an attempt to pressure the Court, to intimidate the Court, or to instruct the Court in the law. Presumably the Court knows the law, and will interpret that law as it sees fit. But the Open Letter, we believe, represents an exercise in participatory democracy that this Republic guarantees every citizen, our critics notwithstanding.

Ken Ringle wrote an inclusive roundup of the controversy which the Washington *Post* published Aug. 16, 1970 under the headline, "Richmond Debates Busing Editorials." It concluded with a quotation from David Tennant Bryan, publisher, "I wouldn't change a damn thing we've done."

JOURNALISTIC SHOP TALK

Debating public issues is a journalistic anachronism which should be encouraged. And the same is true of journalistic shoptalk; that is, consideration of journalistic developments and problems which affect the general public. Newspapers seldom do it, for a variety of reasons, probably the most important of which is their sheer inability to judge the importance of such potential news with the same objectivity that they apply to almost anything else. Democracy would work better if school children became familiar with the operations of the communications media and with their social role. Newspapers cry "freedom of the press" whenever they encounter any interference with news gathering or when a vice president or cabinet member's wife or someone else threatens their reputations. On the whole the public remains indifferent if not hostile. There is a lamentable failure to appreciate the importance of the freedom of the press clause in the First Amendment and a gross ignorance of the attacks on it which are implicit in federal government classification requirements; in injunctions to prevent the publication of supposedly secret information; in proposals to cite reporters and editors, newspapers and television chains for contempt when they refuse to reveal the identity of news sources or to answer subpoenas to produce notes, unused film strips and other material which some judge or congressman or bureaucrat wants to ex-

amine. There should be more editorials like the following from the Chicago *Daily Tribune* of April 19, 1957.

A Few Timely Words About Newspapers

These are great days for the newspapers of America, some of the greatest days in the long history of American journalism.

We are not thinking now of circulation figures and advertising linage, impressive as they are, but of responsibility for the public welfare accepted and of editorial duties faithfully performed.

The tasks have been difficult, costly, and sometimes dangerous, but the recent achievements of the American newspaper press on behalf of the people of this land have been so remarkable as to make the outlay of effort, time, and money seem trivial in comparison.

To choose one example, it is almost wholly to the newspapers of Portland, Ore., that the nation is indebted for the exposure of official graft and union racketeering in the Pacific northwest. Magazines and radio and television stations contributed little to the result and what they contributed consisted, for much the most part, of retelling facts already published in the daily press.

Certainly it was not the local governments, the state government, or the federal government that drew public attention to Dave Beck's betrayal of his trust. That was a newspaper achievement and along with it went the exposure of payments to politicians for the privilege of operating gambling houses and houses of prostitution in and near Portland.

Similarly, the exposure of the Hodge scandals in Illinois was strictly a newspaper job in which every Chicago newspaper man can and does take the greatest pride. There was a time in Chicago when, if one newspaper turned up a scandal, some of the others would almost automatically "throw the story down" as the phrase goes. That is no longer true. Competition for news remains as intense as it ever was, but the public interest is not forgotten in the struggle. The recent murder of Hodge's banker, Leon Marcus, and the revelations regarding Marcus' play-mate, Rado, have found all the newspapers of Chicago keen on the trail.

American newspapers deserve a major share of the credit for defending the tax-payers against the outrageous federal budget that is now being debated in Congress. In this effort to achieve economy, it seems to us, the papers of the middle west, between the Appalachians and the Rockies, have played a particularly important part, but there is no section of the country that hasn't its strong editorial spokesmen for fiscal sanity. Except for what the newspapers have done to stiffen resistance in both houses of Congress, the welfare of the taxpayers would have been forgotten.

Some years ago, in the fullness of his physical and mental vigor, the late Col. McCormick took the trouble to write his definition of the newspaper. It has become the classic statement of what newspapers can be and should be. He wrote:

"The newspaper is an institution developed by modern civilization to present the news of the day, to foster commerce and industry, to inform and lead public opinion, and to furnish that check upon government which no constitution has ever been able to provide."

By their conduct and their achievements the American newspapers of 1957 have proved that this is no description of what they might be but a sober account of what they are and of how they serve their readers and their country.

One of the reasons why there are not more editorials of this sort is implied in an editorial which the crusading Bill Evjue wrote for the Madison *Capital-Times* of Aug. 29, 1950.

But Why Are There Taboos When Journalists Get Together?

The Capital-Times herewith rolls out an editorial red carpet for the teachers of journalism who are now holding clinical studies on the American newspaper in convention at the university. We hope that these faculty members of schools of journalism who will have such great influence in molding

the character of the reporter and the journalist of the future will find their sessions here in Madison productive of much good for a field that has such a great impact on American life.

Frankly, however, we confess to a feeling of disappointment when we survey the programs and the agendas that are so frequently set before those who attend the meetings of organizations associated with journalism,—whether it be the American Publishers' Association, the Inland Press, or the Teachers of Journalism. It seems to us that these organizations too often devote their time to the technical and vocational aspects of the daily job of getting out a newspaper to the exclusion of broader and more fundamental questions that go to the relationship of the present day newspaper to the public welfare and the common good.

For instance, ours is a representative form of government. This presumes, of course, that the people must get the facts and information that are so essential for intelligent decisions on matters pertaining to the public welfare. The press was acknowledged in the fundamental law of the land as the medium through which people could get the facts on public issues. The provision guaranteeing the freedom of the press was placed in the constitution for that purpose. The congress, way back in 1878, passed a law granting preferred mailing rights to newspapers in order that the American people might get facts on which to base their decisions.

But what's happening today at a time when the whole national trend is toward the one-newspaper city? Are the people getting the facts to which they are entitled when there is only one newspaper in a community? Is it a healthy situation when one corporation or one family has the power to control and dominate newspaper policy? This has become the rule in cities all over the United States having populations of 50,000 and running up as high as 700,000.

Another question,—the newspapers today are largely dependent on the three dominant news services—the Associated Press, the United Press and the International News —for news of the outside world. Are these organizations handling news in an objective way? Do they color, suppress, or distort the news? Can the people make intelligent decisions on news that may be colored, censored, or suppressed?

These are questions which seem to be more or less taboo at meetings of newspaper publishers and journalism teachers. Why? Haven't those who are in the field of journalism yet learned the lesson of the last presidential election? Why is there such a big gulf today between the point of view held by newspaper publishers and the point of view of the public?

These are questions that we would like to see on the agenda when newspapermen get together to talk over the problems of their craft.

The Chicago *Daily News* took advantage of an opportunity to make a rather facetious defense of orthodox news judgment in the following from its issue of April 22, 1971.

Happy News in a Glum World

Last weekend's Daily News carried a tongue-in-cheek article by syndicated columnist Art Hoppe about the mythical Euphoria (Kan.) Gazette, an ever-cheerful paper whose forecasts always called for pleasant weather, whose news columns reported only accidents in which no one was hurt, and whose obituary page listed only those Euphoria residents still living.

Absurd, we mused. No one would publish a paper like that.

But now an Associated Press dispatch discloses that there is indeed a good-news-only newspaper: the Aquarian Times, a weekly published in Fair Oaks, Calif.

The Times doesn't distort stories as did Hoppe's Euphoria Gazette (for example, an unemployment rise became an increase in leisure time; a Gallup poll report that 12 per cent were thinking of leaving the U.S.A. was turned around to read "Most Americans won't flee country"). But the Times does studiously ignore calamity in favor of conservationists' triumphs, tax reductions and bedtime stories "where no one is killed, eaten or seriously injured."

Despite its non-Establishment name, The Aquarian Times sounds like a totally straight, upright family publication. Its editor, Bill Bailey, foreswears nudity, cursing and radical polemics in his paper.

"I don't want to get people uptight by constantly treading on our problems," says editor Bailey. "I want to restore people's optimism. We've been caught up in a communications explosion without being able to adjust."

There's no doubt that the media have enlarged the public's awareness of our many ills and, in that sense, contributed to the general uneasiness. However, we can't help but feel that those who carp at the media for accentuating the negative are applying a double standard: They reject news that may make them feel nervous or guilty, but they would hardly settle for such a rosy screening of the bulletins they get over the back fence—"news" about how well-behaved the Smith children are, how happily married the Joneses are, how flawlessly the minister's wife served Wednesday afternoon tea.

We wish editor Bailey happy hunting in his quest for the silver lining. Meanwhile, we'll go on dishing up the news as it comes, and let the reader sort out his own sugar pills.

Also sharing with the general public some of the soul-searching that goes on constantly when journalists get together was the following editorial from the Waterbury (Conn.) *Republican* of Oct. 29, 1949.

The Local Angle

There is nothing new about the idea that local issues ought to claim more of the editorial writer's time and attention. But it always bears mentioning.

How much of newspaper trade talk has a general interest is of course a question. Yet newspapers are so intimate a part of most people's lives, that we have yet to discover a phase of newspaper work that won't interest most people. So we suppose there was more than purely professional importance in the recent news that Morris Ernst advised editorial writers gathered at Columbia University to recapture public interest by tackling local subjects. There was maybe even some sententious head-wagging by readers of this dispatch who told themselves it was high time that writers of editorials got wise to themselves on this score.

Well, we try.

A few years ago we attended a gathering of editorial writers at which a number of editorial pages were the subject of clinical analysis. And one of the discussion leaders touched off a lively debate when he criticized the editor of a paper in a Great Lakes port for giving his chief editorial consideration for the day to contamination of lake beaches instead of to the bisection of India which was proclaimed that same day. Many strongly convinced editors rose to declare that the most world-shaking event abroad didn't stack up as an editorial subject against a really live local issue. In the conclaves of the American Society of Newspaper Editors much is said annually about "Afghanistanism," by which is meant the too prevalent tendency of editorial writers to overlook subjects right under their noses in favor of those half the world away. And Robert Lasch of The Chicago Sun-Times has deplored this tendency by amusingly formulating Lasch's Law, which is to the effect that the positiveness of any editorial varies in direct ratio to the distance of the editorial writer from the scene of what he is writing about.

This is to say that a ringing statement of what the Chinese or the Australians ought to do about their particular problems is cheap. No indignant letters are going to come in from Shanghai and no subscriptions are going to be cancelled from Brisbane. A vigorous and provocative statement on some local issue, however, is going to be heard from, its facts are going to be checked, the persons mentioned in it are going to rise and answer back. Thus the lazy editorial writer tends to let his attention rove leagues away. And it is the conscientious editorial writer who buckles down to conditions closer to home.

Yet certain events at a distance have their importance locally and all editorial flights to Afghanistan aren't escapist. It is only when an editorial page consistently neglects local and state issues to talk about events in a wider area that it gives an unfavorable

picture of the men who make it and loses most of the influence it might have. And such practice is so abject and ill-advised that Mr. Ernst was dead right in inveighing against it.

Again on the seemingly facetious but altogether serious side was the following delightful editorial from the Peoria *Journal-Star* of Jan. 12, 1964.

An Editorial Writer Views a Minister

When editorial writers go to church (and they do) they envy the minister.

They're jealous of the time he has to make his point. Often 30 minutes or longer. He should be able to say something in a half an hour, the editorialist thinks enviously.

But suppose he had only the length of a time an average editorial would take, say, oh, two minutes. Suppose he had to make his point and quit in two minutes? Just stand up there for two minutes, make his point and sit down. Ah, that'd be a different story.

Oh, dream the editorialists, if we only had as much space, say 500 inches, to include examples of what we mean, illustrations of our point, analogies of our theme. Oh if we only had as much room as the minister to pound our point home.

Then people wouldn't misunderstand us, or misread our intentions when we say something. If we could spell it out at length we'd get through to the public. We think.

Yes, we envy the minister. We long for his opportunity to emphasize certain words and de-emphasize others, to go over something when he sees it isn't getting through, and to throw in a gesture here and there when things get dull.

Most of all, we suppose, we envy the minister his captive audience. Now that's a real advantage. Suppose everyone had to read our editorials all the way through?

Deep down, however, we envy clergymen because, most of them, at any rate, do say something in their allotted time. They say something worthwhile, something worth remembering, worth taking home and thinking about.

Probably everyone sees the clergyman through his own specialized eyes—the doctor thinks, "hmmm, he's not looking so well this week"; the lawyer thinks, "that's irrelevant, immaterial and inconsequential"; and the teacher thinks, "wasn't that a grammatical error?" But to the editorialist, the view is one of envy.

A LESSON IN HUMILITY

Never before or since has the public support been solicited more extensively than in 1942 when the Justice Department filed suit against the Associated Press, charging violation of the antitrust laws. This was one of the few suits instigated by Thurman Arnold during his brief tenure as head of the antitrust division, and it ended in victory for the government. That really meant an immediate victory for the Chicago *Sun* which was started Dec. 4, 1941, three days before the attack on Pearl Harbor, by Marshall Field III as a pro-New Deal morning competitor of the Chicago *Daily Tribune,* perhaps the Roosevelt administration's leading journalistic critic. To offset the effect of the appearance of the new publication, the *Tribune* published on the same day what purported to be secret plans for an American military invasion of Canada. Later it was revealed that the plans were the blueprint for war games similar to those which all nations hold as part of the training provided their armed forces.

Although all that Marshall Field wanted was to join the Associated Press, so as to obtain its services for his new venture, he was roundly accused of attempting to destroy it. The government's suit sought to compel the association to open its membership rolls to any newspaper willing to pay the proportionate share of the cost of gathering news in its area. This would mean the A.P. would have to admit Field which, under the old rules permitting regional vetoes, Colonel McCormick could prevent. In support of its position the government declared in its petition in part:

That of the news services supplied by the three news agencies, that of The Associated Press ranks in the forefront in public reputation and esteem . . . the name Associated Press" has long been regarded as synonymous with the highest standards of accurate, non-partisan and comprehensive news reporting.

That without the AP service a newspaper suffers competitive disadvantages and that this service is essential to the survival of any newspaper.

Typical of many editorials on the subject of the suit to appear in the Chicago *Daily Tribune* was the following from the issue of Aug. 31, 1942.

The Suit Against AP

We don't suppose there is any one in the United States so naive as not to know that the action brought by the attorney general against the Associated Press had its origin in spite and anger. The true purpose of the litigation is to show the newspapers of this country that they will take orders from Washington if they know what is good for them. They wouldn't take orders at the recent meeting of the Associated Press in New York and accordingly the complaint has been filed.

The attack is directed against the entire press of the United States—little newspapers as well as big ones. It is intended to disrupt the Associated Press and destroy the values, tangible and intangible, which its members have created in it. The great work of the Associated Press in taking the leadership in the distribution of world news from foreign private agencies that used their facilities, often to damage our country is apparently disregarded as of no consequence.

In their anger the men in Washington have not hesitated to do a very serious injury to the United Press and the International News Service, both of which have long records of usefulness. They are written down as negligible, which they are not. Certainly if the government's allegations are true, these competing services cannot long survive if any one now using them may obtain Associated Press service for the asking. If the government is correct in its contentions, and if it should succeed in its suit, the result of this attack on alleged monopoly would be the destruction of competition in the distribution of news and a complete monopoly for the AP.

In that sense this suit may be regarded as a threat to freedom of the press. In another and more important sense, the threat is the gravest which has arisen since the first amendment was adopted. Here we see the full force of government brought to bear with a view to demonstrating to all editors and all publishers that they must do what Washington tells them to do—or else.

The constitutional guarantee exists primarily to protect those who see the need to criticize public officials and expose administrative derelictions. This action is calculated to intimidate and punish such independence of mind and expression.

The TRIBUNE is a defendant in a suit alleging monopoly. It is not our purpose to try the case in these columns but we feel justified in calling attention to the fact that we have had many competitors possessing membership in the Associated Press but at no time in our long career have we ever bought one of them. The *Times*, the *Record*, the *Herald*, the *Inter-Ocean*, the *Chronicle* were among the papers that couldn't make the grade in a freely competitive market. They folded up. Their memberships lapsed for that reason and only that reason.

In 1945 the United States Supreme Court upheld a lower court ruling that the Associated Press' membership bylaws violated the Sherman Antitrust Act and ruled that the association, in passing on applicants for membership, must disregard possible competitive effects on existing members. The bylaws were then amended to comply. And then the New York *PM*, also owned largely by Marshall Field, asserted that "Associated Press Ruling Reaffirms Freedom of Press" and ran a page in its issue of June 21, 1945 as follows:

Back in 1942, when the Government filed its monopoly suit against the Associated Press, hundreds of member newspapers all over the U.S.A. published editorials defending the AP. The AP got the editorials all together and reproduced them in two fat volumes which were distributed among AP members with a foreword offering additional copies free, on request.

Throughout the Nation, AP editors howled in print about the Government's encroachment on the freedom of the press, complaining that the Constitutional guarantee of free speech was being tossed out the window.

Some of the editorials were original writing, some were paraphrases of statements previously appearing in the powerful AP leaders. The bulk of the editorial blasts on press freedom seemed to follow a pattern set by the powerful journalistic leaders—particularly the Chicago *Tribune*, the Gannett papers and the Baltimore *Sun*—which argued that the suit constituted a *threat* to freedom of the press on the grounds that a Government victory would put AP's competitors out of business, making AP a monopoly which could be regimented.

On this page, some typical freedom-of-the-press blasts are debunked by quotations from this week's Supreme Court decision.

Bunk . . .

If the Government wins, the press services of the United States will be under the thumb of the White House, and the freedom of the American press to do anything save yes-yes the party in power will do a rapid fade-out.

N. Y. Daily News

. . . Because

"The First Amendment, far from providing an argument against application of the Sherman Act, here provides powerful reasons to the contrary. That amendment rests on the assumption that the widest possible dissemination of information from diverse and antagonistic sources is essential to the welfare of the public, that a free press is a condition of a free society. . . ."

More Bunk . . .

The issue that it has made goes to the very roots of American liberty. The attack is fun-

damentally on the people's right to know the truth about public events and to discuss public events freely in an effort to form a sound public opinion.
Indianapolis News

. . . *Because*

"Surely a command that the Government itself shall not impede the free flow of ideas does not afford non-governmental combinations a refuge if they impose restraints upon that constitutionally guaranteed freedom. . . ."

More Bunk . . .

No government, however objective or high-minded, can set up controls over what can or cannot be said in print without throttling the free publication of news and opinion, and influencing newspapers to publish or suppress or color what the government wants published or suppressed or colored.
Minneapolis Star-Journal

. . . *Because*

"Freedom of the press means freedom for all and not for some. Freedom to publish is guaranteed by the Constitution, but freedom to combine to keep others from publishing is not. . . ."

More Bunk . . .

On the outcome of this action, in which the government patently sets out to foster one newspaper and in doing so to destroy the prestige of another, may well rest the fate of a free press in this nation. And the newspapers of this nation, whether within or outside the fold of the Associated Press membership, had better realize that destiny's hour may be drawing near.
Cleveland News

. . . *Because*

"Freedom of the press from governmental interference under the First Amendment does not sanction repression of that freedom by private interests. . . ."

More Bunk . . .

It is also true that Congress has never asserted any right or power to regulate newspapers or news agencies in the collec-

tion and distribution of news, and that under the First Amendment it cannot do so.
Los Angeles Times

. . . *Because*

"The First Amendment affords not the slightest support for the contention that a combination to restrain trade in news and views has any constitutional immunity."

For the editors of *PM*, I. F. Stone composed the following signed editorial in the same issue.

Comes the Revolution, Colonel?

PM addresses this editorial to Robert Mc-Lean, president of the AP.

PM would like to know, as a matter of news coverage, whether the Associated Press intends to obey the ruling of the U.S. Supreme Court in the AP case—or to follow the course suggested by the Chicago *Tribune.*

"It would never do," the *Tribune* said in an editorial yesterday, "for the Associated Press to accept the decree, with its clear threat of censorship, until all remedies have been exhausted, i.e. until Congress has clearly indicated that it accepts the majority interpretation of the Sherman Act."

It was our impression, from a reading of the Constitution, that the court of last resort in this country was the U.S. Supreme Court and that when appeal to it has failed, as it failed in the AP case, all legal remedies *have* been exhausted.

It was our impression that after the Supreme Court has made a final ruling, as the Court did in the AP case it was the duty of every citizen to obey.

Col. McCormick, fighting to perpetuate an extremely profitable monopoly of AP news in the Chicago morning field, is understandably aroused.

But the Supreme Court, and not Congress, is the final interpreter of law in this country. Congress, unlike the British Parliament, is not a court of last resort.

The Chicago *Tribune* has a right to ask Congress to amend the Sherman Act to exempt news association like the Associated Press from the anti-trust laws. But, in the meantime, it has no right—and the Associated Press has no right—to sidestep a ruling of the U.S. Supreme Court.

If this were to become an accepted course of conduct, convicted persons could thumb their noses at the courts while they lobbied for changes in the laws they had violated.

It is true that some Americans—fortunately very few—have taken just such a rebellious and disrespectful attitude toward our highest court in the past.

But if our memory serves us right, such folk get themselves portrayed in the Chicago *Tribune* with whiskers on their chins, and bombs in their hands.

—I. F. STONE FOR THE EDITORS OF PM

The Chicago *Sun,* on whose behalf the suit was brought, was remarkably charitable in its "celebration" editorial June 20, 1945.

Who Is Out of Step
on a Free Press?

The Supreme Court's decision in the Associated Press case invites the publishers of America to search their souls. Justice Black's majority opinion, we think, expresses the conception of a free press held by most laymen and most working newspapermen. It will not coincide with the ideas of freedom held by some powerful newspaper owners. Those gentlemen should now soberly reflect upon who is out of step.

Two years ago the editorial columns of the AP papers were filled with denunciations of the government's action in filing an anti-trust suit. *Editor & Publisher* devoted a special section to these outcries. The AP itself published two volumes of hostile editorial comment. A strenuous and concerted campaign was waged to convince the American people—in advance of a court ruling—that the government had assaulted the constitutional guarantee of a free press.

Some publishers even went so far as to bring pressure to bear in Congress, while the suit was pending, for an "investigation" which would have had the effect of transferring the case from the courts to a congressional committee room.

Now the biggest court of the land declares that it was not the government's action, but the monopolistic practices of the press itself, which threatened freedom. As Justice Black said, the First Amendment rests upon the assumption "that the widest possible dissemination of information from diverse and antagonistic sources is essential to the welfare of the public." Then the court went on to find the AP members guilty of having impeded that widest possible dissemination of information—of having limited the people's access to news by imposing commercial restraints on newspaper competition.

The damage already done to the cause of a free press is incalculable. By grossly misrepresenting the nature of the case, by raising a false cry of "wolf," the dominating members of AP have impaired public confidence in their newspapers. When the court condemns the use of civil liberties as "a shield for business publishers who engage in business practices condemned by the Sherman Act," the people cannot forget that a great many newspapers devoted their power and resources to precisely that purpose.

The harm can be undone only by honest dedication of the press to the service of the people, rather than the narrow interests of a small group of publishers. It would be the blindest of mistakes for the AP members to seize upon Justice Roberts' remarkably weak dissent in an effort to escape the consequences of the court's controlling opinion. Justice Roberts based his opinion on the unstated premise that if any newspaper cannot get into AP, all it need do is set up an AP of its own. Justice Black disposed of that absurdity, and pointed out that the competitive advantage enjoyed by AP members springs not from any superior enterprise or sagacity, but from their collective power.

Unless the AP members promptly accept the decision in good spirit, they will openly confess that interference with free competition is indeed their objective.

Well, the Supreme Court did *not* reverse itself, Congress did *not* amend the Sherman Antitrust Act, the Associated Press did change its bylaws, the Chicago Sun *was* elected to membership and has continued to belong ever since. And the whole experience ought to have a humbling effect on a lot of newspaper men, especially owners but including editorial writers.

THE ROLE OF THE PRESS

The world already is overpopulated and the situation is getting worse daily. The effect on journalism is to make the large metropolitan dailies into national or international publications and to create a need for more small community newspapers, gossip sheets or bulletin boards, to contribute to community life. Here is how one such paper, the Pomona (Calif.) *Progress-Bulletin* expressed its obligation in a July 19, 1966 editorial.

Hometown Paper Essential

In an age when bigness seems to have become a necessity in government, and industry—in fact in virtually any activity you can name—it is gratifying to find one place where size is not necessary to success and has no relationship to quality of service nor the importance of the enterprise. That is the hometown community newspaper.

A national directory of weekly newspapers reports that there are more than 8,000 "hometown" newspapers in the country. These newspapers reach approximately 32 million homes. While metropolitan papers have been beset by circulation troubles, the smaller papers have been flourishing and enjoying steady circulation increases.

The thousands of smaller papers are a bulwark of independent thought. Without them, there would be no freedom of the press. There would be no record of community life, no reporting of important community events, no expression of editorial views or opinions that gradually crystallize into public sentiment on issues of the day.

In fact, without the thousands of editors to give it meaning, the institution of a free press would wither and die and with it the freedom of the people. The local newspaper is an enterprise that does a big job.

Similarly the neighboring Cucamonga (Calif.) *News* editorialized July 28, 1966.

Newspaper Can Be Life Itself

One of the fascinating things about being a newspaperwoman is that the whole range of activities and events in a community is part of "the job."

This brings a good newspaper into touch, at least in part, with every segment of the area it serves.

The newspaper has a great opportunity to help its community in many ways.

First, of course, is to print the news so that the citizens are informed.

Secondly, is to help each part, each segment, to the best of its ability so that the potential of each is realized.

Thirdly, the newspaper can serve a vital function by coordinating or bringing together various aspects so that the community goes along in regular fashion as an entity and not just a few pieces.

        ✿   ✿   ✿

The NEWS attempts to fulfill all three of these.

Sometimes we are a little short of space, as all newspapers are at times, and we don't ever get around to covering all the news we want to each week. But this is very characteristic of a good newspaper that never is satisfied with the job it is doing.

Our best method of helping each group do its best is to print the news naturally, and then to encourage each to take the best available path. Often our editorial comment serves to point out the pit-falls of choices taken or contemplated. This, also, is vital to staying on a progressive path.

And then we try to coordinate and form a high-level plan that encompasses everything in the community. We may pick out an individual, group or activity, but really we keep in mind how it relates to everything in the area.

        ✿   ✿   ✿

Thus we have a wide diversity of interest in Cucamonga.

The affairs of an area and its people are complex and complicated, intertwined beyond belief in detail.

We find being newspaper people the most fascinating business in the world. Where else, in what other field, can an individual find access to every single part of society and environment surrounding himself?

To our mind, there is no business so satisfying as that of newspapering.

It's not an easy profession, but certainly one of the most challenging. But it has its dignity and its goals. It has its rewards.

A newspaper can be life itself. It is with the News.

There are few scenes more melodramatically tragic than those enacted in newspaper plants on the occasions of their deaths. Often the announcement of the demise is delayed until after the final edition has appeared. In the case of the New York *Herald Tribune,* however, it was possible to include an obituary editorial in the last issue which came out Aug. 16, 1966. The editorial follows:

It Was That Kind of Newspaper

Even after the strains of the past decade and the slow, remorseless drain of the last 113 days, it seems impossible to believe that an institution so full of personality and personalities as the New York Herald Tribune should pass from the American scene. The memories of its great days and its great fights, of the vital men and women who made those days great and fought those fights, are too vivid; the selfless dedication that went into the struggle to keep the paper alive is too recent.

Fortunately, the history of a century and a quarter is not completely disrupted; the light that is going out in New York still burns in Paris, and with its association with "The Washington Post," the European Edition has acquired a durability and drive that will allow it to continue as a force in its own right. And in New York, the Herald Tribune tradition will continue as a component of the merged afternoon and Sunday newspapers.

This is not the occasion to hold a post mortem on the New York Herald Tribune, nor to describe those factors, powerful or petty, that, in their cumulative effect, made the Herald Tribune's effort to survive so difficult, and which brought failure in the end. The immediate cause is clear enough: the Herald Tribune had to be able to publish, as one of the merged papers, while there was still a fair chance of picking up the bulk of its old circulation, advertising and skilled staff. And the merger itself had to reach terms with the unions that could make its life in a highly competitive market possible. Between the two imperatives, the lifeblood of the Herald Tribune seeped away while the long disputes went on.

We cannot say that "the rest is silence." What the Herald Tribune was, the whole world knows to some degree. But those who wrote and worked for it, who tasted the fierce pride of accomplishment and the satisfaction of being part of a worthy team, part of a lively and very human institution, will be thinking and talking and writing about the New York Herald Tribune for years to come. They will be contentious, of course. They will dispute over the victories and defeats of the past, and dwell on their personal heroes and personal devils. But just as Mr. Whitney could say of his valiant effort to keep the voice of the Herald Tribune heard in the land: "It was an attempt I am glad to have made," so we doubt whether anyone can ever say "I worked with the New York Herald Tribune" without pride. It was that kind of newspaper.

Finally, perhaps the Era of Personal Journalism is past, but the spirit lives on in memoirs and sketches of many of the powerful editors who promoted the public interest as they saw it while making money in the process. There is no more appropriate way to conclude this book than with the following editorial comment which appeared in *Editor & Publisher* for Jan. 31, 1948.

Josephus Daniels' Will

Bequeathing his Raleigh (N.C.) News and Observer to his four sons, Josephus Daniels stated in his Last Will and Testament, dated Nov. 20, 1946, that he regarded the newspaper "as property, but having an unpurchasable soul."

To the lofty principles set down by Mr. Daniels for the future operation of his paper, we subscribe unqualifiedly. In his will, he wrote:

"If I could look into the future, I would wish those children and grandchildren who will devote their lives to the News and Observer, to receive the chief income that comes from the operation of the paper.

"I leave it as a request that if any grandchildren not actually at work on the paper should at any time be desirous of making a sale of their stock or any portion of it, that preference in purchasing be given to those engaged in managing or editing the paper.

"It is my earnest desire and hope that the News and Observer shall be edited and directed by my descendants, though I do not believe the dead hand should attempt to control the living spirit.

"I recognize that no one can become a good journalist who does not love the calling. For me the joy of work has been my chief happiness and reward, and I could wish the same to be true of my descendants.

"I have never regarded the stock I owned in the News and Observer as property, but as certificates of a trust administered for the common good of the people of North Carolina. I owe to their support and approval the success of the News and Observer. Its future depends upon complete devotion to the ideals that have characterized its course.

"I advise and enjoin those who direct the paper in the tomorrows never to advocate any cause for personal profit or preferment. I would wish it always to be 'the tocsin' and devote itself to the policies of equality and justice to the underprivileged.

"If the paper should at any time be the voice of self-interest or become the spokesman of privilege or selfishnes, it would be untrue to its history."

EPILOGUE

The foregoing chapters fall far short of providing the potential editorial writer with helpful hints for all occasions. It is to be hoped that after he has learned whatever there is to learn from the contents, he will be able to continue his development on his own and not become flabbergasted when confronted with the necessity of making sage comments on situations in fields not specifically dealt with in this volume: agriculture, transportation, urban renewal, pollution, population explosion, mental health, medical research, public housing, city planning, military affairs, race relations, civil liberties, taxation, business and finance, the arts, science, religion and many other fields.

The most important deliberate oversight is the entire field of foreign affairs, international relations and the multiple problems of all of the 200 or so other nations all over the world. The theory has been "first things first," and any newspaper that would start a cub off on an editorial about what to do in Ireland or Pakistan or something of that sort wouldn't be a paper worth working for. It takes time and much effort to learn enough about anything to be qualified to editorialize about it.

The editorial writer's responsibility is great to practice humility and open-mindedness. This book includes many examples of intemperate and/or ignorant editorials. The intention has been to expose them for what they are: exercises in bigotry that nobody should want to emulate. On the other hand, there are numerous literary gems which few professors of English anywhere could equal. Brevity is the soul of wit according to Hamlet, and it also is the necessity for editorial writing. You have to learn how to say a lot in a short space even though you may be tempted to write a book.

There really is no last word except this: *know what you're talking about or keep still.*

Taking his own advice, the author now signs off and will start watching the mailbag hoping it's full of communiqués from readers.

Index